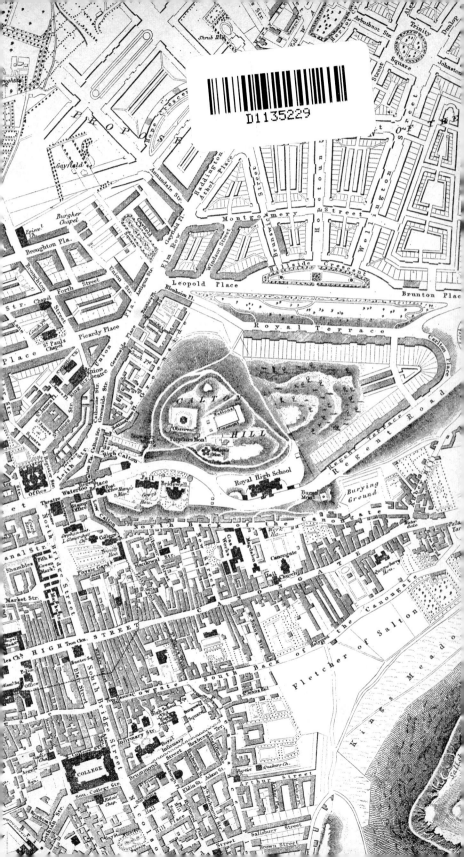

THE CLACKEN AND THE SLATE

The roll-book is closed in the room,
The clacken is gone with the slate.
Robert Louis Stevenson (E.A. 1861–3)

Clacken: a wooden hand-bat or racquet used by
the boys at the Edinburgh Academy . . .
(*Scottish National Dictionary*)

The Clacken and the Slate

Magnus Magnusson

The story of
THE EDINBURGH ACADEMY
1824-1974

COLLINS
ST JAMES'S PLACE LONDON
1974

William Collins Sons & Co Ltd
London · Glasgow · Sydney · Auckland
Toronto · Johannesburg

First published 1974
© Magnus Magnusson 1974
ISBN 0 00 411170-2

Set in Monotype Bembo
Made and Printed in Great Britain by
William Collins Sons & Co Ltd Glasgow

This book is dedicated to all Academy boys,
past, present, and future;
but especially to the memory
of one particular boy
who went to another Academy:

Siggy Magnusson
1961–1973

From *Chronicles of the Cumming Club*

Contents

CONTENTS

List of Illustrations

Preface

THIS book is not an Official History of The Edinburgh Academy. It's not really a history at all – it's a story (though I'm never quite sure of the distinction). It's the story of a great school and its development over 150 eventful, fascinating years. I have tried to place the Academy in its context of time and place, in Edinburgh, in Scotland, in the development of education. I have tried to give an impression of what the School has been like at different periods under different Rectors, with different masters and different boys, as it grew and changed with the passing decades. A great deal has perforce been left out; and Academicals will no doubt disagree over what has been left in. This book cannot be a definitive account; it is a cross-section of time, the story of The Edinburgh Academy as one affectionate Academical sees it. A private book, and yet at the same time a public book – and that's the problem. A school is the sum total of all its parts – and then something more, something that cannot easily be analysed. A great school is a matter of alchemy, not chemistry.

A History of the Academy has been brewing for a long time. Several distinguished Academicals or members of the Academy staff, both past and almost present, have embarked upon it over the years, only to get bogged down in the 1820s when the School was being founded and launched, or to get side-tracked into some area of particular interest, like J. G. Tait who ended up editing the Journals of Sir Walter Scott. But the completion of this book owes much to their pioneering, unfinished efforts.

A host of Academicals, named and unnamed, have helped in the making of this book, through their reminiscences and commemorative articles in the *Edinburgh Academy Chronicle* and elsewhere. From all of them I have borrowed freely, and often without individual acknowledgement. I have also used the standard textbooks on the history of education in Scotland, as well as some unpublished theses which had a bearing on the progress of the Academy down the generations; these are cited individually in the text.

But there are several more personal debts to acknowledge, and I do so with pleasure. To the Directors of the Academy, of course, who allowed me unlimited access to all their confidential Minute Books and archives unconditionally, and who have made no attempt to censor or alter anything I have written. To their original initiative in asking me to do this book, and to their co-operation and forbearance over many months, I owe a great deal. They have worked on the principle that this should not be a committee book, but one man's view, and whether they approved of it or not they have let me go ahead in my own way, and I salute them for it.

Every Academical can imagine what a great debt I owe to the Academy Registrar, Bruce Stenhouse, who has spared no effort to supply me with sources of information and suggest fresh lines of enquiry. He has read the manuscript and proofs with an eagle (and sometimes pained) eye, and has saved me from countless errors and inaccuracies. Whatever blemishes and blunders remain are entirely my fault, not his. I am also indebted to the City Archivist of Edinburgh, Dr Walter Makey, for enquiries he has made on my behalf into the recesses of Edinburgh Town Council activities in the 1820s.

But my major debt of gratitude is to my wife, Mamie Baird, who undertook the enormous task of researching all the relevant (and irrelevant) documents and reducing the great mass of indigestible historical material to manageable proportions and meaningful shape. Without her, as they say, this book would never have been finished; without her, to be more realistic, it would probably never have been started. Looking ahead to the future (dare one say?), she deserves to become the first honorary member of the Academical Club (Ladies' Section)!

Above all, though, my debt is to The Edinburgh Academy itself, where I spent thirteen extremely happy boyhood years; to the Rectors and masters and mistresses and schoolmates who shaped those years; and to my parents for sending me there in the first place. This book is an attempt to repay at least something of that debt. All the proceeds from the sales of the book will be donated to the *150th Anniversary Appeal* for the further development of The Edinburgh Academy.

CHAPTER I

The Scene is Set

Mine own romantic town! (Sir Walter Scott)

OLD Bailie Thomas Blackwood (ex-Bailie Blackwood, as he would be called nowadays) was about to make history, although he did not know it at the time. As far as he was concerned, he was simply on his way to a meeting of Edinburgh Town Council to kick up a row over a proposal to build a school in the New Town. He had been kicking up a row about it for nearly a year, and no one had paid much attention to him. This time, however, he was determined to make them listen; and when Thomas Blackwood, Silk Mercer, of 47 North Bridge, 'Baron Bailie of Canongate and Calton', had his mind made up, he was a man to be reckoned with. It was March 12, 1823.

He had to make his way carefully among the dust and debris of the High Street, side-stepping the wheels of carriages that rattled along the roadway between the towering tenements. He had to dodge sedan chairs supported on the liveried shoulders of sweating bearers, their occupants curtained against the stench of rotten fruit, fish, manure, stale whisky and other odours that wafted from the close-mouths and the stalls cluttering Parliament Square and the entrance to St Giles', the High Kirk of Edinburgh. And as he made his way to the Council meeting, Old Bailie Blackwood was going over in his mind the events of the past few months.

Things had been happening fast – too fast for Old Bailie Blackwood and one or two other members of Edinburgh Town Council who were used to doing things at their own pace, doing what they liked and doing it when they liked. Self-elected, undemocratic, and frequently corrupt, they were like every other town council in Scotland and more power-ful than most, at a time when only the wealthy had a vote and the Scottish Burgh Reform Bill was still a decade away. But Edinburgh Town Council had been moved to haste by two energetic and pro-gressive young men, one of whom was destined to play a large part in the Reform Acts of the 1830's that extended the franchise for

Parliamentary and council elections to middle-class householders. That man was Henry Cockburn (1779–1854). The other was Leonard Horner (1785–1864).

Henry (later Lord) Cockburn, the son of a Baron of the Scottish Court of Exchequer and nephew of the formidable Tory statesman Henry Dundas (Viscount Melville), was an Edinburgh advocate who rose to be a judge of the Court of Session: a wit, sage, and reformer whose *Memorials of his Time* (first published in 1856, two years after his death) are a lively and colourful record of Edinburgh life in the first half of the nineteenth century. Leonard Horner was a linen merchant, a keen amateur geologist, and a pioneer of education for the workers. By this time he had already been instrumental in founding, in 1821, a school for mechanics and tradesmen known as The School of Arts, which over the years has evolved into what is now Heriot-Watt University, and which was the forerunner of many similar 'Mechanics' Institutes in London and the industrial Midlands.

In March, 1823, all that these two friends wanted to do was to open a new school in Edinburgh. Old Bailie Blackwood was just as determined to stop them. Ironically, it was Blackwood's successful opposition to the scheme at the Town Council meeting that March day that turned the dream of a school into a reality. Old Bailie Blackwood was to make history inadvertently, for it was his tactics that ensured the foundation of a school which would lead educational progress throughout Scotland and even farther afield, a school humane and gracious in tone, and liberal and comprehensive in aim, to a degree hitherto unknown in any great school in Britain – a school, moreover, that would make a powerful impact on men and events throughout the world for the next century and a half. For the rest of the nineteenth century, there was to be a tremendous upsurge in new schools for the middle and upper classes; the school that Old Bailie Blackwood tried to stop was to lead the way . . .

To understand how it came about, it is necessary to see Old Bailie Blackwood and Henry Cockburn and Leonard Horner in the Edinburgh of the 1820's. The war with Napoleon had only recently ended. There were men living in Edinburgh whose fathers had fought in the '45 rebellion. Henry Mackenzie (1745–1831), long celebrated as the author of *The Man of Feeling* (1771), had been born on the very day in July, 1745, that Prince Charles Edward Stuart landed in Moidart to raise a Jacobite army; he was a living link with the great literary figures of the eighteenth century like David Hume, John Home the playwright, and William Robertson the historian. Sir Walter Scott's enormously successful historical novels were based on tales of adventure and intrigue in the struggle between Scots and English that he had picked up at first hand from veterans of those battles in his legal visits around the country and from exiled Highlanders scraping an existence in the crowded wynds of Edinburgh's Royal Mile.

Scots and English were just beginning to settle into some kind of feeling of partnership after the troubles that had followed the Union of the Parliaments in 1707. The long Napoleonic Wars, during which the Scots had fought side by side with the English and learned to hate their traditional allies, the French, had drawn the two parts of Britain together. The constant threat of invasion by a common enemy had given them their first sense of unified nationhood. When King George IV visited Edinburgh in the summer of 1822 he was projected as the heir to the House of Stuart, elaborately dressed up in an extravagance of tartan. His visit, the first Royal Visit to Scotland by a reigning British monarch for nearly 200 years, was a spectacular success, thanks mainly to the efforts of that staunch Tory monarchist Sir Walter Scott, who stage-managed the whole affair; but it was also blamed for keeping the Town Council so preoccupied all that summer that there was no time to attend to the urgent matter of a new school that was to give Old Bailie Blackwood his unexpected place in history in 1823.

The king's visit was a symbol of the new entente between Scotland and England. The Industrial Revolution was under way, breaking down national barriers as workers strove to improve their living and working conditions in the face of repressive resistance. 'Revolutionaries' who were sentenced to transportation or even death at Edinburgh High Court were often Englishmen who had come north to rally their Scottish 'brothers-in-servitude'. Scots were moving into influential positions in Government, in the Armed Forces, and in the service of the Honourable East India Company. Wealthy Scotsmen were sending their sons to English boarding schools to help their chances in the competition for entry into these careers, or to be tutored by English dons for entrance to Oxford and Cambridge. Sir Walter Scott, who like all his contemporaries of rank and education in Scotland spoke English with a broad Scots accent and was fiercely proud of his Scottish heritage, was also a dedicated Tory and an ardent supporter of the British monarchy. He could suit his speech to the highest occasions at the English court, he wrote his novels and poetry in the stylised English

of his time, he bought one son a commission in a fine English regiment
and sent the other to Oxford after having him tutored by a Church of
England clergyman.

But the traffic was by no means one-way. Edinburgh's medical
school had for long been famous, but now, since the French wars had
closed the Continent to English students, more and more of them had
been coming to Edinburgh instead of going to Paris, Rome, or Vienna.
English philosophers, English poets and English travellers were writing,
lecturing and preaching, all helping to diffuse the Scottishness of Edinburgh's cultural life.

That life was centred on Parliament House in Edinburgh, in the
halls of justice of Scotland; for the elite of the land in education and
intellect, in talent of tongue and pen, in metaphysics, philosophy
and politics, were the men of law. Sir Walter Scott was an Edinburgh
advocate. So was Henry Cockburn. So was Francis (later Lord)
Jeffrey, co-founder and editor from 1803–29 of the progressive Whig
journal, the *Edinburgh Review*. So was the great law reformer Henry
Brougham (the brougham carriage was named after him), one of the
co-founders of the *Edinburgh Review* in 1802, later to be Lord Chancellor in the Whig administration of 1830–4.

Indeed, the first committee for running the new Edinburgh Academy
when it came about, and the first list of subscribers, read like a legal
drum-roll: Cockburn, Jeffrey, Sir Walter Scott; the Lord Justice-
Clerk, the Solicitor-General, the Deputy Keeper of the Signet, Writers
to the Signet, Advocates, Sheriffs, solicitors . . .

The majority, like Sir Walter Scott, were Tories, supporters of the
Government of the time. The Tory party encompassed most of the
wealth, rank, and public offices in the country. But the two leading
figures in the foundation of the Edinburgh Academy – Henry Cockburn (despite his family connection with the Dundas dynasty) and
Leonard Horner – and many of the friends who supported them, were
Whigs, the Opposition party, the Liberals of their time, the anti-
Establishment, supporters of their former leader Charles Fox whose
birthday they celebrated every year with a dinner. Sheriff's officers
were always sent to the Fox Dinner in Edinburgh to take a note of the
names of those who attended. It could be dangerous to belong to a
party that opposed the Government, and it could have a serious effect
on the prospects of a young man who wanted to make his career at the
Scottish Bar. Whig lawyers who managed to secure a place had a hard
time keeping it. Juniors with Whig sympathies found official doors

barred, judges unkind, agents taking their fees elsewhere. They were never allowed to forget the case of their Radical fellow-advocate Thomas Muir, who had been sentenced to fourteen years' transportation to Botany Bay for sedition in 1793. Henry Cockburn was a particularly able advocate, especially in criminal cases, but for many years after he was called to the Bar in 1800 he received no advancement because of his radical views. Francis Jeffrey, who shared the leadership of the Bar with him, also had his career seriously retarded for years because of his adherence to the Opposition party. It was not until the Whig administration of 1830–4 that these two outstanding advocates came into their own – Henry Cockburn as Solicitor-General and Francis Jeffrey as Lord Advocate. It was they who presented the first Scottish Reform Bill of 1832, which was carried through by Henry Brougham as Lord Chancellor; Brougham himself had found the struggle for promotion at the Scottish Bar hopeless for a young lawyer of radical views, and in 1805 he went to London where he was admitted to the English Bar.

But Scotland's political emancipation that came to fruition with the first of the Reform Acts in 1832 under Cockburn and Jeffrey had been on the way since 1805 with the fall from power of Pitt's political lieutenant in Scotland, Henry Dundas, the 1st Viscount Melville, who had governed Scotland for a generation of almost unbroken Tory rule with a kind of benevolent dictatorship. His nephew, Henry Cockburn, wrote of him: 'Henry Dundas, an Edinburgh man, and well calculated by talent and manner to make despotism popular, was the absolute dictator of Scotland, and had the means of rewarding submission and of extinguishing opposition beyond what were ever exercised in modern times by one person in any portion of the empire.' (*Memorials*, p. 67.)

Variously Solicitor-General, Lord Advocate, Treasurer of the Navy, Secretary for War, President of the Board of Control that ruled India and Secretary of State for the Home Department that ruled Scotland, Henry Dundas was impeached in 1805 during a brief Whig administration and tried for 'gross malversation and breach of duty' as Treasurer of the Navy. He was acquitted of all charges after a trial lasting a fortnight – but the realisation that someone so apparently omnipotent, the very symbol of the Establishment, could have even his motives questioned gave Scots a new sense of freedom. Although the Tories were back in power within a year, reform was in the air. Lord Liverpool, a Tory with liberal views, led the Government from 1812 to

1826, and it became possible for a man to have progressive ideas without being branded a traitor.

By the 1820's the junior lawyers who led the Whig movement in Scotland were being accepted by society and even leading it. Sheer talent had overcome the hostility to their views, and they were all destined to achieve power in their profession. The brightest stars in the brilliant circle of intellectuals who wrote and debated on life and literature and politics in Edinburgh were Cockburn, Jeffrey, and Leonard Horner's more celebrated brother, the economist Francis Horner (another co-founder of the *Edinburgh Review*, who became a barrister at the English Bar and a crusading M.P. against the slave trade). These three represented the cream of Edinburgh's cultural life at a time when the capital was still known as the Athens of the North: the afterglow of the Golden Age of Edinburgh. They had been schoolboys at the High School in Edinburgh, and had studied at Edinburgh University under the great Dugald Stewart, the radical professor of Moral Philosophy (1753–1828). Cockburn wrote of him: 'Flourishing in an age which requires all the dignity of morals to counteract the tendencies of physical pursuits and political convulsion, he has exalted the character of his country and his generation. No intelligent pupil of his ever ceased to respect philosophy, or was ever false to his principles, without feeling the crime aggravated by the recollection of the morality that Stewart had taught him.'

Professor Dugald Stewart excited an interest in philosophy such as neither Scotland nor England had ever known, and pupils were drawn to Scotland from all over to sit under him, among them the future Lord Palmerston. Another was the English clergyman, journalist and wit, Sydney Smith, who was also a co-founder of the *Edinburgh Review* along with Jeffrey and Brougham and Horner. In this journal they expounded their liberal ideas, argued on political topics, reviewed books, criticised sermons, and discussed the scientific discoveries of their time.

Besides the literary giants there were men like David Hume, the nephew of the great philosopher; Archibald Fletcher, the 'father of burgh reform'; George Joseph Bell, whose *Mercantile Commentaries* was the standard work then on Scottish jurisprudence; and John Clerk, later Lord Eldin, one-time Solicitor-General and a knowledgeable patron of the arts. As young men, most of them (including Sir Walter Scott) belonged to the Speculative Society in Edinburgh (founded in 1764), where animated weekly debates produced sparkling speeches and great thoughts on every subject under the sun from Irish rebellion to the merits of Mr Wordsworth's latest poem (but not, apparently, the question of setting up a new classical Academy in Edinburgh).

Journalism, too, was beginning to flourish. The *Edinburgh Evening Courant*, which supported the Tories, and the *Caledonian Mercury*, which supported the Whigs, had been established for a century, but in January, 1817, *The Scotsman* was founded as a respectable Liberal weekly and did much to enliven the journalistic scene. The Tories replied by rejuvenating the failing *Scots Magazine* as *Blackwood's Magazine*, in which Whig opponents were lambasted with breathtaking scurrility by Sir Walter Scott's son-in-law and biographer, John Gibson Lockhart, and even more so by John Wilson, soon to be Professor of Moral Philosophy at Edinburgh University, writing under the pen-name of 'Christopher North'. Paisley-born John Wilson was the most flamboyant and rumbustious figure in Edinburgh even in that rumbustious age; he was described by a friend as 'a sixteen stoner – a cocker, a racer, a six-bottler, a twenty-four tumblerer – an out and outer – a true upright, knocking-down, poetical, prosaic, moral, professorial, hard-drinking, fierce-eating, good-looking, honourable, and straightforward Tory'! In 1821 another Tory journal was launched, the *Beacon*, which was so spectacularly slanderous that its contributors were sometimes attacked in the street; in 1822, indeed, one of its writers, Sir Alexander Boswell (the son of Dr Johnson's biographer) was shot dead in a duel with a man he had defamed, James Stuart of Dunearn, W.S., an ardent Whig.

It was in this exciting and excitable cultural climate, in an Edinburgh where the young Thomas Carlyle was taking private pupils and immersing himself in German literature, an Edinburgh in which, according to Sydney Smith, people even did their courting in terms of metaphysics – it was in this Edinburgh that Henry Cockburn and Leonard Horner had their dream of a great new school, and Old Bailie Blackwood made his way to a Town Council meeting on March 12, 1823.

THE SOCIAL BACKGROUND

In a morning after seven o'clock it stinks intolerably ('A Gentleman')

The proposed new school was the last thought in the minds of the ordinary Edinburgh citizens whom Old Bailie Blackwood passed on his way to the City Chambers. In 1823, mere survival was their main preoccupation in the damp closes and stinking wynds of the over-crowded, disease-ridden 'lands', or tenements. Crime, vagrancy, dirt and drunkenness throve in the narrow streets. Whisky cost 10d. a bottle, tea 8s. a pound, and 10s. a week was a good wage for those who were lucky enough to find work.

The last Scottish famine had occurred in the winter of 1782-3. Since then, improved farming methods and trading prosperity had ensured that there was plenty of food for those who could afford to buy it, but employment was uncertain, and as the Industrial Revolution brought more and more people flocking to the towns in search of work, not even all the canal-building schemes and new cotton mills and water projects and gas works could absorb the available labour, and destitution, hunger and malnutrition were rife.

Typhus was known as 'the poor man's friend' because it regularly cut down the number of hungry mouths to feed. Cholera was on its way and was to take a terrible toll in four epidemics in the next fifty years. Smallpox was endemic, although vaccination had been practised successfully since 1801. Without public services of any kind, with sanitation unheard of, no piped water, and sewage chucked from windows into the streets, doctors battled in vain against disease. General hospitals, run on charity, were incapable of coping with the victims of plague. Volunteer societies did their best: there were soup kitchens, sickness and funeral societies, friendly societies and dispensaries handing out medicines for the poor. But hospitals were just as ignorant of sanitation or hygiene as the populace. Joseph Lister with his antiseptic system would not be born until 1827. James Young Simpson was a twelve-year-old in Bathgate and a quarter of a century away from the discovery of anaesthetics – which was no consolation to those requiring amputations in 1823.

It was the time of the body-snatchers. Burke and Hare were prowling the Edinburgh streets of the 1820's, and Dr Robert Knox, the young anatomist for whom they provided corpses for dissection, was about to be made Conservator of the new museum of the College of Surgeons in Edinburgh. Henry Cockburn was to defend Burke's 'common law wife', Helen McDougal, at their murder trial in 1828.

Gas lighting had been introduced, but only the wealthy could afford it. The friction match had not yet been invented. There were still no trains. Travel was by coach (eighteen hours from Edinburgh to Carlisle), while shorter journeys were made on horseback, by private carriage, or sedan chair. Glasgow and Edinburgh each had a theatre.

There were travelling players, circuses and menageries, prize-fighting and cock-fights. People were roused in the mornings by a six o'clock bell, and an eight o'clock curfew warned children off the streets at night.

Scotland's population was now increasing fast. At the first official Census in 1801 it was 1,608,000 – double the estimated population at the time of the Union of the Parliaments in 1707. And as people came crowding into the towns, the well-to-do of the other Scottish cities began to move out. The Glasgow merchants built themselves mansions in the West End; middle-class Aberdonians put up rows of villas beyond the Den Burn; prosperous Dundee families moved out to Newport. Only the capital resisted the necessity to build beyond the limits of the old city walls. Perched on its rocky ridge with the Castle at one end and the Palace of Holyroodhouse at the other, protected by a drowned valley to the north (the Nor' Loch, now Princes Street Gardens), Edinburgh hugged itself for as long as it could to the Royal Mile (Lawnmarket, High Street, and Canongate) and the adjoining closes and wynds. Unable or disinclined to move outwards, Edinburgh had to build upwards – ten storeys, fifteen storeys of towering tenements, with all classes and types piled on top of one another – the poor in the cellars and attics, the noblemen and lawyers and ministers and doctors in between. Thirty years before Old Bailie Blackwood took his historic walk to the City Chambers there were two dukes living in the crowded Canongate along with sixteen earls, several lords and judges, and an assortment of lawyers, merchants, clerks and tradesmen. An English traveller had written: 'In a morning after seven o'clock, it stinks intolerably; for after ten at night it sounds very oddly in the ears of a stranger to hear all passers-by cry out as loud as to be heard to the uppermost stories of the houses . . . "Hoad yare hoand"; that is, "Hold your hand and throw not till I am past".' (*Tour in Great Britain*, by A Gentleman, 1753). A hundred years later the conditions were to be just as bad, if not worse.

But at long last the stubborn civic authorities were persuaded that no marauding army was going to assault their battlements if they built a bridge connecting the Old Town with the lands to the north of their protective water-filled valley. With the completion of the North Bridge in 1772, the better-off citizens began to move out of the huddle on the hill and build fine houses on the line of what is now Princes Street. The Theatre Royal and Register House went up at the east end of Princes Street; Queen Street and George Street took shape, then

Charlotte Square. The Nor' Loch was drained early in the nineteenth century and a rampart raised in it to make the Mound – another link between the Old Town and the new residential area.

By 1823 the elegant lines of the New Town had spread from Queen Street down to Great King Street. By 1831 the population of the New Town had risen to 40,000 out of a total Edinburgh and Leith population of 162,000. The Old Town residences had been abandoned to the poorer folk, and in 1823 there were still around 50,000 people crowded into the old cellars and attics and the deserted flats of the noblemen. The overcrowding and filth were now worse than ever, but the judges and lawyers and merchants who now enjoyed more gracious living in the Georgian terraces of the New Town were far from being insulated from the discomforts they had left behind in the Old Town. The Old Town was still the heart of Edinburgh. The courts, the High Kirk, the university, the offices and the markets were all still there. Every day the occupants of New Town and Old met in one great heaving noisy throng, now made all the more hazardous by the increased traffic of coaches and carriages hurrying across the bridges that linked the two sections of the city.

Into this disagreeable mêlée the New Town dwellers had to send their children to be educated at the High School on the far side of the High Street, beyond the Cowgate, at the bottom of Infirmary Street. These youngsters had to dodge the carriages, rub shoulders with the destitute, breathe the fetid air of the close-mouths, and make their way homewards on winter evenings through darkened wynds where footpads and other perils might lurk. No wonder that Cockburn and Horner wanted a new school on their own side of the tracks . . .

EDUCATIONAL BACKGROUND

Leonard Horner and I had often discussed the causes and the remedies of the decline of classical education in Scotland . . .   (Lord Cockburn, *Memorials of His Time*)

Nowadays, when local authorities provide buses or even taxis to save children long or dangerous walks to school, it is easy to appreciate why the New Town dwellers of Edinburgh in the 1820's should be anxious to have a New Town school. For reasons of health and safety alone they had good reason for wanting an alternative to the old High School, which had been founded in 1578 during the reign of King James VI. But the founders of the Edinburgh Academy had more serious objection to the old school than simply its remoteness from the New Town or its insalubrious location at the High School Yards near Kirk o' Field.

Their dissatisfaction with the High School was a reflection of their dissatisfaction with the whole state of education in Scotland. They were concerned that Scotland was not going to be able to compete with England for the top positions in running the rapidly spreading Empire. They were well aware of the changes that were taking place in many Scottish schools to meet the demands of the Industrial Revolution, but they were afraid that the new trend would confine Scots to a second-class position in British affairs. They knew that the average Scot was better educated than the average Englishman, and that a far higher proportion of Scots than English attended University. This was all very well for turning out droves of advocates, village dominies, doctors, and unheard-of poets and philosophers; but for those wanting to make a real mark in British scholarship, there was an undoubted advantage in having taken a degree at Oxford or Cambridge, where Latin and Greek were compulsory as entrance qualifications. This meant competing with the only people who aspired to that standard of education in England, the products of the six elite Public Schools – Eton, Harrow, Charterhouse, Winchester, Westminster or Rugby, where boys were put through an intensive process of specialisation in Latin and Greek until the age of eighteen or nineteen; whereas Scottish boys were attending university at Edinburgh, Glasgow, St Andrews or Aberdeen at the age of fourteen or fifteen, or even as young as twelve.

The problem was that there were few rules and no regulations governing education in Scotland in those days. Although John Knox's *First Book of Discipline* in 1560 had pledged 'a school in every parish', by 1715 only one out of three males and one out of twelve females in the county of Fife could sign their names; by 1720 scarcely anyone in Galloway could read; in the 1730's there were twelve parishes in the presbytery of Ayr without a single school, and as late as 1758 there were 175 parishes in the Highlands without school or teacher. And this was in spite of continual efforts at legislation by the Scottish Parliament, including the 1696 *Act for Settling of Schools*, which gave Scotland a head-start over England in educational legislation by decreeing that in every parish not already provided for, a school should be established and a schoolmaster provided at the expense of the heritors or land-owners of the parish.

Although many landowners chose to ignore the law, parish schools multiplied throughout the country and were the basis of the tradition of democratic education for which Scotland became famed. The laird's son and the tinker's son sat at the same desks, and the 'lad o' pairts' could go straight from his village school to the Humanity (Latin) or Divinity classes of the nearest University.

The parochial system did not extend to the burghs, yet despite the absence of legislation there had been grammar schools in all the towns of any consequence in Scotland since before the Reformation. They were now run by the town council, with the Church (as in the case of the parish schools) seeing to it that the schoolmaster was an adherent of the Church of Scotland. The burgh generally supplied the school building and a small stipend for the teacher out of the Common Good fund. Burgh primary schools, which instilled the rudiments of education (the three Rs) were, like the parish or rural schools, co-educational. But the grammar schools, whose main concern was to teach Latin in order to prepare pupils for University, were mainly confined to boys. The Universities, of course, were barred to women.

Some of these grammar schools were run entirely by the town councils, some by private subscription, and some by a combination of both. There were 'sessional schools' founded and managed by kirk sessions of the Church of Scotland, of which the most celebrated was the one founded in connection with the Tron Kirk in Edinburgh by John Wood (later a Director of the Edinburgh Academy) in 1813. There were private Academies, endowment schools, Trust schools, hospital schools.

Until the latter part of the eighteenth century, Latin was practically the only subject taught in the larger grammar schools; this was because lectures were still being conducted in Latin at the Scottish Universities until the middle of the eighteenth century. Francis Hutcheson was the first professor in Scotland to give a lecture in English, on his appointment to the chair of Moral Philosophy at Glasgow University in 1729. The Scots clung to Latin as the language of academic discourse long after most of the rest of Europe – chiefly, perhaps, through a reluctance to accept English, with all its bitter associations from history.

But as Scotland's commercial prosperity increased towards the middle of the eighteenth century, the demand grew for a more modern type of education. Schools which were comparatively remote from the dominating influence of the universities began to introduce French, German, arithmetic, mathematics, navigation, and drawing. Writing or Commercial Schools were opened, teaching book-keeping, arithmetic, and mathematics. Ayr Grammar School broadened its curriculum in 1746 to prepare pupils for a business career by adding mathematics, navigation, surveying, book-keeping and natural philosophy to its traditional diet of Latin and Greek. Perth Academy was opened by the Town Council in 1761 in response to a public petition advocating the advantages of science against a knowledge of dead languages. It was an entirely new type of school; all the teaching and exercises were in English, there was no provision for instruction in languages, and the curriculum was confined entirely to mathematics, natural science, astronomy, physics, English, civil history, and religion, and later chemistry, drawing, and painting. This complete turn-about from the classical tradition was followed by the setting up of similar schools in Dundee, Inverness, Elgin, Fortrose, Ayr, and Dumfries.

There is no doubt that the new educational trend served a useful and necessary purpose, if the Scots were to be in the forefront of the Industrial Revolution. But what alarmed people like Cockburn and the other founders of the Edinburgh Academy was that this tremendous surge of educational reform was not being balanced by an improvement in the quality and conditions of teaching in the schools that were the bastions of the old classical tradition – in particular, the High School in Edinburgh. As Cockburn wrote in his *Memorials*: 'Leonard Horner and I had often discussed the causes and the remedies of the decline of classical education in Scotland; and we were at last satisfied that no adequate improvement could be effected so long as there was only one great classical school in Edinburgh, and this one placed under the Town Council, and lowered, perhaps necessarily, so as to suit the wants of a class of boys to more than two-thirds of whom classical accomplishment is foreseen to be useless.' (p. 235).

The High School, like Edinburgh University, had been placed 'under the Town Council' because Mary Queen of Scots had granted ground known as the Kirk o' Field to the City of Edinburgh for the express purpose of establishing Colleges, Schools, and Hospitals. The University was not opened until 1583, but a school for teaching the rudiments of Latin and Greek was founded in 1578 and replaced by a new building in 1777. To this new High School the magistrates of Edinburgh, as patrons, gave their sanction and the sum of £200 from the civic funds to help pay for the school-house. The rest of the cost was raised by public subscription. The only other financial responsibility borne by the Town Council was to pay a small annual salary to the Rector and masters, whose main source of income, however, was the fees paid by the pupils. The Rector had the largest class: the bigger the class, the higher the income. The result was that the High School crammed pupils into its classes indiscriminately until by 1822 it had become, according to the founders of the Academy, hopelessly over-crowded, despite desperate attempts to create extra seating space by dividing even the school Hall into separate classrooms.

It had been built to hold 450 boys. By 1809 the roll had increased to 630, and by 1820 it had reached a peak of 890 pupils, which made it possibly the largest school in Britain at the time. These pupils were divided among four masters and a Rector, whose class in 1823 (when the total roll had begun to fall) nevertheless reached an all-time record of 257. These great mobs of boys sat in long rows that rose upwards in tiers, with the cleverest at the top and the slower boys 'sitting boobie' on the lowest benches. They droned their Latin verbs and declensions en masse with 'ushers' (monitors paid by the masters out of their own pockets) 'hearkening' each row and helping to dispense punishment to the slow or inattentive.

It is significant that, right from the start, the founders of the new Academy, all of whom had been educated at the High School, were agreed that corporal punishment should only be administered for serious acts of misbehaviour and never for scholastic backwardness; many an Academy teacher was called to account for striking a pupil – and this at a time when the appallingly brutal floggings at English public schools were accepted with a shrug as a fact of life.

Cockburn remembered his days at the High School without pleasure: 'Out of the whole four [sic] years of my attendance there were probably not ten days in which I was not flogged, at least once. Yet I never entered the class, nor left it, without feeling perfectly qualified, both in ability and preparation, for its whole business; which, being confined to Latin alone, and in necessarily short tasks, since every one of the boys had to rhyme over the very same words, in the very same way, was no great feat. But I was driven stupid. Oh! the bodily and mental weari-ness of sitting six hours a day, staring idly at a page, without motion and without thought, and trembling at the gradual approach of the merci-less giant. I never got a single prize, and once sat *boobie* at the annual public examination. The beauty of no Roman word, or thought, or action, ever occurred to me; nor did I ever fancy that Latin was of any use except to torture boys.' (*Memorials*, pp. 3–4.)

Yet Cockburn still believed in 1823 that 'there is no solid and grace-ful foundation for boys' minds like classical learning, grammatically

learnt.' But he asked – 'How is it possible for the elements, including
the very letters, of a language to be taught to one hundred boys at
once by a single lecturing professor?'

How much more must he have been concerned about the High
School Rector's monstrous class of 257 in the session of 1822–23! And
he was not the only one to be concerned; the parents were beginning
to show their disapproval, too. Although the Rector's class had reached
a new peak, the younger classes were beginning to decline rapidly in
numbers, and the total roll of the school in 1823 had shrunk to 694 from
its high of 890 in 1820. Yet the private academies which had sprung
up in the New Town were showing no equivalent rise in numbers.
Where were the boys going?

Some were having private tutors. Some were being sent farther
afield, to Mr Langhorne's small private preparatory school at Stoney
Hill in Musselburgh (soon to become Loretto), or to schools south of
the Border. Cockburn and his friends wanted to arrest this dangerous
drift away from Edinburgh. They believed that it could only be done
by means of a school situated right inside the New Town, with smaller
classes than at the High School and with a much greater emphasis on
the teaching of Greek. If Cockburn despaired of the Latin teaching at
the High School, he was even more concerned about the attitude in
Scotland to the teaching of Greek.

Greek had always been regarded as the prerogative of the universities in Scotland. The Professor of Greek at Edinburgh had a class
of beginners, and since his income depended on the fees paid by
students who enrolled in his class, he greatly resented schools sending
boys to university so proficient in Greek that they could bypass his
class and go straight to the Philosophy classes; as a result, very little
Greek was taught at the High School in Cockburn's time there (1787–
1793). By 1809, however, it had been established as part of the six
years' course of study, and Archibald ('Bowsey') Carmichael, who
taught first at the High School and then at the Royal Academy of
Inverness as Classical Master before joining the staff of the new Edinburgh Academy, could claim: 'It cannot be disguised that for a long
period the study of ancient languages was conducted almost nowhere
in Scotland with reasonable skill and ability, save in the High School of
Edinburgh.' From 1814 onwards, the Town Council awarded a gold
medal to the boy at the top of the Greek class, and there is no doubt
that during the Rectorship of James Pillans, who had taught at Eton
and went on in 1820 to become Professor of Humanity at Edinburgh

University, the High School was in the forefront of Greek teaching amongst Scottish schools. Indeed, it occupied a unique position in Scottish education, with a standard of instruction that was closer to university levels than to normal burgh schools. When Dr J. Griscom, Professor of Chemistry and Natural Philosophy in the New York Institution, made an educational tour of Europe in 1819, he had nothing but praise for the High School of Edinburgh: 'We were highly gratified with the evidences of intelligence and attainment which the boys displayed when collected into one room, and examined before us by the Rector. The superiority of their instruction appeared not only in the facility of their translations, but in the readiness with which they recited parallel passages, and referred to the illustrations of different classical authors, and in their acquaintance with the geography, chronology, etc., of the historical passages, which were given to them as extemporaneous exercises . . . With such advantages of intellectual and moral instruction, is it surprising that Scotland should have taken such an elevated stand among the nations for the intelligence, industry and sobriety of her people?' (*A Year in Europe*, by J. Griscom.)

But this fulsome accolade could not mask the fact that Greek still came a poor second, even at the High School; Greek instruction only amounted to one hour three times a week, with another hour on the Greek Testament, compared with the four hours a day that were devoted to Latin. Clearly this was not nearly enough to compete with the standards achieved by Winchester or Eton; and it was their kind of attention to the teaching of Greek that Henry Cockburn and Leonard Horner had in mind one April day in 1822 when they went for a walk on the Pentland Hills . . .

CHAPTER II

The Scheme for a New Academy (1822)

'. . . from topmost Allermuir,
Or steep Caerketton, dreaming, gaze again.
Far set in field and woods, the town I see
Spring gallant from the shallows of her smoke,
Cragged, spired and turreted, her virgin fort
Beflagged. About, on seaward-dropping hills,
New folds of city glitter . . .'
(Robert Louis Stevenson, E.A. 1861-63)

HENRY COCKBURN always felt that there had been something symbolic in the fact that he and Leonard Horner had made their decision to found the Edinburgh Academy while they were out walking on the Pentland Hills: '. . . One day on the top of one of the Pentlands – emblematic of the solidity of our foundation and of the extent of our prospects – we two resolved to set about the establishment of a new school.' (*Memorials*, p. 235.)

A century and a half later, surrounded as we are by the machinery of State and the paraphernalia of bureaucracy, conditioned to being passive onlookers as the wheels of progress are inexorably turned by faceless departments of government, that far-off walk in the hills conjures up an impression of freedom of thought and action, a spirit of adventure as heady and refreshing as the breeze that whipped the faces of the two men that day. What a nerve they had! What vision! What big hearts! 'To set about the establishment of a new school' – just like that! Two men scarcely in their middle age (Cockburn was forty-three, Horner thirty-seven), brought up in security and comfort, doing well in their respective careers, graciously housed in the New Town, busily occupied with convivial society, clever talk, and congenial debates – these men could so easily have sent any sons they had (Horner had none, but Cockburn had six) to private tutors or English boarding schools and reserved their progressive ideas on education for some sparkling paper to be read to the Speculative Society. They must have known that they were letting themselves in for a lot of trouble. There would be opposition on all sides. As Whigs they were under permanent suspicion among members of the Establishment. The campaign for social and electoral reform was under way, and they were its leading advocates. Political feelings were running high. They would be accused on the one hand of founding a hotbed of Whiggery among the youth of the city, and on the other of providing a school for the exclusive use of the privileged upper classes. They would probably be opposed by the powerful Town Council, who would see the new school as a direct challenge to their own High School. They had no promise of money. From that day to this, the Academy would never know the luxury of a really rich benefactor. There was never a major endowment. No tycoon has ever left his millions to the Edinburgh Academy.

But Cockburn and Horner were undaunted. Having made up their minds, like excited young undergraduates planning a new magazine, one can just see them striding down from the hills and back to Edinburgh to start their new school.

Leonard Horner was good at starting things. He possessed that rare combination of high principles and exceptional energy. He had been educated at the High School and at Edinburgh University, where he studied chemistry and developed an interest in geology. At the age of nineteen he became a partner in the family business (his father was a linen merchant with interests in both Edinburgh and London), and in 1804 he left Edinburgh to live in London. There he distinguished himself as an amateur geologist (he was elected a Fellow of the Geological Society of London in 1808, and a Fellow of the Royal Society at the age of twenty-eight, and he was an intimate acquaintance of Charles Darwin). When he returned to Edinburgh in 1817 he became prominent in Whig political circles, and became totally involved in the cause of educational reform. Of The School of Arts (now Heriot-Watt University) that he was instrumental in founding in 1821 'for the instruction of mechanics', Cockburn wrote: 'The whole merit, both of its conception and of its first three or four years' management, is due exclusively to Leonard Horner. His good sense, mildness, and purity made it a favourite with the reasonable of all parties and classes.' (*Memorials*, p. 224).

Horner was appointed the first Warden of the newly-founded University of London in 1827, and occupied this post for four difficult and tension-racked years; when he resigned in 1831 he had to spend two years convalescing in Italy. In 1833 he was appointed one of the first four Inspectors of Factories for Britain under the provisions of the Factory Act of 1833, and for the next twenty-five years he did a tremendous amount to improve the conditions of factory workers in Britain. The Inspectors' work soon led to the banning of the employment of women in mines, a reduction in working hours and a half-holiday on Saturdays, and to the fencing-in of dangerous machinery. It also led to a rapid increase in the number of schools and in Government expenditure on schools (from £30,000 in 1839 to £663,000 in 1858), because the 1833 Act had limited the employment of children under the age of thirteen to eight hours a day and of children under eighteen to twelve hours a day, and had also laid down that children must attend school; and since there were no schools available, Horner set about providing them.

Throughout those years as an Inspector, when Horner was in charge of the four northern counties of England (an area which then contained 1,484 mills), he continued to work for the Edinburgh Academy and help in its decisions wherever he was. 'Leonard Horner, Merchant' was a Director of the Academy for a relatively short time, from 1823-7 and again from 1834-6, but even when he was not on the Board he was frequently consulted by the Directors on matters of school policy: and he loved visiting the school he had helped to found. In June, 1841, for instance, he wrote to his wife: 'I went to Cockburn's at two and we bent our steps to the Academy . . . Cockburn says that everything is going on admirably well . . . I looked upon the flourishing state of my work with great satisfaction.' (*Memoir of Leonard Horner*, edited by one his daughters, Katharine M. Lyell). In July, 1855, he wrote after another visit: 'I was at the Academy from ten to three, and have been much gratified with everything.' His final visit to the Academy was in July, 1863, the year before his death, when he was Chairman at the annual end-of-session Exhibition: 'I have had great satisfaction in my visits to the Academy, and have even been of some use, for I am in close communication with the Directors about some important improvements in our system of teaching.'

Cockburn, writing in the 1820's, called him 'the most active and enlightened of our citizens, and with a singular talent for organisation'. At his death in March, 1864, the Directors of the Academy wrote: 'The Academy has lost one of its oldest and best friends. He was one of the few survivors of the band of eminent men by whom the school was founded . . . Neither absence from Edinburgh, nor employment in some branch of the public service, diminished Mr Horner's warm interest in the Academy.'

He was described as 'short and stocky in appearance with high forehead and deepset eyes; his strong mouth and determined jaw proclaimed him a man of ruthless energy and deep conviction – ideally suited for the part he was called upon to play'. (*The Early Factory Legislation*, by M. W. Thomas, 1948).

Such was one of the founders of the Edinburgh Academy. What of Henry Cockburn, who has always enjoyed rather more of the limelight, the man who was described by the Directors of the Academy at his death in 1854 as 'emphatically the father and founder of the School'? He was born in 1779 in one of the high 'lands' on the east side of Parliament Close. His father also owned a small estate about eight miles south of Edinburgh called Cockpen (which, presumably, made him the Laird o' Cockpen); he was Sheriff of the County of Midlothian and later Judge Admiral and a Baron of Exchequer as Lord Cockburn.

Young Henry spent six years at the High School ('notorious for its severity and riotousness'), then went to Edinburgh University, became an advocate, was appointed Solicitor-General in the Reforming Whig administration of 1830, and later became a Scottish judge of great distinction.

But Lord Cockburn, the man who left us such scintillating glimpses of the characters and happenings of his day, had no great word to say about himself. The *Edinburgh Review*, on the other hand, described him as 'one of the most popular men north of the Tweed. His was not the popularity of a great name . . . It was good, honest, personal liking . . . Nor was this popularity confined to Edinburgh. He was known to all classes over Scotland; and from Aberdeen to Wigtown no assemblage of Scotsmen, young or old, could be gathered, in which his lineaments were not known and recognised, or in which his approach was not a signal for a vociferous welcome'. (*Edinburgh Review*, January, 1857.)

That, of course, was written after his death, in a Whig journal. He didn't inspire the same vociferous welcome in the minds of Old Bailie Blackwood and certain other Edinburgh citizens in the months that followed the walk on the Pentlands.

Thomas Carlyle described him in his *Journal* as 'small, solid, and genuine . . . a bright, cheery-voiced, hazel-eyed man; a Scotch dialect with plenty of good logic in it, and of practical sagacity; veracious, too. A gentleman, I should say, and perfectly in the Scotch type, perhaps the very last of that particular species'. J. G. Lockhart (Sir Walter

top left: Henry Cockburn
bottom left: John Russell

top right: Leonard Hor
bottom right: Sir Walter Sc

THE NEW EDINBURGH ACADEMY.

Scott's biographer) in his *Peter's Letters to his Kinsfolk*, was also very impressed by Cockburn's eyes – 'in colour a rich clear brown and capable of conveying a greater range of expression than almost any I have ever seen.' The *Edinburgh Review* noted that he was 'rather below the middle height, firm, wiry, and muscular, inured to active exercise of all kinds, a good swimmer, an accomplished skater, and an intense lover of the fresh breezes of heaven. His face was handsome and intellectual; a capacious brow, which his baldness made more remarkable, large, lustrous and, in repose, rather melancholy eyes which, however, when roused by energy or wit, sparkled like a hawk's, and a well-formed nose, were the principal characteristics of a very striking personality'.

He was eccentric in his dress: 'His hat was always the worst, and his shoes constructed after a cherished pattern of his own, the clumsiest in Edinburgh – so uniformly that they became identified with the springing step and picturesque figure of the man. He despised great-coats and umbrellas, and down to the last year of his life constantly wandered forth at midnight, in defiance of rheumatism and lumbago, to enjoy a solitary hour's meditation, or a chatting stroll with any companion, of any age, who might be fortunate or weatherproof enough to accompany him.' (*Edinburgh Review*.)

He believed passionately in the freedom of the spirit, and 'detested all that was finical and prudish'. As an eminent advocate, and even as Lord Cockburn the judge, he could be found careering gleefully along the pavement slides in winter, and 'giving as much sly countenance to a snowball "bicker" as a well-disposed citizen might decently do'. He took special delight in 'leading the liberated urchins to shouts' when the Academy broke up for the summer holidays. He was always popular with the boys, and every July he would appear in the Academy playground scattering invitations to a feast of strawberries and cream at a tea-shop in the West End of Queen Street.

He was also an outstanding orator, with 'a finely modulated voice, an unlimited choice of happy and concise expression, and a command of the human passions in all their phases . . . Before a Scottish jury he was all but irresistible'.

TRIUMVIRATE: COCKBURN, HORNER – AND RUSSELL

In the early days of the Academy we worked almost daily together, and we had but one mind to all that concerned it.   (Leonard Horner, January, 1862)

Cockburn and Horner realised that if their scheme was to succeed they must not only have the support of the Tories, but that Tories must be allowed to take a prominent part in the management of the school. What they needed in particular was a Tory to be Honorary Secretary – 'a good active man in whom all parties would confide.' They knew of just the very man; and, as Horner wrote, 'we fixed upon John Russell, Writer to the Signet, as eminently qualified.' They met over supper in Cockburn's house and discussed the matter, and 'agreed as to a course of proceedings . . .'

John Russell (1780–1862) was the prototype Edinburgh solicitor. He was a member of the Society of Writers to the Signet, as his father and grandfather and great-grandfather had been: conscientious, shrewd, able and utterly respectable. He had an extensive practice, and he held a good position in Edinburgh society, on intimate terms with all the great names of the time – Sir Walter Scott, Francis Jeffrey, Cockburn, Horner, and the others – even though he was on the other side of the political fence from some of them. That was his great value in the eyes of Cockburn and Horner. In its obituary of Russell on January 31, 1862, the *Edinburgh Evening Courant* wrote: 'It spoke well for Mr Russell that, though always a steady and consistent Conservative, his politics never alienated him from friends who respected his opinions, sincerely held and ever mildly expressed, whilst they disagreed with them.'

This was the man who was to become the third man in the triumvirate of founders of the Edinburgh Academy, the lynch-pin of the school's affairs for twenty years first as Honorary Secretary from 1823–1831 and then Honorary Treasurer from 1831–43 (he remained a Director until his death in 1862). One of the first pupils at the Academy, J. M. Stuart (E.A. 1824–6), who became a journalist on the *Morning Post*, recalled his 'kindly paternal face' in an article he wrote fifty years after the school was founded: 'No Secretary of State could be a much greater, certainly a much more dignified, personage than our own secretary, Mr John Russell.' And no one connected with the Academy under-estimated the great debt the school owed him; when he gave up the post of Honorary Treasurer in 1843, the Directors wrote: 'No remuneration could have procured a greater amount of zeal, attention and judgement, than what has been bestowed by Mr Russell gratuitously during the twelve years in which his Treasurership has extended . . . There has been no greater benefactor to the Academy.'

When he died, Leonard Horner, the last survivor of the triumvirate, wrote of him to the Secretary of the Directors: 'When the idea first occurred to Lord Cockburn and myself, he was the first man we went to, and to his zeal, good sense, and influence with the leading men who afterwards became the first Directors, the success of the scheme was mainly owing . . .'

These three, then, set out to muster support for a new school, and discovered, according to Cockburn, 'that the conviction of the inadequacy of the High School was far more general than we supposed.'

Sir Walter Scott was then at the peak of his fame and fortune, his authorship of the Waverley Novels publicly acknowledged and the disastrous bankruptcy that ruined the last years of his life still three years away. Dyed-in-the-wool Tory though he was, he promised his support 'eagerly' to those interesting Whigs, Cockburn and Horner. At the Academy's Jubilee Dinner in 1874, Principal John Campbell Shairp of St Andrews University (E.A. 1829-32) recalled how 'the great Sir Walter joined heart and hand with Cockburn and Jeffrey and others, to whom in most other public questions he had stood in lifelong antagonism . . . It is one of the most benign influences of Learning and Literature that they can unite those whom nothing else can'. Busy as he was with his writing and his socialising at Abbotsford, Scott yet found time to campaign vigorously for the first Rector of the Academy, to make the principal speech at the Opening ceremony, and to attend many meetings as a Director (1823-32), even though he was latterly working desperately to pay off the crippling debts he had shouldered. But despite the 'benign influence of Learning and Literature', he always retained a most profound suspicion about the motives of Cockburn and the other leading Whigs among his fellow-Directors, and he was constantly worrying in letters to his friends about what they might be getting up to behind his back.

Others who promised support were the Lord Justice-Clerk (Lord Boyle); the Solicitor-General (John Hope); Sir James Fergusson, Bart.; Francis Jeffrey (soon to be elected Lord Rector of Glasgow University for the second time, before becoming Dean of the Faculty of Advocates, Lord Advocate, and ultimately a judge); and Sir Walter Scott's close friend, Colin Mackenzie of Portmore, the Deputy Keeper of the

Signet and Principal Clerk of Session. In no time at all, Cockburn, Horner and Russell had gathered a list of twenty-six eminent men who were prepared to become immediate Contributors (share-subscribers) to the new school; nearly all of them were advocates or solicitors.

One of the early subscribers was the architect William Burn (1789–1870), the designer of North Leith Parish Church and St John's Episcopal Church in Princes Street, and the towering Melville Monument in St Andrew Square commemorating Cockburn's uncle, the 1st Viscount Melville. Burn, who was a Tory like Russell, was asked to draw up a rough plan for a school. He estimated they would need about £12,000, so they decided to raise that amount in 240 shares of £50 each. They also had their eye on a piece of ground on the north side of the New Town and within five minutes' downhill walk from George Street, and a few inquiries satisfied them that they would be able to acquire about three acres there on which to build their school at an annual feu-duty of fifteen guineas per acre.

The three met day after day, in snatched moments between business at Parliament House or in more leisurely sessions at one another's homes, getting their proposals down on paper. And on June 3, 1822, barely two months after that walk on the Pentland Hills, they held the first meeting to be recorded formally in the first Minute Book of the Directors of the Edinburgh Academy. This is what John Russell (appointed Secretary that day *ad interim*) wrote in his beautiful copperplate hand, the ink brown now after 150 years but every word still legible:

Minute of a Meeting held at Edinburgh the 3 June 1822 for the purpose of considering a Scheme for the Establishment of a School in the New Town of Edinburgh similar to that of the High School.

Present

Colin Mackenzie Esq Deputy Keeper of the Signet
Henry Cockburn Esq Advocate
Alexander Wood Esq Advocate
William Trotter Esq of Ballindean [*future Lord Provost*]
Leonard Horner Esq
Richard Mackenzie Esq W.S.
John Russell Esq W.S. who also appeared for Sir James Fergusson Bart
Dr John Abercromby

Roger Aytoun Esq W.S.
William Burn Esq Architect

Colin Mackenzie Esq was elected Preses.

There was laid before the Meeting a Scheme for the Establishment of a School in the Newtown of Edinburgh on a plan similar to that of the High School which having been read over and discussed by the meeting they were of [the] opinion that the same should be printed for the consideration of the Gentlemen present as well as such of the other members of the Committee therein named as are absent, and that proof sheets thereof should be circulated among them. And the meeting adjourned till Friday next the 7th instant at 3 o'clock, when they will resume consideration of the proposed Scheme, and the other members of the Committee shall be requested to attend that meeting.

'The Scheme' discussed at that first meeting was gone over again at the meeting on June 7, when the Lord Justice-Clerk (Lord Boyle) and the Solicitor-General (John Hope) were added to the Committee and Dr John Abercromby withdrew. There was a good deal of discussion and some alterations and amendments were made (one notable amendment was that the name that had originally been suggested, *The New Town Academy*, should be changed to *The Edinburgh Academy*); eventually this was the Scheme which was ordered to be printed and circulated:

Since the present High School was built, Edinburgh has at least trebled in extent and population. The consequence has been, that the only great Public School of the City has become too distant from many parts of the town and far too much crowded for the advantage of the Scholars. This has induced some individuals to turn their thoughts to the Establishment of another School in the immediate neighbourhood of the New Town, which may be free from the Objections to which the existing Institution must always be liable while it continues the only great Seminary of the Place.

It is accordingly proposed to erect a great public School which shall comprise such accommodations contrived with all the benefit of experience, as the most improved method of conducting great Schools requires. Nothing can show the demand that there is for such an Establishment more strikingly than the fact, that in spite of the great zeal and ability with which the High School has long been and still continues to be conducted, there are at this moment about 500 Boys who are obliged to receive their education at detached Private Seminaries in the New Town.

A piece of Ground containing ample space for play ground, on the north side of the New Town and within five minutes walk of George Street, can be acquired, and a School containing all the requisite accommodation may be erected at an expence in whole of about £12,000. It is proposed that this Sum shall be raised in 240 Shares of £50 each. The Subscribers to be formed into a Corporate Body and an Act of Parliament or Royal Charter to be got bestowing the necessary powers upon them for managing the School and the Funds in the most efficient manner.

In order to pay the interest of the capital, as well as small Salaries to the Masters and the other expences of the Establishment, it is proposed that each Scholar shall pay annually such a sum, not exceeding £3.3 in name of School Fund as shall from time to time be fixed by the Directors, which shall be applied exclusively for those purposes. The other remunerations of the Masters shall be derived solely from the fees of teaching.

This School Fund of £3.3 supposing 500 boys at the School would produce		£1575
Deduct salaries to Rector £100 and four other Masters at £50,	£300	
Feu duty and Taxes	50	
Repairs and other Expences	250	
		600
Balance out of which the Interest on the £12,000 will be paid and the remainder applied as shall be afterwards arranged		£975

(In actual fact no interest was ever paid to the original subscribers and shareholders, or to those who at various times down the years subscribed shares in order to help the Academy out of financial straits. Eventually the Charter had to be changed to remove the profit-making clause in its constitution, which hampered efforts to raise money.)

The following General Regulations are suggested for the present, leaving it for the Subscribers to adopt such farther and more special Regulations as may be best adapted for the objects in view.

1st. The School to be called 'The Edinburgh Academy', and to be taught in five Classes by a Rector and four other Masters as in the High School, with a condition that the Directors may require the Masters to employ Ushers according to Circumstances.

2. The whole management to be placed in the hands of Fifteen Directors, to be chosen by the share-holders from their own body, three of whom to go out of office every year by rotation but who may be re-elected and two of them always to act by appointment of the Directors as Visitors.

3. The Directors for the time being to have the entire regulation and controul of the School including the appointment or removal of Masters, Janitor, and all other persons employed in the Establishment, but being bound to enter all their proceedings regularly in a book for the inspection of Subscribers.

4. The sum of £12,000 required to buy the ground and build the School house to be raised in 240 shares of £50 each, which shares shall be transferable. The shares to be paid by equal instalments at Martinmas 1822 and Whitsunday 1823 with interest on each instalment from these periods until paid. Any subscriber holding four shares may have two votes but no Subscriber to have more than two votes, and every Subscriber may vote by proxy. The number of shares may be increased if it shall be thought necessary.

5. An Annual Meeting of Subscribers to be held shortly before the last public examination of the School for the season, for receiving the report of the Directors for the preceding year, and for electing three new Directors in place of those who retire, and to fill up other vacancies.

6. An Act of Parliament or Royal Charter to be obtained for forming the Subscribers into a Corporate Body, and conferring on them full powers as to their holding property, the management of their Funds, the framing and enforcing such regulations with regard to these points, and to the conducting of the School as shall be adopted by the Subscribers and with a power to the Subscribers at a General Meeting to be called for that purpose of terminating the Establishment and disposing of the property and dividing the proceeds thereof in case, from any unforeseen circumstances, that measure should be deemed expedient.

7. As soon as 240 shares shall be subscribed for, a General Meeting of Contributors shall be called, for the purpose of making the first election of Directors, who shall thenceforth carry forward the business till they be relieved by successive annual elections as above.

In the meantime the following Gentlemen shall act as a Committee, until the first General Meeting of the Contributors:

The Lord Justice Clerk	Alexr Wood Esq Advocate
The Solicitor General	Alexr Munro Esq
Sir James Fergusson Bart	Henry Cockburn Esq Advocate
Colin Mackenzie Esq Deputy Keeper of the Signet	Richd McKenzie Esq W.S.
	Leonard Horner Esq
Roger Aytoun Esq W.S.	Francis Walker Esq
James Skene Esq Advocate	William Burn Esq Architect
Willm Trotter Esq of Ballindean	John Russell Esq W.S.

Colin Mackenzie Esq to be Convener of the Committee
Thomas Kinnear Esq to be Treasurer
John Russell Esq to be Secretary

It is of the utmost importance that those who approve of this measure and intend to become Contributors shall signify their intention on or before the 1st of July next. If the Subscriptions shall be completed before that period the Committee can undertake that the School-house may be built and ready to be opened on the 1st of Oct 1823.

With the publication of the Scheme this small group of men set themselves on a course that was to demand from them, and a long line of volunteers over the next 150 years, a degree of devotion and dedication that is truly admirable. They would give up their leisure and a great deal of professional time that might have been more profitably employed in earning a living, in order to attend meetings, visit the school, serve on special committees, interview candidates, worry over financial crises, and sort out all manner of day-to-day problems ranging from faulty drains to parental complaints. A tiny fraction of the troubles that have confronted the Directors down the years would have been enough to make most people give up the whole idea. But right from the beginning they showed a remarkable ability to cope with all manner of crises without being shaken from their purpose.

It all seemed plain sailing at first. By July 1, 1822, some 160 sub-scribers had agreed to take £50 shares to the value of nearly £9,000, 'and there appeared every probability that the whole sum of £12,000 would soon be obtained.' But the first crisis was not far off, in the shape of Edinburgh Town Council, and Old Bailie Blackwood in particular.

CHAPTER III

The Opposition (1822-23)

Old Bailie Blackwood dissenting.
(Edinburgh Town Council Minutes.)

The founders of the Academy knew that Edinburgh Town Council would inevitably feel concerned about the effect a new school might have on the reputation and financial standing of the High School; so before circularising the Scheme they 'communicated their intentions to the Lord Provost'. The Lord Provost, William Arbuthnot, who had already received alarmed representations from the Rector and masters of the High School, requested a joint meeting with the High School men and the Academy committee, who appointed a sub-committee of Sir James Fergusson, the Solicitor-General (John Hope), Colin Mackenzie, Richard Mackenzie and John Russell to meet the Lord Provost and Magistrates. A courteous exchange of views at this meeting showed that the City Fathers were very concerned indeed about the scheme for a new school.

As Colin Mackenzie, D.K.S., reported to the Academy Committee at a meeting in the MacEwan Rooms, Royal Exchange, on June 26: 'The great anxiety expressed by the Magistrates related to the Interest of the Masters of the High School which it was feared might be injured and also to the reputation of that excellent School which it was thought, would suffer if the proposed School were instituted on a plan of higher School fees.'

The Academy men had replied that it was 'far from the wish of the promoters of the New School to trench upon or injure the High School, which indeed they thought would not be materially affected by their project or in any way worthy of being considered in competition with the great advantages which were contemplated'.

As for the fees, though it was impossible to state anything precise, 'the assurance was given [by the Academy sub-committee] that there was no intention of raising these to a higher rate than necessary, and especially no intention of doing this with a view to rivalship with the

High School or to rendering Education unnecessarily expensive.'

Mackenzie said that the meeting with the magistrates 'led in fact to no result except the interchange of mutual civilities and expressions of reciprocal respect and good will'. But there had been one pointer which made the committee sit up. Reporting that no specific proposition had been made by the magistrates, Mackenzie added that 'the only thing they seemed to point at was the selling the present High School and erecting a new School upon the East Side of the Mound, but it was obvious that no definitive views even as to this had been formed'.

A new High School on the east side of the Mound! Since that meant it would still be in the Old Town, it could not satisfy the aims of the Academy committee; but the mere fact that the penny-pinching conservative Town Council should have been moved even to consider building a new school showed that they were taking the threat very seriously.

This preliminary initiative by the Town Council was immediately followed on July 3 by a letter from the Lord Provost which took it even farther: 'Several most respectable Inhabitants have stated to me, that in consequence of the great increase of population of Edinburgh they conceive there is an absolute necessity, that (without abolishing the present High School) a new High School should be built in the New Town, but they are desirous that both Schools should be precisely on the same footing with each other. And I now beg to inform you that I this day brought the subject under consideration of the Magistrates and Council and that (trusting to receive considerable aid from their fellow Citizens in the way of Donations to promote so desireable an object) [they] have come to the resolution of building a new High School in the New Town, which they have no reason to doubt they will be enabled to compleat before the end of next year, as they will immediately set about carrying the measure into effect.' In this manner, 'the plan now in agitation would be given up, or a fair competition would be kept up so as to prevent the present High School from being thrown into the background'. In Provost Arbuthnot's view, funds for building the new school could be provided by charging pupils at both Schools an annual entrance fee of a guinea, as well as by private donations.

This was a real turn-up for the books. What the Town Council was now saying was – 'Forget about your Scheme. We will build your new school ourselves in the New Town. We will raise the money.'

But Cockburn and his colleagues did not feel inclined to leap at this opportunity of relieving themselves of the massive responsibility they had undertaken. In a report of events to the subscribers, the Committee stated that they were 'unwilling at once to give up the objects they had in view, without obtaining some satisfactory assurance from the Town Council on the following points which they deemed of considerable importance:

1. The accommodation for the Boys both in and out of School.
2. The situation of the School.
3. A certain Co-operation in the management, with a view to improvements in the mode of Education.
4. The precise time within which the School is to be completed.

Another sub-committee was appointed to confer with the Lord Provost and Magistrates on these four points, and a meeting was held on the very next day, July 4. This sub-committee duly reported back on the Town Council's reaction to the four points:

1st. With regard to the accommodation for the boys, both in and out of School, the Sub-Committee received a distinct assurance that the accommodation in School should be similar to those proposed by the Committee as appearing from Mr Burn's drawings which were produced by Mr Russell; that the Size and number of the Rooms should be not inferior and that the Space for buildings and Play Ground should not be less than three Scotch acres in extent.

2. The Situation of the School it was stated was proposed to be either that field which had been selected by the Committee or a part of the adjoining field to the East of it belonging to Heriot's Hospital.

3. With regard to a certain Co-operation in the management with a view to improvement in the mode of Education: The Lord Provost expressed that the Magistrates would not admit into their Scheme any right of Interference on the part of private Individuals, but that they had no objection to establish such right of Co-operation as was proposed in the persons of the four learned Judges presiding in the Courts of Session, Justiciary and Exchequer, and Jury Court with the addition of the Lord Advocate, Solicitor General, Dean of Faculty, and Keeper or Deputy Keeper of the Signet all for the time being, and to extend this Co-operation to the present High School as well as to the New School, it being always understood that the right of Patronage in both Schools should remain exclusively and

unfettered in the Lord Provost, Magistrates and Town Council.

4. As to the precise time within which the School is to be completed, the Lord Provost undertook that the Contractor should be taken bound under a suitable penalty to have the School completed and ready for occupation on or before the 1st of October 1823; and to provide proper Teachers so that the School should be opened by that time.

Finally the Sub-Committee received a distinct assurance that tho the Magistrates hoped for aid by Subscription from Individuals the undertaking was altogether unconditional and not dependent on the fulfillment of these hopes.

The Academy sub-committee sent a draft of their report to tne Lord Provost to ensure that they had it quite right, and then presented it to their full committee, who decided to call a General Meeting of the Contributors in the Waterloo Hotel on July 10 'to obtain their authority for giving up the proposed Scheme'. The feeling of the Contributors was that 'since the Lord Provost and Magistrates had undertaken to build a new High School in the New Town, and had given such assurances on the important points before specified, it is unnecessary to persevere in the Scheme formerly proposed by them'. Sir Walter Scott took the chair at this meeting to report the triumphant outcome of their parleys with the Town Council, and the committee congratulated the Contributors and their fellow citizens 'on their having obtained a great advantage to the Community by prevailing on the magistracy without delay to undertake a measure which has been long called for and which must prove of great and essential benefit to the City by improving and extending the means of Education'.

But the Contributors were still leaving nothing to chance. Just in case the City Fathers should falter in their new-found determination, a clear warning was sounded in the resolutions that were passed unanimously at the meeting:

'. . . That upon an explicit and unqualified determination being intimated by the Lord Provost, Magistrates and Council to proceed without delay in terms of the Report of the Sub-Committee . . . the Scheme of the Subscribers shall be abandoned as unnecessary;

'. . . That . . . in case such explicit and unqualified determination shall not be duly intimated to them on or before Thursday the 25 day of this month [*July*], to call another meeting of Subscribers to consider of the measures proper to be taken . . .'

Over now to the Town Council, who held a meeting a week later, on July 17, to consider the report of *their* sub-committee who had been having all the dealings with the Academy committee. The Proceedings of the Town Council take up a lot of space in the early pages of that first Minute Book of the Edinburgh Academy Directors; but they give little hint of the arguments, the angry exchanges and recriminations that were bandied about both inside and outside the Council chambers, as Lord Provost Arbuthnot, who was clearly in sympathy with the aims of the Academy Contributors, fought to persuade the Council to take over the Scheme and keep this proposed new school under the patronage of the magistrates. Meanwhile the Contributors, arrested at the very moment of putting their scheme into action, could only sit back and watch and wait while the grinding wheels of local government turned the matter over.

First the Town Council had to get legal advice as to whether they would be entitled in law to charge every scholar 'a certain sum of entrance money' towards paying the building costs of the new school. Under the existing system the annual amount paid by each High School pupil was £3 6s., made up as follows:

4 quarters at 10/6	£2	2s
Candlemas [*gift*]		10s 6d
The Rector		5s
The Janitor		5s
Coal money		2s 6d
Library		1s
	£3	6s

The Council's legal advisers gave their opinion that the Council would be fully entitled to charge an extra entrance fee, not exceeding one guinea, for all pupils at both the old and the new High Schools. The Council now felt it safe to go ahead, and at that meeting on July 17, 1822, they passed a resolution 'to proceed in the erection of an additional School connected with and precisely on the footing of the High School, and in order to raise the funds requisite do now Enact and Declare that there shall be levied for this purpose from each Scholar attending the High School of this City now in existence as well as the School about to be built, a Sum not exceeding One Guinea of entrance money; and Remit to the Committee appointed on the third instant to carry the measure into effect, by procuring ground, obtaining plans and setting on foot a public Subscription in aid of the measure'.

Old Bailie Blackwood protested against the resolution, but protested in vain. He protested again at the next meeting, on October 16, on the ground that his protest at the July 17 meeting had not been recorded in the Minutes. No other moves seem to have taken place in between these two meetings, for now Edinburgh was preoccupied with the business of the royal visit by King George IV to Edinburgh in August, during which Lord Provost William Arbuthnot became a baronet. The proposal to build a new school, which had excited so much urgency during June and July, now hung fire for several weeks. The Town Council approved the acquisition of the 'Academy Site' on October 16 at a feu of fifteen guineas per annum, and invited building contractors to submit tenders for the building of the school to the specifications drawn up by the Academy architect, William Burn; but it was not until December 2 that the Town Council sub-committee on the new school project met to consider the tenders. There were twelve estimates up for approval, but none of them was accepted: the highest was £19,423 and the lowest £15,200 (exclusive of land or furnishings), compared with the original £12,000 (including the cost of the ground) estimated by Mr Burn. The Town Council committee, which included the Lord Provost and Old Bailie Blackwood, now declared that it was impossible to proceed with the project until the expense had been reduced 'most materially', and that it would be 'proper to open a communication with the body of Subscribers'.

So once again the Academy Committee met in the Waterloo Hotel, on December 11, 1822, to consider a copy of the Town Council's Minute over costs; and as a result Mr Burn was asked to modify his plan so as to keep within the original estimate of £12,000. The revised plan, which involved the cutting out of a large upper storey that had been envisaged for the original structure, was delivered to the Lord Provost on February 8, 1823, with a request for a further meeting as soon as possible, 'as the Session is drawing to a close when some of our members may probably be going to the country.'

The Town Council met on February 18 to consider the revised plan, and declared that 'unless the plans can be so reduced as to bring the expense of building the School to £8,000, being the amount originally contemplated between the Town and the Subscribers, it will not be prudent for the Town to go on with the plan'. The revised plan was thereupon remitted back to the Academy men for further revision.

The quoted figure of £8,000 came as a complete surprise to the Academy Subscribers, who claimed that no such understanding had ever been arrived at, and that the capital necessary to build the school had always been estimated at £12,000. The Academy men now decided to apply a little pressure. They were getting impatient, for there was now no chance at all that the new school could be completed and ready for opening by October, 1823, as Cockburn and Horner had originally hoped.

So Russell now wrote direct to the Lord Provost on February 24, 1823: 'The Sub Committee are extremely anxious in consequence of the frequent applications to them on the part of their Constituents to be able to report to them that some definitive arrangement has been entered into between the Town Council and them, so that the School may be commenced without delay . . . I am desired to request your Lordship . . . that we may have a definite answer on or before the 5th inst [sic], whether the Town Council are willing to undertake to erect the new School, so as to be ready by the 1st Oct 1824 . . . We are very unwilling to appear too urgent in this matter, but after the unavoidable delays that have occurred we think it absolutely necessary to call a meeting of the Subscribers before the Session rises in order that they may determine whether in the event of the School not being likely to be immediately erected under the auspices of the Town Council, it may not be necessary for them to lay aside the expectation and resume their original plan.'

This letter with its elegantly phrased but unmistakable threat did the trick, and the Town Councillors were galvanised into immediate action. The Council sub-committee met on February 26 and resolved (Old Bailie Blackwood dissenting, of course): 'That this Committee do now recommend to the Town Council instantly to proceed with the building of the High School containing accommodation similar to that exhibited in Mr Burn's reduced plan.' They also recommended that the committee be given powers 'to accept any estimate which shall not exceed the sum of £9,000, including all expences in finishing the building and enclosing the ground.' (The committee had shifted ground again, and were now narrowing the difference between the original £12,000 and their arbitrary figure of £8,000).

A full meeting of the Town Council was held on the same day, February 26, 1823, to consider the sub-committee's report. True to form, Old Bailie Blackwood moved an amendment; he recognised that the High School was badly situated, but his remedy was to build

The first Rector: Dr. John Williams

top left: John Hannah   *top right:* J. S. Hodson

bottom left: Thomas Harvey   *bottom right:* Reginald Carter

one great new school on a more central site. He argued that since the estimated number of boys doing Latin in Edinburgh did not exceed 1,000 (if that), this would not be enough to maintain two schools; nor were the classes at the High School so crowded as to justify a step that must lead to the destruction of the old school. Furthermore, he claimed that a new High School would materially injure the income of the Rector and masters at the existing High School, and that they would thereby be entitled to sue the Council, as patrons, for breach of contract, which would lead to the discredit of the patrons. The establishment of a new High School in the New Town, he urged, would create separate institutions for different classes of people, and would thus destroy one of the proudest characteristics of Scottish education – its democratic equality of opportunity.

But his arguments did not sway the rest of the Council on this occasion, and the amendment in favour of a single central school was heavily defeated. The Council then approved the report of the sub-committee by nineteen votes to four.

On February 28, 1823, the Town Clerk sent John Russell a copy of the report by the committee, and confirmed: 'The Report has been approved of by the Town Council and a remit made to the same Committee to proceed as proposed therein.'

At last it was there, in black and white. The Town Council had finally made up its mind. The waiting was over. The new school had been given the go-ahead. And that should have been the end of the idea of an independently-run school for Edinburgh, the end of The Edinburgh Academy. But those who thought that had reckoned without Old Bailie Blackwood.

OLD BAILIE BLACKWOOD

Baron Bailie of Canongate and Calton. (*Directory*.)

Old Bailie Thomas Blackwood was against the building of a new school in the New Town right from the beginning. He was against it being built by private individuals, and he was against it being built by the Town Council. He voiced his opposition in the Town Council and at every meeting of the sub-committee which was appointed to meet the Contributors to the Academy and carry out the negotiations for getting the new school under way.

'Old Bailie Blackwood dissenting'. 'Old Bailie Blackwood protested'. But if his objections were loud in the Council Chambers, they were no louder than the voices that were raised both for and against the idea in Parliament Close, in the coffee-shops and ale-houses and round the fashionable dinner-tables as soon as the Academy Scheme was circularised. There were letters to the *Scotsman* and the *Edinburgh Evening Courant*, and in the fashion of the day those who had a lot to say and could afford it had their views printed in pamphlet form to hand out to friends and acquaintances.

One of these pamphlets, written by a Mr Alex Peterkin in 1822 and grandly entitled *A Letter to the Lord Provost, on the Mischievous Tendency of a Scheme for Abolishing the High School – 'Et tu, Brute!'*, called upon the Lord Provost to do something quickly before the Academy project should 'destroy entirely the High School under the patronage and protection of the Magistrates'. Mr Peterkin, who signed himself 'Scotus' ('because I am unwilling to obtrude myself personally on public attention'), put forward the same arguments that were raised time and time again by Old Bailie Blackwood in the Town Council: granted that the High School accommodation was unsatisfactory and there was need for a new and bigger building, but there must not be two High Schools. The Town Council should scrap the old school and build a new High School in a central position, preferably in the region of the Mound on the new land formed by the filling in of the old Nor' Loch.

This was the idea which had come up originally as the Town Council's first reaction to the Academy Scheme when the Academy sub-committee had their first meeting with the magistrates: 'The only thing they seemed to point at,' Colin Mackenzie had reported, 'was the selling the present High School and erecting a New School upon the East Side of the Mound.' This was what Old Bailie Blackwood had wanted, but he was quickly talked down by the other members of his committee, and within a week the Town Council had resolved to take over the Academy Scheme and build a second High School in the New Town. From that moment on, Old Bailie Blackwood never let up in his efforts to win over a majority of the Council to his belief that there should be only the one High School, run by the Town Council and situated centrally between the Old Town and the New. He maintained that there was no need for two schools. He challenged the figures put forward by the Academy supporters who argued that (including the boys who had to be sent outside Edinburgh for their schooling) there were between 1,000 and 1,500 sons of Edinburgh residents now receiving a classical education. Old Bailie Blackwood contended that many parents who sent their boys to private seminaries in the New Town would continue to send them there, no matter where the new school was situated. A new High School in the centre of the city would not have to accommodate more than 800 or 900 boys at the most, and the High School system was perfectly adequate to cope with that number. If the school were built in the New Town, human nature being what it was, parents would opt for the new building in the fashionable district despite the educational worth of the old school. Deprived of the greater part of their fees, masters would follow the boys to the new school and the old one would die, leaving only one school, once again overcrowded and now inconveniently situated for boys from the Old Town and the southern areas of the city.

Old Bailie Blackwood's opponents believed that with the population of the city steadily increasing, and with boys even being sent from England to be educated in the 'Athens of the North', there was ample room for two large schools in Edinburgh. Besides, there was no central site that was ideally suited for a school. The Nor' Loch region was not only insalubrious, but subject to severe building restrictions by the proprietors of Princes Street. Another suggestion, the Excise Office site in St Andrew Square (now occupied by the Royal Bank of Scotland), was much too small; and they refused to take seriously 'the east side of the Calton Hill . . . as a fit situation for a central School'.

But after the Town Council meeting of February 26, 1823, public opinion began to harden against the proposal for a second school. It was pointed out that the proposed Academy site at Canonmills Park was itself not particularly convenient, and that access to it involved the crossing of many and busy thoroughfares; that there were possible dangers to boys from the Water of Leith in times of flood, while the tannery at Silvermills and Haig's Distillery at the rear of the site could hardly be said to provide a pleasant or savoury environment.

But the one major objection that bulked larger than all the others was the prospect of destroying the old Scottish tradition of democratic education. The *Scotsman*, which supported the Academy project, summed it up in a leading article (or 'disquisition' as it was called in those days) on January 14, 1824, when the Academy was already being built: 'It is known that one objection, and one only of any weight, has been urged against this New Academy from the start – that it would assume a Patrician character.' Mr Peterkin had declared in his Open Letter to the Lord Provost: 'The projected Scheme is calculated to separate, by a line of distinction very marked and very mischievous, the higher (or rather the wealthy) from the humbler classes of the community.' And a letter from 'A Plebeian' in the *Scotsman* of April 16, 1823, put the same point more crudely: 'However manly and liberal may be the opinion of many encouragers of the novel scheme, I am sufficiently uncharitable to suspect that it derives a very powerful support from the aristocratic feelings of many of the papas and mamas whose hearts sicken at the thought of Master Tommy being obliged to trudge through dirty streets jostled by all sorts of low and crude people; triumphed over in school by the son of the shoemaker and beaten when out of it by the son of the butcher, and associating with vulgar companions.'

(It is worth noting, perhaps, that the Dux of the Academy in 1853, a brilliant and popular boy called George R. Luke, was the son of a Stockbridge master baker. But he was an exception; and it would seem idle to deny that the Edinburgh Academy, from its birth, reflected a degree of social or class orientation, and that it did represent the first major break with the democratic traditions of Scottish education.)

Even Henry Brougham, fellow-Whig and former High School pupil along with Cockburn and Jeffrey and other Academy founders, frankly raised the bogey of class distinction and criticised the divisive nature of the Academy at a dinner in his honour in 1825 that was presided over by Cockburn: 'What I have to say of the High School of Edinburgh, and say as the grounds for the preference I give it over others, and even over another Academy lately established in this city, on what is said to be a more improved principle, [is that] a school like the Old High School of Edinburgh is invaluable; and for what is it so? It is because men of the highest and lowest rank of society send their children to be educated together – noblemen, sons of shopkeepers in the lowest part of the Cowgate, one or two sons of menial servants in the town . . .' Brougham had unsuccessfully supported a scheme for national education in 1822, so he was being perfectly consistent; but his twenty-one years in London had possibly given him a somewhat rose-coloured memory of conditions at the High School. Cockburn and his friends wanted to educate their sons in Scotland, and though they were just as proud of their *alma mater* as Brougham, they were much more aware of its inadequacy to provide the standard of education that could compete with the best in England. They argued that the New Town was not wholly composed of the rich, and that their fees would be only about £2 10s. more than those of the High School. Their objection was not to letting their sons sit side by side with the sons of shoemakers, but that the High School was catering to so many different needs that the standard of classical education was being lowered, as Cockburn put it, 'to suit the wants of a class of boys to more than two-thirds of whom classical accomplishment is foreseen to be useless.'

'Class' was not an objectionable word in the 1820's. Different levels of society were accepted as a fact of life. Discounting the destitute, who were too poor to go to anything but the 'Ragged Schools', there was not much to choose between the schooling of an advocate's son or a shoemaker's son when it came to coarseness and crudity. Cruelty, bullying and drunkenness were the order of the day at places like Winchester and Rugby, and the descriptions of the sanitary conditions at the new Edinburgh Academy, as well as the fights that took place during and after school, would give today's New Town papas and mamas a fit.

It was the standard of education, and that alone, that concerned Cockburn. If the sons of the gentry could not be instructed in Latin and Greek at the High School to the level that would take them to positions of influence in the affairs of Britain, then another school must be provided which would be unrestricted by having to cater for boys with less ambitious careers in view.

The Town Council, anxious to retain their power as patrons of the leading school in the city, were at first eager to take over Cockburn's scheme. But Old Bailie Blackwood insisted from the beginning that the kind of education that Cockburn wanted to provide at the new school would not only cost the Town Council too much but would reduce the beloved old High School to the position of a poor sister. There should be one school for all and it should be here, in the Old Town, among the people.

Old Bailie Blackwood wasn't a radical or a premature Socialist. The Whigs were the leftists of their day, and to be an Edinburgh Town Councillor you had to be a prosperous burgess, representing a Trade Guild or Association. Blackwood was the prototype Town Councillor of the past – obstinate, close, conservative. Besides, he was convinced that it was no business of the Town Council or the High School to run an exclusive, upper-class school in the New Town, and he has to be admired for the way he stuck to his guns. Anyway, he inadvertently did the Academy a good turn by refusing to accept defeat even after all seemed lost on February 26, 1823, when the Town Council had decisively voted 'instantly to proceed' with the building of a second

High School in the New Town, and rejected, by nineteen votes to four, the Old Bailie's amendment to have the old High School moved to a central site to cater for both Old Town and New.

That should have been that. But Old Bailie Blackwood wasn't finished yet. As he made his way to the Council Chambers on March 12, 1823, he was determined to make a last-minute attempt to bring the Council round to his point of view. The Minute of the last meeting on February 26 would be up for approval as a matter of course – a mere formality, normally; but Old Bailie Blackwood planned to use this technicality to re-open the discussion and try to persuade the Council to reconsider their previous decision.

And this time, in the new climate of opinion, he managed it. Despite protests from the Lord Provost, Sir William Arbuthnot, he persuaded the Council to agree, by sixteen votes to eleven, 'to suspend their approval of their Minute of February 26, and to appoint a committee to investigate thoroughly the propriety and possibility of erecting a new school in a central situation, to which the present High School could be removed, and that this committee be empowered to meet with the gentlemen with whom the agreement was made, in order if possible to obviate their objections to a central school.'

Perhaps what finally swayed the Town Council that day was the uneasy suspicion that by setting up a second High School in parallel to the old one, they would be landing themselves with a heavy financial burden. Whatever the reason, 'the gentlemen with whom the agreement was made' heard the news next day of this spectacular volte-face 'with the utmost astonishment'.

Their astonishment was echoed by the consternation of the group of Town Councillors, led by Lord Provost Sir William Arbuthnot, who had always favoured building a second High School along the lines of the Academy Scheme. They published their five *Reasons of Dissent from Old Bailie Blackwood's Amendment*, basically on legalistic lines – that the Town Council was morally obliged to fulfil the engagement they had entered into with the Academy Contributors.

Meanwhile the Committee of Contributors held two urgent meetings to prepare for a meeting that had been requested by the Blackwood Committee for March 29. They drew up a Memorandum of five resolutions, in which they rejected the idea of a single central school as being inadequate and impractical and affirmed their intention of reviving the Academy Scheme on their own unless the Town Council reverted to their original decision of February 26. Armed with this uncompromising document, they went to the meeting with the Blackwood Committee on March 29.

Old Bailie Blackwood himself was now content to take a back seat, and it was left to the chairman of the committee, Bailie John Waugh, to address the Contributors. He made an extremely lengthy speech, apologising for the inconvenience that might have been caused, but claiming that the Town Council had been rushed into a decision the previous year without being given time to consider the full consequences of building a second High School in the New Town – namely, 'the annihilation of the old school.' The Academy committee withdrew to consider his remarks, but when they returned they said they had heard it all before and still believed there was room for two great classical schools in Edinburgh. The Academy convener, Colin Mackenzie, read out the five resolutions that his committee had already agreed, reiterating that the Contributors would not attempt to take legal advantage of the Town Council but would go ahead with their Scheme if the Council did not. It seems that the meeting became heated, but both sides were now so entrenched in their positions that no real attempt was made to reach agreement or compromise, and the meeting ended in deadlock.

The Town Council met in full on April 9 and heard the lengthy report of the Blackwood Committee's meeting with the Academy Contributors on March 29. In a last bid to defeat Old Bailie Blackwood, the Lord Provost had approached a banking firm for a loan of £9,000, and had sought alternative designs from the architect who would later design the new High School on Calton Hill. Now he moved that 'that part of the Minute of February 26th last, which had been suspended by the Minute of March 12th, be now approved of'. But the motion was defeated, once again by sixteen votes to eleven, on an amendment that the Blackwood Report be approved; and so the Town Council confirmed its decision to rebuild the High School on a central site in Edinburgh.

The Town Council, having admitted that the present site of the High School was unsuitable, were now committed to rebuild the High School, if only to meet the threat posed by the Academy. In the event, the new High School was opened in June, 1829, on a site on the south-east side of Calton Hill. It was a magnificent classical building modelled on the Athenian Temple of Theseus, and clearly designed to outdo the Academy in grandeur; but the total cost was over £34,000, compared with the estimated £12,000 of the original Academy

Scheme that Old Bailie Blackwood had successfully opposed. (In 1968, the High School moved again, to new premises in Barnton.)

Old Bailie Blackwood's opponents weren't quite finished, however. Two of them – Old Treasurer Thomas Kinnear (a banker who had joined the Academy Scheme as Treasurer in June, 1822) and Deacon William Wood, a surgeon – published a list of *Reasons of Dissent against the Decision of the Town Council adopted at the Meeting of 9th April*, 1823, to which the Lord Provost and three other councillors also adhered. They argued that 'since the guardianship of the education of the Youth of this City *cannot* now be exercised through the same limited means which have sufficed during the last century, it has become the duty of the Town Council, in selecting other means, to act on the great fundamental principles of the present system, namely, 1st, To preserve to the Magistracy the control, and to charge them with the responsibility of the public system of education; and 2nd, To keep open equally to all classes of the community the same Seminary or Seminaries in which that system of education is carried on'. They argued that the new school, if privately run, would soon become the successful opponent of the High School and reduce it to secondary importance; and that it would tend to become exclusive, to the detriment of the 'lower classes of citizens'. The only way to prevent this happening, they claimed, would be for the Town Council to build the second school themselves, for this would inhibit and render unnecessary the establishment of an independent school.

But it was too late for arguments now, however cogent – and soon both Thomas Kinnear and William Wood would become Directors of the new Academy.* On May 14, 1833, a General Meeting of Subscribers to the Academy was held in the Waterloo Hotel. Of the 111 Subscribers who attended, half were members of the legal profession. The meeting decided 'in view of the Council's decision to have a single, central High School, to go ahead with their original plan to establish an independent school in the New Town'.

Old Bailie Blackwood had done it. The Edinburgh Academy was under way.

---

*The identification of the two dissentient Town Councillors with two of the first Academy Directors of the same name is nowhere made explicit. But the City Archivist of Edinburgh, Dr Walter Makey, tells me in a letter that 'I personally feel that the identification is sound.'

CHAPTER IV

Starting a School (1823-24)

. . . in a field to the north of the New Town, and within ten minutes' walk from the most distant part of it. (*Statement* by the Directors, December, 1823.)

HOW do you start a new school? The founders of the Edinburgh Academy seemed to know exactly what to do, and they got down to it at once. They got their go-ahead from the Contributors at the meeting in the Waterloo Hotel on May 14, 1823. There and then they elected fifteen Directors, to hold office until the time of the Public Examination at the end of the first school session in 1825. The first fifteen were:

James Skene of Rubislaw, Advocate
William Wood, Surgeon
Thomas Kinnear, Banker
Sir John Hay of Smithfield and Hayston, Bart.
John Russell, Writer to the Signet
Robert Dundas of Arniston, Advocate [*the Advocate Depute*]
Colin Mackenzie of Portmore, Deputy Keeper of the Signet
Henry Cockburn, Advocate
Alexander Wood, Advocate
Sir Robert Dundas of Beechwood, Bart.
Leonard Horner, Merchant
Alexander Irving, Advocate, Professor of Civil Law at Edinburgh
    University
Richard Mackenzie, Writer to the Signet
Sir Walter Scott of Abbotsford, Bart.
Roger Aytoun, Writer to the Signet.

This first Board of Directors was drawn predominantly from the legal profession, like so many of the Boards that succeeded them down the generations. But it is also noticeable that there was no representative from the Church on it. From the very first, the founders of the Academy showed no interest in a sectarian approach to religion and were content that the life of the school should be broadly and soberly Presbyterian; but what is a little surprising is the deliberate way in which the founders eschewed any formal connection with the Established Church. No place in the timetable was allotted to religious education. Leonard Horner was to write, in 1824: 'It may perhaps surprise you, that in such an establishment, there is no churchman in the management. They certainly were not excluded, but they are in general in this place – I speak chiefly of the ministers of the Established Church – so little distinguished for classical or literary attainments of any sort, that they hold no station in society, or possess no influence that should have led the promoters of this scheme to consult them.' (Letter to Dr Samuel Parr in *The Works of Samuel Parr, LL.D.*, 1828, vol. VII, p. 302.)

Once the Directors had been elected, the energy with which they threw themselves into the task was amazing. The tirelessness, the efficiency, the thoroughness – and above all the speed – with which they tackled this daunting prospect would put today's school builders to shame. Consider the timetable:

On May 16, the Directors held their first meeting in Gibson's Rooms, which they decided to hire for all their meetings for £10 a year. Robert Dundas of Arniston, the Advocate Depute, was elected Chairman, and three committees were formed, involving every member of the Board:

1. To obtain a plan and estimates for the building;
2. To negotiate for the acquisition of the ground;
3. To prepare the draft of a Charter, and (later) a scheme of education to be followed at the school.

All three committees were to report back within a week, by May 21.

On May 21, the First Committee reported that Mr Burn had produced the sketch of a building plan for the Academy. The Third Committee, on the draft of a Charter, produced some suggestions for discussion, and agreed to defer for further consideration. The Second Committee, on ground purchase, produced a Petition to the Governors of Heriot's Hospital for a feu of the piece of ground which had been promised to the Town Council for their abortive New Town school project – the site originally chosen by Cockburn and Horner. It lay beyond the northern limits of the city, hard by the Water of Leith and between the two villages of Stockbridge and Canonmills, on land known variously as Canonmills Park or Distillery Park. To the west of it, Saxe-Coburg Place and Claremont Street were beginning to take shape, and between it and Fettes Row lay the hamlet of Silvermills, mostly occupied by extensive tanneries. One track joined Stockbridge to a toll-gate in Pitt Street (now Dundas Street), and another from Stockbridge to Canonmills was lined by a picturesque row of red-tiled cottages (now Henderson Row, named after Lord Provost Alexander Henderson, who died in 1827). The Town Council had acquired three Scots acres of this site for the school, and two adjoining acres had been earmarked for the Deaf and Dumb Institution that was to be built alongside; and Mr Russell was now instructed to lodge the petition with the Governors of Heriot's Hospital without delay.

On May 5, after many alterations and modifications, the Directors approved a plan for the school that 'would not exceed £9,000' and instructed Mr Burn to get working-plans out to builders' firms for tenders.

By June 12 they had secured the feu of three acres of Canonmills Park at the rate of 'twelve bolls of wheat and ten pounds Sterling in money per acre, the wheat to be converted and accounted for according to the highest fiars (*prices*) of Midlothian, and a composition of double the feu duty to be paid every 25th year.' (Clearly, the rapid development of the New Town had led to an increase in land-values in adjoining areas.) There and then the Directors decided that the Foundation Stone of the Academy should be laid on June 30 at three o'clock – less than three weeks later.

On June 19, the building plans were ordered to be put on view for inspection by the Contributors; and a draft of a Charter, as well as a preliminary plan for the mode of education to be adopted at the Academy, were discussed and remitted for further consideration.

On June 20 – the following day – the members of the First Committee (Plans and Estimates) met Mr Burn, the architect, at Canonmills Park, and chose a site for the school-house in the centre of the ground.

On June 21 – the following day – the revised draft of the proposed Charter, incorporating the suggestions made two days earlier, was approved and ordered to be circulated amongst the Contributors. And Messrs Horner and Kinnear were asked 'to prepare the Inscription for the Foundation Stone of the Academy and to forward all the preparations for laying the same'.

On June 27, the plans for the Academy were approved with some slight alterations.

And on June 30, the Foundation Stone was duly laid, right on schedule. The prodigious time and energy that had been devoted to the service of the Academy by busy men in those hectic few days fore-shadowed the selfless dedication of successive Boards of Directors down to the present day.

Three men in particular provided the main drive in the early days of the Academy. One was the Secretary, John Russell, who had con-ducted all the tortuous negotiations with the City Fathers, and who acted as Secretary until 1831 and as Treasurer thereafter from 1831 to 1843. Another was the first Treasurer, Thomas Kinnear, the banker, who was to provide the financial security that the Academy so badly needed in its early days. (Kinnear's own story ended in tragedy, for after his death in 1831 his heirs recalled all his loans, which led to the collapse of his banking house in 1834.) But the man to whom the members of the original Board gave the main credit was the indefatig-able Leonard Horner. In an unsolicited testimonial they wrote of him, four years later: 'From the first moment that it was contemplated, Mr Horner has had the chief charge of settling the principles of its con-stitution and of organising all its details, and the Directors have no hesitation in declaring that in doing so he has uniformly evinced the most signal talents for such a task, insomuch that they ascribe the complete success which has attended their new and very difficult under-taking principally to his unwearied zeal, literary tastes, bland manners, good sense, and great powers of method.' (*Minutes*, May 23, 1827.)

If the Foundation Stone of the Academy is ever disinterred, it will be found to contain three bottles filled with various contemporary documents, maps, and plans, as well as a lead casket with the names of the Directors and Architect incised on one side, and on the other the following inscription, penned by Horner and Kinnear:

UT NUMERO PARENTUM in urbe Edinburgo in dies crescenti et ampliorem quam qui suppetebat locum UBI AETAS PUERILIS ad humanitatem informari posset jamdiu efflagitanti consuleretur HANC AEDEM docili juventae sacratam quidam cives pecunia collata exstruendam curaverunt et primum lapidem posuerunt Prid. Kal. Jul. MDCCCXXIII.
[To meet the needs of the ever-growing number of parents in the city of Edinburgh who have long been clamouring for an ampler place than was previously available, where the rising generation could receive a liberal education, certain citizens, having contributed the necessary money, made arrangements for the construction of this

building dedicated to the teaching of the young, and laid the Foundation Stone on the day before the Kalends of July, 1823.]

On July 4, a General Meeting of Contributors at the Waterloo Hotel approved the draft of the Charter, subject to any minor alterations that might occur later.

On July 10, it was agreed to insert advertisements in the Scottish and English newspapers inviting applications for the situations of masters at the school.

On July 16, the First Committee (Plans and Estimates) met to consider the five building estimates that had been received. The highest was for £9,191, the lowest was for £8,162 7s.

Next day, on July 17, the Directors met in Gibson's Rooms and agreed to accept the lowest offer – £8,162 7s. – from Mr Walter Stuart Dinn, and instructed Mr Burn to employ a Clerk of Works. The contract provided that the work was to be completed by August 15, 1824.

On August 7, and again on August 9, the Building Committee met to discuss a possible shortage of stone from the Collalo Quarry in Fife, which had been stipulated for certain parts of the building.

On August 16, a special meeting was called to consider whether to add a special Writing Room to the school plans, at an additional cost of £1,130. This was subsequently approved on August 28.

And on August 22, 1823, the Contract between the Directors and Mr Dinn for building the Academy was read over and duly signed. The detailed specifications cover eighteen painstaking pages of the Directors' Minute Book in cursive copperplate. Nothing was overlooked; the quality and thickness of every piece of stone from the foundations and drains up to the slates on the roof were specified, right down to the last door knob and even the thickness of the wood that was to frame the privy seats:

> The whole Ruble stone will be got from Craigleith or Hailes Quarry. The Portico steps and whole landing within the Portico . . . and all the other stair steps and landings will be executed with the best Craigleith Stone . . . The hearth of fireplaces and the Floors of small entrance lobbies will be done with Dundee or Arbroath pavement, and the whole ashlar work (Portico, Pilasters, mouldings, base, etc.) on the principal front and East and West returns will be executed with the best liver rock from Collalo quarry; the remaining

fronts being done with the best liver rock from Denny or Redhall Quarries . . .

The whole stone of whatever description used in the building must be laid upon their natural beds, and the lime will be mixed up with clean sharp pit sand and pure fresh water. The whole walls and ceilings in the building will be finished with three coat plaster . . . The plaster lime must all be mixed up with hair of the best quality, and be prepared at least six weeks before it is laid on the walls . . .

The lead used in every part of the work must be cast and all of the best quality. The whole roofs of all the buildings will be covered with the best Welsh Queen slates, hung with malleable iron nails, steeped in linseed oil when hot and laid on a shouldering of haired lime . . .

And with that, the building of the school began.

PLANNING A MODE OF EDUCATION

Could it be managed, I should like there were a separate master for English . . .
(Sir Walter Scott, E.A. Director.)

Throughout the summer and autumn of 1823, after the Directors meeting of June 19, the Third Committee (Mode of Education) had been working and thinking hard on the preliminary report they had presented. The original scheme had proposed that the new school would be established on a plan similar to that of the High School, but the Directors did not feel themselves so tied down to the letter of that statement as to preclude the adoption of any other system, provided that it was obviously advantageous to do so. Right from the start, Cockburn and Horner had talked of achieving an 'improvement' of classical education in Scotland to make it more compatible with career prospects in England; and the first priority would obviously have to be the raising of standards in the teaching of Greek. But the Directors were also concerned to provide a broader, more complete system of education than was currently available at the High School; and one of them, Sir Walter Scott, pressed hard for greater attention to be paid to the teaching of English. In the autumn of 1823 he wrote to an un-known correspondent (presumably a fellow-Director): 'Could it be managed, I should like there were a separate master for English reading, orthography, geography, and history . . . I am convinced that by thus mixing the knowledge of the English language and Modern History with classical instruction, the most useful impression would be made on the youthful mind. We still carry the pedantry of former times a little too much into education, and boys are apt to think that learning Latin is the exclusive business of life and that all other acquisitions are of little consequence in comparison. Now though I am quite aware of the value of a classical education, yet I would not have it like Aaron's serpent swallow up all other attainments, and in my opinion in order to form the *Vir bonus* domestic history and an acquaintance with our own language should be kept abreast of the acquisitions to be made in classical knowledge.' (*Letters*, vol. VIII, p. 415.)

And now, in the late autumn of 1823, when the first flurry of getting the building operations started had subsided, the Directors sat down to consider 'the very important matter committed to them, viz, the plan of education which should be adopted at the Academy'. On November 20, and again on December 4, December 11, December 15, and December 18, the Directors hammered out a framework; and eventually, on December 29, the committee's Third Report was approved and ordered to be issued in 1,000 copies as a forty-page *Statement by the Directors of the Edinburgh Academy Explanatory of the Scheme of that Institution*. It set out in minute detail the background to the decision to establish this new school, the method by which funds were raised, the proposed 'Plan of Instruction', the time-tables for the various classes, the dates of the holidays, the school fees and masters' salaries, and the 'conditions upon which Masters are to be engaged'. This was, in effect, the first Prospectus of the Academy.

While the general system of instruction was to be based on that of the High School, with a Rector and four Classical Masters (each class remaining with its master as it moved up through the school for four years before graduating to the Rector's class for two), there were to be some highly significant modifications:

1. A more extended instruction in Greek, by all the Masters.

2. In addition to the four under-masters, a Master for English, who shall have a pure English accent: the mere circumstance of his being born within the boundary of England not to be considered indispensable. The object of this appointment is to endeavour to remedy a defect in the education of boys in Edinburgh, who are suffered to neglect the cultivation of their native tongue and literature during the whole time that they attend the Grammar Schools, and in most cases

to a much later period. It will be the duty of this master to give instruction in Reading, Elocution, and modern History . . .

3. A regular attention to Geography in all the Classes.

4. The Writing Master is to be bound to provide assistants in proportion to the number of his pupils, so that each teacher shall not have more than 35 boys under his care at one time.

5. Arithmetic is to be taught by a separate master, who is to be a well-educated mathematician, and who is to provide assistants, in like manner, in proportion to the number of his pupils.

6. The boys of the highest class are to be carried as far in the Elements of Algebra and Geometry as their time and previous knowledge will allow.

Thus, the standards of Greek, Geography, Writing and Arithmetic were all to be raised, and English was to be made a compulsory subject, with a separate master for English teaching all classes, as Sir Walter Scott had urged. (This was in advance of any English public school, where Classical Masters taught all other subjects too.) For the present, Writing would be optional from the 1st to the 5th class, and Arithmetic from the 4th class onwards, and it would be a long time before boys or parents could be persuaded to take English seriously as a subject. Latin was to be taught 'according to the accustomed mode of pronouncing that language in Scotland' – the European method, as it was called – but in later years the boys would also be made 'as familiar as is practicable with the English mode of pronunciation'. The Directors believed 'that to attempt to introduce any other branch of education would interfere with the success of the direct object of the Institution, which is to be a school for Classical Instruction'; but two years after the school opened, French, Astronomy and Natural Philosophy would be introduced as additional subjects.

The Rector and masters were to draw up a detailed Plan of Tuition for the whole school, with printed lists of books to be studied in each session. The Plan of Tuition had to receive the approval of the Directors, who insisted that the work of all classes should be closely supervised and correlated. This was a considerable departure from the practice at the High School, where individual masters had free responsibility for the ground covered and the methods of tuition. But there was an even more striking innovation in the way in which the school as a whole was to be run. Unlike the High School and most other schools, where the Headmaster had no jurisdiction over the other masters, and often very little contact with them, the Rector of the Edinburgh Academy was to be responsible for superintending the work of all the under-masters, and any failure on their part to carry out his instructions and recommendations was to be reported to the Directors. The idea of a Rector as superintendent of the staff, all of whom were required to work to an overall Plan of Tuition, represented a degree of control and central organisation hitherto unknown in Scottish schools, and made the choice of the first Rector crucially important to the whole tone of the school.

The question of school discipline had given the Directors much thought. Cockburn and all the other Directors who had been pupils at the High School held strong views on indiscriminate corporal punishment, from bitter experience: 'We do not think it would be prudent to lay down any fixed rules on the subject, but we are of the opinion that the frequent infliction of it should be discouraged, and that it should be reserved as much as possible for extreme cases, or for serious moral offences.' However, from the frequency with which the tawse was used, it seems likely that 'palmies' – strapping on the hand with a tawse – were exempted from the concept of corporal punishment in those days; it probably applied mainly to floggings inflicted on the body. Only the Rector was authorised to use a cane, although many did not take advantage of the privilege. The staple instrument of punishment used by the masters was the tawse, a leather strap cut into two or more thongs at one end. It is part of the canon of school dogma that tawses manufactured in Lochgelly, Fife, have always been the most efficacious.

Since one of the original reasons for wanting to establish a new school was the overcrowding at the High School, great stress was laid on the acceptable size for classes at the Academy. The High School, under Rector James Pillans, had recently introduced a monitorial system of teaching whereby large classes were divided into sub-classes under the care of a monitor: 'The Rector superintends the whole, and decides all questions of dispute when appeals are made to him against the decisions of the monitors. In each room is a *custos morum*, who watches the behaviour of the scholars, and notes every instance of remissness . . . The 23 classes all recite the same lesson at the same time. The noise they make is unavoidably great, but it is the sound of useful activity.' (Griscom, *A Year in Europe*). Nonetheless, the Academy never adopted the monitorial system, and the Directors decreed that admissions to the school would be limited so that the junior classes should not exceed 110, and the Rector's classes 160 combined, making a total of 600.

The First Class would have a play-time from eleven to eleven-forty-five in the morning and a quarter of an hour in the afternoon. The Directors were also of the opinion 'that between every change of occupation there ought to be an interval in all the Classes; a run of five or ten minutes in the play-ground will be quite enough to renovate the relaxed energies both of body and mind, and make the boys come with fresh vigour to their new employment, and will materially conduce to their health'.

The Directors constantly showed an unusual (for those days) concern for the health of the boys who would be entrusted to their care. Wet-weather shelter for the playground 'breaks' was to be provided by a covered way that ran from the Masters' Lodge and the Janitor's Lodge up the sides of the boundary walls, and then at right angles to join the east and west lobbies of the main building, where the outlines of the original shelter-roofs could still be seen until new porches were built about ten years ago. A remnant of the original shelter with its iron supports survives to this day as cover for the school notice-boards.

A lunch interval was not considered necessary in those days when the main meal of the day was taken just after school, at 4 p.m.; but snacks could be brought from home or purchased at the Janitor's Lodge to be consumed during breaks.

On Saturdays, school was to finish at 11 a.m. It was not until 1851 that compulsory classes on Saturdays were eventually abandoned.

School holidays would be two months in the summer, and a week at Christmas, but no Easter holidays. In addition, the Rector was empowered to grant four days a year as 'Rector's Holidays', and there were to be four days twice a year at 'the preachings' – the four days in November and May set aside by the Church of Scotland for the administration of the Sacraments.

On the vexed question of fees, the Directors were very conscious of the criticisms that had been voiced in the Council Chambers and elsewhere that the lower classes would be effectively priced out of the kind of education offered by the Academy: 'In fixing the rate of fees, we have felt the full importance of keeping them as low as possible, consistent with the practicability of carrying the plan into execution in such a manner as is calculated to fulfil the intentions of the Contributors in establishing the Academy. And although the gross amount of the fees is somewhat greater than what is paid at this moment at the

High School, yet it is humbly conceived, that the excess will not appear unreasonable to the public, when it is considered that additional branches of Education are one cause of the increase, and that the accommodation of a great Public School in the New Town, which has been provided at the expense of private individuals, must necessarily be paid for.' Fees paid by Academy boys over a six-year course, including Writing and Arithmetic, would average out at £9 12s. 10d. a year, compared with £6 18s. paid by boys at the High School – about forty per cent more. For that extra £2 14s. 10d., 'the boys at the Academy will have the additional instruction of English Reading, Elocution, and Modern History during the whole period of six years; Geography will be an object of attention during the whole period; Greek will be taught from the commencement of the Third Year; and in all probability the elements of Geometry will be taught in the Sixth Year'. These fees would also cover all the costs that parents were expected to meet; for it was specifically laid down 'as an absolute rule' that no master should 'under any pretence take fees of a higher amount from any of the scholars', and that 'there shall be no Candlemas gift or any other gratuity whatever to the Masters'.

The fees included an entrance payment by each boy of two guineas for the First Class and three guineas annually for each of the other Classes. Out of this the school would pay a salary of £100 to the Rector and £50 for each master; the rest of their income would depend, as in all other schools, on the fees paid to them directly by the boys. With a roll of 500 boys, the Rector would earn an income of £700 and the masters £400, but until the numbers built up, the Directors would guarantee the Rector an income of £400 and the masters an income of £200 each. The remainder of the money from entrance fees (with 500 boys, it would total annually £1,480 10s.) would go to paying feu duty, the Janitor's salary (£50 a year), three women cleaners at 3s. a week, heating (half a ton of coal a day for seven months at 10s. a ton, totalling £45 a year), school prizes, repairs, and so on.

As for the Rector and masters themselves, the Directors were determined to cast a wide net and set the highest standards. There were no formalised qualifications for teachers in those days – no teacher training schemes, no colleges of education, no teaching diplomas. Teachers started straight from university, either in schools or as private tutors, or tutors attached to schools. In England they were liable to be clergymen, taking pupils to augment a meagre living, or taking posts in schools until such time as they might be called to some higher rank in the church. The Directors of the Academy carefully listed a number of 'inquiries to which all candidates are required to give a distinct answer:

1. The Age of the Candidate. It is highly desirable, in an establishment such as this, especially where a new system is to be organised, that the Masters should be in the full vigour of life . . .

2. Testimonials of moral character, and *most particularly of temper.*

3. Where he has received his education.

4. Whether he has gained any literary honours at any of the Universities.

5. Whether he has had any experience in teaching, where, of what kind, and to what extent.

6. Whether he can name any persons whom he has taught, who have afterwards distinguished themselves by their attainments, either at the Universities or elsewhere.

7. To name persons to whom the Directors may make personal application for such further information as they may require.

8. Whether he belongs to the Church, or has any views to that profession.

'Before engaging any Master, it will be absolutely necessary for the Directors to ascertain that his general health is good, that he is not subject to attacks of any violent disease, such as fits, and whether he has any marked natural deformity, and what that is.'

The Latin and Greek masters would require testimonials of their competence in composition, prose and verse, the English Master of his 'particular attention to the genius and structure of his own language', and the Writing Master would be expected to produce specimens of his penmanship.

The *Explanatory Statement* was now sent off to the Principals of the four Scottish Universities, the Vice-Chancellor and Heads of all Colleges at Oxford and Cambridge, the Provost of Trinity College, Dublin, and each of the Headmasters of all the great Public Schools of the United Kingdom – 'this, it is supposed, will be sufficient to secure a free competition for Candidates from any part of the United Kingdom.'

Applications and testimonials had to be lodged by March 15, 1824; but 'if a very highly qualified person should offer for the situation of Rector, we shall not hesitate to elect him before that period; for there can be no doubt that the success and character of the Academy will be very materially affected by the talents and attainments of the person who fills that office . . .' But probably not even the Directors of the Edinburgh Academy realised just how important that first appointment would turn out to be.

FINDING A RECTOR

I think *his* superintendence will be the making of our School.
(Colin Mackenzie, D.K.S.)

In the middle of December, 1823, even before the *Explanatory Statemen* was circulated, Sir Walter Scott wrote to his old friend Richard Heber, the English bibliophile who had secured a place for Scott's elder son at Oxford; now Scott was seeking his help in finding a Rector for the new school:

'I promised to several of the Committee to mention this business to you, knowing your zeal for learning all over the world . . . This would be a very desirable situation for a man of learning and preceptorial talent should such a person of desert be within the sphere of our knowledge and we look to England to obtain candidates for the situation . . . I should think Oxford abounded with young men of learning and talent to whom this would be a Godsend and if such were presented in time (there is no absolute hurry) I think he would be the winning horse . . .'

Scott was making an early move to try to ensure that a candidate from England would be selected, and preferably a Tory at that; for although he said there was no absolute hurry, there was a note of anxiety in his letter: 'The majority of the committee and great majority of the Subscribers are Tories, and to speak truth in your private ear we are rather afraid that the others who are always very active mean to palm a Whig upon us . . . I know these gentry pretty well and have good experience how loud they can sound their horns when they have a mind to sell their own fish, but I should be sorry were a Whig to be fairly cramd down our throat for want of a man of good principles in church & state to pull against him.' (*Letters*, vol. VIII, pp. 132–3.)

Meanwhile another Tory among the Directors, Colin Mackenzie of Portmore, the Deputy Keeper of the Signet and one of the hardest-working members of the original committee, was also busy soliciting candidates. He had written for advice to a man whom both he and

Scott admired tremendously, a young Welsh scholar and divine called John Williams. The Rev. John Williams was then thirty-two years old, the son and pupil of a notable Welsh schoolmaster at Ystrad-meurig in Cardiganshire. He had started his teaching career at the age of fifteen in a school at Chiswick, but had later gone up to Balliol College, Oxford, where he took a First Class degree in 1814 along with the future Dr Arnold of Rugby. For the next four years he had been personal assistant to the Headmaster of Winchester, Dr Henry Gabell, and then taught at another school in Winchester for the next two years. Since 1820 he had been vicar of Lampeter in Cardiganshire and Headmaster of Lampeter School. Williams had been at Balliol with Scott's son-in-law, Lockhart, and on Lockhart's recommendation Scott and Colin Mackenzie and other prominent Scotsmen had sent their sons to him as private pupils to be tutored for Oxford.

And now, when the first half dozen applications for the post of Rector had already been lodged and reported to the Directors, Scott was delighted to receive from Williams not a recommendation of some other suitable candidate for the Rectorship, but a letter offering himself for the post. On that very same day, February 18, 1824, he dashed off an excited letter from Abbotsford to Colin Mackenzie in Edinburgh:

'My dear Colin – The enclosed is of such importance that I forward it immediately, for no *Deus ex machina* ever came more *apropos* to our Academy. I only wish it were better worth Williams' while, but I have no doubt that his acknowledged scholarship and power of communicating information will at once render the Academy respectable and his own situation valuable. Having been three years in correspondence with Mr W I can bear witness to the careful and regular attention which he bestows on his pupils, to his attention to their peculiar bent and the dexterity with which he renders learning lively. Charles [*Scott's younger son*], who was idle, conceited and impracticable at home, is now a steady hard-reading student and passionately fond of his teacher . . . Of course this is a matter that cannot be hurried, but yet we cannot have better bread than is made of wheat, and I should [like] to have Mr Williams' claim considered soon after his certificates are brought forward, for a man of proved talents & scholarship in the prime of life, an enthusiast in his profession, though possessed of a private independence which makes him completely respectable, seems to be the very man we want.' (*Letters*, vol. VIII, pp. 183–5).

Colin Mackenzie, who had also received a letter from Williams, was just as excited as Scott. He wrote to Sir Walter by return of post: 'I feel exactly as you do about Williams. I think *his* superintendence will be the making of our School. I had asked his help in finding us a Rector & was delighted to get a letter from him offering himself. A Committee met yesterday before which I laid his letter, adding my own opinion – and we are all concurred in the disposition to prefer him to every other Candidate.' (*Ibid.*, p. 185, note 1.)

But it was not to be as easy as all that. One of the Directors raised a point which caused the Whigs on the committee deep concern – the allegation that Williams was said to be a close friend of Lockhart and John Wilson (Christopher North), those notorious lambasters of Whigs in *Blackwood's Magazine*. Wilson was by this time the rumbustious Professor of Moral Law at Edinburgh University, but he had got the chair in 1820 in the teeth of fierce Whig opposition. Mackenzie was well aware of the possibility that this would endanger Williams' chances: 'Skene spoke of Lockhart and Wilson as Williams' friends,' he continued in his letter to Scott, 'which I felt, as you do, was not likely with some of us to promote his claims, but to do Horner justice it did not make him swerve. I told the opinion I know you entertained of him, and my own on a shorter acquaintance but with the advantage of having seen him. I would have referred to Sir Wm Hamilton [*who had been Wilson's chief rival for the Edinburgh chair*] but did not, for having once talked to him of Williams I observed a little leaven which seemed to me to arise from his being Wilson's friend . . .'

Poor John Williams. A little 'leaven' was frequently observed to arise when his name was mentioned, as Leonard Horner was to find when he went to London on business early in March. Nonetheless, Whig though he was, Horner had been reassured by Scott and Mackenzie and was prepared to settle for Williams as Rector even without waiting for his testimonials to arrive. The lobbying was now on in earnest; several other Directors were persuaded to accept Williams, and even Thomas Kinnear, the banker, who had a friend from Cambridge to propose, 'yielded the pass to Williams' superior pretensions.'

But the struggle for the Rectorship was only beginning, and the Directors knew that it could create problems and divisions. At a meeting on February 12, Secretary Russell had suggested that because 'in the course of the discussions that may arise among the Directors in regard to the merits of the respective candidates, it would be of importance that they should feel themselves at liberty to communicate freely and unreservedly to each other the information which they may receive, it would therefore be expedient that the Directors should enter into a resolution that whatever shall pass at their meetings or in conversation with each other respecting the candidates shall be strictly confidential and shall on no account be divulged to any person whatever'; and all the Directors had signed this Minute individually. Mr Russell also declined to take the responsibility for answering individual applications, and for this task a special advisory committee was appointed. Mr Russell wasn't a lawyer for nothing! At the same time it became clear that the Directors would not exercise their option of appointing a Rector before the closing date for applications on March 15.

Meanwhile Leonard Horner had to go to London on business, and he took the opportunity of 'asking around' in academic circles there about this fellow Williams who wanted to be Rector of his beloved new school in Edinburgh. What he heard so alarmed him that he rushed post-haste up to Oxford to make some further inquiries. He came away from there dismayed and determined that Williams should not get the job, and went straight to Cambridge to interview Kinnear's candidate, John Hutton Fisher, a Fellow of Trinity College.

What had Horner heard? Already there were rumours circulating that Williams was a Tory and had actually contributed one or two articles to the hated *Blackwood's Magazine*; but now Horner brought back to Edinburgh horrifying accounts that charged the Rev. John Williams with coarseness of mind, impropriety of language, violence of temper, repulsiveness of appearance, unpopularity with boys, and even responsibility for the outbreak of the notorious 'schoolboy rebellion' at Winchester in 1818 when the whole school had locked themselves in and occupied the roof, and the military had had to be called out. (Student sit-ins are by no means an exclusively twentieth-century phenomenon. In 1595, for instance, an Edinburgh bailie, John McMorane, was shot in the head and killed when leading a force of Town's officers trying to break into the Edinburgh High School when the pupils staged a 'barring out' after a request for a holiday had been turned down.)

In fact, as it turned out, it was the Winchester connection that was at the root of all the trouble. Winchester had been founded by the English churchman and statesman William of Wykeham in the fourteenth century, and for centuries it had been run exclusively by the Wykehamists of New College, Oxford (another Wykeham foundation). The appointment of non-Wykehamist John Williams by the Headmaster, Dr Henry Gabell, as personal assistant in 1814 was resented by the New College governors and by boys whose fathers and grandfathers and great-grandfathers had all been Wykehamists; for although Williams tutored only boys in Dr Gabell's house, known as Commoners, he had a Master's jurisdiction over all the rest of the boys. To make matters worse, Williams was a disciplinarian; that is to say, he believed that diligence in study was of prime importance, and that boys should show respect for authority. This made him less than popular with the prefects, the elegant young Flashman-type thugs who ran the school under a reign of terror. The rebellion in 1818 was neither the first nor the last student uprising there, but non-Wykehamist Williams was made the scapegoat and was forced to resign. In his letter applying for the Rectorship of the Edinburgh Academy, Williams had merely commented that 'in July 1818 I resigned my appointment under Dr Gabell in consequence of the displeasure of the Senior Fellows at the New College, Oxford, who were dissatisfied that a non-Wykehamist should have so much influence and authority in the School'.

Perhaps it is understandable that Horner, Cockburn and Russell, unfamiliar with the ferocity of the tribal wars in English public schools, should find it hard to believe that so much odium could attach to a young man simply over a politically tactless appointment. At any rate, they completely turned against Williams and his candidature.

This was the signal for Sir Walter Scott to swing into massive action. He fired off a broadside of letters in all directions, soliciting personal testimonials, mobilising support, lobbying busily amongst Williams' former pupils (with the help of his son Charles), vilifying poor Leonard Horner, and everywhere suggesting a vicious Whig plot to discredit an able Tory candidate. Time was now of the essence: could the damage be undone before the crucial meeting at which the Directors would formally appoint a Rector?

On March 8 he wrote to Dr Gabell, who had left Winchester the previous year; and Dr Gabell replied by return post: 'That Mr John Williams was hated and slandered by certain persons at Winchester, whom I do not wish to name, & that he became, in consequence, unpopular among many of those boys who were not his pupils & did not know him; and also that on account of these things, he was finally induced to relinquish his very uncomfortable situation, these are undeniable facts. Yet, believe me, under all the circumstances of the case, these transactions redound to his honour . . . Mr John Williams was the first man that was ever appointed Tutor in Winchester School,

who was not a Wykehamist. The appointment, from the first, gave
umbrage to several persons. But no sooner did he begin to discover his
great parts, & great attainments, & the ascendancy which those high
qualifications gave him over the minds of his pupils, than they felt
their own merits to be obscured by the superior lustre of his, and with
their mouths full of deference & submission to him in his presence,
hated, calumniated & persecuted him. The rest followed of course.
Yet under these provocations he *showed no ill temper*, but comported
himself with a strength and dignity of mind which served only to
inflame the hatred of his enemies. That the effects of their rancour
should still pursue him, & tend to obstruct his progress towards the
high honour to which he now aspires, fills me with indignation . . .'
(*Letters*, vol. VIII, pp. 205-6, note 2.)

The plotting and intriguing continued. Scott to James Skene
(March 13): 'I had not the least doubt from the beginning that there was
party at the bottom of this opposition. Horner's letter showed the
cloven hoof in every line . . . I never knew the match of the Whigs for
talking *up* and whispering *down* their friends . . . To secure the strong-
hold of education has been a part of the Whig tactics for twenty years
past. They have not the wealth or numbers to found schools, but by a
constant system of manœuvres they endeavour to intrigue us out of our
natural influence in these matters.' Scott to Colin Mackenzie (March
13): 'It is and has been long their *tactique* to get and keep possession of
public schools and they make up by assiduity and union what they want
in influence to accomplish their object. They do not scruple to employ
our best and most honourable feelings on these subjects – to appeal to
our candour, our humanity, our sense of honour, and whenever they
gain a trick it is always by making some well-natured Tory take the
lead. I suspect you will find Hay (*fellow-Director, Sir John Hay of
Smithfield and Hayston*) has been humbugd in this manner.' Scott to
Skene (March 26): 'Adieu, sleep with one eye open.' Scott to Skene
(March 28): 'Your order of battle is excellent, and by adhering to it we
shall be secure of victory.'

Despite his almost pathological suspicions of Whig machinations,
it seems that it was Scott himself who was doing most of the plotting.
Nothing in Leonard Horner's voluminous correspondence suggests
anything but devotion to duty and utter fair-mindedness in his interviewing of candidates. At various Directors' Meetings throughout
March at which Sir Walter Scott was present, it was invariably agreed
to postpone discussion of the applications, from March 4 to March 10,

from March 10 to March 18, from March 18 to March 22, from March 22 to April 3. This gave Scott and his friends time to amass a formidable weight of testimonials in Williams' favour, from two local landowners in Cardiganshire, from Richard Heber (refuting the Wykehamist smear), and from twenty-three former pupils, full of praise for his scholarliness, his power to communicate knowledge, and his gentlemanliness.

On Saturday, April 3, 1824, fourteen of the fifteen Academy Directors met to elect the first Rector and staff. There were sixteen applications for the Rectorship and nearly a hundred for the four Classical Masters and three other masters, and eleven for the post of Janitor. Sir Walter Scott, who in an earlier letter to Colin Mackenzie (March 13) had said, 'If I thought there was any difficulty of carrying Williams I would sprain my ancle on purpose and stay where I am,' was there, and fighting fit.

Cockburn, Horner, Russell and three other Directors voted for the Cambridge candidate, John Hutton Fisher. But the Rev. John Williams scraped through against him by a narrow majority. The 'Whig plot', if there had ever been one, had been defeated, and Williams was duly appointed as the first Rector of the Edinburgh Academy: not an Englishman but a Welshman, and hardly a Tory either, for he rejoiced with the best of them by giving the School a holiday when the Reform Bill was passed in 1832! Even Scott had the grace to admit (in a letter to Lockhart on May 2) that Williams suffered no hostility from his former opponents when he later came north: 'He has been most kindly received at Edinburgh – even by those who least wished him there.' Scott himself, meeting Williams in person for the first time, found that 'there is no rudeness in his manner – none whatever – and he is the only schoolmaster whom I have ever found totally free of pedantry – full of information besides and a very pleasant companion' (which must have come as a relief, considering the ardour with which he had championed Williams). Leonard Horner, too, showed his usual fair-mindedness, in a letter to Russell on May 11: 'The more I saw of Williams, the more I liked him. He appears to be thoroughly master of the duties of a schoolmaster, as far as we have yet had the opportunity of judging, and there is a clearness of head and promptitude which gives me great hope that he will inspire his undermasters with a proper confidence in him.'

[John Hutton Fisher of Cambridge, the defeated candidate, never took up teaching after his failure to get the Academy Rectorship. It was probably his lack of teaching experience as much as Sir Walter Scott's machinations that cost him the job. Henry Cockburn annotated the copies of the testimonials he was sent, and these, or at least those of the 'more respectable of the candidates', are now in the British Museum. On Fisher's application he wrote: 'Good certificates. This gentleman is almost the only real competitor against Mr Williams for the office of Rector. His defect (and it is a great one) is that he has not been accustomed to *teach*; of which Williams has had great experience.' Fisher was Vicar of Kirkby Lonsdale, Westmorland, from 1831 to 1860, and died at Cambridge in 1862.]

Williams's under-masters were also chosen at that meeting on April 3. The applicants were a motley collection of teachers, tutors and clergymen from all over Britain from Islay to Cambridge, and included the Rector of Dumfries Grammar School, the Headmaster of Watson's Hospital, the Rector of Moffat Academy, and the Rector of Montrose Academy. All the candidates presented a bunch of testimonials, printed at their own expense, and the Directors paid particular attention to the opinions of men they knew personally, like their former Headmaster, Dr Pillans of the High School, who was now a Professor at Edinburgh University. Cockburn's laconic annotations provide an invaluable glimpse into their way of thinking: 'It is curious and satisfactory to see so many well qualified persons in the country for such places.' He also noted that one of the candidates who was not seriously considered was an English clergyman who 'very candidly admitted that he was lazy and not very learned, but that he "hoped that by due attention he would always be able to keep pace with his pupils".' There are two intriguing mysteries about the original applications that cannot now be answered: an earlier would-be historian of the Academy, Dr J. G. Tait (E.A. 1871–4), who eventually edited *Scott's Journal*, appealed in the *Chronicle* of July, 1923, for information about 'the letter of Coleridge recommending De Quincey' and 'the letter written by Macaulay in 1824 recommending a candidate for the Rectorship'. The future Lord Macaulay was then a newly-elected Fellow of Trinity College, Cambridge, and presumably he had written a letter in support of a Cambridge candidate whom he knew; but this document does not survive in the extant testimonials, if it ever existed. The reference to Coleridge and De Quincey is even more interesting. An earlier *Chronicle* (October, 1915) had made a casual reference to it: 'We are informed that a testimonial from S. T. Coleridge recommending De Quincey as the original English Master was still preserved in

1898.' Alas, no knowledge or trace of this document exists today. De Quincey, who was then enjoying a certain notoriety as the author of *The Confessions of an Opium-Eater*, which had appeared as a serial in *The London Magazine* in 1821, was certainly eager to come to Edinburgh: he eventually settled in Edinburgh in 1828 and stayed there until his death in 1859, writing articles for *Blackwood's Magazine* and other journals. It is perhaps hardly surprising that the Directors did not take his application for a job in 1824 seriously enough to record it formally (if it ever happened): De Quincey, the hippy writer of his time, would have been considered as grossly unsuitable as Henry Miller today, even when championed by Samuel Taylor Coleridge, who by then had achieved the respectability of mature years, if nothing else. It is fascinating to speculate on what De Quincey might have done to the fledgeling English Department at the Academy had his application been taken seriously . . .

The masters eventually appointed were:

Classical Masters:	Archibald N. Carmichael, teacher of Latin and Greek in the Academy of Inverness.
	George Ferguson, assistant master in the Grammar School, Selkirk.
	Robert Mitchell, M.A., Rector of the Grammar School, Kirkcudbright.
	William Henry Marriott, B.A., of Trinity College, Cambridge.
English Master:	Charles Barker, B.A., of Trinity College, Cambridge.
Writing Master:	James Glover, Writing Master in the Academy, Hope Street, Liverpool.
Mathematical and Arithmetical Master:	James Gloag, Teacher of Mathematics in George Heriot's Hospital, Edinburgh.

The first Janitor to be elected was no ordinary man, either. He was an Edinburgh book-binder and antiquarian called John Howell who wrote an *Essay on the War Galleys of the Ancients* and a *Life of Alexander Selkirk* (the original of Robinson Crusoe); later, the Directors were to buy from him 'some very ingenious models of an ancient galley, a Roman Camp, Caesar's bridge over the Rhine, and of some machines described in the classics'. Howell was also to construct a flying machine, in which he made an unpremeditated descent into the school grounds at the cost of a broken leg.

The team was now ready, and it was a young team. The masters were all in their twenties, and the Rector himself was only thirty-two.

CHAPTER V

The Opening: October 1, 1824

And wise Sir Walter made the speech. (Poem in the *Chronicle*.)

HAVING met the Directors and most of his future colleagues on the staff and drawn up a General Plan of Tuition, Mr Williams returned to Wales to settle his affairs in Lampeter, promising to return in July or August. The Directors were now left with four months in which to have the school ready for opening on October 1st. All the necessary formalities had been completed: a Warrant of Charter of Incorporation was signed by Robert Peel on February 6, 1824, and on April 24 the Royal Charter was sealed at Edinburgh, and the Subscribers (all 240 of them) were now incorporated into a body politic and corporate with the name and title of 'The Proprietors of The Edinburgh Academy'. Total capital was not to exceed £12,000, with the provision that it could be increased to £16,000 in case of need.

But there were a thousand and one things still to be done, and the Directors were kept frantically busy all summer. They held meetings galore, they visited the site on countless occasions to confer with the builder, they took legal decisions about share transfers, they ordered a brass school bell from Armstrong's Foundry and a clock for each classroom, they arranged for trees and shrubs to be planted to screen 'the necessaries' (the lavatories, or 'down the hill', to use the euphemism that the Academy has used for 150 years), they negotiated for a dry access path from the Toll Gate on Pitt Street to the Masters' Lodge, they agreed on the design and supply of coat-racks and hat-pegs, they chose the six-seater desks and benches for the classrooms (they plumped for backs on the benches for the benefit of pupils who were weakly).

The building estimates were going up – by July, the costs already contracted for had risen to nearly £11,000 – but they decided nevertheless to go ahead with the scheme for providing a covered way round the sides of the playground. However, they reckoned it would cost too much (£700 or £800) to build a wall to serve as bounds for playing ball-games against, and settled instead for a railing to be erected to close off the steep bank at the north end of the playground (the windows, however, were to be prudently protected by trellises).

The Plan of Tuition drawn up by Mr Williams was amended to suit parents who wanted Arithmetic introduced in the Third Class instead of the Fourth; but care was taken to ensure that the Arithmetical Master would not gain any undue increase in his income. The Classical Masters managed to wrest some time off the English Master in order to give the First Class extra Latin; he, poor soul, offered to make up for the time taken from him by holding classes in the summer term between 7 and 8 a.m., but the Directors left the offer in abeyance until nearer the time. In a last-minute inspiration, probably at the pious suggestion of the Rev. Rector Williams, it was decided that a chapter of the Bible should be read aloud in every class each Monday morning, and Bibles were hurriedly ordered for the purpose.

There was some discussion about the feasibility of introducing gymnastic exercises into the curriculum, but they decided that there was no hurry about it and agreed to look for someone who might be interested in coming to Edinburgh to run optional gymnastic classes in the school. (Later that year they decided to delay this innovation until a more suitable time, and it was not until 1827 that a Drill Sergeant was employed to hold classes three times a week on an entirely optional basis).

And should they have boarding-houses belonging to the school to accommodate the sons of parents who were abroad or lived inconveniently far from Edinburgh? They couldn't decide about this, and left the matter meanwhile.

They kept sending letters to Mr Williams asking him to come and help interview boys for admission to the school (277 pupils had been entered for the Academy by July), but July and August passed and still Mr Williams did not arrive. He had already advised on the books he wanted for the boys, so the Directors discussed them with the masters who were on hand and arranged to have them supplied to the school at trade prices. The Janitor, himself a book-binder to trade, was to sell them from his Lodge at retail prices, and the profits were to go towards forming class libraries.

The Janitor was authorised to sell bread, biscuits, milk, gingerbread, and balls, marbles or other toys, but nothing must be sold on credit, and he was strictly forbidden to sell fireworks or gunpowder. He must on no account accept any fees or gratuities from the boys. He must be constantly on the look-out to prevent them injuring themselves by climbing walls, and in the terms of his Instructions, 'you will prevent them injuring or defacing any part of the building.' But whatever resistance the boys might offer, or whatever provocation they gave him, he must on no account strike any boy 'on pain of immediate dismissal'.

Detailed Instructions were also laid down for the Rector and the masters, mainly concerned with the questions of punctuality and strict adherence to the schedule of instruction sanctioned by the Directors; but the matter of corporal punishment again loomed large in the Directors' minds: 'The Directors are desirous to impress upon all the Masters their most anxious wish that the practice, which is not only degrading to the boys but derogatory to the dignity of the Master, should as far as possible be banished from the Academy: and that the Masters should earnestly endeavour to devise methods of maintaining subordination which shall act upon the honour and good feelings of their pupils and thus gain their respect and affection rather than give authority by inspiring terror . . . At all events, if corporal punishment is ever to be inflicted, let it be an invariable rule that an interval of one hour at least shall elapse between the discovery of the offence by the Master and the infliction of the punishment, that the boy may never be chastised in anger.'

But the main cause of concern throughout that summer was whether the school buildings would be ready in time for the Opening. The builder, Mr Dinn, was deluged with letters and exhortations and frequent visits from anxious members of the Building Committee, and Mr Burn, the architect, more than once had to assure the Directors that the classrooms and Hall would be ready and the plaster completely dried out in plenty of time (it was a good dry summer that year); but there were difficulties in obtaining sufficient of the golden-yellow Collalo stone for the portico, and it became clear that the school would have to be opened with its handsome classical portals unfinished (the portico was not, in fact, finished until the middle of the first session).

Crossing their fingers, the Directors went ahead with their plans for the opening ceremony and a subsequent banquet in the Royal Hotel. The Chairman of the Board, Robert Dundas of Arniston, agreed to deliver the opening speech. Old Henry Mackenzie, the 'Man of Feeling', was also booked for a speech, even though he was now in his eightieth year. Invitations were sent out to six Lords of the Court of Session, the Lord Advocate, the Solicitor-General, six baronets, a bishop, the M.P.s for the city and the county, a clutch of University Professors and the Lord Provost and two Bailies; and the Rev. Sir Henry Moncreiff, the minister of the parish of St Cuthbert's in which the Academy was situated, agreed to be the officiating clergyman.

Leonard Horner, who was frantically busy conferring with masters, ordering books and desks, getting estimates for window-blinds, negotiating with painters, and sending 'Come quickly' letters to the absent Rector, was also given the job of having cards printed with the list of fees, to be given to each boy on Opening day. The fees, it had been decided, should be paid to a clerk and not, as was the custom in some other schools, directly to the masters.

At last, on September 15, the Rector arrived in Edinburgh and was instructed to be in attendance every day from the 20th to the 30th at Thomas Kinnear's house in Great King Street with 'Bowsey' Carmichael, the Classical Master who would be taking the First Class, in order to examine prospective pupils privately and 'ascertain their state of proficiency previous to their parents fixing upon the Class to which they are to be sent' (the Rector could only *advise* parents on the right class – the parents were not bound to accept his advice). An advertisement announcing the Rector's interviews was rushed to the newspapers to be added to the advertisements that had been appearing regularly about the Opening of the school and the sale of books.

As Opening day approached, the tempo of activity increased and became positively hectic. But with a wary eye on the danger of bad publicity at this late stage, the Directors found the time to devote a lot of attention to a complaint from a Mr George Bell, who had been going round town alleging that the backless benches in the Writing Room could cause accidents. Several Directors went to the school with their sons to try out the benches for themselves, and at the last meeting before the Opening, on September 30, they earnestly discussed the safety of the seats and instructed that Mr Bell should be sent a copy of the Minutes which reassured all parents that the seats occasioned no cause for concern and promised that experts would be commissioned to report if they weren't satisfied. Their last recorded task at that eve-of-opening meeting was to approve the appointment by Messrs. Russell and Horner of 'three persons for the purpose of cleaning and sweeping the different classrooms'.

One late change of plan had been forced on them. The Chairman of the Directors, Robert Dundas of Arniston, had intimated that his official duties as Advocate Depute would detain him in Glasgow on the day of the Opening, and he would be unable to make the principal speech. So Colin Mackenzie approached Sir Walter Scott to fill the breach – 'Dundas will be absent & we look all to you as our head on the occasion . . . and we shall be much the better of an address from such lips as yours to grace our outset.' Scott was doubtful – he was expecting visitors at Abbotsford that weekend, including the Foreign Minister, George Canning. But the visit was cancelled at a late hour, and Scott wrote to James Skene: 'My time is at my disposal, and therefore I put it at yours on the 1st October. I am, I own, no particular friend to this species of blow-out . . . I hope you expect no forenoon oratory.'

Came the great day, Friday, October 1, 1824. The Directors and masters met at 10 a.m. in the Masters' Lodge, and from eleven o'clock onwards carriages and pony-traps clattered down from the New Town terraces as the 372 enrolled boys arrived and were shown to their classrooms to have their names taken down by their respective masters, while the parents went to take their seats in the narrow, hanging gallery that went all the way round the handsome, oval-shaped Hall with its tiers of benches rising from a central well. The Hall was originally an amphitheatre, and there was no Rectorial dais as there is today – that is a remnant of a false floor that was laid when the Hall was used as a dining hall for a few years at the turn of the century. The Hall, which to Academicals is the crowning glory and nostalgic focus of the Academy, followed very closely the lines of St Cecilia's Hall in Niddry Street, off the Cowgate, which had been built in 1762 by the Musical Society of Edinburgh on the model of the Opera House at Parma. The characteristic elliptical cupola was added at the Directors' insistence, and later required the addition of steel bars to keep it from collapsing. St Cecilia's, which is now rectangular and not oval, was used as a dance hall for many years, but has once again been restored to use as a concert hall.

At 12.30 the five classes marched direct into the Hall from their adjoining classrooms, and the boys took their places on the tiers of benches adjacent to their rooms. The masters sat round a covered table in the central well, facing their classes. The Rector was seated at the north end of the table with his class behind him and facing the Directors' Box, which was sited where the glass partition at the main entrance is now. He was a resplendent figure in flowing academic gown, a snowy white stock knotted high under his chin, brown hair curling round his ears and down his cheeks in the kind of ample sideburns that are fashionable again 150 years later. He was a good-looking young man, short in build and inclined to plumpness of face and figure, but handsome enough to make the New Town ladies sorry to hear that he was already married. His sonorous Welsh voice carried right round the Hall as he exhorted the boys to conduct themselves with decorum during the ceremony.

At 12.45 a procession of Directors and V.I.P.s led by Leonard Horner and the secretary, John Russell, marched diagonally across the Yards from the Masters' Lodge to the Hall. The V.I.P.s took their seats in the well of the Hall and the Directors filed into their Box, and Sir Walter Scott opened the proceedings by calling upon Sir Henry Moncreiff, who duly obliged with 'an eloquent and fervent prayer'.

Academy boys and Academicals have always had a penchant for penning verses about notable school occasions, and the Opening duly received its accolade in doggerel seventy years later from Rector R. J. Mackenzie (1888–1901):

> Weel nigh four hunder laddies thrangs
> Upon the bonny opening day,
> Moncreiffs, Bells, Balfours, Woods and Langs,
> And Aytoun o' the mellow lay,
> And Tait wha hid (the clever chap)
> A muckle mitre in his cap.

(This was a reference to Archie Campbell Tait, the future Archbishop of Canterbury, sitting that morning among the fourteen-year-olds in the Rector's Class.)

> And gude Sir Harry raised the prayer,
> And wise Sir Walter made the speech;
> Frae Wales he'd brocht a man o' lair,
> The weel-faured eident lads to teach.
> 'He'll schule your bairns,' quoth Scott, 'for he
> Has skelpt my ain successfully.'

'Wise Sir Walter' spoke at some length, despite his distaste for 'forenoon oratory' (his speech was printed in an *Account of The Ceremony at opening The Edinburgh Academy*, which was circulated by the Directors). He outlined the proud history of education in Scotland and gave a tactful account of the aims and motives behind the foundation of the

Academy. He scoffed at any suggestion that there was any intention to ruin the old High School:

'The effect of the present Institution,' the *Account* quotes him as saying, 'would only be to relieve the High School of a few superfluous Scholars, and thereby leave the hands of its Teachers more at liberty to educate those who were left. He trusted he should hear nothing more of such an unworthy motive. He was sure there would be no petty jealousies – no rivalry between the two Institutions, but the honourable and fair rivalry of Scholarship . . . He was convinced Palinurus would not slumber at the helm, while he beheld another vessel striving to gain the port behind him.' (Applause.)

While Scotland was the best informed country in Europe, he said, it had not of late produced many eminent Classical Scholars, and, sturdy Scotsman as he was, he had to admit that there was some truth in Dr Johnson's observation 'that in learning, Scotland resembled a besieged city, where every man had a mouthful, but no man a bellyful'. The Directors were anxious to wipe off this reproach, and for this purpose had made some additions to the course adopted in the High School, 'to lay a foundation for a thorough knowledge of the Latin tongue, by the most precise and careful study of its fundamental principles', conjoined with the study of Greek to a greater extent than hitherto was customary in Scotland. 'At no moment was the study of that beautiful language so interesting as at present, when the people among whom it was still in use were again, as he trusted, about to emancipate themselves from slavery and barbarism and take their rank among free nations' (a reference to the Greek struggle to throw off the Turkish yoke).

But Sir Walter wanted the boys of the Academy to be taught 'to venerate the Patriots and Heroes of our own Country, along with those of Greece and Rome; to know the histories of Wallace and Bruce, as well as those of Themistocles and of Caesar; and that the recollection of the fields of Flodden and Bannockburn should not be lost in those of Plataea and Marathon'. (Applause.) To this end there would be a class for the study of English – 'not to be found in any other literary Academy'. This would avoid the error of creating 'scholars who can express themselves better in Latin than in English'.

Turning to the rows of boys shuffling on the hard new seats, he exhorted them to give their whole souls and minds to their studies: 'Next to a conscience void of offence towards God and man, the greatest possession they could have was a well cultivated mind.' And with a further flourish of high-flown sentiments and exhortations he sat down to loud applause.

The new Rector then said a few words, leaving no one in any doubt that in the short time he had been in Edinburgh he had become as enthusiastic as the Directors themselves over the aims of the Academy. All he asked for was 'one boon from an enlightened public – that they would not be hasty in their censure, nor premature in their applause. The system would require time, before it was seen in all its parts. A fair experiment would not be made until those boys who now filled the First Class had passed through his [*the Rector's*]. But when that period arrived, he trusted they would not shrink from a comparison with the proudest Institutions of the South – not even with Eton in Latin Versification – nor with the Charter House or Winchester in Greek. (Applause.) The genius of Scottish Youth would, he trusted, not stop at the porch of Grecian literature, but come into its recesses, and there see its harmony, its proportions, and its taste; their youthful minds would thus acquire the necessary knowledge to fit them for becoming the future Statesmen, Orators, and Heroes of the age – that they would reflect glory on this Seminary, and render it classic ground to future ages . . .'

It was a long business for the boys on the benches, for old Henry Mackenzie was next, thin, shrivelled and yellow, his voice so weak that the reporter from the *Edinburgh Evening Courant* had the utmost difficulty in catching what he said. But this would probably be the last time he would make a speech in public, and the distinguished audience strained to hear the words of the man who had known David Hume, Adam Smith, Goldsmith, and all the great writers and philosophers of Edinburgh's Golden Age to which he himself had contributed three novels and a successful play as well as founding the Royal Society of Edinburgh and the Highland Society. It was he who had been the first to recommend to the Edinburgh *literati* the poems of 'a genius of no ordinary rank . . . Robert Burns, an Ayrshire ploughman' in an article in *The Lounger* in 1786.

And now, on the Opening day of the Academy, he recalled that it was seventy years since he had been in the Rector's Class at the High School. 'Young men speak from feeling, old men from memory.' He gently chided his illustrious friend, Sir W. Scott, for quoting Dr Johnson, observing that Dr Johnson was 'but little acquainted with the particular circumstances of the Country, otherwise he would have known that here there was less of that exclusive, and what might be termed esoteric, attention to learning which is paid to it in England.' He gently warned the 'Learned Rector' to eschew a defect he had noted in the educational system in England, 'namely, an elaborate attention to the *words* of the Authors read in their Classes, to the latinity of the Roman and the atticism of the Greek, but little notice or observation was communicated to their Pupils on the subject matter, or the ruling ideas of their works. This seems to me an omission of considerable importance . . .' He made some grateful references to the High School and looked forward to 'that useful and honourable competition which would be equally beneficial to both Establishments'. He ended by hoping 'that this Institution may continue to flourish, to the great advantage of our posterity, long after the tongue that now ventures to address them is silent in the grave'. And with that, the 'Man of Feeling' sat down from his last public address.

When all the applause was over, the boys marched back to their classrooms, and the Directors took the distinguished visitors on a tour of the school, and 'were glad to find that the whole arrangements of the Academy met with unqualified approbation'. (*Minutes*, October 1, 1824). The sentiments of the Lord Provost, Alexander Henderson (Arbuthnot's successor), are not recorded, for he had been 'prevented from attending'. But soon his name would be indissolubly linked with the Academy, when Henderson Row was named after him.

Thereafter the Directors took their visitors off to a celebration banquet at which toasts were drunk to the old High School, where all the Directors had been educated, and to the success of the new Academy.

Certainly, its immediate success was impressive – and it does not seem to have been gained entirely at the expense of the High School. Only fifty-seven boys of that first roll of 372 can be definitely shown to have attended the High School the previous year, according to an unpublished thesis by Peter N. Grainger (*The Challenge to the High School*, 1971, p. 80.) The opening of the Academy did not have the disruptive effect on the High School that Old Bailie Blackwood and the pamphleteers had claimed. The High School roll remained constant around 600 before climbing to 700 a few years later, and the combined rolls of the High School and the Academy were higher than even the peak year of 890 at the High School in 1820. Presumably the extra pupils were coming from the rash of private seminaries in the New Town, as the Directors of the Academy had foreseen.

But the Academy certainly seems to have fulfilled another of Old Bailie Blackwood's fears – that it would cream off the upper social strata of Edinburgh. Of the 372 boys who started at the Academy on the Opening day, listed in *The Edinburgh Academy Register 1824–1914*, sixty-seven were sons of men in the legal profession. Of the remaining fathers, twenty-seven were in the Army or Navy, twenty-seven in business, twenty-six were connected with the land (either as farmers, lairds, or titled landowners), twenty were doctors, nineteen were merchants (four of them abroad), eighteen were with the Honourable East India Company, eleven were in the Church, seven were on the staff of a University, two were Government officials, and two were in local government. There was an architect, a writer, and a painter, and seventy-nine entries did not specify the father's occupation. (Peter N. Grainger.)

(*The Edinburgh Academy Register 1824–1914* was and is a magnificent work. It was begun in 1908 and took six years to compile; it attempted to list not just the names but also the careers of every single boy and member of staff who ever attended the Academy. The original editor was Arthur Stanley Pringle, advocate (E.A. 1887–96), who had to relinquish the task from pressure of work after two years, whereupon the editorship was undertaken jointly by Thomas Henderson, W.S. (E.A. 1879–84) and Philip Francis Hamilton-Grierson, advocate (E.A. 1892–1901). They were helped by a Consultative Committee consisting of Professor John Hepburn Millar (E.A. 1874–81), who was a Director of the Academy (1906–29) and who also contributed the Historical Introduction; Dr John S. ('Mucky') Mackay, Mathematical Master at the Academy from 1866–1904; the surgeon A. A. Scot Skirving (E.A. 1879–84); advocate Sir Frederick Thomson (E.A. 1886–94), Honorary Secretary to the Directors from 1906–19 and a Director from 1919–35; publisher S. C. Freeman (E.A. 1884–7); and the Clerk and Treasurer, C. E. W. Macpherson, C.A. (1885–1931). The *Register* was published in 2,000 copies. As a definitive record of Academicals it had many unavoidable gaps and omissions and errors, which were corrected bit by bit in subsequent issues of *The Edinburgh Academy Chronicle*; but it is a priceless mine of information for the historian. It is a matter of real regret that the Academy has never summoned up the nerve to embark on the compilation of another *Register*; the various *Edinburgh Academy Lists* that have been published since the war are bloodless and uninformative shadows by comparison – designed only, as the archivist of another school put it cynically, to keep a record of former pupils' addresses to which to send appeals for more money.)

The Edinburgh Academy clearly provided serious competition to the High School, and no doubt there were those amongst the City Fathers who resented it. But there seems to be no truth in one of the hoariest legends of Academy life – namely, that the massive St Stephen's Church was deliberately sited at the foot of St Vincent Street by a vindictive Town Council to blot out the view of the Academy's handsome frontage from George Street. It's a good story, and it *ought* to be true. But in fact, St Stephen's was thought of even before the idea of the Academy was mooted. The Town Council had bought the land in March, 1822 – the month before Cockburn and Horner took their walk on the Pentland Hills – and by April, 1823, the architect, W. H. Playfair, had been commissioned to prepare a design, for a fee of £155 5s. The building was eventually started in 1826. From the Academy point of view, the only suspicious aspect is that in July, 1826, for no stated reason, the architect was instructed to add to the height of the tower!

CHAPTER VI

Rector Williams: The First Years (1824-28)

... A figure short and rotund, in flowing college gown, his felt hat in one hand, his staff in the other, with head reverently bowed to address a brief petition to Him who had safely brought us to the beginning of that day, the morning sun casting an oval shadow of impressive breadth and magnitude on the white wooden floor, his was a form that held the eye, even as the sonorous voice, filling out the words, and snapping the ends of his sentences in Cymbrian fashion, did amply fill the ear.

(*Chronicles of the Cumming Club.*)

'THE Edinburgh Academy opened under circumstances unparalleled in the History of British Education,' wrote Rector Williams in his first annual *Report to the Directors* (July, 1825). 'Above three hundred and fifty pupils met together for the first time, in one day, under the same roof. They came from various Schools; they had been taught by various Masters; and according to various systems of Tuition. The acquirements even of those who were destined to pursue their studies in the same Class, were most dissimilar. While some were not only adequately, but excellently prepared for the business of their Class, others were totally unfit and unable to pursue their studies with any advantage to themselves, or with the hope of any credit to their Teachers ... The Masters themselves had been selected from distant parts of the Kingdom, and were consequently unknown to each other previous to the commencement of the Session. It therefore required no common exertion, and no inconsiderable part of the Session, to reduce the discordant mass of Pupils to a unity of feeling and of conduct ... This unity, however, prevails at present in every part of the Institution, and gives every reason to hope that the difficulties of next year will be but trifling, in comparison with the difficulties encountered in the course of the present Session.'

In that first eventful year, the Directors found that running a school was no less worrying and demanding than building one. They were kept extremely busy in the first days and weeks coping with the myriad problems that cropped up. Maps were needed for the Geography lessons – Leonard Horner was commissioned to order them in

London. Slates had to be ordered, too. Then the expensive air-flue heating system devised by the Sylvesters of Derby at a cost of £285 failed to perform adequately, the boys complained of the cold, and the Janitor was ordered to light open fires in the classrooms. Someone wrote an anonymous letter complaining about some unwholesome sweetmeat being sold by the Janitor, and he was informed that he must restrict his food sales to 'wheat and ryebread biscuits and ginger-bread'.

Then there was the matter of an inscription for the facade of the Portico. Rector Williams produced several edifying slogans for consideration; and eventually the Directors chose the Greek inscription incised there to this day: *Η ΠΑΙΔΕΙΑ ΚΑΙ ΤΗΣ ΣΟΦΙΑΣ ΚΑΙ ΤΗΣ ΑΡΕΤΗΣ ΜΗΤΗΡ – Education is the mother of both Wisdom and Virtue.*

There were staff problems, too. It was reported that both Mr Gloag, the Mathematics Master, and Mr Glover, the Writing Master, had each engaged an Assistant without consulting the Directors. Secretary Russell was instructed to 'signify the disapprobation' of the Directors to Messrs Gloag and Glover, dismiss the Assistants, and advertise for others. Later they had their first taste of an industrial dispute when they tried to get rid of Mr Glover and his new Assistant, Mr Gray. The two Writing Masters simply did not have what it took to cope with the huge classes of boys, and Gray got into real trouble with the Directors when he lost his temper with a boy and hit him in the small of the back. At first he was 'severely admonished', but after more complaints from parents the two of them were asked to resign. At first they refused. Then they demanded compensation, the Directors made an offer, and eventually Mr Glover and Mr Gray, the Academy's first Writing Masters, agreed to resign.

In the midst of all these diversions, one man was quietly but inexorably stamping his personality and authority on the school: the Rector, John Williams. The boys all called him 'Punch', though no one knows the origin of his nickname. It just seemed to suit his jovial round face and his well-fed, easy-going dignity. He was soon a familiar figure striding the precincts of the new school, his cloak flying open to reveal a comfortable paunch, felt hat on his curling locks, a staff in his hand.

He was unquestionably in command from the very beginning: confident, imperious even, utterly dogmatic when it came to the matter of his beloved classics, a subject on which only two or three men in the country were able to keep pace with him. He could recite Homer from memory at such length that people found it hard to believe he didn't have the book open in front of him. Only Mr Gladstone was said to be his equal in this feat, but Rector Williams used to complain in later life that the great statesman was guilty of 'cribbing without acknowledgement' from Williams' own magnum opus, *Homerus* (1842). But he said it with a smile; and his engaging good humour always made people forgive his somewhat despotic manner. He was interested in everything and kept the conversation flowing from topic to topic in the Masters' Lodge, where he displayed a prodigious omniscience, stopping now and again to jot down a note when someone made a suggestion that might turn out to be useful for the school.

He was soon in great demand in Edinburgh's intellectual and literary circles: 'Brilliant talkers, when they knew they were to meet Archdeacon Williams at a dinner-party, were put on their mettle, and fain to gird up their loins and prepare to do their best.' (*Cumming Club*, p. 70.) Of course he was always a welcome guest at Abbotsford with Sir Walter Scott, and he renewed his undergraduate friendship with Lockhart, but it was not long before those staunch Whigs, Cockburn and Jeffrey, had become his close friends as well. Although he was an Anglican, and looking to further advancement in the Church of England, he was no sectarian bigot and the Celt in him took easily to Edinburgh's presbyterianism. He often preached in local churches on Sunday mornings, and people deserted their own churches to hear his sermons. He never lost an opportunity of extolling his native language and race, and the story is told that he once said the Lord's Prayer in Welsh in St Paul's Church in Edinburgh – although the congregation all thought he was speaking in Greek.

He was held in great awe by the younger Academy boys, especially the Geits (the Scots word for 'child' by which the youngest group of classes of the Academy Upper School is known to this day), but they were well aware of the friendliness under the air of authority, and he seldom, if ever, inflicted punishment. He might occasionally pull a boy's ear, or send him out into the playground in disgrace, or even dismiss him to his home for the rest of the day, but he never had any trouble in keeping order. In a day when dignity was all, he was the only master who would stop in the playground to take a flying kick at a ball that came his way. One day he sent a ball over the wall into a carpenter's yard on the opposite side of Henderson Row. The boys surrounded the Janitor (the Janitor at the time was a cheerful little one-armed man called Adam Pinkerton who augmented the amputated stump of his arm with an impressive steel hook) and managed to slip the big bunch of keys off his hook and open the gates. They all charged across the road, which was strictly out of bounds during school hours, and burst into the carpenter's yard to retrieve their ball, all yelling and whooping in a way that should have brought terrible retribution. But the Rector merely looked on contentedly, and they knew he was in a good mood when they got back into class because he was rubbing his knees with the palms of his hands. He always did that when he was in a good humour, so that over the years the knees of his trousers were rubbed to a fine polish, like satin. But he could not bear idleness, mumbling, cribbing, careless writing, or false quantities in prosody ('then he would almost cry out as if in pain'), although he always took trouble over the backward boys and never omitted to praise any of them who made progress: 'You may not be a great scholar,' he would say, 'but I'm sure you'll be a good man.' He spent a long time watching the boys at play, to get a better insight into what made them tick.

No man of lesser energy, confidence, ability or scholarship could have achieved what he did in the first year of the life of the Academy – or, come to that, in the first twenty, for he was Rector until 1847 with a brief interregnum in 1828–29. Sir Walter Scott had certainly been justified in insisting that here was the 'heaven-born teacher' who could take this conglomerate of boys, masters, and a new building and mould them into a school.

One of his problems was that parents insisted on their boys entering the class of their age group, regardless of whether they were fit to keep up with the work, whereupon they would automatically move up through the school lagging farther and farther behind their contemporaries. Although the classes were relatively small compared with the crowds that were taught at the High School, they were vast by today's standards: the First Class had already reached its permitted maximum of 110, while the smallest, the Fourth Class, had fifty-seven boys. It was impossible for a master to give special attention to the misfits, who languished at the bottom of the class learning little or nothing. 'A similar state of things cannot again take place,' the Rector wrote in his first *Report*. 'To place a pupil in a class to the studies of which he is unequal is an act of great injustice both to the pupil and his teacher.' But Rector Williams was too far ahead of his time in recognising what to us now seems an educational axiom. It was to be all of sixty-five years before the Directors could persuade parents to allow their sons to advance by merit rather than age. The boys on the bottom benches were naturally resentful, disinterested, and badly behaved, and the tawse was used more often than the Directors would have liked, or probably knew.

But the Rector claimed at the end of the first session that discipline had been maintained 'without any severe application of corporal punishment', and he thought that there would have been no need for any at all if the boys had not been under the impression that corporal punishment was completely banned at the Academy and had tried to take advantage of the fact. But Williams had to admit: 'As long, however, as there exists a spirit of indolence, not to be stimulated by the love of approbation, not to be roused by the fear of disgrace, so long, unfortunately, must bodily pain be held forth as the only remaining corrective of the evil.' In 150 years, the basic problem has not changed.

Williams introduced an alternative to the tawse by establishing an incentive – a daily Register which kept a record of every pupil's progress, behaviour, and position in class; and he found that most boys were so keen to earn a good report at the end of the session that they were led to 'the cultivation of order, decorum, tranquil subordination, and gentlemanly habits'.

The Directors had evolved an extremely humane and forward-looking system of prizes that was designed to encourage the more backward boys. By dividing each class into divisions of sixteen and allotting a prize for each division, they hoped that the lowest boy would 'see a premium within the limits of his sensible horizon' by having to contend with only fifteen competitors instead of eighty or more. The prizes for diligence and good conduct were not to go to the highest boy in the division but to the boy 'of whom it can be said . . . that he has done the best he could'. And to obviate any charge of favouritism on the part of the master, the boys themselves were to choose the prizewinner by secret ballot – although the master had the power to veto the choice. (Over the years, a large number of specially-endowed prizes has been added to the list. The first was the Mitchell Medal, which is now awarded to the best in Mathematics in the Vth Classes; it was endowed in 1837 by the Trustees of one of the original Classical Masters, Mr Robert Mitchell, who died in 1836. Mr Mitchell was a much-respected teacher. When he had applied for the post at the Academy, Cockburn had noted on his testimonials: 'A very good-mannered, sensible person. His certificates are not so good as he deserves; for they don't adequately explain the substantial fact that he prodigiously improved the Kirkcudbright Academy. Keep this man in view.')

There was also to be a Gold Medal for the Dux of the Rector's Class (the Dux of the School, in effect), and Silver Medals for the Dux of the other Classes, and books and maps for the lesser prizes. The Rector suggested the economy of awarding cheap medals and merit tickets for some prizes, but the Prizes Committee thought this would not work effectively: some day the boys might learn to work hard for the sole honour of doing well, but in the meanwhile prizes had better have intrinsic value if they were to be an encouragement to diligence. The total intrinsic value of that first year's prizes was £107 11s.; and thus encouraged, the boys worked their way through a programme of study that sounds horrifyingly onerous to modern ears.

The 110 small boys in the First Class were coaxed, drilled, bullied and bored through the standard Latin primer of the time, Ruddiman's *Rudiments*, 'embracing all the parts usually taught, with the exception of the Defective Verbs, and the Rules of Syntax on the construction of the Relative and the Gerunds.' For light relief they read 'a considerable portion of Valpy's *Latin Delectus*, and committed a considerable number of Latin primitive words, with their translation, to memory'. They also worked on Murray's *Introduction to the English Reader*, the outlines and leading features of the map of Europe 'with considerable minuteness', and had an hour-long Writing lesson three times a week.

The Second Class of seventy-four boys, whose average age was nine and a half, tackled the first 140 pages of Adam's *Latin Grammar*, the first 143 pages of *Grammatical Exercises*, the first three books of *Phaedrus* (plus the 4th and the 5th if you were one of the top pupils), and the *Lives* of Miltiades, Themistocles and (partly) Pausanias by Cornelius Nepos, while the top ten boys took home for private reading the *Lives* of Aristides, Epaminondas, and Hannibal. They all had to learn the regular declension of nouns, adjectives and pronouns in the Charterhouse *Greek Rudiments*; and their relaxation from the ancient languages consisted of studying the general outlines of the four Great Continents, and Murray's *English Reader*, and practising Writing for five hours a week.

The Third Class (sixty-five boys, average age eleven) were on to Caesar's *Gallic Wars* (Books 2, 3, and part of 4) and Ovid's *Elegiac Works* on top of Adam's *Latin Grammar*, and made a start on Latin versification. As well as the Charterhouse *Greek Rudiments* they had Sandford's *Greek Exercises* and the first six fables from his *Greek Extracts*. Their Geography added the map of England and ancient Gaul to the four Great Continents (Europe, Asia, Africa and America), and they started on the elementary rules of Arithmetic – addition, subtraction, multiplication and division, simple and compound; and reduction, with the necessary arithmetical tables. The Senior Division advanced to simple and compound Proportion, Practice, and a slight sketch of Interest. All the pupils had five three-quarter-hour Writing lessons and two chapters of Murray's *English Reader*.

The Fourth Class (fifty-seven boys, aged twelve) read the first three Books of Virgil's *Aeneid*, while the upper part of the class were exercised in Latin compositions both in prose and verse (hexameters and pentameters). They mastered the whole of the Charterhouse *Greek Rudiments*, and worked on Sandford's *Greek Exercises* and Greek Testament *Extracts* and the *Odes* of Anacreon. In Geography they studied Ancient Italy and modern Britain; and in English, the inevitable Murray's *English Reader*. The Arithmetic was only slightly advanced from the Third Class, though the top boys were tackling Interest, Fractions (vulgar and decimal), Duodecimals, and Extraction of the Square Root. They had three Writing lessons a week.

The Rector's Class, all sixty-six of them, were the big boys of the school, with an average age of fourteen, some of them going to University the very next term. They were led by Mr Williams through Virgil's *Aeneid* (Books 6 and 9), the four Books of Horace's *Odes*, and the 21st Book of Livy's *Roman History*, and were assiduously exercised in Latin versification. In Greek, the Junior division read Moore's *Greek Grammar*, twelve of Lucian's *Fables*, and fourteen of Anacreon's *Odes*, while the Senior division also read the First Book of Xenophon's *Anabasis*. To the geography of Italy, Ancient and Modern, they added the March of Cyrus to Cynaxa, and the March of Hannibal into Italy. The Mathematics showed no advance on the Fourth Class, except that the senior boys started on the first book of Euclid's *Elements of Geometry*. And they could all read and recite from, unerringly, Murray's *English Reader*!

It's not hard to see which subject was the poor relation of the syllabus: English was an also-ran, and a poor one at that. 'The success of the English Department,' the Rector reported, 'has not been such as to answer his expectation.' He blamed the failure mainly on 'the light estimation in which the study of their own language is held by the

Pupils. Hence arises a serious difficulty in fixing their attention, and exciting their minds to exertion in the pursuit of it'. He held that the parents were just as much to blame for failing to impress on their children 'the vital importance of attention to this most necessary branch of education'.

The main victim of this situation, apart from the English language, was the English Master, Mr Charles Barker, fresh from Trinity College, Cambridge. Leonard Horner had thought him 'the beau ideal of what we want'. The Rector described him as being 'highly qualified by his education, by his talents, and by his elegant acquirements for efficiently conducting the department assigned to him'. The Directors had thought so highly of him that they had given him precedence over the other masters, next to the Rector. Poor Mr Barker! He must have found it utterly soul-destroying to have to wade through Murray's *English Reader* hour after hour, day after day, with great masses of boys whose broad Scots speech he could hardly understand, who despised his refined English accent, and who looked upon the study of English as a childish exercise beneath the contempt of grammar school boys. He never had a separate classroom of his own, and 'his wandering from Class-room to Class-room has been found a serious obstacle in the way of acquiring influence and authority'. Nor was he helped by the books at his disposal. Murray's *English Reader* and its companion *Introduction to the English Reader* were, according to the Rector, 'peculiarly unfortunate, although of great modern celebrity. The Books possess no attraction, and are singularly destitute of everything likely to communicate information, or to gain the attention of a Pupil'.

A better selection was planned for the next session. But that was too late for Mr Barker, who lost heart and resigned, to the great regret of the Directors. But at least his resignation led to improved conditions for his successor, Mr John Dyer, another Englishman. To make things easier for him the Directors turned over the Writing Room to the English department, with a section set aside for a Library, and ordered the building of a new Arithmetic and Writing Block in the north-west corner of the site.

The widespread antipathy to English would continue to plague the unfortunate English teachers for many years. But from the Arithmetic and Writing Block emerged two masters who stand out from the others in the recollections of the early Academicals. The one was the Mathematics Master, James Gloag; and the other was his Assistant, who was also appointed Writing Master after the departure of Glover and Gray – Robert Familton.

Mr Familton did not remain Mr Familton for very long. The boys soon decided that he ought to be called 'Hamilton', and he got so used to hearing himself being called 'Hamilton' that he started using the name himself, and that is how he is described in all the Academy records, apart from the early Minutes which recorded his appointment (he was Clerk to the Directors as 'Mr Hamilton' from 1825–50). To the boys, of course, he quickly became known as 'Hammy', and 'Hammy' he stayed, for twenty-eight years, despite a sticky period in 1832 when he was threatened with dismissal by the Directors for incompetence. 'Hammy' was a very easy-going man, and as a general rule, boys could do pretty much as they liked in his class; but if he were ever provoked beyond endurance he could use the tawse with the best of them, and because he was an exceptionally hirsute man, his fury could be distinctly alarming to behold. *Hairy Hammy, Loves to pammy.*

Mr Gloag started his career at the Academy inauspiciously, when he was provoked by a boy's impertinence into giving him two or three blows on the side of the head. The boy's father, a doctor, angrily reported the assault to the Directors; Mr Gloag was solemnly admonished by Cockburn and warned that any recurrence would mean instant dismissal. The Rector was asked to remind the staff yet again that 'it was a sacred principle of the School that though corporal punishment should not be absolutely prohibited, it should be very sparingly resorted to and never practised except with such publicity and deliberation as excluded the idea of its being inflicted in anger, or of its not making a deep impression on the minds of the spectators'.

Yet Gloag was a born teacher, and the Directors knew it. He was to stay on at the Academy for forty years, a stern disciplinarian but much respected and even liked by his pupils, amongst whom his dexterity with the tawse (despite Cockburn's solemn admonition) was to become legendary.

MR GLOAG

Greasy Gloag
Delights to floag.

The Directors of the Edinburgh Academy never carried out their threat
to dismiss James Gloag, 'Master of the Arithmetical and Geometrical
School', if he were ever found guilty again of striking a boy in anger.
They had opportunity enough the following session, when a boy
accused Mr Gloag of belting him about the head and sides and legs 'not
less than thirty times' with the tawse. Gloag said he had only hit him
about ten times, and that was just to encourage him to put out his
hand and take his punishment for insubordination. The Directors
made exhaustive inquiries and came to the conclusion that Mr Gloag
had made an 'error of judgement' in not referring the matter to the
Rector; but apart from another reminder of the school policy on
corporal punishment, and a warning from the Rector to 'be more
circumspect in future', nothing more was heard of the incident.

Clearly the founders of the school had recognised in James Gloag
a master they could not afford to lose – 'a most honest, zealous and
energetic teacher' as he was later described in a Rector's *Report*. Cockburn had noted that he was 'a sensible-looking man, with a pale face,
and hoarse voice. Gentle and amiable' – an opinion of his character
that forty years of Academy boys tended to dispute at first. The fact
that he was much the strictest disciplinarian in the school, and deadly
with the tawse withal, was offset by his indisputable fairness and
impartiality, a gruff kindliness under the irascibility, and the growing
evidence that the boys learned well under him – once they had got
over their initial terror of him.

He was a heavy, short, thickset man, with a long oval face that was
described as being like a bulldog's, deepset eyes, short black hair and
close-cut whiskers; not exactly handsome, but far from ugly, with a
deep, sonorous voice. He always wore a black suit with tail-coat, and
was perpetually covered in dust from the huge chunks of chalk with
which he covered the blackboard with neat rows of sums. He was still
a young man in his twenties when he came to the Academy. He had
been teaching maths at George Heriot's Hospital, but he had been born
farther south, at Gretna in Dumfriesshire, although no one could
really tell from his accent. At the Academy, where dialects were thick
and strong and ranged from the Borders to Aberdeenshire, none was

quite as broad as Mr Gloag's. He had a way of pronouncing vowels like nobody else. For instance, the word 'road' he pronounced 'rod', and 'rod' became 'road', so that 'Get out of the road' came out as 'T'oot o' the rod', and a spine-chilling roar of 'Fatch the road!' was only too easily translatable as 'Fetch the rod!' (a short but heavy wooden pointer).

A boy was a 'booie'; the board was the 'boord'; chalk was 'chack', and paws became 'pas', so that a visitor to the classroom would be asked by Mr Gloag to excuse his 'chacky pas'. His remedy for defaulters in subtraction or multiplication or for inattention was invariably the same – 'Copy doon the first sax sums on the boord an' bring them nicely written oot in the mornin'.' He always had a supply of punitive sums ready on the back of the 'boord', which could be swivelled round to reveal them at any moment. His first task every morning was to roll up his cuff and chalk up a nice selection in readiness for the first offender.

But that was only after he had had what he called 'a bit prayer' with his class. Even after the practice of class prayers had been abandoned in favour of collective school prayers in the Hall in 1847-8, Mr Gloag continued to say the Lord's Prayer with whatever class was starting the morning with him. But the real business of the day was never forgotten. At the side of the blackboard stood a big wooden basin full of bits of slate-pencils or 'skeelies'; and one morning in the middle of Mr Gloag's 'bit prayer' a boy stuck out his foot and knocked the basin over, spilling the pencils all over the floor. With hardly a break in the rhythm of his intonation Mr Gloag opened one eye and demanded 'Wha skailt the skeelie bowl?' and went on devoutly to the end of the prayer before dealing with the quaking culprit. His piety was never quite proof against his devotion to maths, for he would always finish the prayer with '. . . the Poo'er and the Glory, for ever and ever (tak up yir slates), Amen.'

Thereafter the boys would sit in fear and trembling lest a wrong move brought down the wrath of Mr Gloag on his head or the wooden 'road' on his knuckles. But that was only for minor offences like letting a slate fall; the most awful sin was making a screeching noise on the slate with the slate-pencil. Even the tiniest squeak of a skirl would bring the 'road' down sharp and sure; but a real lingering skirl would send Mr Gloag reaching for his tawse in a paroxysm of rage. The worst sounds were produced by the sharpest pencils, so Mr Gloag disapproved of the sharpening of slate-pencils by any other means than the old-fashioned rubbing on a stone (preferably a particular stone located 'down the bank' behind the school), which produced a softer point. Sharpening with a knife was an abomination in his eyes.

One day a new boy called Matthew Heddle produced a magnificent pocket-knife with which he proceeded to sharpen his pencil lovingly to a rapier-sharp point. He was working away eagerly at his sums when – tragedy! – the pencil produced the father and mother of all skirls. Mr Gloag whirled round –

'What booie was that? Was't you? Was't you? Was't you? Haw, it was *you*, Haddle!'

Poor Heddle, unaware of Mr Gloag's paranoiac hatred of skirls, explained that his knife had made the pencil too sharp.

'Lat's see the knife, Haddle! That's a pretty knife, Haddle, a varra pretty knife!' And he opened out all the blades and showed them to the class.

Years later, Professor Matthew Heddle of the Chair of Chemistry at St Andrews University recalled the fate of his beautiful pocket-knife: 'Gloag, laying hold of the mere fringe of my collar with the tips of his thumb and forefinger, leads me to the fireplace, and treating me to a last fond look at my treasure . . . drops it into the centre of the glowing embers.'

But that was not all. Mr Gloag did not like the expression on the victim's face as he watched his knife disappearing in the flames: 'We're no' din yit,' he said. 'Fatch the tawse, Haddle!'

For a long time afterwards, Mr Gloag would associate all skirling noises with the unfortunate Heddle. 'That's Haddle!' he would roar. 'Come aloang, Haddle. You an' me's wal acquant, but we'll be batter acquant yit. Fetch the tawse!' It was not long before pranksters in the class realised that all they had to do to land Heddle in trouble was to squeak their pencils on the slate. But they tried it once too often: Gloag realised what was happening and caught the offender, and terrible was the tawsing that ensued.

But he still had his doubts about Heddle. He would look at him almost wistfully from time to time and mutter, 'Streinge booie, streinge booie – sully fuil!' Years later when Professor Heddle, by now vice-president of the Edinburgh Geological Society and president of the Mineralogical Society of Great Britain and Ireland, revisited the Academy he met Mr Gloag in the playground and asked if he recognised him. 'Haud off, haud off, till I look at ye,' said Mr Gloag, peering at the professor's luxuriant beard. 'It's the appandages, the appandages.

It canna be Smith? – Naw. Nor Thomson? – Naw. Than ye maun be Haddle!' And he warmly grasped the hand which had so often felt the full force of his unrivalled dexterity with the tawse.

(It should perhaps be borne in mind that Professor Heddle had the reputation of being the most spectacularly mendacious story-teller of his day, and his stories about Gloag should perhaps be regarded as impressions rather than strict history.)

His pupils always felt that Mr Gloag took a particular pride in his own proficiency with the tawse, and executed a delivery with a perfection of timing, a unison of hand and eye, that was almost artistic. One of his most brilliant pupils, Peter Guthrie Tait (E.A. 1841–7), who became Senior Wrangler at Cambridge and Professor of Natural Philosophy at Edinburgh University from 1860 to 1901, once analysed his old master's technique: 'To use a well-known cricketing phrase, Gloag could get "more work" on the tawse than any of the other masters. His secret was in great part a dynamical one.'

Whatever the dynamical secret of his tawsing, Mr Gloag certainly knew how to turn out brilliant scholars. Professor Guthrie Tait was only one of a long line of outstanding scientists and mathematicians nurtured by Gloag in his forty years at the Academy. The Rector's *Report* of 1854 noted that in the previous seven years, the Academy had recorded one Senior Wrangler (Tait in 1852), two 2nd Wranglers, one 9th, one 14th, and one 30th – and this at a time when the Senior Wranglership at Cambridge was held to be the highest university mathematical distinction in Britain. Mr Gloag took the most intense pride and delight in his former pupils' successes; but unlike many masters who concentrated almost exclusively on the cleverest boys and let the others languish, Mr Gloag's sense of duty impelled him to try and make mathematicians out of even the most backward. In a way his tyranny was a sign that he cared about them all – the constant vigilance that ensured that he never missed a turn of a head and could switch his attention in a twinkling from a problem in Higher Mathematics at the top of a class to a boy struggling with vulgar fractions on the lowest bench.

Despite the discipline he imposed, there were also occasional moments of fun, as when interlopers (even the Rector) came nosing into the sanctum of a Maths class. One day, to the great entertainment of the class, Mr Gloag said, 'Now, booies, we'll give the Ractor an equation to solve,' and proceeded to cover the blackboard with an incomprehensible mass of symbols. 'Now, Ractor!' he challenged. But the Rector was quite equal to the occasion, according to the Rev. W. H. Langhorne in his *Reminiscences* (but not according to the gossipy compiler of the *Chronicles of the Cumming Club*): 'His answer consisted in a very hearty laugh at being made a boy of again, attended by the usual rubbing of his knees, so that even the imperturbable Mr Gloag was unable to resist the fun, and for a minute or two laid aside his sternness, eyeing the Rector with a sardonic smile.' (pp. 161–2). The Rector took his departure amid much cheering, and the boys heard him still laughing as he passed by the open window, where he could hear Gloag concluding the episode with the observation, 'Ha! booies, we tucked the Ractor up there!' (The second-hand version in the *Cumming Club* is much less flattering to the Rector, and makes him out to be a ninny, which he certainly was not.)

Another of his pet aversions was the nobility. He had no time for the sons of dukes and baronets and other Scottish aristocrats who were fairly thick on the ground during his time at the Academy. Pity help the boy who fell foul of Mr Gloag if he were unfortunate enough to have committed the extra sin of possessing a title: 'You think,' he would roar at Lord Archibald Campbell, son of the 8th Duke of Argyll – 'you think because your faither's a duke you can mak' a moke of me!'

After thirty years as a teacher at the Academy, Mr Gloag was given a Testimonial – and a purse of 150 sovereigns subscribed by 205 of his former pupils. In his last ten years he taught Moral Philosophy as well, and his fame spread far beyond Edinburgh as the boys he had taught won honours around the world. In 1848, Edinburgh University conferred on him the degree of LL.D. When he eventually retired from the staff, in 1864, he was awarded a pension of £100 a year for life, and his former pupils subscribed for the Gloag Medal for Mathematics to be established in his honour. They came from all over to his retirement Dinner, which was always referred to thereafter as the Gloag Banquet, and he was a frequent guest of honour at the annual dinners held by the various Class Clubs which became a striking feature of Academical life.

Old pupils visited him at his house in Duncan Street and discovered depths and interests in the old man they had never suspected in the classroom. He loved to talk of the old times at the school, but he seldom went back to visit it, for there had been great changes.

'It's nothin' but a hert-brek,' he would say. 'A hert-brek.' He died in 1870, only six years after he retired.

END OF THE FIRST YEAR

Fat Punch
Likes his lunch.

It was a momentous year, that first session of the Edinburgh Academy of 1824–5 – and not just for the Academy. In November, just six weeks after the opening of the school, Edinburgh woke to find a heavy black pall of smoke over the city and a terrible fire raging in the heart of the Old Town.

Sir Walter Scott wrote: 'I have witnessed a horrible calamity – a fire broke out on Monday night in the High Street, raged all night and great part of the next day catching to the steeple of the Tron Church, which being wood was soon in a blaze and burned like regular fireworks till all was consumed. All this while the flames were spreading down to the Cowgate amongst those closes where the narrowness of the access and the height of the houses rendered the approach of engines almost impossible. On Tuesday night a *second* fire broke out in the Parliament Square, greatly endangering the courts of Justice and the Advocates' more than princely library. By great exertions it was prevented approaching this public building, and Sir William Forbes' bank also escaped. But all the other houses in the Parliament Square are totally destroyed, and I can conceive no sight more grand or terrible than to see these lofty buildings on fire from top to bottom, vomiting out flames like a volcanoe from every aperture and finally crashing down one after another into an abyss of fire which resembled nothing but hell . . . Between the corner of Parliament Square and the South Bridge all is destroyed except some new buildings at the lower extremity, and the devastation has extended down the closes which I hope will never be rebuilt on their late form.' (*Letters*, vol. VIII, pp. 427–8).

But he noted a silver lining, too: 'Upon the whole I believe the conflagration will be followed by its own advantages as such evils usually are. A large space is cleared which though in old times it form'd the abode of the learned, the noble and the gay has latterly become the cells of misery and often of vice.' (*ibid.*, p. 438.)

There was a determination abroad to make a fresh start; and this mood was reflected in that first session of the Academy, a pioneering mood that tended to make light of all the formidable difficulties of the project. Not that it really concerned the boys who ran about in the Academy playgrounds round the school buildings – the Yards, as they have always been called, from the Anglo-Saxon word for 'enclosure' – whooping and shouting as they made up nicknames for their new teachers and composing scurrilous rhymes like 'Greasy Gloag, Delights to floag' or 'Hairy Hammy, Loves to Pammy.' They had no idea that they were taking part in the making of a legend. They were too busy trying to cope with an unfamiliar new system of education; they couldn't wait to be released from school at three o'clock so that they could run wild again.

In the first weeks their games had spilled over into the street, and the boys would push and jostle their way to neighbouring shops to buy things that weren't on sale at the Janitor's Lodge – until it came to the ears of the Directors that they were buying 'unwholesome articles' and picking up bad language from a sweetie pedlar who hung about outside the Yards; so the Directors decreed that the school gates were to be locked at ten past nine every morning and kept locked until it was time to go home, and the police were asked to remove the foul-mouthed pedlar. The boys had to be content with the Janitor's shop where his wife, 'Mrs Jenny', sold them bread, biscuits, milk and ginger-bread, as well as balls, marbles, and 'clackens'* – wooden long-handled bats with round-headed ends like flattened spoons that were used for the favourite playground game of 'Hailes'; it's an old Scots ball-game akin to shinty, which the Academy inherited from the High School and which is still played once a year in the Academy Yards. Every boy in those early days carried his clacken to school as naturally as he did his slate. It came in handy for all manner of uses apart from Hailes, not least as a weapon in playground battles and in skirmishes with local boys (the 'keelies', or 'cads', as they were contemptuously called) on the way to and from school. It was also indispensable for trailing along iron railings, and other noisy pleasures. The boys also bought their school books from the Janitor, who had to find a guarantor to stand

---

*A clacken was defined in *The Encyclopaedia of Sport* (1898) as consisting of 'a piece of wood about 18 inches long, and has a head about 4 inches wide and $\frac{1}{2}$ inch thick; just short of the head, the bat is thinned down to about $\frac{1}{4}$ inch from back to front, and again the head is thinned off towards the tip to make it easier to raise the ball from the ground. The thinned neck of the clacken is known as the "spring", and a good spring is essential to success in carrying the ball poised on the clacken. The ball is somewhat larger than a lawn-tennis ball, made of india-rubber, and collapsible, to prevent it bursting if trodden upon . . . In general appearance the "clacken" is very like the shorter rounder-headed form of the "fives-bat" – not the "Rugby" form – but differs from it in being thinned away at the tip to assist in lifting the ball from the ground, as explained above.' (Vol. II, p. 141, under *Public School Games*.)

bond for him to the tune of £500 before the Directors would entrust
him with this responsibility – even though all the profits (£108 in that
first year) went towards the school library. And the Janitor's wage
was only 19s. 2¾d. a week!

But the Directors were desperately anxious to avoid getting too far
into debt. Already, the building costs had reached well over £12,000,
and not all the bills were in yet. With a roll of 372 boys, they still had
a long way to go to reach the optimum roll of 600 on which their sums
for running the school had been based, using the income from class
entrance fees and leaving something over, as they fondly imagined, to
pay a dividend to the shareholders, or Proprietors as they were now.
And there were a lot of extra expenses to be met, quite apart from the
cost of building the new Writing and Arithmetic Block.

There were the Dux medals to be struck, for instance. The indefatigable Leonard Horner had been making inquiries about the cost
of having dies cut by an artist in Paris, but in London he found a Scot
called Bain – 'an artist of very great merit' – who agreed to cut the die
for the gold medal at a reduced rate of thirty-five guineas; a Mr Wyon
of the Mint was commissioned to cut the silver medal die for forty
guineas. The Rector had wanted to have on the medals the head of
George Buchanan, the great seventeenth-century Scottish education-
alist, but the Directors eventually plumped for the Louvre bust of
Virgil for the Gold Medal and the Townley bust of Homer from the
British Museum for the Silver Medals.

Then they had to print tickets and invitations to the Public Examinations, which were held over five days, one for each Class, a fortnight
before the end of the session. The Public Examinations must have been
a real ordeal for the boys. With their fathers or guardians and invited
guests looking on from the gallery in the Hall, the pupils were questioned on the year's work by examiners from the university 'competent
to judge of the progress of the pupils'. The examiners could choose any
boy at random from the school register, although the actual questions
were put by the Rector or the masters. No wonder there was always a
sudden outbreak of indisposition on examination day.

But Exhibition Day, held on the last day of the summer term,
was the great occasion of the year when, as the Directors decreed,
'those boys who were distinguished at the previous Examination of the
Classes, are to be brought forward to exhibit such specimens of their
attainments as are suited to such an occasion; and when the prize essays
and poems are to be read and recited; and at the conclusion of the

Exhibition the prizes are to be delivered to those who have gained them, in the presence of the whole boys attending the Academy, and of the parents and others who shall be present on the occasion.'

It was not only the great occasion of the year – for the Directors and staff it was a thoroughly exhausting one. A later Secretary to the Directors, Andrew Beatson Bell (E.A. 1841–8), recalled the sort of day it had become by the 1850s: 'Two social functions used to coincide with the Exhibition, one the breakfast of the Academical Club, the other the Dinner of the Directors – both now long abolished. At the Academical breakfast a number of "old boys" used to attend – the guests were the masters, and the principal prize-takers among the boys. The youngest was the Dux of the Geits, whom Lord Cockburn used to have by his side and carefully to watch over. The banquet, to our schoolboy notions, was a veritable feast of the gods, and I have no doubt it was really very good. I remember John Thomson Gordon, the Sheriff of Midlothian [E.A. 1825–8] who was looking after me, commending to my notice fresh peaches and cream, saying I ought never to miss a chance of partaking of the delicacy. I remember it as excellent, but I am not aware of ever since having had an opportunity of repeating the experiment. The Dinner of the Directors took place on the evening of the Exhibition. The Director who had presided in the Hall was the chairman, and the principal guest of the evening was the Father, or nearest male relative, of the Dux of the whole school. There was generally a pretty large number of prominent citizens present as guests, in addition to the Rector and masters, and the toast list was long and elaborate. Altogether the Exhibition day, commencing with breakfast and winding up with the dinner, was about the longest day of work I have ever gone through, and after the dinner-party had separated at a pretty late hour I used to go up to the *Courant* office and revise the proofs of the report of the proceedings in the Hall. The *Courant* was always a good friend of the Academy, and gave long reports of the Exhibition. The *Scotsman*, I do not know why, has never done so.' (*Reminiscences*, in the Academy archives.)

The first Edinburgh Academy Exhibition was held on July 29, 1825. It was a brilliant scene in the splendid Hall (which was only used for such public occasions in the early days), with tier upon tier of boys scrubbed and shining, their linen collars sparkling white over Eton jackets of blue broad-cloth, white trousers of spotless 'Russia duck' gleaming like satin, many of them wearing white gloves. The Directors were ranged in their Box with the piles of prize books and medals in front of them, the masters and Rector resplendent in ceremonial academic robes, the gallery packed with proud parents, guardians, shareholders and distinguished guests, including the Rector and masters of the High School.

The first Dux of the School was a fourteen-year-old called Alexander Wood (he was later to be called to the Bar, and died as Sheriff-Substitute of Berwickshire in 1861); he came forward to accept his gleaming Gold Medal, and recited his prize Latin poem, 'Maria Regina in Scotiam Reversura Galliae Valedicit'. The runner-up was thirteen-year-old John M. Balfour (later to change his name to Balfour-Melville, a Writer to the Signet, who was to play a tremendously important role in Academy and Academical affairs for the rest of his long life), who now recited at great length his 'Desertion of Athens on the Approach of Xerxes'. Archibald Campbell Tait (the clever chap with the muckle mitre in his cap) came third and won a merit prize for the best English Essay, 'On the Advantages Derivable from the Study of History', which he now proceeded to deliver. Only the comforting thought of the holidays ahead and the steely gaze of such as Mr Gloag could have kept the smaller boys in check as fourteen-year-old Tait, A. C., solemnly assured them that 'the mind is enlarged, and its faculties developed as we contemplate the invention and improvements of arts, the progress of science, and the completion of plans devised by Wisdom, and executed by Patience and Perseverance'. With what patience and perseverance they sat through the long Latin recitations and earnest soliloquies, while the shareholders stole a quick look at the printed Rector's and Directors' *Reports*. The latter informed them that the school had finished its first year £1,371 17s. 2d. in the red, but that the Directors were confident that the deficit would soon be wiped out as the school numbers increased (they expected to reach the target of 600 in another three years); and 'in the course of a very few years . . . the Proprietors will receive interest on their Shares'. How could the Directors guess that they would still be in debt 150 years later, or that no dividend would ever be paid, or that their Charter would eventually be altered to ensure that no shareholder could *ever* receive a return on his investment?

So it was on a note of high optimism that the Directors reported that 'their first year's experience affords them the strongest reasons to hope that all their anticipations of the benefits to be derived from this Institution will be amply fulfilled'.

NEW DIRECTIONS

All Sir Walter Scott's sympathies were, of course, with the Scottish pronunciation [of Latin], but his common sense carried the day. I cannot doubt that he was right in saying that they should adopt the English pronunciation. Of course that pronunciation was all wrong. (*Laughter*) But the question as to what might be done was a matter of expediency . . .   (Viscount Finlay of Nairn, Centenary Dinner, 1924)

When the Edinburgh Academy opened for its second session on October 1, 1825, a total of 440 boys had enrolled – a useful increase of sixty-eight on the first session. Keeping to the plan that had been adopted from the High School, each master now moved up one stage with last year's intake until the Fifth year was reached, whereupon he would hand over his class to the Rector and start again with the First or 'Geits' Class, while still assisting the Rector with the Fifth. Thus, a boy who started in the Geits would theoretically spend his first four years under the care of one particular Classical Master before joining the Rector's Class for two years. As the years went on and the Academy masters acquired individual reputations, the beginners' roll would swell noticeably in a year when a popular master was starting a new Geits Class. Parents would engage tutors to push their children on at home, so that they would be ready to join the favoured teacher per-haps a year younger than it had been intended to send them to the Academy; or a boy would be kept on a year longer at his preparatory school to wait for a particular teacher's turn to take the Geits. This is perhaps why the Geits Class of 1825–6 was very much lower than the previous year's intake – only eighty, compared with 110. The Rec-tor's first *Report* had made it clear that the master of the Fourth Class, Mr William Marriott of Cambridge, had had a lot of trouble; his class had clearly been the bad boys of the first session – 'a mass of ignor-ance and idleness truly deplorable', the Rector had reported, although the class had also contained some excellent scholars. Mr Marriott had been unable to cope (the prescient Henry Cockburn had scribbled on his testimonials the terse comment – 'Not accustomed to teach'), and at the end of this second session he would resign in relief to return to less arduous pastures south of the Border (he was ordained a deacon in 1826, and died in 1832).

The Rector himself now had a Sixth Class as well as a Fifth, totalling ninety-three pupils; the new Sixth was made up of boys from last year's Fifth who were staying on for another year, like Archibald Campbell Tait, who won the Dux Medal in this second session. A new

English Master had been appointed to replace the unfortunate Mr Barker – another Englishman, Mr James Dyer, who now had his own classroom and several class libraries handsomely stocked from the profits of the school book sales; he was to prove rather more successful than Mr Barker, and survive for seven years, although he would then leave under a cloud and with the bailiffs on his tail. (The first really successful English teacher would be the Rector's nephew, Theodore Williams, a man of inspiring presence who ran the English department with much skill and enthusiasm from 1834–46.)

The Directors were concerned about the problem of housing boys who came long distances to school. With the horse and coach the only means of travel (though some boys from Fife and the north coast sailed to Edinburgh at the beginning of term, and others arrived by horse-drawn barge along the Forth and Clyde Canal), many boys lived with relatives or guardians in Edinburgh, or were boarded with individual Academy masters (later the Rector, too, took boarders into his house). Others, as young as nine years old, were established in lodgings during term-time, and little boys whose parents were abroad in India and other outposts of Empire were entirely dependent on landladies for comfort, guidance and care when they were ill or merely homesick during the ten long months of the school year. The early lists of Prize-winners, first published in 1832 with places of residence included, suggest that a high proportion of boys winning prizes would today have been Boarders. The Academy was clearly catering for a large number of boys who came from all parts of Scotland and from much farther afield. One prize-winner in 1834 came from Moscow. In 1841, the Rector in his *Report* noted the arrival of two pupils, one from Australia, the other from St Petersburg.

The Directors went into all the pros and cons of starting School Boarding-houses, which would make the Academy even more like an English public school. This course was strongly urged by Secretary John Russell. A group of Directors worked out the building costs and running costs, and even took the lease of feus in what is now Saxe-Coburg Place (where the Rector lived) with a view to creating suitable dormitories for thirty boys each, but they shrank from the risk of losing money on the project. The cost of building the new Writing and Arithmetic Block, and finishing off the main buildings, led to a debt of £4,127 in the second session, and the idea of building School Boarding-houses was shelved. It would be the end of the century before they came into being at last, with the opening of the first two

Houses in 1899. Meanwhile, individual masters continued to keep boarders in their homes, and were in some cases reputed to have made fortunes of a most unschoolmasterly size as a result!

Another matter for concern was that a number of boys were not taking the Writing and Arithmetic lessons which had been set down in the original Prospectus as optional subjects. The Rector was finding that these boys were having a disruptive effect, either running around idle during Writing and Arithmetic periods or having to be allowed out of school to attend private lessons in town – quite apart from representing a loss of potential revenue. So now the Directors decided that, as from next session, the whole course of study would be compulsory for every boy – a completely new concept in day-school education in Scotland.

The Directors also decided to establish a Seventh Class to encourage boys to stay on for a third year with the Rector and to keep them from enrolling too young at Scottish universities or going on to English public schools in order to be able to compete with the much older English boys for places at English universities. This move had been adumbrated in the *Explanatory Statement* of December, 1823 ('It may be advisable, hereafter, to make arrangements for a more advanced instruction, should it be found that parents are disposed to keep their boys for a longer period at the School than six years'); but now, in their *Report* on the second session, they argued their reasons for putting it into effect immediately. They declared that 'It had been long a subject of regret with many Parents in Edinburgh, that by the present System of Instruction, their Sons are obliged to terminate their School Education at an age much too early for their entering with safety upon the comparatively independent life of a College Student. Their Classical Education usually begins when they are Seven or Eight Years old, and the Six Years' course of the High School, or the Academy, brings them to the University at Fourteen, freed at once of the regular discipline of a School, where the idle are compelled to work by the terror of confinement or the rod, and the indolent are roused to exertion by the daily excitement of change of place, and the distant hope of honour and rewards at the Public Examination – securities for industry which no College can afford.'

In the Seventh, which is still such an individual feature of Academy life, the boys would extend their reading and develop their composition, but in addition they would advance farther in algebra, geometry, trigonometry and practical matters; and for the first time they would be taught French. To this end a Frenchman, M. Buquet, was appointed French teacher, to take the Seventh for an hour a day in French grammar and selections of French literature, sufficient 'to enable the majority of the Pupils to read and understand Grammatically the more easy authors in that language' (soon afterwards, in 1829, French was extended to the Sixth as well, and in 1834, it became a voluntary extra subject, after school hours, for members of the Fourth and Fifth Classes).

Given the pressing need of the Directors to cover their expenditure by income, the start of the Seventh was clearly a sensible move, even though university professors would undoubtedly jib at the prospect of losing even more novices from their elementary Classics classes. The Directors also pointed out, shrewdly, that in return for a year's fees the boys would have ten months of instruction at the Academy compared with only six months at the university. But apart from the strictly financial considerations, the start of the Seventh can now be seen as part of the inexorable development of the Academy into a public school on the English pattern, to keep the boys longer at school and prevent them entering university at too young an age, as was the custom in Scotland.

But the problem that caused the most public interest and stir during that second year of the Academy and the year that followed was over the pronunciation of Latin; and this, too, highlighted the question of the extent to which the Edinburgh Academy was becoming anglicised. It caused a great deal of heart-searching in committees, in the letter columns of the *Scotsman*, and at the dinner tables of the New Town, and led to the first and only recorded disagreement between the Directors and the Proprietors (shareholders) of the Edinburgh Academy. However unimportant it may seem to us today, the matter of how Latin should be pronounced summed up the basic dilemma that faced the Directors of the Academy in trying to establish a school which they hoped would provide the best of both worlds on both sides of the Border. They were attempting to combine the good, solid excellence of a traditional Scottish education and the more specialised, refined niceties of the kind of classical education to be gained at Eton or Winchester.

There was a distinct difference between the ways in which a Scots schoolboy and an Eton schoolboy pronounced Latin words, particularly the vowel sounds, which were much broader in the Scots version than the clipped English rendering. The Scots would say *curahtor*, the English would pronounce it *curaytor*. The Scots version was claimed to be much closer to the original Roman pronunciation, and Scots who went to the Continent were reported to experience no trouble in making themselves understood to French, Italian or Dutch scholars. An Englishman, on the other hand, however brilliant he might be at versifying in Latin, was often incomprehensible to a Continental because the Latin sounds had been anglicised beyond recognition. The Academy Directors were well aware of this; but they also knew that a Scot competing at Oxford or Cambridge, or appearing at the English Bar, or in the House of Commons, was at a real disadvantage, even an object of ridicule, when he pronounced Latin in what the English considered to be a barbarous manner. There was the case of the pawky Scottish advocate, John Clerk of Eldin, who was pleading the cause of a 'curator bonis' in the House of Lords. When Clerk said *curahtor bonis*, the Lord Chancellor interrupted pompously '*curaytor*, I suppose you mean, Mr Clerk'. Whereupon, quick as a flash, Mr Clerk retorted, 'I'm varra proud to be correctit in my quantities by such a splendid *oraytor*, such a brilliant *legislaytor*, and such a learned *senaytor*, as yir Lordship,' dwelling long on the long *a* in each word.

The Academy founders wanted to produce scholars who could equal the English at their own game as well as retain the ability to speak in the old Scots way, so in their original Prospectus for the Academy they had proposed that the Scots pronunciation should be the accepted one, but that in their later years at school the boys should be introduced to the English style as far as possible. But this compromise only produced confusion amongst both boys and masters, and in 1826 the Directors took one more step in the English direction by agreeing that the English method should be taught occasionally in the Fourth Class and almost exclusively in the Rector's Classes, the pupils being 'occasionally required to pronounce in the Scottish method'. At the same time any boy in the Junior Classes who was already used to the English method (and there were many English boys at the Academy) was to be allowed to use it throughout. In this way, said the Directors in their *Report* of 1826 (hoping to appease everyone), pupils leaving the Academy 'will have acquired as much of the English pronunciation as is practicable while they retain the ordinary dialect of Scotsmen, and sufficient for those occasions when in after-life they may be called on to pronounce Latin and may wish to avoid the pronunciation of Scotland'.

C.S. H

But it was all very confusing, and became even more so when the Seventh Class was introduced, with half the school learning the English pronunciation and the other half the Scots, and the three Classical Masters now assisting the Rector with his three top Classes were having to teach Scots vowel sounds at one lesson and English vowel sounds at the next, while all the boys were expected to learn Scottish vowel sounds from an English Master who was an Englishman trained to speak English and Latin in the Eton manner.

The Rector was understandably annoyed at the effects all this confusion was having on results, and he complained so strongly that the Directors allowed him to go ahead and introduce the Eton pronunciation into all the Classes. There were no complaints from parents, boys, or masters, even though the Classical Masters were now all Scots (Mr Marriott had meanwhile been replaced by an old High School boy, James Cumming, who was to make a considerable mark on the Academy in the next twenty years). But the public, and more especially the Proprietors, began to grow restive as the year went on and word of the English 'take-over' got around.

Letters began to appear in the newspapers, reviving the bitter antagonism expressed by a certain Mr Peter Reid in his original hostility to the establishment of the school: 'It seems the New Town gentry, not content with the absurdities already existing, have, in their rage for cudgelling out the brains of boys, called in an English Rector to assist them, who, no doubt, is preparing to do his best to give us a cut extraordinary, after the English fashion, that Scotch teachers may see what they still have to learn.' (*Letter to the Patrons of the High School and the Inhabitants of Edinburgh on the Abuse of Classical Education*, 1824.)

The Directors found themselves the targets for unprecedented criticism. On January 24, John Russell and Leonard Horner went to ask for advice from Sir Walter Scott, the Grand Old Man of Scottish letters. On the next day, Sir Walter wrote in his *Journal*: 'Thought during the watches of the night and a part of the morning about the question of Latin pronunciation, and came to the following conclusions – That the mode of pronunciation approved by Buchanan and by Milton and practised by all nations excepting the English, assimilated in sound, too, to the Spanish, Italian and other languages derived from the Latin, is certainly the best, and is likewise useful as facilitating the acquisition of sounds which the Englishman attempts in vain. Accordingly I wish the cockneyfied pedant who first disturbed it by reading *Emo* for *Amo*, and *quy* for *qui*, had choked in the attempt. But the question is, whether a youth who has been taught in a manner different from that used all over England will be heard, if he presumes to use his Latin at the bar of the senate; and if he is to be unintelligible or ludicrous, the question [arises] whether his education is not imperfect under one important view. I am very unwilling to sacrifice our *sumpsimus* to their old *mumpsimus* – still more to humble ourselves before the Saxons while we can keep an inch of the Scottish flag flying. But this is a question that must be decided not on partialities or prejudices.' (*Journal*, 1827–8, pp. 12–13.)

It says much for the interest that this (to modern eyes) somewhat esoteric question aroused, that Sir Water should spend so much time on it when he was in the immediate throes of the financial crash that shattered the last years of his life.

The Directors were surprised at the fervour with which the question was brought up at the Annual General Meeting of the Proprietors on July 2, 1827, and agreed to hold a special meeting on the 25th at which the Directors would present a *Report* on the whole matter. (This was the only occasion in the history of the Academy in which the Proprietors attempted to intervene on matters of policy and administration of the School.) The Rector and masters were asked to give their views in writing, and these were also included in the *Report* which was circulated to all the shareholders before the meeting (*Report on the Pronunciation of Latin*).

In this *Report* the Directors first of all defended themselves against the accusation that by allowing the English pronunciation to be taught in all classes they were breaking the terms of the original Prospectus for education at the Academy. They agreed that it was intended that 'Latin shall be taught according to the accustomed mode of pronouncing that language in Scotland, and that this shall be the acknowledged system of the School'. But the Prospectus had also stated that '*the Boys are also in the latter years to be made as familiar as is practicable, with the English mode of pronunciation*'. But if this 'statement' was to be held to be a positive contract, from which it would be a breach of faith to deviate, 'the whole scheme of the Academy may be considered as destroyed; because, experience has always been suggesting improvements – and the Directors never understood, that every change that has taken place is liable to be set aside, merely by producing a passage in the original statement (necessarily prospective and hypothetical) with which that change is inconsistent.'

Not for nothing was the Board of Directors crammed with dis-

tinguished legal minds. They went on to point out that in 1826 the
Proprietors had unanimously approved the improvement of introducing the English method into the Fourth Class. They had also approved
the establishment of a Seventh Class, and it was this class that had put
the cat among the pigeons – or, as the Directors put it, 'by exhibiting
the English pronunciation among a higher Class of young Gentlemen,
it made it popular all over the School.' Having a Seventh Class also
necessitated having three of the Classical Masters teaching the Upper
Classes for half a day as well, 'obliging these Masters to pronounce
upon opposite and inconsistent principles every two hours'. When the
Rector had pointed out that so much confusion was 'rapidly tending
to the formation of a mongrel pronunciation', the Directors had given
him permission to do whatever he thought best, and the result had been
the introduction of the English pronunciation into all the Classes. The
Directors were highly gratified by the result. It was impossible for any
unprejudiced person to go into the Academy 'without perceiving a
higher tone of elegance and refinement than is generally to be met with
in a Scotch School'.

The Directors claimed that 'their only, or at least their chief, object
in introducing the English pronunciation of Latin was, to facilitate the
pronunciation of the English Language . . . The English pronunciation
ought now to be made *the standard* for all the Classes . . . The teaching
of English literature, *including a proper English articulation and accent*, has
always been one of the main objects of this Academy'. But can boys
from eight to twelve years of age, they asked, 'be expected to make any
approach towards an English utterance when their efforts, at that early
age, are counteracted by a far greater portion of their time being spent
in the exclusive use of ordinary broad Scotch?' The Directors were
satisfied 'that the exclusive Scotch pronunciation of Latin, in the four
Junior Classes, can only be obtained by a corresponding sacrifice of the
English mode of pronouncing the language of England'. The boys
themselves seemed to associate 'ideas of refinement with the habitual
and unaffected use of the English accent . . . and it does seem somewhat
hard to chain them down upon system to those sounds which are
beginning to be deemed vulgar even among the lower orders'.

The Directors also pointed out: that the Latin of a Frenchman or a
German is less like that of a Scotchman than is often supposed; that
any similarity between the Scotch and Continental pronunciations was
an advantage which could be useful to only a very small number of
boys (not one in a hundred would ever have occasion to have inter-

course with Continental foreigners, and probably not one in a thousand would ever wish to converse with such foreigners in Latin); that any Scotchman who was likely to hold communication with a foreigner in Latin could easily prepare himself for the task in a very few weeks in spite of the training at the Academy; that, as regards the supply of trained masters and the expressed fear that it would limit that supply to masters from England, it was much easier to find Scotch masters trained to the English method than English ones trained to the Scotch.

Finally: 'The Academy was planned . . . not only to educate the higher classes of native Pupils [and] save these the necessity of going, as usual, to England after they left School, [but] to attract Pupils . . . from the south. This scheme has, as yet, promised to succeed perfectly; in so much that at least one School in the North of England . . . has suffered very materially from its competition from the Academy. The Directors have not the slightest doubt that this most valuable source of supply must be greatly narrowed by establishing Scotch as the standard of pronunciation for four entire years.'

It speaks volumes for the persistence, the eloquence, and the force of personality of the Rector that he had managed to win the Directors so thoroughly over to his way of thinking – and not only the Directors but the Classical Masters who, as the Directors pointed out to the Proprietors, 'are all Scotch by birth and education, and some of them originally leant to a different opinion. Their present conviction has been forced upon them in opposition to their national partialities, by experience and reflection.' In their written views, the masters supported to the hilt the Welsh-born English Classicist who so dominated the Masters' Lodge at the Edinburgh Academy.

Rector Williams wrote: 'If there was once a close resemblance between the vowel sounds of the standard vernacular language of Scotland and those adopted by it in pronouncing Latin, Time has entirely destroyed it . . . The language of the English Court has become the standard language of Scotland, and the Scottish dialect has disappeared in her own higher circles. All classes seem desirous that their children should, at least, read with a pure English accent. In the meantime, the Latin pronunciation has remained unmodified and still retains those sounds which, however familiar from infancy to the courtiers of James the Sixth of Scotland, can only be acquired by study by the great body of George the Fourth's British subjects.'

He was certainly making no concessions to the kailyard sentimentalists: 'Most of the European nations seem to have adopted the vowel sounds of their own languages as the basis of their Greek and Latin pronunciation . . . The English, perhaps more than any other nation, refused to make any concession in favour of the more universal principle, and made their own language the sole basis for pronouncing the Greek and Latin . . . Eton, placed in the immediate vicinity of the Court, and under the eye of Royalty, and most frequented by the sons of the Nobility and Gentry, was early regarded as the standard school for English pronunciation, and its Latin and Greek pronunciation, formed on the most refined method of teaching the English language, finally became triumphant in the South, and banished all the broader sounds of the vowels from all respectable Schools.' Moreover, the pupil learning Latin and Greek on the Eton plan tended to become more perfect in his English pronunciation: 'To this must be referred that peculiar rhythm and intonation of high bred and highly educated English speakers, the absence of which so instantly strikes an English audience, and for the want of which nothing but the greatest genius and the richest vein of eloquence can compensate. In fact, a peculiar fastidiousness of ear has been a distinguishing mark of high mental culture in all ages, and a false argument has often been pardoned where false pronunciation has proved fatal.'

But the Proprietors were not convinced, at that meeting of July 25, 1827, by the Rector's powerful appeal to their more exalted, or more snobbish, instincts. Nor were they entirely convinced by a final appeal by the Directors themselves to leave the matter in their hands and not let it become the subject of a public slanging match: 'The Directors again entreat the Proprietors to observe that all necessity of any public discussion at present is superseded, *by its being now distinctly and authoritatively announced, that if the Directors be left on this, as on other occasions, to exercise that discretion, without which no persons in their situation can act, they engage to teach the Pupils of the Academy that mode of Scotch pronunciation, which is thought to be desireable by some Proprietors.'*

However, the Proprietors insisted that the Directors should appoint a committee to work out a way of 'redeeming our pledge to the Proprietors', and on September 18 a compromise was agreed: for the first three school years, a 'softened' mode of the Scottish pronunciation would be taught, which would come close to the European mode of Latin without spoiling the ground for the teaching of the Eton system in the four senior Classes.

But clearly, the compromise was not adhered to for long – Rector Williams was too dogmatic and forceful a character for that. By 1844 the English method had long been adopted for use throughout the school, and Lord Cockburn (as he was by then) was writing in his *Journal*: 'There are Scotch schools (the Edinburgh Academy, for example) from which Scotch is almost entirely banished, even in the pronunciation of Greek and Latin . . . I could name dozens of families, born, living and educated in Edinburgh, which could not produce a single son or daughter capable of understanding even *The Mouse* or *The Daisy*. English has made no encroachment upon me; yet, though I speak more Scotch than English throughout the day, and read Burns aloud, and recommend him, I cannot get even my own children to do more than pick up a queer word of him here and there.' He went on: 'Scotch cannot be obliterated without our losing the means of enjoying some of the finest productions of genius, and of understanding the habits and characters of one of the most picturesque of European nations, and of losing an important key to the old literature, even of the south. Above all, we lose *ourselves*. Instead of being what we are, we become a poor part of England.' (*Journal*, vol. II, pp. 88–9.)

It's rather sad to hear Cockburn in his old age mourning the effect that the school he had founded was having on something he held dear about Scotland. Twenty years later, another renowned Academy name, the great D'Arcy Wentworth Thompson (ch. 10), who was edged out of his post at the Academy in 1864 for his unconventional teaching methods, published his own comments on the English pronunciation of Latin ('unmusical in verse, absolutely ludicrous for prose'): 'There is no doubt that in the familiar handling of the classic tongues – of Latin especially – we are far behind Germany, Holland and Italy . . . Is there any chance then of amendment in our great public schools? In those of England, I think there is none; in those of Scotland, there is a possibility of change . . . In Scotland, a servile imitation of what is bad in English scholarship has nearly led to the extinction of a music, which, at the commencement of the present century, might have been heard in every parish school.' (*Day-Dreams of a Schoolmaster*, pp. 114–15.)

It was not to be for nearly fifty years after the arguments and compromises of 1827 that the Scottish mode of pronunciation was finally vindicated and adopted in England – in 1871, when it was also revived at the Academy while Dr Harvey was Rector. Meanwhile, back in 1827, the compromise solution of 'softening' the Scotch pronunciation seemed to satisfy everyone, on the surface at least. The third session of the Academy ended in a blaze of glory. Henry Cockburn was happy to present the Gold Medal for Dux of the School to Archibald Campbell Tait, who was winning it for the second year in succession. The reporter from the *Scotsman* waxed ecstatic: 'Trammelled by no ancient rules – enslaved by no venerable prejudices – stiffened by no official inconveniences – arisen in an age fertile of improvements in the science of opening the human mind – and guided by men who cannot possibly have any interest but to discover and adopt every useful invention in that science – it may be the glory of this institution to reform the hitherto very imperfect system of Scotch classical education. It has, indeed, already done so, to an extent quite sufficient to attest how much the success of our classical learning is involved in its prosperity.' (*Scotsman*, August 4, 1827.)

The Directors, in their annual *Report*, were hardly less enthusiastic: 'The Directors have again the pleasure of congratulating the Proprietors of the Edinburgh Academy on the increasing prosperity of the Institution; and they have much satisfaction in informing them that the experience of this last year, being the third of its progress, fully justifies the hopes that were held out at its first formation.'

But a shock was in store that no one had conceived even as a remote possibility: Rector John Williams, the man who had set the Academy on its successful way, suddenly resigned.

CHAPTER VII

Interregnum: Mr Sheepshanks (1828-29)

The Satyrs of our day all Satyrs surpass,
With the shanks of a sheep and the head of an ass.
(Schoolboy, *Anon*)

THE bad news came just as the Directors were breathing a sigh of relief that the heat had been taken out of the Latin controversy and were still congratulating themselves over the success of the third session. The roll had increased yet again, to 519, and enrolments for the fourth session were holding steady, at 521. With numbers like that, the Directors no longer had to make up the masters' salaries to the guaranteed minimum, so the school was now reaching a financially viable level as far as running costs were concerned. True, the accumulated building debt had risen to £5,843, but that represented once-and-for-all capital schemes like the new Writing and Arithmetic Block, and the Directors sounded confident that ways of reducing the debt would be found. The money was owed to their Treasurer and banker, Thomas Kinnear, and since the Charter did not allow the Academy to borrow money, the Directors had been discussing the possibility of a personal loan, with the Directors themselves standing as guarantors, so that Mr Kinnear could be paid back. A special committee was also busy investigating 'the propriety of applying to the Nobility and Gentry of Scotland to patronise the School by taking shares'.

Several noblemen and 'other persons of consideration and literary attainments from England' had visited the school, and all had 'expressed themselves in terms of great satisfaction with the plan of education and the manner in which it is carried on'. The experiment of making the whole curriculum, including Writing and Arithmetic, compulsory was working satisfactorily: 'Some complaints have been made . . . but the small number of these makes the Directors think these come from very few individuals . . . The Academy is founded on the idea that an enlightened system of instruction has been devised; and to allow this system to be broken up at the discretion of individual

parents, would be at once to ruin it, or to render it impracticable.'
A measure of physical training had been introduced, in that a Drill
Sergeant had been engaged 'to conduct classes in these preliminary
exercises which are conducive to the health of the boys, by opening
the chest, and giving flexibility to their joints; and which tend to
improve their carriage and appearance', and 200 boys had attended his
classes voluntarily. (This experiment was abandoned the following
year, but later a Fencing teacher, George Roland, was allowed to set
up classes in the Academy.) The Rector had turned in a glowing *Report*
in which he pointed to the achievements of the new Seventh Class
(thirty boys) in Classics, French, and Mathematics as evidence of 'how
simultaneously the great branches of education may be carried on';
and he claimed that the progress of the Geits Class was 'the most
successful experiment in preliminary education' that he had ever
witnessed. The masters considered that in teaching at the Academy they
enjoyed 'advantages rarely if ever before enjoyed by public teachers'.

And, in their turn, the Directors gave the credit for the success to the
'zeal and ability of the Rector and Masters', while paying a special
tribute to Leonard Horner, who had just left to become the first
Warden of the new London University: it was largely thanks to him,
they said, that the Academy had been placed 'on such a footing as to
entitle it to the rank which it now holds among the classical schools of
Great Britain'.

It was at this moment, on August 30, 1827, that the Rector informed
the Directors that he was applying for the post of Professor of the
Roman Language and Literature in the newly-opened University
College in London – and had no doubt that he would get it: 'It would
be unfair,' he wrote to the Directors in his engagingly immodest way,
'to state that I had any doubt of the success of the application.' But he
went on to assure the Directors 'in the strongest terms' that Mr Leonard
Horner, the new Warden at London, had nothing to do with his
decision to apply for the appointment – 'I assure you that he appeared
more alarmed than pleased with the communication.'

He was well aware of the blow he was dealing the Directors, and
tried to soften it: 'I have only to regret exceedingly that this opening
did not occur 3 years later, which would have enabled me to conclude
the Academical cycle with the original First Class . . . As it is, my colleagues are perfectly acquainted with my system of tuition, and if my
successor be elected to join me on the first of March, I have no doubt
(if he be a proper man) that after six months careful inspection, he will

be enabled to carry on the School in October, 1828, without any change of system.'

This was more than just a setback when the wind had seemed set fair; it was little short of catastrophic. The Directors had known that Mrs Williams had not taken kindly to Edinburgh and that her husband would not be content to spend the rest of his days in Scotland. His ultimate goal was advancement in the Church of England and it was understood that one day in the future, perhaps, after retirement from the Academy, he would want to return to England and his vocation as a churchman and classical scholar. But Mr Williams' ambition had been much more immediate and burning than any of them had realised. He saw the University College appointment in London as a heaven-sent opportunity to establish himself in England and make history by forging a link between a new non-denominational University and the Church of England. He could hardly wait to get started.

The Directors were shattered. Sir Walter Scott called it 'a sad slap in the face to the Academy. He was a heaven-born schoolmaster, and I believe that I shall never see such another.' But the Directors, in the quiet, matter-of-fact way in which they had faced up to Old Bailie Blackwood and would go on to handle angry parents, various wars, plagues and financial crises during the Academy's first 150 years, contented themselves with politely recording their regret in the Minutes, and went on to discuss the damage that boys were doing to the new school furniture. But when Mr Williams announced in November that his application had been successful, and formally tendered his resignation, they expressed 'unfeigned regret' and published a fulsome tribute to him in their annual *Report*, giving him the credit 'in a great degree, for the almost unlooked-for success which has attended the Academy'. Then they had to set about the wearisome business of finding a successor, and gladly accepted Leonard Horner's offer to interview candidates for them in England.

Meanwhile the Rev. John Williams continued to run the school and everything went more or less smoothly. There was some discontent over the standard of teaching in the Writing and Arithmetic departments and a few boys were withdrawn from the school by their parents, but the only fault reported by a committee set up to investigate the trouble was 'Mr Gloag's excess of zeal, which leads him to push the boys with too much rapidity'. And M. Buquet, the French master, was having trouble keeping order in the difficult Class that Mr Marriott had found so trying – that 'mass of ignorance and idleness truly deplorable'. But there was good news of striking successes by some of the first 'old boys' of the Academy, who were carrying away 'some of the highest prizes at the Universities of Edinburgh and Glasgow', and it was obvious from the interviews with candidates for the Rector's post that there was a growing respect for the new Academy in scholastic circles throughout the country.

At last, on June 13, 1828, the new Rector was appointed, when the Directors unanimously elected the Rev. Thomas Sheepshanks. He was thirty years old, the Headmaster of Falmouth Grammar School, a graduate of Trinity College, Cambridge, and a former assistant to Dr Samuel Butler, the Headmaster of Shrewsbury School (and later Bishop of Lichfield and Coventry). Mr Sheepshanks had been an unsuccessful candidate for one of the Classical Masterships when the Academy opened, but now the Directors chose him for Rector in 'the most unhesitating belief that his talents and conduct will amply justify the propriety and fitness of their choice'. In this belief, as it turned out, they were ludicrously mistaken.

But now events took another and equally unexpected turn: because only a few days after Mr Sheepshanks had been appointed Rector-elect, Mr Williams resigned from his new Chair in London before he had even had time to occupy it. He had discovered that the Church of England had no desire to see any link forged with 'that godless institution in Gower Street', and that University College was intended to be a London University from which theology was to be totally excluded. In his eagerness to accept the appointment, Mr Williams had neglected to look into the religious intentions of the new University, and now he found that to take the Chair would rule out any chance of future ecclesiastical preferment: 'When the Church came forward to establish a similar institution [King's College] on her own principles, my occupation was gone. There could be no linking in such a case.'

There now developed an extraordinary tug-of-war between London and Edinburgh over Mr Williams. Leonard Horner withheld acceptance of the resignation from London University, and asked his old friend Henry Cockburn to try to persuade Williams to reconsider it; and meanwhile Mr Sheepshanks gamely offered to stand down and let Williams have the Rectorship of the Academy back again. A deputation of Directors, consisting of Sir Walter Scott, Colin Mackenzie, John Russell, and Cockburn hurried off to Saxe-Coburg Place on July 4 and asked Williams to stay on at the Academy. But for once the normally self-assured and decisive Williams was in an agony of indecision. He asked for time to think things over, and the Directors gave him three days, until two o'clock on July 7. In the event, he decided to adhere to both his resignations: he did not want the London University post now, and he did not want to return to the Academy in case the Church of England had him in mind for the new King's College in the Strand.

In fact this hope came to nothing, even though Sir Walter Scott provided him with a fulsome testimonial: 'With his singular command over the human mind he has made himself fully obeyed through a numerous school, where he is equally beloved by the subordinate Masters and by the scholars. He has great personal strength of body and constitution, and has been quite an Atlas to our little state.' Privately, however, Scott seems to have thought that Williams had made rather an ass of himself; in his biography of his father-in-law, Lockhart claims that Sir Walter had told him, 'I am glad it confirms a theory of mine, that no schoolmaster whatever existed without having some private reserve of extreme absurdity, which I think Taffy Williams, whom I always supposed an exception, has most plainly evinced.

> '*Friend Williams falls with heavy thump*
> *Upon his reverential rump.*'
> (*Life*, vol. II, p. 30.)

But while Mr Williams sat on his reverential rump in Saxe-Coburg Place getting on with the notes for his *Life and Actions of Alexander the Great* (1829) and his beloved *Homerus*, Mr Thomas Sheepshanks was just around the corner trying to get on with the job of running the Edinburgh Academy. And if ever a man was unfitted for the task he had taken on, it was Thomas Sheepshanks, that 'transient and embarrassed phantom' as the *Edinburgh Academy Register* called him. Everyone knew it. The boys all knew it, and quickly managed to make his life a misery; the Fifth Class in particular did their best to establish superiority over the gormless intruder and behaved in a manner 'tumultuous and subversive of good discipline'. The masters all knew it, and before long they submitted a *Memorandum* to the Directors proposing reforms that would have deprived the Rector of his authority over them and withdrawn the teaching of Greek from him. Too late, the Directors realised that they had made an appalling mistake.

How they came to make such a mistake is hard to understand. They based their decision mainly on the testimonial from Dr Samuel Butler of Shrewsbury, who was at that time considered the most successful headmaster in Britain. But they must have forgotten all about Mr Sheepshanks' original application for an under-mastership in 1824, only four years earlier. (So unlikely had it been that Cockburn had not bothered to file it with the others.) He had not even written it himself. He had got his uncle to do it for him, with the plea: 'It has occurred to me more than once in life to set my mark too low, and to forbear, from motives of my own inadequacy, applying for things which have afterwards been obtained by men decidedly inferior.' His uncle seemed to think that this letter in itself would impress the Directors, for he had enclosed it with his application on Thomas's behalf; and he had added what must be the most left-handed recommendation ever in support of a candidate's scholarly claims – that Mr Sheepshanks had competed several times for the medals given for Greek and Latin verse at Cambridge but 'was uniformly, I think, either a day too late or a stanza or two unfinished', but that if these exercises could be produced they would show him to be 'an excellent writer of Latin verse, and good, but not super-eminent, in Greek'.

It seems incredible that no one amongst the Directors remembered this bizarre application when the name Sheepshanks cropped up again in 1828. The name itself must surely have given the Directors pause, knowing the propensity of boys to make fun out of even the most everyday names; indeed, Sheepshanks told Dr Butler that when he called on Leonard Horner on his way to take up his post at the Academy, Horner had advised him to change his name. Most men would have resented the suggestion, but Sheepshanks, whose diffidence suited his name all too well, was quite ready to concur; but as he explained, 'The precaution would have been fruitless, for an idle quondam pupil of yours and mine, yclept Hogg, recognised me, and my name was soon known.' And it was not long before the boys were chanting:

> The Satyrs of old were Satyrs of note,
> With the head of a man and the legs of a goat;
> But the Satyrs of our day all Satyrs surpass,
> With the shanks of a sheep and the head of an ass.

(It is an index of the contempt in which he was held by his pupils that this verse was said to have been handed to him in person as a school exercise on English *Satires*.)

No one could have been more different from the confident and bouncy Mr Williams, who had written to Sir Walter Scott when applying for the Rector's post – 'I have an impression that the Directors would never have cause to repent were they to choose me.' Whereas Mr Sheepshanks wrote to Dr Butler just before leaving for his interview in Edinburgh: 'I certainly should not have dreamt of proposing myself as a candidate, taking it for granted they would have men greatly superior. I somewhat doubt my own adequacy to so important an office, but should I be elected and find myself in difficulties, I may perhaps beg for a little of your assistance.'

Difficulties he certainly had. The biggest was a painful sense of inferiority regarding the reputation and popularity of his predecessor, whose presence just around the corner in Saxe-Coburg Place was a constant reminder of his own inadequacy. He also found the 'high degree of celebrity acquired by this Institution in the course of a few years' daunting rather than inspiring. He was painfully honest about it all in his first and only *Report* to the Directors: 'It was my misfortune to be an entire stranger in this country, personally unknown to Directors, Masters and Pupils. The very idea of the chief authority in the Academy had long been identified with the person of another . . . This difficulty would exist even in a case where the attainments and experience of the two Masters were upon a par; and must necessarily be greatly increased wherever the superiority of talent and power of teaching is greatly in favour of the original Master.'

In his humility, he could even be self-effacing about the gross misbehaviour of the Fifth Class: 'I do not conceive that this misconduct had its origin in any peculiar ill-feeling towards myself, but that it was an attempt to gain the upper hand of a new Master, and that any other gentleman, coming as Rector when I did, would have been subjected to the same trial.' And he also found that 'a strong sense of honour seems to pervade the pupils of the Academy in general, and that their laudable desire of occupying a good place in their respective classes is scarcely exceeded by their anxiety to see industry or talent in a classfellow obtain its reward, even to their own temporary loss'.

In his *Report*, he revealed the large difference that still existed between the educational aims and standards of the English public schools and the Edinburgh Academy. He thought the style of translation at the Academy too free, and advocated that it should be strictly literal, 'rendering each Latin or Greek word into its corresponding one in English'; and he also thought the boys should be able to parse each word with almost mathematical exactness. 'In these two very essential points I perceive a large portion of the upper boys of the Academy to be deficient, and behind boys of equal scholarship in English schools.' But he found the Academy boys to be far superior in knowledge of Greek and Latin vocabulary, 'defective in chronology, fair proficient in History, and good Geographers', while 'the knowledge of Arithmetic and Mathematics possessed by boys of the Academy is unquestionably far superior to that even of the highest boys at English schools of classical celebrity.'

But Mr Sheepshanks had had enough by then. The writing had been on the wall almost from the beginning. Only a couple of months after Mr Sheepshanks had arrived at the Academy, Sir Walter Scott was writing to his son-in-law, Lockhart, on November 20, 1828: 'I think if Edinburgh Rectory should be open again, which is very likely, he [*Williams*] will do wisely to slip into his hole again where [he may] convert his spheroidical form into a globular one with great comfort.' (*Letters*, vol. XI, p. 45.) On May 25, 1829, Mr Sheepshanks sent in his resignation. Richard Mackenzie, one of the Directors, went straight round to Saxe-Coburg Place, and Williams accepted re-appointment as Rector at once, promising to remain at the Academy at least until the next year's Geits Class had been right through the Academy seven-year course. 'I have not been very happy since the separation took place,' he said. 'I think the second election has found me a wiser man than the former.'

Mr Sheepshanks may not have been a wise man, but he was honest and sincere, and whatever other good qualities he possessed have been obscured by his blinding failure as Rector of the Academy. One cannot help but feel sorry for him. The Directors wrote to him expressing 'in the strongest terms, their regard for you as a gentleman, their respect for your high attainment as a scholar'. And they added: 'In all their intercourse with you . . . they have met with nothing but the most perfect honour, candour, and propriety of demeanour on your part.'

His troubles at the Academy were over. He went on to become headmaster of Coventry School, and Rural Dean and Rector of St John's Coventry, and died in 1874 at the age of seventy-six.

CHAPTER VIII

Dr Williams: Years of Fruition (1829-47)

Occasional obstacles and perplexities, of course, arose; but they were all met by the energy and sagacity of the Rector . . . (Directors' *Report*, 1847)

THE Rev. John Williams had promised that he would stay at the Academy for at least seven years. In fact he stayed for the next eighteen – eighteen years in which the Academy settled down to become an institution, in a world in which change and challenge had to be faced and overcome at every turn.

His return to the helm in 1829 was welcomed by masters and boys alike. He pulverised the arguments of the masters' *Memorandum* in a crushing letter, and immediately reasserted the unassailable authority of the Rector. But he was in no mood for radical changes. He was content to continue, more or less unaltered, the system of education which he and the Directors had evolved and found so successful in the early years. His justification was the annual list of honours and prizes won by Academicals at universities all over Britain. Writing in 1852, Lord Cockburn said that it would probably be found that more Academy pupils had gained honours at Oxford and Cambridge than all the pupils of all the other schools in Scotland since the Edinburgh Academy began. Meanwhile, the Rector flourished and grew fatter, even rotund, but he lost none of his ebullience. He became even more renowned in Edinburgh society and literary circles. He received a Doctorate of Divinity from Oxford University in 1831 and was appointed Archdeacon of Cardigan in 1833 (albeit an absentee Archdeacon). He ruled the Academy with a genial despotism, and praised it unreservedly in his annual *Reports* to the Directors. He seemed content to devote all his teaching career now to the Academy, although in 1838 he applied, unsuccessfully, for the post of Headmaster of King Edward I's Free School at Birmingham.

The year 1831 was in a way a watershed. It was the end of the first full cycle of pupils from Geits to the Seventh. At the Opening of the school in 1824, the Rector had asked that judgement be suspended until the first cycle was complete – 'The system would require time, before it was seen in all its parts.' Now, when that day of judgement had arrived, Dr Williams was uncharacteristically diffident in his 1831 *Report* to the Directors: 'Much, assuredly has been done during the last seven years, but much more, he feels confident, will be achieved during the second curriculum.'

He spoke compassionately about the kind of humane atmosphere that was wanted at the Academy: 'The Founders of the Academy felt a strong conviction that harsher modes for enforcing school discipline, and securing the attention of the pupil, were oftener adopted than either humanity permitted or the ductile minds of youth required. Hence sprung the frequent and earnest applications of the Directors to the Masters on the advantages of diminishing, as far as possible, the motives to industry resulting from fear and pain, and of increasing the natural stimuli arising from the love of knowledge and approbation, and from the powerful impulse of honourable emulation. In short, to render education as much as possible an act of love.'

The Directors, in their own *Report* to the Proprietors, expressed themselves as having 'every reason to be satisfied with the result'. But there is a muted note of anxiety to be read between the lines of the Minutes of Directors' meetings and the Directors' *Reports* throughout the 1830's. There was to be constant concern about the numbers of boys enrolled, on which the school's income depended, and during this difficult decade the numbers sank to perilously low levels. There was to be constant concern about the state of the school debt, which stayed obstinately above the £5,000 mark despite severe economies; such was the concern that after 1831, the annual Directors' *Reports* became more and more laconic, and even omitted from the printed version the lengthy discussions of the accounts which were presented verbally to the Annual General Meetings of Proprietors. The Directors also lost the services of some of their most experienced men: Thomas Kinnear, the banker who was their Treasurer, died in 1831 with £5,500 still owing to him; John Russell, the indefatigable Secretary who had founded the school with Cockburn and Horner, resigned in November, 1830, because of pressure of business, but took over the Treasurership for the next twelve years; and Sir Walter Scott died in 1832. Despite his personal financial troubles, he had remained assiduous in his attention to Academy affairs. At his funeral at Dryburgh Abbey it was the man he had championed – Dr Williams – who conducted the burial service.

Under the circumstances, it's hardly surprising that the Directors were reluctant to make any radical changes in the school system. They were too busy trying to keep the Academy's head above the financial waters, especially when the Kinnear banking house collapsed in 1834 and the Directors had to make urgent emergency arrangements with the bankers Forbes & Company to survive the crisis. Finance was a constant and complicated chore: juggling with the dwindling income from fees and dispensing it according to a salary scale dependent on the number of boys enrolling; cutting the Janitor's wages, firing the cleaners, and paying the Janitor to do their work; reducing the payments to the Mathematics and Writing Masters, and dismissing two of their Assistants; taking out a mortgage on the school and arranging a system of regular instalment payments of the debt; fighting off a proposal to erect a slaughter-house in front of the school; coping with an unusual number of staffing problems in the minor masterships – in 1832, the English Master, Mr Dyer, had to be bailed out of serious financial trouble with £10 to help him escape the sheriff's officers and return to London.

Most of the trouble was caused by changes that were taking place in the educational world. The State was beginning to exert more control over education, and the first steps were being taken to prise schools away from the grip of the Church. At the same time, new schools were springing up, privately endowed or financed by public subscription: Madras College in St Andrews (incorporating the Grammar School), the Bell-Baxter in Cupar, Milne's Institution in Fochabers, Morrison's Academy in Crieff, the Bathgate Academy. Dr Langhorne moved his little private prep school from Stoney Hill to Loretto, where it was later to blossom under the great Dr H. H. Almond. Merchiston Castle School, which had begun modestly in 1828 under the ownership of Charles Chalmers (brother of the great theologian Dr Thomas Chalmers, one of the founders of the Free Church) in a large private house on the present site of the McEwan Hall, moved out to the old Merchiston Tower on the Borough Muir in 1833 as a small boarding school.

But in Edinburgh it was the opening of the Edinburgh Institution (later to become Melville College) in 1832 by the former head of George Watson's Hospital, the Rev. Robert Cunningham, that constituted the main threat to the Academy – and to the High School; because the Institution offered, in addition to the classics, a wide curriculum of modern languages, practical and theoretical mathematics, English Literature, history, geography, astronomy, natural philosophy, chemistry, and drawing. The keynote was that 'a critical knowledge of Greek and Latin was not indispensably requisite'. The curriculum was not compulsory, as at the Academy, nor based on a hard-core course of classics, as at the High School, and this made it less expensive for middle-class families. From a standing start of sixty pupils in a leased flat in George Street at the start of the first session in 1832, the Institution had risen to 241 pupils by 1836, and been forced to move to larger premises, in Hill Street. (It was to move again, to Queen Street, in 1853.) And as the numbers at the Institution went up, so the numbers at the Academy and the High School came down. In that same year, the High School only enrolled 371 pupils, compared with the 739 who had enrolled for the first session in the magnificent new buildings on the Calton Hill in 1829, while the Academy had just over 300 pupils, compared with the early peak of 521 in 1827. It was to be late in the '30s before the numbers at both the classical schools began to climb again.

At first the Directors of the Academy did not see, or admit, any real threat to the school in the kind of broad-based education that was offered by the Institution. They still believed that there would always be enough parents willing to patronise an almost exclusively classical school. When the numbers dropped in 1829, they might have seen it as a result of the counter-attraction of the new High School. When the numbers showed no appreciable increase in 1831, they reckoned it was 'very much attributable to the state of the times and to the prevalence of cholera'. When the numbers dropped again in 1832, they repeated in the annual *Report*: 'The state of the times is sufficient to account for the diminution in numbers, and the Academy is not singular in this respect, for every other seminary of education has suffered from the same cause.' (In actual fact, the High School numbers hardly dropped at all that year.)

They could take some comfort from the reassuring accounts of academic success reported by the Rector, who claimed in 1834 that the Academy now had 'a far more comprehensive system of education than was ever proposed in any Public School within our Island' – despite the fact that the oldest boys were only sixteen, compared with eighteen or nineteen at the great English schools. His Seventh Class was achieving 'the highest degree of scholarship ever attempted in any school in Scotland'.

But was that what parents still wanted? On October 5, 1834, Henry

Cockburn was writing in his *Journal*: 'The tide is setting strongly against classical education. The Grammar-School of Glasgow had scarcely above 100 boys last winter. Our High School has sunk in three or four years from nearly 800 to about 400. The Academy has descended from about 450 to 320 . . . Meanwhile, other establishments, both private and public, are springing up now, which as yet have in general succeeded chiefly, as it appears to me, because they disdain these two languages [*Latin and Greek*], and profess to teach what they call useful knowledge, which means modern languages, chemistry, civil and natural history, physiology, astronomy, navigation, and in Edinburgh phrenology. All this and everything else is not only capable, it seems, of being taught to *children*, but it is peculiarly easy to them; and the classics, it also seems, are not only not learned where they are professed to be taught, but when learned are pernicious, inculcating an unchristian morality and erroneous taste. Absurd as all this is, it will probably go on, and I should not wonder if amidst other new eras we are on the verge of one which will consist in making the languages of Greece and Rome not the staple of our schools.' (*Journal*, vol. I, pp. 69–71.)

Cockburn was right, but it would be many years before the Academy bowed to the inevitable and gave a serious place in its curriculum to science and the arts. During the Rectorship of Dr Williams and for a long time thereafter, although small changes were introduced here and there and small concessions made to the trend towards more practical education, the Academy doggedly kept the flag flying for Homer and Virgil.

The Rector had made one slight concession in his *Report* of 1833: '. . . It cannot be denied that many parents who design their children not for the learned professions, but for the practical business of life, have complained that the learned languages have too exclusively occupied the attention of the pupils, at the sacrifice of their greater proficiency in common Arithmetic, Algebra, and Mathematical Studies . . . The Rector, therefore, suggests the expediency, if not the propriety, of commencing Arithmetic in the First Class and of making attendance upon the Arithmetic class compulsory upon the pupils both of the First and Second Class.'

It wasn't much, but at least it was something – even though next year the Directors were to turn down a suggestion that German instruction should be started (in the event, German wasn't started until 1843–4, and then only on a voluntary basis after school hours, as the

Directors were 'unwilling to lay too heavy a burden on the young gentlemen in their care'. It was made a compulsory part of the curriculum of the Seventh in 1847). However, French was introduced to the Fourth and Fifth Classes on an optional basis, and one of the Directors, Mr John Wood of the Sessional School, undertook to polish up the image of another problem department, English, and teach there himself without fee; he at least managed to attract the interest of the boys by introducing more stimulating text-books.

Despite these minor remedies, the numbers at school still went down the following year, and in their *Report* of 1834 the Directors noted, a shade desperately: 'Every institution of a similar nature throughout the country has lately suffered more or less from a vulgar and, it is to be hoped, a temporary abatement of the conviction of the value of classical literature as a principal object in the education of youth.'

The Rector was asked to give a course of public lectures on *The Theory and Practice of Education*, in the hope that 'it may have some effect in removing the dangerous and narrow-minded prejudices against Classical Education which have lately threatened to disgrace Scotland'. The hope was not fulfilled, and the numbers went down again in 1835 and 1836. But then the tide began to turn, and the Directors reported that 'there are already some symptoms in the public mind of an abatement of that prejudice against Classical Education, from which this Institution, in common with others of a similar nature, has of late suffered'. The recovery began to show in the numbers for the 1837–8 session (332), with a further increase to 360 the following year and another, unspecified, increase in 1839–40.

The worst seemed now to be over, for the time being at least, although the numbers never approached the 500-mark which had been estimated as being necessary to make the school pay its way. In all these difficult times the Directors were never panicked into abandoning their original plan, but quietly sweated over the business of trying to make ends meet (by deciding to increase the capital from £12,000 to £16,000, for instance), while continuing to give Dr Williams their full support in his efforts to consolidate the unique academic character the school was evolving, based on all that had been best in the old High School, with the refining influence of English public school training, all leavened by a sprinkling of modern subjects, a dash of wholesome Celtic good humour from the Rector, and the humane effect of the boys' daily contact with the warmth of home and family instead of being school Boarders.

In that vein the Edinburgh Academy entered the calmer domestic waters of the 1840's. In their 21st annual *Report* of 1845, the Directors celebrated the landmark without fanfare, simply noting with satisfaction that the school 'continues quietly and steadily to follow out that course which has already secured for it the confidence of the public, and an eminent position among other seminaries of education'. Rector Williams contented himself by noting that he thought that 'the objects of the Founders have been fully attained'. The school was on an even keel again, and the numbers of boys remained remarkably steady around the 360 mark throughout the '40s. Archdeacon Williams' Rectorship was drawing to a serene close, as year by year he was able to point proudly to the academic distinctions that were being earned by his more gifted former pupils.

But if there was tranquillity at the school, the outside world was seething with change and turmoil, and new social eras were being ushered in. During Williams' Rectorship at the Academy, George IV was succeeded by William IV and Queen Victoria came to the throne in 1837. The repeal of the Combination Acts made Trades Unions legal in Britain. Spanish America became independent, Nicholas I became Czar of Russia, Beethoven died, and Greece gained her independence. The Catholics were emancipated in Britain, and the Metropolitan Police force was established. The Reform Bill was passed, and when the news reached Edinburgh, Mr Williams was so delighted he almost polished a hole in his knees and gave the school a holiday. Belgium broke away from Holland. The British Association was founded, Faraday discovered electro-magnetic induction, the electric telegraph was invented by Morse, the first steamship crossing of the Atlantic was made by the Dutch vessel *Curacao*, and the first railway was opened between Darlington and Stockton. The First British Factory Act was passed. The 'Tolpuddle Martyrs' became the first victims of the British working-class struggles. The word 'socialism' was first heard. The Municipal Reform Act reformed local government in Britain, and the Chartists produced their People's Charter.

The Boers made their Great Trek from British South African territory. Texas achieved independence of Mexico. The National Gallery in London was opened, the first Afghan War began, Aden was annexed by Britain, and the Penny Postage was instituted. The Opium War with China started, and the last convicts landed in New South Wales. Britain acquired Hong Kong, the Corn Laws were repealed, and the British Museum opened its doors in Great Russell Street.

That was in 1847, the year that Archdeacon Williams retired from the Rectorship and went back to his native Wales to become the first Warden of Llandovery College. The Directors accorded him handsome tribute in their *Report* of 1847:

He undertook the Rectorship when the Academy was first opened, and under all the difficulties implied in its novelty, and in the necessity of working it by Directors and Masters who had never acted together before. Occasional obstacles and perplexities, of course, arose; but they were all met by the energy and sagacity of the Rector, who never made any difficulty himself, and subdued obstructions which would have dismayed any zeal less judicious or efficient than his. In this, as in all efforts, he was no doubt powerfully seconded by the other Masters, from whose portion of merit the Directors are very far from meaning to detract. But these Masters who best know the facts, will be strongest in attesting what they and the Academy owe to the peculiar and unabating enthusiasm of their chief.

The result has been the production of a system and of a School of which the only apparent misfortune is, that it is, perhaps, superior, not we hope to the ultimate, but to the present taste of Scotland. No modern scholastic establishment has done so much to avert the decline of classical education in this country, and to elevate the reputation of Scottish tuition at the English Universities. In so far as mere education, chiefly classical and mathematical, is concerned, it has extinguished whatever necessity there ever was for sending Scotch boys beyond Scotland.

All concerned are entitled to their share of the merit of having thus realized the object for which the Academy was instituted, but the merit of the Rector has always been pre-eminent. He leaves the School, matured chiefly through him, in an admirable system. He has exhibited in his own Classes a model of perfect teaching, and he has established witnesses of his kindness, vigour, and success, in grateful and eminent pupils, scattered over every quarter of the globe.

Ill-health forced Archdeacon Williams to retire from Llandovery College in 1853. He died at Bushey, in Hertfordshire, in 1858 at the age of sixty-six; and the man who ministered to him at the end and conducted the service at his funeral was his favourite and most distinguished pupil, Archibald Campbell Tait, then Bishop of London but shortly to become the first Scotsman to be Primate of All England.

Later, when Tait (now His Grace the Archbishop of Canterbury) presided at the Jubilee Dinner of the Edinburgh Academy in 1874, he said of his old headmaster: 'As a strong man intellectually improves those amongst whom he lives by the very conversation which is his pleasure, so this man taught us in a way that none but a very able man indeed can teach. He had his faults, as who has not? And many may conceive that these faults, as he grew older, predominated. He had, indeed, a strong opinion of his own powers . . . He was a man, and a real man; he taught as none but a man of great intellectual power could teach; and he fascinated his pupils as none but a man of feeling could those with whom he has to do.'

Throughout the whole of his Rectorship, it had never proved necessary to expel a boy – in itself a remarkable tribute to the disciplined but humane atmosphere he had fostered. His own educational ideals, both as a teacher and Rector, he had expressed firmly and clearly: 'The great object of Education is to form habits of intellectual exertion, to inspire an eager thirst for knowledge, to kindle the imagination, to chasten the judgement, to refine the taste, and to render the Pupil anxious to distinguish himself in after life as an intelligent and rational being.'

When he had come to it as a young man of thirty-two in 1824, the Academy was a brand-new building and a disparate collection of boys and inexperienced masters. When he left it in 1847, he left a school – a living, breathing entity of character, personality, tradition, reputation and influence. Now the time had come to find another man to carry on the tradition – and it was going to be no easy task to follow him.

It was a subject that greatly exercised the thoughts of Lord Cockburn, now nearly seventy years old but still as vigorous and downright as ever, and still as deeply concerned about the destiny of the school he had created. A century later, in 1947, a letter came to light that gives us a vivid insight into the old man's mind. It was found in Liverpool in a collection of disregarded family papers by an Academical, Dr Gerald Wallace (E.A. 1878–85), whose mother's first husband had been another Academical, James Mitford Morison (E.A. 1836–43), later Sheriff-Substitute for Lanark. When the question of a new Rector for the Academy had come up early in 1847, Morison, who had been Dux of the School in 1843 and was now a student at Exeter College, Oxford, had written to Cockburn pressing the claims of a possible candidate for the Rectorship, the Rev. George Rawlinson of Oxford (later Canon of Canterbury). Lord Cockburn's reply of February 25, 1847 (now in the Academy archives), was typically robust:

'I hope Mr Rawlinson will come forward, tho' I beg you to *observe specially* that I don't mean by this to hold out anything approaching to an invitation; for at present no Titius has a better chance than any Marius. I only wish that we may have plenty wheat to pluck the tares from.

'And observe our peculiar danger in reference to a learned Oxonian. Their friends always attest their prodigious learning! universal knowledge!! high principles!! etc., but they *never* say a word about the one thing needful, their *experience* in the *practical teaching* of *masses* of *boys, at once*. A learned and elegant pundit who has converted a few old blockheads, by private tuition, into double firsts or double quadruples, is utterly wasted upon us. We don't [want] to hear of an Oxford Candidate's power of *acquiring* – which however is the only thing attested – but of his power of *communicating*. Did Rawlinson ever look fifty boys in the face in his life? If not, *you know* that his being your best Lecturer and Sub-Rector does not even *tend* to shew that he is fit for us. Indeed for a *Provincial School*, however high, it seems to me that there is a certain English University perfection which positively *disqualifies* a man by its mere eminence, and the fineness of its habits. We have never succeeded yet in obtaining a single Oxford, or indeed English, scholar, who has done well in the Academy. I don't except Williams, for he is not English, but Welsh, and was bred up to *teach* a large *school* of *boys* from his youth.

'I hope we shall succeed now; but certainly not by mistaking a scholar for a teacher.

'Now what do you say to this? Answer, and *speedily*. Does Tate know Mr Rawlinson? – for he knows us, and his opinion would go far. I hope he is aware of the exact nature of our place. If he fancies he is to have £5,000 a year and be bowed to as if his thighs had a black apron across them, he will be mistaken . . .'

There is no record of what Lord Cockburn thought of the appointment when it was eventually made on May 26 'after a mature and anxious deliberation'; for the new Rector of the Academy was a young man who seemed to stand for everything Lord Cockburn disliked. His name was John Hannah.

CHAPTER IX

Dr Hannah: Masters and Boys (1847-54)

... The cry was raised "The Rector! The Rector!" And we saw away in the distance a little black figure making straight for the scene of the battle at full running speed. Instantly the whole school took to flight in the opposite direction. It was a triumph of the moral over the physical – one man putting hundreds to flight with an innocent umbrella ...   (*Chronicle*, 1900)

W HEN the Rev. John Hannah was appointed Rector of the Edinburgh Academy in 1847, he was only twenty-nine years of age, younger even than Mr Sheepshanks had been, and many of his friends wondered why on earth he should choose to give up a thriving tutorship in Oxford to run a boys' school in Edinburgh. But J. H. Overton, Canon of Lincoln and Rector of Epworth, who wrote 'A Clerical Study' of Dr Hannah in 1890, had an answer:

'The post was an honourable and lucrative one ... Next to Oxford and Cambridge, there was no place in the United Kingdom which a man of literary tastes and talents would select for his home sooner than Edinburgh. The natural and artificial beauties of the city, the fame of its literary society, its fresh sea-breezes, so wholesome alike for body and mind, would all render it attractive to a cultivated man ... The Rector had all his afternoons after three o'clock, all his evenings, and every Saturday and Sunday free; so the work allowed ample room for social and literary pursuits. The material upon which he had to work was good; for the Academy had always had a succession of hard-headed, clever boys, and industry was the tradition of the place ... So tempting a post was with good reason eagerly sought; and Hannah had to compete with a number of exceptionally able candidates, among whom may be especially named the late Dr Mansel, afterwards Dean of St Paul's; Mr George Rawlinson, now Canon of Canterbury; and ... Sir Francis Sandford, of the Education Department, and Under-Secretary for Scotland. There was a close contest between the last-named and Hannah, but in the end Mr Hannah was elected.' (*John Hannah*, pp. 49–50.)

In fact, as the Directors were pleased to note in their *Report* of 1847, among the candidates 'there were no less than five who had obtained first-class honours at Oxford – a fact quite unprecedented in the history of any Scottish institution'.

He was born in Lincoln in 1818, the son of a Wesleyan minister, and was educated at St Saviour's School, Southampton, and Oxford. After graduating from Brasenose and Corpus Christi, he had taken up a country parish at Woodford, near Oxford, but in 1845 he had returned to Oxford as a Fellow of Lincoln College, where he became the leading science and logic tutor in Oxford. There he coached students whom Overton described as 'the picked men of all England, who were being prepared for by far the most severe and eventful ordeal in the way of examination which they would ever be called upon to pass' – the Classical Finals (Greats).

From all this John Hannah came to take over the Edinburgh Academy, so youthful-looking that more than one parent had grave doubts about his suitability for the job, and when he preached in Portobello one Sunday he was described by a member of the congregation as 'a fine lad'. He was small, slender, and delicately built, with long raven-black hair, fine features, an aquiline nose, bright eyes and alert movements. What a stir there was among the ladies who were invited to be present, when he appeared at his first Exhibition Day, immaculate as always in clerical garb with snow-white linen and lilac gloves, and moved about the crowded Hall, his flowing black hair standing out against the shining white tie and shirt-front. But alas for them, he was already married.

Despite the slightness of his build, he had no difficulty in establishing his authority as Rector over the boys, especially when he introduced a little black notebook in which misdemeanours were noted for future reference. He could reduce the boldest of offenders to abject repentance by pointing out the evil of their ways with a fund of moral earnestness, and no junior could be summoned before him without being over-awed by his presence and tones. An anonymous member of the Trotter Class of 1846–53, writing in the *Chronicle* (October, 1900) could still vividly remember an occasion when nearly all the pupils had gathered after hours in an open place near Pitt Street to watch a forbidden fight between two of the boys: the merest glimpse of the Rector's small black figure racing down towards them from school brandishing his umbrella was enough to put the whole school to headlong flight. It was, said the writer, 'a triumph of the moral over the physical – one man putting hundreds to flight with an innocent umbrella as completely as Samson in earlier days had killed his thousand Philistines with the jaw-bone of the ass.'

But he was considerably less successful when he resorted to using the tawse against the senior boys, some of whom were taller than himself: 'I remember one case when this was done, and when we had to witness the little man rising on his little toes, and endeavouring with his infantile muscles to inflict severe corporal chastisement on a lad who towered above him, and on whom his worst efforts were quite ineffectual to cause serious pain. The rest of us were like boys with a broken rib bound round and round with flannel: we dared not laugh, and yet the whole spectacle was irresistibly absurd and indescribably funny.'

But in all other ways he took the greatest care to maintain his dignity and the dignity of his position; for instance, he would never pronounce a French word in case his pronunciation was not quite up to the mark and would thereby expose him to ridicule.

But despite these entertaining glimpses of his personality, Dr Hannah remains a curiously insubstantial figure compared with his flamboyant predecessor. He only stayed at the Academy for seven years, and he made two unsuccessful applications for jobs elsewhere (the first, for the Headmastership of Rugby, only two years after he came to Edinburgh) before he was appointed Warden of Trinity College, Glenalmond, in 1854; and when he left, somewhat abruptly, he had hardly any further association with the Academy. Yet he was a brilliant teacher – everyone was agreed about that. And in his short time he did a great number of good things for the Academy, and initiated a number of innovations which brought immense and far-reaching benefits to the school – in particular, the acquisition of the first Academy playing-fields (p. 165).

Perhaps, after all, he was too young when he got the job; for it was only after he left the Academy for Glenalmond that his real genius for Headmastership came to the fore. It emerged then that he was a marvellous *manager* of a school – and if there was one thing that the Directors desperately needed, and were going to need even more desperately, it was a Rector who was also a business manager. Perhaps if he had been a little older when he came to the Academy, or if he had been allowed to exercise his real talents to the full earlier, he would have stayed on to become one of the truly great Rectors; he would certainly have steered the Academy through its later troubles more adroitly than most.

As it was, it is not Dr Hannah but the masters and boys from the 'forties who make the most immediate impression on the mind.

There were some formidable members of staff at the Academy at that period. No fewer than four of the Classical Masters became University Professors: Patrick Campbell MacDougall (1836–44) as Professor of Moral Philosophy at Edinburgh University, and Dr Payne Smith (1847–53) as Regius Professor of Divinity and Canon of Christ Church, Oxford, while two others got chairs at Aberdeen – George Ferguson (1824–47) as Professor of Humanity at King's College, and Dr Robert MacLure (1846–52) as Professor of Humanity at Marischal College.

One long-serving Classical Master had recently died in harness when Mr Hannah started as Rector: Archibald N. Carmichael, known as 'Bowsey', who had been one of the original Masters appointed in 1824. Henry Cockburn had had no very high opinion of him at the original interview: 'I have seen him,' he noted on Carmichael's testimonials. 'Looks ill, vulgar, ill-fed and dour; very like an intense under-Dominie. Yet Pillans raves about him.' The testimonial from Dr Pillans, former Headmaster of the High School, had carried the day, and Mr Carmichael went on to serve the Academy faithfully and well, and was later to gain, posthumously, the accolade of a couplet from Rector Mackenzie:

> *Carmichael ruled a hunder' Geits*
> *A' fechtin', flytin', tumblin' brats.*

He also had a quiverful of sons who were all educated at the Academy. In a way, these five sons were a microcosm of the Academy world, both educational and professional, of the time. The eldest, John Carmichael, took over his father's class after his death as interim teacher in 1857, and went on to gain renown at the High School as the redoubtable 'Bunkie' Carmichael. One brother became a solicitor, another a banker in the Far East, a third, William, who was Dux of the School in 1852, became a surgeon to Royalty. The second eldest, James ('Skinny'), who was runner-up for the Dux medal in 1846, became the first Academical to be a master at the Academy and was one of its longest-serving members of staff, from 1856 to his death in harness, like his father, in 1894. He was a much-loved teacher, even though badly prepared homework was an abomination to him. He was a gentle, kindly man, rather delicate in health (he sometimes had 'bales of cotton wadding adorning his ears', one of his pupils recalled), with a nervous, highly-strung temperament. Yet he had a way of keeping impeccable order in class without ever having to throw his weight about. When the present system of allocating the boys into four Divisions for games and other purposes was instituted in 1905, one of them was named in his memory (the others are *Cockburn*, after Lord Cockburn; *Houses*, for the boarders; and *Kinross*, named after Lord Kinross, Lord President of the Court of Session, Dux of the School in 1855 as John Blair Balfour, first President of the reconstituted Academical Club from 1900, and a Director of the Academy from 1882 until his death in 1905).

In 1909, 'Skinny' Carmichael's name was further commemorated by the institution of a prize for the runner-up in classics in the Classical Sixth – the *Carmichael Class Club* (1859–66) *Prize*, nowadays awarded as the Carmichael Prize for the best in 1st Year Classical VIIth. A marble memorial to him was designed by one of his former pupils, Sir Robert Lorimer (E.A. 1877–82), the architect of the Thistle Chapel in St Giles' and the National War Memorial in Edinburgh Castle. It was originally in the Hall, but is now set into the wall of the porch of what used to be his classroom (No. 9).

Another Classical Master whose name was long commemorated among Academicals was John Trotter – 'Old Trot'. He was a shepherd's son from the Lammermuirs, who had been taught by a renowned country dominie in Duns, in Berwickshire, and he had risen to be Rector of Musselburgh Academy before he joined the Edinburgh Academy in 1846. He was a tall, spindly-legged man with spectacles, whose hair always seemed to be standing on end as if to illustrate one of his favourite Latin verbs – '*horreo*, I stand on end, I bristle up, I am erect through fear.' He was a homely, down-to-earth man with a broad Scotch accent and no pretensions about himself; he was never too vain to admit it if he came across a Latin passage he did not fully understand at once. When translating, he would harangue the author: 'Coom, Mr Tacitus, coom, give us another word to help us. Ye're most vexatiously terse the day,' or 'Oh, Mr Cicero, ye're most partial to that word *videatur*.' He covered himself with glory one morning when the two members of staff in holy orders were absent from school, and he had to step into the breach to conduct Prayers; everyone was entranced with his inspired adaptations of the polished phraseology of the printed prayer-book into couthy Scots, whereby 'Prevent us, O Lord, with Thy most gracious favour' became, in 'Old Trot's' vivid rendering, 'O Lord, swape us not away with the beesoms

of destruction.' He was not the most polished scholar on the staff, nor
the most imaginative teacher, but he was successful and deservedly
popular, and forty years after his death in 1861 the anonymous member
of his Class of 1846–53 still remembered him with great affection in the
Chronicle in 1900. The most brilliant pupil of that Class, George R.
Luke, the son of a Stockbridge master baker, took all the available
prizes from the Seventh Class while he was still in the Sixth, and became Dux of the School when he reached the Seventh himself the
following year; and he was complimented at the Exhibition for never
having been assisted by a private tutor during the whole time he had
been at school (a rare distinction in those days). Luke had a spectacular
academic career at Glasgow University, 'where he distanced all competitors, while his magnanimity disarmed their jealousy,' and also at
Balliol College, Oxford; had he not drowned in 1862 at the age of
twenty-five he might well have become the most distinguished
Academical scholar of them all. And from his last Class of 1854–61, Mr
Trotter produced one of the greatest scholar-journalists of the nineteenth century, Andrew Lang, who wrote a host of books on history,
mythology, anthropology and literature, and translated the *Iliad* and
the *Odyssey*.

But it was another Classical Master from the 1840's who gets most
prominence in any history of the Edinburgh Academy, because in a
way he made history himself: in 1850, Dr James Cumming gave his
name to the most renowned Class Club to be formed.

MR CUMMING

A high-minded honourable gentleman of large attainments and wide sympathies . . .
(Chronicles of the Cumming Club)

When the unfortunate Mr Marriott had retired to Cambridge, defeated,
after two years of trying to cope with his unruly Class in 1824 and
1825, the Directors did not look for another Englishman as his successor. Instead they chose a Scot. James Cumming had been born in
Edinburgh in 1800; his father, who came from Morayshire, was a
Classical teacher in Edinburgh, and James went to the High School and
Edinburgh University before becoming head teacher of the Quakers'
Seminary in Darlington. He stayed on at the Academy for twenty
years, and only left in 1846 on being appointed 'Rector of a Seminary
about to be instituted in Glasgow' – the Glasgow Academy, in fact.

top left: Archbishop Tait *top right:* James Clerk Maxwell
bottom left: Viscount Finlay *bottom right:* Robert Louis Stevenson

International Match, 1886; Charles 'Hippo' Reid is the forward in the right foreground runni[...]
back in support.

Academy 1st XV, 1910-11; the captain (holding the ball) is H. F. W. W. Buchan, on his ri[...]
is W. M. Crabbie, directly behind him is N. G. Salvesen. Second from the left in the b[...]
row is W. M. Wallace. On the right of the front row is A. T. Sloan.

Mr Cumming was Rector of Glasgow Academy for only five years, and is not remembered in the centenary history of *The Glasgow Academy 1846–1946* with any great enthusiasm, for when he resigned in 1851 to become one of H.M. Inspectors of Schools for Scotland, the school was in serious financial trouble, and there was to be no Rector at all at the Glasgow Academy for the next ten years. But Mr Cumming never lost touch with his old Edinburgh Academy pupils, and in 1850, the year he was made an LL.D. of Glasgow University, thirteen young men met in the Café Royal in Edinburgh under the presidency of Sir George Home, Bart, where it was resolved: 'That those present do form themselves into a Club to be called *The Edinburgh Academy, 1841– 46, Cumming Club*: that all those who attended Dr Cumming's First Class in 1841, and Fifth in 1846, or any one or more of the intervening years, be entitled to admission; that the design in instituting the Club is to promote good feeling generally among the members of the Class, to stimulate friendship by intercourse among those of them who have had the good fortune to be still within its reach, to revive mutual interest with those whom circumstances have dispersed, and to testify the respectful regard which they cherish for their former teacher.' By the end of the year, twenty-two of that Class of ninety-seven had joined the Cumming Club.

The originator and first secretary of the Cumming Club was Doyle (later Sir Doyle) Money Shaw, who was then a medical student and ended up as Inspector-General of Hospitals for the Navy. One of the members of the Club was a young man who was to serve the Academy well for the rest of his long and distinguished life – Andrew Beatson Bell of Kilduncan, advocate (E.A. 1841–8), who was Dux of the School in 1848, Secretary to the Directors from 1857–62 and thereafter a Director from 1862 until his death in 1913 as Chairman of the Prison Commissioners for Scotland. In some *Reminiscences* written for the Academy archives in 1905, Beatson Bell recalled: 'We looked upon ourselves as Cumming's boys, and our relationship to all the other masters as a thing of very minor importance. This had the effect, I think, of increasing our *esprit de corps* and to form friendships in the class which in many cases have proved life-long. We were very fortunate in our Class Master, Dr Cumming. He had an excellent way with the boys and won their hearts. He was a licentiate of the Free Church of Scotland, but I think never held a charge, and I do not remember that he was ever called "the Rev."'

There were to be many Class Clubs formed down the years, cementing the social cohesion of the one-master classes, but the Cumming Club also had the distinction of having its history written and published in 1887 by one of its members, Lt.-Col. Alexander Fergusson (E.A. 1841–6). His *Chronicles of the Cumming Club* are a vivid and chatty account of those early years at the Academy.

Col. Fergusson recalled his first day at the Academy in 1841, when the school had been in existence for seventeen years. There was an unusually large crowd of small boys gathered to join the Geits Class that day because of the reputation of the master who was starting it: 'Mr Cumming had secured for himself the reputation of a high-minded honourable gentleman of large attainments and wide sympathies, which took the form of the most genial and kindly bearing towards his boys.' Certainly, his pupils liked him; he was firm without being harsh, kind without being weak, and above all he was fair. He demanded discipline in class, but he tempered it with humour. When he cuffed a boy for dazzling another with a bit of looking-glass in the sun, he softened the blow by remarking, to the delight of the boys, that he allowed nobody to 'cast reflections' on his class. And there were amusing moments during the time that efforts were being made to 'soften' the Scotch pronunciation of Latin: when a new boy pronounced 'Menelaus' with the broad Scots *a*, Mr Cumming asked, 'Who is Mene*laws*? I only know an excellent tea-merchant of that name.'

He sometimes threatened 'a tremendous flogging' but his heart was never in it, and the boys knew they could always rely on his absolute fairness. Col. Fergusson remembered an occasion which left a great impression on him and his class-mates. During the headlong rush of boys down the steps to the Yards after school, the boys at the front tried to stop to let Rector Williams past but were pushed from behind, so that one of them tramped heavily on the Archdeacon's toes. It was useless to speak of being shoved from behind: Archdeacon Williams took the two front boys back to their class and angrily reported to Mr Cumming 'a most deliberate and unprovoked aggression'. In vain did the two boys protest their innocence: the Rector had seen everything and, as it was late, Mr Cumming had to promise them the tawse first thing in the morning. With resignation the boys made their way to the tan-yard opposite the Academy gates and immersed their hands in the liquid in the tan-pit which was optimistically believed to be especially efficacious in hardening the palms against the ravages of the tawse. Sadly, they acknowledged that faced with Punch's evidence,

Mr Cumming had no alternative but to carry out the punishment. But next morning, when they were called out by Mr Cumming, to everyone's surprise he merely told them to go back to their seats and 'take care another time'. The verdict of the class was that their shrewd and fair-minded teacher had seen through the Rector's excitable account of the incident to the real truth of the matter. Mr Cumming was more firmly in favour than ever.

Violence was an accepted part of the life of a schoolboy in those days, and the younger boys had to suffer much at the hands of the bullies of the upper classes, who, wrote Col. Fergusson, 'wove unto them cunning (and cutting) lashes of hard whip-cord, which, attached to the shafts of "clackens", became as scorpions in their hands.' The only way the smaller boys could get their own back was when a crowd of them happened to meet one of the big boys on his own after school: 'Then did his shin-bones click, and his toes resound with a dull thud, under the sharp impact of the "clacken's" edge, wielded by small but determined hands!' (*Cumming Club*, p. 23).

There were also pitched battles ('cad-fights') on the way home between local lads and the Academy boys, who banded together for the perilous walk through Stockbridge with look-outs posted ahead and clackens ever at the ready. Another favourite home-going pastime was navigating the Water of Leith in the days before it was embanked. From Stockbridge upwards to Bell's Mills the stream deteriorated into a series of stagnant pools choked with weeds and filth, and the game was to play follow-my-leader, leaping from rock to rock up the slippery bed of the river. By the time the Dean Bridge was reached there were few, if any, who had not fallen in, and many a boy had to go home soaked and coated with green slime.

On hot days the whole school would retreat to the sloping green banks behind the Academy building to play 'Knifey', a game which later became very popular in America. It consisted of seeing who could best drop the knife, blade first, into the ground from various positions – the end of each finger, or each knee, the tip of each boot, the point of the nose, indeed from every possible angle and with numerous complicated gambits. The penalty for the loser was to have to pull out with his teeth a sharpened peg of wood driven into the ground by the winner with a single kick of his heel.

Football was played in the Yards, but according to Col. Fergusson it was 'a game of the most primitive kind; crude, and devoid of regulation or rule; hardly recognisable in the complicated manly

Rugby game now played at the Academy. In those days the most cruel "hacking" with iron-toed and -heeled boots was allowed, and suffered, in what was called a "muddle" – the modern "maul".' The ball was a raw bladder, *fresh* – but that is hardly the word – from the butcher's hands, enclosed in the leather case. The "blowing" of this contrivance was a disgusting operation in which a quill was used as a mouth-piece. The process was taken in turns as a necessary, but repulsive, duty – one not without risks. Consequently it was considered prudent to perform the operation of orally inflating the bag *at home*, because, as certainly as anyone attempted to do so at school, somebody would watch his opportunity and, when the bag was three-quarters filled, *squash* the whole thing flat. The effect of the foul blast from the unsavoury interior of the ball, thus forced down the throat of the unhappy blower, is not to be described.' Nor, apparently, was the smell when the loose gravel of the Yards (ah, the marks those sharp flints made on generations of small Academy knees!) wore a hole in the leather through which the bladder pushed its way and burst.

For cricket, however, a ball with thick coarse leather was used to withstand the effect of the stones. Sir J. H. A. Macdonald, Lord Justice-Clerk of Scotland and later Lord Kingsburgh, who was in Mr Cumming's last Geits Class in 1846, tells in his *Life Jottings of an Old Edinburgh Citizen* (1915), how the boys used to chalk the wickets on the walls of the Yards, and use the chalk itself as umpire: 'The batsman was out when there was a chalk mark on the ball.' (*Jottings*, p. 153.) The first recorded school cricket matches, against the High School and the Scottish Naval and Military Academy (both of which the Academy won), took place in 1832. By the 1840s, Col. Fergusson reported an annual match between each class of the Academy and the corresponding XI at the High School, and an annual encounter between the School XIs. These matches were played at the upper end of Bruntsfield Links, and once the boys had taken off their jackets and laid them in a heap, the game was on: 'There were no flannels, fielding jackets, cricketing caps, pretty ties, nor newspaper paragraphs in those remote ages. Pads were rarely used, and hardly necessary, seeing that the bowler's hand was strictly kept down by law. Much of the bowling was "under hand". But while the attack has been revolutionised, and doubtless improved, it is not certain that the graceful game of Gavin Young, or the slashing bat-play of Henry McVitie – those Anakim of "the Seventh" – has been surpassed.' (*Cumming Club*, p. 55.)

In his *Reminiscences*, Andrew Beatson Bell recalled playing Hailes and a form of fives, using clackens, against the walls of various class-rooms, and he found that when lawn tennis came into vogue, long after he had left the Academy, 'to my astonishment I found myself at once a tolerable player, a fact which I attributed, rightly, I believe, to previous clacken practice in the Yards. With the clackens we learned to hit a small racket-ball with considerable accuracy, and the larger tennis racket and ball came comparatively easily.'

He also recalled a game called 'Prisoners' Base' which they had played in the Yards: 'There was no ball used, and it was a sort of more highly developed "tig". Sides of equal number were chosen and they occupied two "dens" as I think they were called. A boy from one side went in front of the other, which was called giving "Cavé". He was immediately pursued by one of the enemy, he again by one of the side which gave "Cavé", and so on till one was touched by his pursuer. He was then put "in prison" a good way out, and could be rescued by being touched by one of his side, if the rescuer could escape touch from the opposition. It was an excellent game for warming the boys during the short interval.'

'DAFTY': JAMES CLERK MAXWELL

> Dear auld Academy! Queer auld Academy!
> A merry lot were we, I wot,
> When at the auld Academy!
> (*Academy Song*, by James Clerk Maxwell)

There was one small boy who took no part in these playground games. He was in the class above Mr Cumming's, but he was the same age as Cumming's boys and was friendly with one of them, Peter Guthrie Tait – as friendly, at least, as he ever got to be with any boy in his early years at the Academy; for James Clerk Maxwell was a loner, a strange, sad-looking boy with a long face, a high forehead, and an awkward, gangling gait that earned him the nickname 'Dafty' almost as soon as he arrived at the Academy in 1841 from his home in Kirk-cudbrightshire, dressed in the most outlandish fashion.

He was ten years old then, the son of an Edinburgh advocate, but he had spent most of his childhood in the wilds of Galloway. His mother died when he was eight, and thereafter James spent most of his time with his father, who had a consuming interest in nature and scientific matters. Young James used to spend hours on his own watching butterflies in the sunshine, or playing with a kaleidoscope or with his favourite toy, a *diabolo* or 'devil on two sticks' – a game in which a two-headed top is spun, tossed and caught on a string attached between two sticks held one in each hand. James, who looked so awkward and ungainly alongside more athletic boys, was extremely skilful with his hands, and he could do almost anything with the *diabolo*, which was his constant companion. He could jump over it and bring it round him without letting go of the sticks, and he could keep it going behind his back. He was fascinated by its possiblities, as he was intensely curious about how everything worked. His favourite expressions as a child were 'Show me how it *doos*' and 'What does it *do*?' or 'What is the *go* of that?', followed by 'But what is the *particular* go of that?' He had an amazing memory, and at eight he could recite all of the marathon 119th Psalm.

But as far as the other small boys at the Academy were concerned, 'Dafty' was only good for a laugh, especially when he turned up on his first day at school wearing a rough tweed tunic, with a skirt, and a frilly collar, and home-made square-toed boots with brass buckles. Boys never make allowances for domestic circumstances, and within an hour he was in his first fight and arrived back home minus the skirt and with the frilly collar in tatters. Then the boys discovered that one of 'Dafty's' strange skills was the ability to squat and jump like a frog, and the bullies with their whips would goad him into jumping back and forward over a handkerchief until he was exhausted. Once he exploded into such a fury that even the biggest boys got a fright, and he was left alone after that. But the games he played by himself – watching butterflies, pole-jumping, doing wild gymnastics in trees, and making friends with frogs and water-rats – only confirmed their impression that he was daft, especially since he wasn't very good at his lessons. He was a poor scholar at first and had great difficulty with his classical studies. The highest position he achieved in class was four-teenth – until he reached Mr Gloag. Then it became obvious that this boy had a brain for mathematics, and his self-confidence grew so much that he also began to do well in Latin and Greek. Even before starting to do geometry at the age of thirteen, he wrote to his father to say that he had made 'a tetrahedron, a dodecahedron, and two other hedrons whose names I don't know'. He was soon leading the maths class, and he took the Mathematics Medal in the Fifth, as well as first place for English. Next year, at fifteen, he wrote a paper which was read to the Royal Society of Edinburgh on 'Ovals of the form $mr + nr^1 = $ const, and practical methods of drawing them'; this was a development of the familiar idea of drawing an ellipse with the help of two pins and a piece of thread. He just missed being Dux of the School in his final year in 1847; he was beaten to it by the brilliant classical scholar Lewis Campbell, later Professor of Greek at St Andrews University, who after his schoolboy rival's death wrote the *Life of James Clerk Maxwell* (1882).

For 'Dafty' turned out to be a genius; the ugly duckling grew into an intellectual swan. He went on to Edinburgh University with Peter Guthrie Tait, and there he studied mathematics, physics and moral philosophy, continued his private experiments on polarised light that he had found so absorbing with his kaleidoscope, and wrote another paper for the Royal Society, on rolling curves, when he was not yet eighteen. When he was nineteen he attended a meeting of the British Association in Edinburgh and astonished the audience by standing up and arguing a point with Sir David Brewster, the eminent Scottish physicist who had won distinction for his discoveries on the polarisation of light. This brought Maxwell to the notice of Lord Kelvin, another great scientist and then Professor of Natural Philosophy at Glasgow University, whose experiments in the field of electricity, along with those of Michael Faraday, became the stimulus for Clerk Maxwell's tremendous contribution to that field of physical science.

After three years at Edinburgh he moved to Cambridge, where he and Peter Guthrie Tait, now his inseparable friend, took the Mathematical Tripos. But whereas Tait achieved the coveted first place as Senior Wrangler (and a dinner in his honour given by the Cumming Club, with his old Maths Master, Dr Gloag, sharing his triumph), Clerk Maxwell, two years later, only managed Second Wrangler. As always he was hampered by his inability to rein in his galloping intelligence and to set down his thoughts in coherent terms understandable to ordinary minds. Besides, the work for his Tripos was only a small part of his boundless activities. He was conducting his private experiments all the time. He was reading, arguing, expounding his theories in letters and papers. He wrote poetry, both serious poems and light, jocular verses, for he always had a tremendous sense of fun. He walked, swam, and sculled. And, as it was when he was a boy, while he played he worked, and work was play. His mind was always searching, always finding answers.

And just what answers did he find that made his contribution to scientific knowledge so important? To quote from *Chambers's Biographical Dictionary*: 'In 1873 he published his great *Treatise on Electricity and Magnetism*, which treats mathematically Faraday's theory of electrical and magnetic forces considered as action in a medium rather than action at a distance. He also contributed to the study of colour vision, and to the kinetic theory of gases, but his greatest work was his theory of electromagnetic radiation.' Basically, he discovered theoretically the connection between electricity and light – that light is electrical in nature. The electromagnetic waves he predicted were later discovered in the laboratory – the 'wireless waves' that carry radio, television, radar and so on.

To the unscientific lay mind, one simple achievement seems impressive enough: in May, 1861, he made the first colour photograph (of a tartan ribbon) and showed it at the Royal Institution in London. But his work was also the inspiration that stimulated Einstein to present the world with his Theory of Relativity. A contributor to the *Chronicle* in 1931, Clerk Maxwell's centenary year, cited Professor Sir A. S. Eddington from the Observatory at Cambridge, who had visited Einstein in Berlin and noticed that there were just three portraits on his study walls, those of Sir Isaac Newton, Michael Faraday, and James Clerk Maxwell: 'Your former Academy boy was famous in his lifetime, but his genius is far more appreciated now.' One of the leading physicists in America, Professor R. A. Millikan, described him as 'one of the most penetrating intellects of all time'.

Clerk Maxwell was Professor of Natural Philosophy at Marischal College, Aberdeen; Professor of Natural Philosophy in King's College, London; first Professor of Experimental Physics at Cambridge University. He was President of Cambridge Philosophical Society; F.R.S.; Rumford Medallist; LL.D. of Edinburgh University; and D.C.L. of Oxford. He was only 49 when he died in 1879.

It's an astonishing coincidence that two of the giants of nineteenth-century physics, James Clerk Maxwell and Peter Guthrie Tait, should have come from the same age-group in the same school (I wonder what the mathematical odds against that are?). Yet James Clerk Maxwell was just one boy – and an unpromising one at that – from just one class at the Edinburgh Academy in its early years. Every year, boys left the school to make their mark to a greater or lesser degree on a world which was expanding in every direction – in science, the arts, industry, transport, navigation – and rumbling to the sounds of gunfire as nations struggled for independence and Queen Victoria's dreams of empire made heroes out of Mr Gloag's 'booies' . . .

HEROES

> Domi suboles est nota
> Atque loca per remota
> (*Floreat Academia*)

One of the Rector's most pleasant duties was reading out the annual list of awards and honours and appointments gained by Academicals around the world. It made a thankful change from the reports of falling numbers, rising fees and a rapidly increasing debt as the hard-pressed Directors strove to cope with the embarrassed state of the Academy funds. Fire, thunderstorms, cholera epidemics, the collapse of the school's source of credit (the Kinnear banking house in 1834), salary demands by the masters, prejudice against classical education, and a national slump, all contributed to bring about a financial crisis so severe that an Appeal had to be launched in 1849 for £2,000 to save the school from imminent closure (pp. 159–60).

But the Directors were always cheered and encouraged by the Rector's annual *Reports* of Academical achievements. It had always been so since Archibald Campbell Tait, that golden boy, the son of a W.S. from Clackmannan, had gone off with his two Dux Medals (1826 and 1827) to win Glasgow University's first prizes in Latin Verse and Metrical Translation from Latin, the Blackstone Examination, and the Silver Medal for Latin and Greek. He then beat twenty-two contestants, including the Dux of Charterhouse and four distinguished pupils of the great Dr Butler of Shrewsbury, for a scholarship to Oxford. From then on, successive Rectors were gratified to announce his Snell Exhibition at Balliol, his B.A. there, his Fellowship there, and his consequent stream of appointments and honours: Junior Dean at Balliol; Tutor and Logic Examiner; Classical Examiner; LL.D. of Glasgow University and D.C.L. of Oxford; successor to the great Dr Arnold as Headmaster of Rugby, where he introduced some Academy ideas with good results; Dean of Carlisle; Bishop of London; and then finally – the highest prize of all – Archbishop of Canterbury (1869–82).

It is an extraordinary coincidence that one of Tait's classmates in that first year of the Academy, Henry Davidson (E.A. 1824–6), became the father of *another* Archbishop of Canterbury. His son, Randall Thomas Davidson, who went to Harrow, became chaplain to Archbishop Tait and Queen Victoria, married Tait's daughter, and was himself Archbishop of Canterbury from 1903–28. In 1891, he wrote a *Life* of Archbishop Tait, his father-in-law.

The other Tait, Peter Guthrie Tait (no relation), from Dalkeith, followed up his Senior Wrangler triumph at Cambridge by becoming Professor of Mathematics at Queen's College, Belfast, at the age of twenty-three, then Professor of Natural Philosophy at Edinburgh when he was twenty-seven (beating his friend James Clerk Maxwell for the Chair). He produced twenty-two books and 365 papers, his most famous publication being the *Treatise on Physics* in collaboration with Lord Kelvin. He held the chair at Edinburgh for forty-one years, almost until his death in 1901, as one of the most renowned scientists and mathematicians of his time in Europe.

In the Cumming Class of 1841–6 with Peter Guthrie Tait was Henry Charles Fleeming Jenkin, son of a naval officer from Kent. He organised a Philosophical Society when he was in the Rector's Class, and at meetings round his mother's mahogany table in Northumberland Street, boys who had never had a science lesson at school read papers to one another on geology and chemistry, and held scientific outings on Saturdays to quarries and hillsides in search of fossils and other geological and botanical specimens. Fleeming Jenkin left the Academy to study engineering on the Continent, but returned to be Professor of Engineering at Glasgow, London, and Edinburgh Universities. He supervised the laying of the first cable across the Alantic, the Red Sea cable, and cables from Singapore to Batavia, and Malta to Alexandria. While mending one cable he discovered the fact of living organisms existing at a depth of 1,200 fathoms. He took out patents on many electrical appliances, bridge work, hydraulics, gearing and caloric meters. He was also a first-class amateur actor, and he and his wife presented French comedies and Greek plays at their house in Edinburgh.

One Dux of the School created a tremendous stir, as 'The Case of the Dux who didn't drown in the Danube' – George Drysdale (E.A. 1834–41), the Dux of 1841, who was the son of a Lord Provost of Edinburgh, Sir William Drysdale. In his annual *Report* for 1845, Rector Williams announced with sorrow that Drysdale, 'one of the most distinguished pupils of the Academy', had drowned the previous summer while bathing in the Danube; and one of the prize poems recited that year at the Exhibition was a set of Latin elegiacs – *In Juvenem Danubio Flumine Absumptum*. The evidence of his drowning had been purely circumstantial, however (his clothes had been found discarded on the riverbank), and a couple of years later the 'dead' Dux turned up again in Edinburgh, undisputably alive. He admitted that he had deliberately faked his own demise because he was overwhelmed by the high expectation of a brilliant career that any Academy Dux had to bear, and had felt himself unable to live up to it. In his new-found obscurity he took a degree in medicine at Edinburgh University and became a general practitioner in London, where he died in 1905. There is no other recorded instance of a Dux of the Academy finding the medal round his neck turning into such a millstone.

The Directors kept the school informed of the progress of their own sons who had been in the very first classes at the Academy. The son of James Skene of Rubislaw, who headed the first list of Directors, became Vice-Consul of Constantinople, was with Lord Stratford in the Crimean War, and became known in the deserts of Syria as Sheik ul Arab (Chief of the Arabs). Secretary Russell's son became a W.S., like his father and grandfather and great-grandfather before him. The son of William Wood, the surgeon, became a coffee planter in Brazil. Roger Aytoun's son, William, published a book of poetry, *Poland and Other Poems*, when he was seventeen, and became Professor of Rhetoric and Belles Lettres at Edinburgh University at the age of thirty-two, and a prolific writer and poet (including the celebrated *Lays of the Scottish Cavaliers*); he married the daughter of the flamboyant Professor John Wilson ('Christopher North'). Alexander Irving's son, George, became an advocate and vice-president of the British Archaeological Association. And Cockburn's six sons? Archibald William (E.A. 1824–30) became a doctor in London and a Government Inspector of Lunatic Asylums; James (E.A. 1824–30) just got married, according to the *Register*; George Fergusson (E.A. 1825–7) joined the Honourable East India Company's Service in Bengal, and became the Commissioner of Patna; Henry G. D. (E.A. 1828–34) died in Canada; Laurence (E.A. 1831–7) became a sheep farmer in Australia: and Francis Jeffrey (E.A. 1833–9) joined his big brother George in the H.E.I.C.S. in Bengal, and became Judge of Dacca and Judge of Sylhet.

Of that first crop of Academicals, one became a political agent in Karachi, one became first Superintendent of the Vernacular School of Medicine in India; another was Factor to the Duke of Sutherland at Scourie. There was a manager of the Bank of Madras, and a Governor of the Military Prison at Aldershot. One boy went on to publish *Tables of Logarithms* for use in insurance offices, one painted the portraits of Louis Napoleon and Archbishop Tait, and one went to Australia 'and was never heard of again'.

John Irving was lost on the Franklin Expedition in search of the North-West Passage in 1848. James Macaulay was the founder of the *Boys' Own Paper* and the *Girls' Own Paper*, and became Editor-in-Chief of all the Religious Tract Society's publications. Allan Duncan Stewart (E.A. 1841–7) did the mathematics of the Forth Bridge. Sir Edward James Harland (E.A. 1842–4) built up the great Belfast shipyard of Harland & Wolff. Marcus Dods, D.D. (E.A. 1843–8) became one of the foremost divines and Biblical scholars of the Free Church of Scotland. Lord Francis W. B. Douglas (E.A. 1859–62), the son of the Marquis of Queensberry, was killed on the way down after the first successful ascent of the Matterhorn in 1865.

They fought wars from China to Constantinople, across the deserts of Africa and the plains of India. Mr Marriott's unruly Fourth Class of 1824 contained no fewer than five future Admirals – Admirals W. E. A. Gordon and David Robertson-Macdonald, Vice-Admiral W. R. Rolland, and Rear-Admirals James Horseford Cockburn and James Dirom. Dr Payne Smith's Class of 1852–9 contained two future V.C.s who were both killed in the Afghan Campaign of 1878–9 – Major John Cook and Captain James Dundas. Twenty-seven of the Cumming Class of 1841–6 went into the Services and won thirty-nine military decorations, including 'six British and Foreign knightly *Orders*'. They had been well trained for battle by Mr George Roland and his sons, who taught gymnastics and swordsmanship at the Scottish Naval and Military Academy as well as at the Edinburgh Academy, and held a competition, known as the 'Assault', among all their pupils once a year in the Music Hall. The memory of the elegant figure of Mr Roland, looking like an old French Marquis in black silk stockings and knee breeches with short black jacket and rose-silk lapels, demonstrating the Quatre and Tierce, inspired many a young subaltern in the Crimea or the Punjab. They wrote to him frequently, describing cuts and thrusts that had saved their lives against swordsmen at Moodkee, Ferozeshah and Sobraon; and on such occasions old Mr Roland would go about for days radiating happiness.

George Burnes won glory with the 1st Bombay Fusiliers at the 'Forlorn Hope' assault on the Fort of Multan in 1848, and the surrender of 30,000 Sikhs at Poonah, but came to a tragic end in the Indian Mutiny. Naval Lieutenant Francis Grant Suttie, second son of Sir George Grant Suttie of Balgone in East Lothian, won the Order of

Medjidie of the Fifth Class, and the Crimean and Turkish War Medals for his conduct in the trenches before Sebastopol. Alexander Strange, of Balcaskie in Fife, helped to quell a rising of the Moplahs in Southern India, and was mentioned in despatches in the New Zealand War of 1863–5. William Clephane, fourth son of the Sheriff of Fife, died of cholera in the Punjab. Lt.-Col. Alexander Fergusson, son of the governor of Sierra Leone (and author of the *Chronicles of the Cumming Club*), helped in the capture of the Persian Army's camp in 1856. Henry Alexander Cockburn, grandson of Baron Cockburn of Cockpen, was wounded twice during the Indian Mutiny and finished up a General. Patrick Heron Watson of Burntisland served as a surgeon in the Crimea and specialised in amputations necessitated by frost-bite; he had trained at the Edinburgh Royal Infirmary under Professor James Syme, whose treatise on *The Excision of Diseased Joints* was published in 1831, and Professor James Young Simpson, who had discovered chloroform in 1847. William Maitland Heriot (E.A. 1827–31), later Vice-Admiral William Maitland-Dougall, served with distinction during the first Chinese War, and played golf with equal dash when he settled in Scotland; it is recorded that he won the King William IV Medal of the R. and A. in 1860 after spending all morning in the local lifeboat, pulling the stroke oar for five and a half hours in the bay in a gale of wind.

Those who survived came back to tell their tales at the annual dinners of the Cumming Club in Daunie's Tavern in Fleshmarket Close. Chief guest of honour was always Dr Cumming himself, who after his Rectorship of Glasgow Academy became one of Her Majesty's Inspectors of Schools. His after-dinner party-piece was always a rendering of the old song 'A wee bird cam' to oor ha' door', while Dr Gloag, who was also a regular guest, one night solemnly presented to the safe-keeping of the Club, amidst rapturous applause, that former scourge of his hosts, his tawse – hard, thin, black and sinister. It was put under lock and key by Harry Cheyne, W.S., along with a fragment that some bold spirit had cut off it many years before and sent to the Club from India. There was hilarious discussion on whether the word *tawse* was singular or plural; many years later when an English-born Rector, Dr Ferard, asked the same question in his early days in Edinburgh, he would be informed that it was 'singular at one end and plural at the other'.

Another honorary member of the Cumming Club was 'Hammy', Mr Hamilton, the Writing Master, whose free-and-easy classes were a haven in which boys could chat to each other as they executed copper-plate scripts decorated with highly ornamental capitals, for which they mixed their own colours from poppy petals and other plants gathered on the way to school. And M. Senebier, the French master (1840–50), often came too. 'Snibby' was a congenial dinner companion, far removed from the peppery Monsieur of the classroom. Rumour had it that he had been taken prisoner at Waterloo, and when he used the tawse the boys believed he was avenging himself for the humiliation he had suffered on the battlefield.

'Hammy' died in harness in 1852, and they drank a toast to his memory at the Cumming Club. But by that time, Class Clubs were beginning to sprout all over the place, and changes were coming thick and fast at the Academy . . .

CRISIS AND RESPONSE

I did not expect to survive the Academy.   (Lord Cockburn, October, 1848)

The financial crisis which burst on the Academy at the beginning of John Hannah's Rectorship had been building up ever since the opening of the school. The Academy had started its life in debt, because the cost of the buildings had exceeded by £1,371 the estimated £12,000 provided by the subscribers. The Directors had had it all neatly worked out: the subscriptions (shares) would pay for the buildings, the tuition fees would pay for the staff, and the class entrance fees would pay for the maintenance and running of the school. But the initial capital deficit, increased to £4,127 by the building of the Writing and Arithmetic Block, had knocked all their reckonings out. Two loans were taken out in the hope they could be paid off from the annual profits, but as the numbers of boys fell away, the fees failed to produce the required surplus, and all sorts of unexpected expenses arose – flaws in the new building, storm damage, wear and tear by the boys – and the debt obstinately refused to go away. In fact it grew. At one stage, in 1833–4, when the numbers started to plummet from 430 to 340 in two years, the kitty was so low that the Directors were unable to pay the Rector and masters their salaries to bring them up to the guaranteed minimum. The following year the Directors each advanced £67 10s. to guarantee the staff's incomes, and the masters declared themselves 'prepared to bear new losses' even though the Directors still owed them £413.

The staff's sense of involvement in the Academy's struggles for survival was illustrated again in the crisis of 1848–9 when they donated £100 towards reducing the debt. Were they just trying to preserve their own jobs, or were they already caught up in the feeling of loyalty to the old school which has kept the Academy going through so many vicissitudes? Certainly their standard of living, particularly that of the Rector and Classical Masters, was enviable at a time when children were being pushed up chimneys or down coal mines for a few pence a day, and a man had to keep a family of ten or twelve on less than 10s. a week. As late as 1874, the master jobbing gardeners of Edinburgh were reluctantly agreeing to increase the wages of their workmen from 1d. to 1¾d. per hour, and to reduce their working hours from fifty-six to fifty-one hours per week!

In 1831, the Academy Rector's income was £723 14s. and the Classical Masters earned an average of £357 11s. 11d., not counting their extra income for taking in school Boarders. For this they taught nearly five hours a day. Mr Gloag got £300 for just over four hours a day; the English Master got £311 for 4½ hours, the French Master got £162 for two hours, and the Writing Master £250 for nearly three hours. Constant and complicated efforts were made by the Directors to evolve a more equable system of distributing the tuition fees, but the Classical Masters were always the favoured ones in any such scheme, with a guaranteed salary, whereas Mr Gloag, the Maths Master and the only survivor in 1847 of the original staff, was always dependent on the number of fees.

One of the first of Mr Hannah's undertakings after his appointment was to try to get some sense into the system. 'I cannot see,' he wrote to the Directors, 'why a competent mathematician, able to conduct admirably that most important part of our teaching, should be placed on so much lower a level than the Classical Masters' (Mr Gloag's income was £220 that year, compared with £300–£350 for the Classical Masters). Mr Hannah went on to say that if it hadn't been for the temporary guaranteed salary arrangement he had with the Directors his own income that year would be £375 – rather less than the Classical Masters earned in some years. At this time the Rector's Seventh Class was down to five pupils, and the Directors agreed to allow him to start a Higher Seventh to include boys who had left school and wished to take extra coaching from the Rector.

In order to stabilise the system and iron out the anomalies, Mr Hannah proposed, at the masters' request, that the school fees should be raised. At this time they averaged £9 5s. 8½d., compared with

£8 10s. plus at the High School, where there was no English Master. A course at the Scottish Naval and Military Academy 'precisely like our higher classes' cost £27 14s. 6d. a year. The fees at English minor schools which catered for 'the smaller gentry, merchants and professional men at the very best' were double those of the Academy – yet, as the masters pointed out through the Rector, the Directors of the Academy had always sought, and obtained, qualifications in their teachers as high as those required at any English school. And the Rector concluded: 'A School of more than 300 boys, who are almost entirely taken from among persons who hold a good position in society, should support its masters in comfort and independence.'

In response to this plea the Directors duly raised the school fees in order to help the staff, but there was nothing left over from the increase to relieve the school Debt. It now stood at over £6,000, which included a loan of £2,000 from the Lord Justice-Clerk (Lord Hope) secured over the ground and buildings. And now disaster struck; for the Lord Justice-Clerk called in his loan of £2,000.

Behind the measured tones of the Minutes, the Directors were clearly in a frenzy of near-despair. They made desperate attempts to secure another loan, but their only security was the Academy itself, and possible guarantors were put off by the terms of the feu, which stipulated that the ground could only be used for a school and nothing else. Lord Cockburn wrote to his son-in-law, Thomas Cleghorn, a fellow-Director, on October 4, 1848: 'The state of the Academy fills me with sleepless alarm. I have thought of nothing else since I last saw you. But, except in one course, I see no ground for hope . . .' He went on to suggest that some temporary arrangement be made with the creditor and that by the following summer enough should be raised by donations to pay off the whole loan. 'Unless the debt be paid, the Academy must be abandoned and the buildings and ground ceded to the creditor . . . Possibly this is all nonsense; the dream of one who has all along been in a fright about this unfortunate debt. If it be, I only hope that those who have always seemed to treat the burden as immaterial, will have something better to propose. I did not expect to survive the Academy.' (*Academy Archives.*)

An appeal to the Lord Justice-Clerk brought them six months' grace, and the Directors organised an *Appeal to the Friends of the Academy* for £50 subscriptions or donations of any kind. Unless £2,000 were forthcoming very quickly, 'the results may be such as seriously to endanger the continuance of the school.' This Appeal, containing a full

Rector R. J. Mackenzie

The School Hall

statement of the financial situation, was marked 'Private and Confidential' and sent only to selected people whose discretion the Directors
thought they could trust. They were terrified that if the general public
got to know of the Academy's parlous situation, parents would lose
confidence in the school. This was what had held them back time and
again from making a public appeal for funds. But though the Directors
started the ball rolling with a combined subscription of £500, and the
masters chipped in with £100, the Friends of the Academy were slow
to respond, and with the total subscriptions at only £1,150 the Directors decided that their 'scruples about making a public Appeal must be
overcome'. A meeting of Proprietors gave its blessing, and an Appeal
was announced in the newspapers.

A certain amount of harm, inevitably, was done. In the spring of
1849, rumours swept Edinburgh that the Academy was about to close
at the end of the session. The Rector called on the Directors to do
something positive to assure people that the rumours were unfounded.
The Directors decided to put another advertisement about the Appeal
into the newspaper at once, and word it in such a way as to allay
people's fears; and as a result, they were able to announce in their
annual *Report* of 1849 that £2,266 15s. had been subscribed. The
£2,000 bond had been discharged, and the immediate crisis was over.
But they hoped that they would continue to receive 'from those who,
on various grounds, are interested in the continued prosperity of the
School, such assistance as will facilitate the gradual extinction of the
remaining debt . . .'

The disaster had been averted. For the meantime all was well. But
the Report also announced the resignation of the Treasurer, William
Young – it must have been a harrowing business being Treasurer of the
Academy in those days. Into his shoes stepped an Academical, John
Mackintosh Balfour (later known as Balfour-Melville), who had been
runner-up to the Dux of the School in that first session of 1824–5. He
was a Writer to the Signet, the son of James Balfour of Pilrig, W.S.,
and had been elected a Director in 1845. He would remain Treasurer
until 1860, and serve as a Director for a total of thirty-eight years –
from 1845–60, and then from 1870 to his death on his 82nd birthday in
1893. His appointment as Treasurer of the Academy brought about
one of those remarkable family associations which has so often stood
the Academy in good stead; for in 1845, his younger brother, Robert
Balfour (E.A. 1827–34) had been appointed secretary of *The Edinburgh
Academical Club*, an office he was to hold until his death in 1869.

THE ACADEMICAL CLUB

Of benefactors we have none whose pious memory we can celebrate, as, I am happy to say, the benefactors of the school are not only still alive, but belong to a body which is likely to remain with us as an immortal one, in as much as like the sovereign of the realm, they never die. I need not say that I refer to the sole benefactors of the Academy, The Academical Club.   (Rector Hodson, Exhibition, 1867)

The 'Accie Club' had been founded in 1828, and had been steadily growing into a potent factor in the development of the school itself. In 1846, Rector Williams had called the Club 'the best patrons of the Academy', and a later Rector, Dr Hodson in 1867, was to call it 'the sole benefactors of the Academy'. In 1849, during the great financial crisis, it leapt to the school's support by donating to the fighting fund all the subscriptions it had been collecting to found an Exhibition for university-bound Academy boys of £100 a year for four years.

The Academical Club had been founded 'to consist exclusively of students of the Edinburgh Academy'. Like so many other far-reaching innovations in those early days, the idea was first suggested by Rector Williams; he put it to members of his Seventh Class of 1826–7. The Minute Book of the Club reads: 'A Meeting of that Class was accordingly held in the Academy on the 28th of July, 1828, when John M. Balfour, Esquire, was called to the Chair.' (John Mackintosh Balfour was then nearly seventeen years old, and had left school a year earlier.) 'That Gentleman in an able and eloquent Address explained the purpose for which they were assembled, and concluded by moving "That there should be instituted a Society to bear the name of the Edinburgh Academical Club to be confined exclusively to Students of the Edinburgh Academy". Which motion was carried by acclamation.' The first Annual General Meeting of the Club was held a few months later, on January 10, 1829, and elected as its first president Archibald Campbell Tait (who else?), the future Archbishop of Canterbury. The Academy Directors gave enthusiastic support to the Club, as well they might; Sir Walter Scott, in particular, recognised that an association of prosperous and influential Old Boys could be of immense benefit to the school itself, and expressed 'his entire approbation of its Institution and his warm wishes for its success'.

Among the first actions of the Club was to found the *Academical Club Prizes* which still feature on the Academy prize-list. The first prize was awarded in 1831 for 'a copy of Latin Verses', and was won by James Rannie Swinton, who was to become the most fashionable portrait painter of his day in London (he painted Archbishop Tait and Louis Napoleon, amongst others). The prize continued to be awarded annually for a composition in prose or verse, Latin or English, to be written at leisure at home; but in 1846 this was changed (at Rector Williams' suggestion) to an annual prize for the best in *all* subjects based on *written* examinations held in school. These examinations were voluntary, and were open to all members of the three senior classes. 'The branches of study were divided into five departments, viz., Greek, Latin, Mathematics and English, with French, Geography, History and Scripture Biography; and printed Examination Papers, containing questions and exercises on each of these, were successively put into the hands of the Competitors, who returned written answers, without leaving the school-room, and without assistance of any kind. There were thirty-seven competitors, and the Examination occupied three separate days.' It was won in that first year by Lewis Campbell, who was then in the Sixth Class and who beat that year's Dux of the School, David Scott Dickson, into second place, with Peter Guthrie Tait third and James Clerk Maxwell sixth. (Lewis Campbell also won a Silver Medal for Geometry awarded that year for the first time by the Academical Club.)

By 1848, competition for this annual prize had become so keen that two distinguished members of Oxford University were engaged to prepare and mark the exam papers for the competition, which now lasted six hours a day for four days and was made compulsory for all senior boys. This was really the start of the Oxford and Cambridge examination tradition which still pertains at the Academy; and it was a dramatic extension of the written examinations, set and marked by outside examiners, that Rector Williams had introduced for members of his Seventh Class in 1836.

The old *viva voce* type of examination was gradually being abandoned. Senior boys were now to write their examination essays at school instead of at home, but the juniors were soon also to have monthly written exams so that the Rector could keep a check on their progress (this was one of Rector Hannah's first educational innovations). There would be oral exams as well, but the written tests 'would give more control over boys in their daily work ... In the oral examination it is not very difficult for an indolent boy to pass without actual discredit in the crowd'.

Alongside the new emphasis on written exams there was a new emphasis on the study of history. And now that the written com-

petition for the best in all subjects had become a compulsory part of the
school curriculum, the Academical Club gave instead a prize for history, which was another of Rector Hannah's innovations. Saturday
morning history lectures were started, and the boys had to write an
essay during the week on what they had learned. What's more, they
were to do actual research into history, rather than just repeat facts fed
to them by the master. All the emphasis was on writing, as distinct
from the old method of reciting everything parrot-fashion. Thus, the
annual Academical Club Prize was now awarded for a new kind of
history exam to help the Rector 'in the attempt he is now making to
introduce into the Academy the study of history . . . not merely the
communication of general and somewhat vague and desultory facts . . .
but an attempt to communicate to them the power of examining auth-
entic materials themselves . . . the study of history on this plan is little
known in Scottish schools . . .' Once again the examiners were from
Oxford, and they reported of the Seventh Class papers: 'They would
do credit to candidates for scholarships at Oxford.' The Academical
Club also presented its library to the Academy, which added the books
to the school's own collection.

In 1867, Rector Hodson paid the Club handsome tribute for its
pioneering educational initiatives in his annual speech at the Exhibition,
when he referred to the Club as the Academy's 'sole benefactors'. He
went on to say that apart from the *Mackenzie Prize* (endowed in
1849–50 by an anonymous donor who expressed a desire only to be
known as 'an admirer of the genius of the late Henry Mackenzie', of
Man of Feeling fame), all the 'great prizes' were provided by the Club,
which had also been responsible 'for originating in Scotland the system
which up to a recent date was, I believe, unknown on this side of the
Tweed, of having the examinations conducted by persons wholly un-
connected with the school . . . Here till very recently the examinations
were conducted by the professors or masters who had taught the
students or boys . . . The example set for the first time by the Academy
is gradually being imitated even by the Universities . . .'

There can be no doubt that the prime mover in this close co-operation with the school and its educational aims was the Club's secretary,
Robert Balfour, C.A., who held office for twenty-four years. Dr
Hodson's tribute to the Club was spoken only two years before
Balfour's death in 1869 at the age of fifty – a death which 'cast a gloom
over all connected with the Academy, which he loved and served so
well'. Working in close association with his brother, John M. Balfour,

the Treasurer of the Academy, he had done an enormous amount to bring School and Club into a dynamic and creative relationship; one of the last things he achieved was to launch, in 1868, the long-delayed Academical Club Exhibition to the universities, whose initial endowment funds had been diverted to the Academy fighting fund in 1849 (the sum now raised was £1,130, sufficient to endow an Exhibition of about £50 tenable for three years). After his death, his friends established the *Balfour Prizes* for French and German (now for German only) in his memory; but the Academical Club itself lost much of its impetus, and did not regain it until the amalgamation with the Academical Cricket Club and Academical Football Club in 1900. As the *Edinburgh Academy Register* put it with refreshing candour, 'After manifesting all the symptoms of senile decay, it rose like a phoenix from its ashes in 1900, and became the powerful organisation which we know today.'

But long before then, Robert Balfour and Rector Hannah between them had launched a scheme that was to prove equally vital for the all-round development of the Academy as an educational institution, and was to set another important precedent for day-schools in Scotland: they had acquired a cricket-ground for the Academy.

RAEBURN PLACE

After an examination of the different fields in the neighbourhood of the Academy, one of them, situated between Comely Bank and Stockbridge and within a few minutes walk of the School, seemed so suitable, that although considerably larger than was required, a lease of it was taken for six years.

(Academical Club General Meeting, July 24, 1854)

The Rev. John Hannah, that slight and scholarly gentleman, was the last person you would expect to take an initiative in school sports. He had never been particularly fond of games. At his funeral service in Brighton in 1888, Canon Gregory was to say of him: 'As a boy he was shy, with no love for the ordinary games and active pursuits in which most boys delight. He much preferred taking a book and going over it to any kind of games, and I do not suppose he ever played a game of football or cricket in his life.'

Bookworm he might have been as a boy, but as a headmaster he had a shrewd nose for success. Cricket had been growing apace in popularity ever since the first Eton *v*. Harrow match in 1822 and the first Oxford *v*. Cambridge match in 1827. In Scotland, cricket was becom-

ing firmly established at the Academy and was a major spectator-sport
in the early 1850s; the Grange Cricket Club had started organising
annual visits to Edinburgh by the All-England Eleven in 1849, and in
1851 no fewer than 7,000 spectators turned out to watch the All-
England XI play against a twenty-two of the Clydesdale Club at
Kinning Park in Glasgow. Spectators, for the main part, were wealthy
people (newspaper reports referred to a 'splendid display of private
carriages'), and Hannah must have realised that these were all potential
parents of boys for the Academy.

And so in April, 1853, he wrote to Robert Balfour, secretary of the
Academical Club, to say that he was 'anxious to secure a field for the
use of the Pupils for Cricket, and should wish to know whether the
Club would be disposed to aid in accomplishing this object'. The
Club Committee met to discuss the letter and decided that the object
was, indeed, a desirable one. A committee of Club members met the
Rector and a number of masters and pupils, and together they examined
various fields in the vicinity of the Academy. They eventually decided
on a large field on the Estate of Inverleith immediately behind Raeburn Place. It extended to ten Imperial acres, which was much larger
than they thought they would ever need, and was practically flat apart
from a large hillock (the celebrated Mound). A lease was available for
six years at a rent of £53 17s. 4d.; the cost of levelling and resowing
six acres of the field to make it fit for cricket came to £87 10s. 5d.

In his annual Report for 1853, Hannah announced his scheme for
'providing a cricket-ground for the exclusive use of the Academy, in
which boys may enjoy their exercise without the chance of interrup-
tion'. He paid tribute to the Academical Club for its help; but the Club
itself was not involved financially. Instead, Hannah and three individual
members of the Club (Robert Balfour the secretary, Kenneth Mackenzie (E.A. 1824–8), who was later to become Treasurer of the
Academy, and Thomas Cleghorn, Lord Cockburn's son-in-law) agreed
to 'take upon themselves the whole pecuniary responsibility' for the
initial expenses, and a committee of two Directors, the Rector, two
masters, several Club members and seven pupils was appointed to run
things.

The Field was duly opened on May 17, 1854, and was an instant
success. During the first year, nearly 200 Academy pupils paid the field
subscription, which had been set at 6s. for the senior boys and 4s. for
the juniors; Academicals paid 10s. In April, 1855, the School XI beat
an Academical and Masters XI by one wicket, and the *Edinburgh*

Evening Courant noted that 'a number of ladies and gentlemen were present as spectators, and among others we noticed the Lord Advocate, Lord Ardmillan, Colonel Gordon, H.E.I.C.S., etc., etc.' The *Academical Club Report* for 1855 commented that the Field has 'attracted a considerable amount of public attention . . . and in the plan of the Academy as published and issued by the Directors, it is now recognised as one of the distinctive features of the School'.

But there was opposition early on to the idea of Academy boys playing *away* matches. In 1856, when it was suggested that an Academy XI should travel to Glenalmond to play cricket there (Dr Hannah was Warden by then), Robert Balfour himself declared strong opposition to the scheme; he wrote to the Secretary of the Directors, John Marshall (afterwards the second Lord Curriehill): 'I think it ought to be stopped, and this ought to be done through the boys themselves. I *know* that some of the parents of the Eleven, though they might be unwilling to prohibit their sons from going, would greatly dislike it.' And another Director, James Mylne, W.S. (not an Academical), protested against it 'not only on account of the Expence (which would be considerable for a thing of the sort), but also because I think such matches are calculated to bring Schoolboys too much forward, and to give them higher ideas of their own competence than is good for them.' But by now there was nothing that even Robert Balfour could do to rein in the movement he had helped to unleash.

Rector Hannah's instinct had been right. He had sensed the way the wind was blowing and had harnessed it for the benefit of the Academy long before other schools recognised it. Fourteen years later, the Royal Commission on Education of 1868 stated: 'With the single exception of Irvine Academy, which has three acres in extent, there are not to the best of our recollection, two acres of grass set aside for the use of any of the schools, except the Cricket Field of the Edinburgh Academy.'

The first Academy 'Games' – the annual athletics meeting – were held at Raeburn Place in 1858. In 1882, the Field was acquired by the Grange and Academical Trust. Until the opening of New Field in the 1890s, Raeburn Place was the hub of all the school's sporting activities. But it was also the pace-setter for Scotland as a whole; for Rector Hannah's field was to become the cradle of Rugby Football in Scotland, the scene of the first International Football Match in 1871, and Scotland's International Rugby Football ground for twenty-four years, as well as the home of the oldest school-based Cricket Club in Scotland and one of the oldest Rugby Clubs in the world. The full story of this historic Field and the sporting occasions it has witnessed can be read in *One Hundred Years at Raeburn Place 1854–1954* and *The Edinburgh Academical Football Club Centenary History* (1958) – and a truly splendid story it is.

But not even Rector Hannah could have had any idea of the immensity of the thing that he and Robert Balfour had started. Nor did he stay to witness it. For only two months after Raeburn Place was officially opened in May, 1854, Hannah resigned as Rector of the Edinburgh Academy.

DEPARTURE FOR GLENALMOND

The most severe blow the Academy ever sustained.
(Andrew Beatson Bell, E.A. Director)

There was always an air of impermanence about John Hannah's Rectorship. Only two years after he came to Edinburgh, he applied for the Headmastership of Rugby when Archibald Campbell Tait was appointed Dean of Carlisle in 1849. Two years later, in 1851, he applied for the Chair of Greek at Edinburgh University. Mr Hannah did not get either job, and the Directors heaved a sigh of relief each time. Things were going better at the Academy. Although the debt, like the poor, was always with them, the Directors felt they had it under control. Numbers at the school were increasing. Mr Hannah's energy was unflagging. He toiled unsparingly to get the last ounce of effort out of boys and masters alike.

He seemed happy enough in Edinburgh. He got on well with the Directors. The Academical Club was always ready to listen to his ideas for improving educational standards at the Academy and to give the financial support that the Directors simply could not afford to provide. He enjoyed the intellectual society of Edinburgh and the warm friendship of notable men like Lord Cockburn and leading figures in the church and society.

But there were some aspects of his job that he positively disliked. He hated having to take in school boarders (in fact, he almost turned down the appointment in the first place on this count). He was a sensitive, nervous, fidgety person, as Canon Overton described him, and although he was a family man (he had a son and a daughter) the close proximity of schoolboys in his home was an invasion of his domestic privacy to which he never became reconciled. Yet he probably appreciated the Directors' point of view in requiring the Rector and masters to take out-of-town boys into their homes: it was an inducement to parents who might otherwise have sent them to boarding-schools elsewhere. Academy boys were now coming from every corner of Britain and many far-flung parts of the world. They came from Yorkshire, London, Linlithgow, Calcutta, Kent, Sutherland, Madras, Moscow, Bombay, Bengal, Northumberland, Suffolk, British Guiana, Antigua . . .

So Mr Hannah accepted boarders, but their presence was a constant irritation. He was also a little out of his element in the easy-going Presbyterian climate of the Academy. He was no theological bigot, but he was first and foremost an Anglican clergyman. What Canon Overton does not mention in his biography of Hannah is that Hannah asked permission from the Academy Directors to take only Episcopalian boarders, and the Directors refused – a clear indication of their continuing determination to keep clear of inter-denominational problems. Hannah, who at his first meeting with the Directors after his appointment had tried to emphasise to them that he was a High Churchman, had to limit his religious energy to gathering the whole school every morning for Prayers in the Hall, instead of the brief classroom ceremonies that had previously been held by individual masters. There was not much scope for an Anglican zealot at the Academy.

So, born teacher though he was, he was always looking for a niche in which he could be the clergyman or theologian first and the teacher second. But he obliged the Directors as far as his conscience would allow. For instance, they wanted him to be dignified with the title of Doctor, particularly since he looked so young that there were still people who wondered whether he could possibly have the qualifications for the responsible post he occupied. He was too young to take the degree of Doctor of Divinity, and he refused an honorary D.D. from another university, but he took the degree of Doctor of Civil Law at Edinburgh University in 1853 instead.

But while he kept an eye open for fresh pastures, he never relaxed in his efforts to improve or tighten up the system at the Academy. There was the question of Saturday school, for instance. In 1850, at the request of some parents, backed by the masters and with the Rector's agreement, the Directors decided to make Saturday a holiday for a trial period of a year: 'If it becomes an occasion of relaxation of discipline . . . a recurrence to the former system may be inevitable.'

Mr Hannah pointed out to the Directors, in advocating free Saturdays: 'Nothing is so hurtful to the spirit of diligence as this restless longing to be free.' However, by the end of the session he was requesting Saturday morning classes during the winter months, while sixty parents wrote asking for holiday Saturdays to be continued. The Directors compromised, and agreed to Saturday school in the winter, Saturday holidays in summer. It was not until the following year that compulsory Saturday classes were abandoned completely, to the delight of the pupils, although voluntary art classes were started in their stead.

The Rector's main interest, however, was in keeping expenses down. When suggesting a change, he would frequently make the point that it would represent an economy. When the German Master resigned in 1851 he suggested that instead of appointing another one, the Directors should ask the French Master, Mr J. G. E. Macleod (a Scot educated in Paris) to take over the German class, too. Then, in order to 'modify' the Writing and English departments, Mr Macleod was asked to teach English, too, and be known as Master of Modern Languages and Literature. The English Master was demoted to Master of Elocution. In one stroke he had given the Directors three teachers for the price of one, and he was soon looking for a rise in his own salary – only to be told 'Next year, if we have the funds.'

What the arrangement did to the status of English at the Academy was never assessed. 'We may hope to see the happiest results from the endeavour to bind together Modern Languages, as we have always treated Ancient Languages . . . into one organised whole,' wrote the Rector when he announced the new scheme. And after a year he reported that 'the amalgamation of English, French and German fulfils all hopes'. This was the classicist speaking, seeing English as a subordinate branch of Latin and Greek, or as just another modern language. Relegating the English Master to teaching the boys to recite in refined English accents was a distinctly retrograde step in the Academy's constant battle to find a foothold for English as an important subject in the school curriculum. On the other hand, Hannah extended the curriculum in other ways; in 1853 he introduced a 'Course of Instruction in the Elements of Science' (described as 'the principles of Natural Philosophy') into the Fifth, Sixth and Seventh Classes.

The year, 1854, in which Dr Hannah left, was a poignant one for the Academy. At the Directors' Meeting of May 4, only two subjects were discussed. The one was the opening of Raeburn Place. The other was the death, on April 26, of Lord Cockburn. The Directors wanted to attend his funeral as a body, along with the Rector and masters, in order 'to pay that last tribute of respect to the founder and never tiring friend of the Academy'. But Lord Cockburn had left written instructions that his funeral should be 'as strictly private as possible', so the Directors had to be content with appointing Messrs. Charles Neaves (later Lord Neaves) and George Dundas (later Lord Manor) to prepare a Minute expressing the feelings of the Directors. This is what they wrote:

'Any language the Directors can employ will but inadequately represent the grief occasioned to everyone connected with the Academy by the removal from among them of one who was emphatically the father and founder of the school, and who, from the hour when the idea of its establishment first occurred to his mind, down to the latest day of his life, was its most zealous, and its most valuable friend and supporter. The blank is indeed a great one which the death of Lord Cockburn will cause in Edinburgh and throughout the whole country; but nowhere beyond the limits of his own family will his loss be more severely felt or more sincerely mourned than in the Councils of an Institution which for thirty-two years had the benefit of his wisdom to direct all its proceedings, and the success of which, attributable in a great measure to his fostering care, was among the highest pleasures of his benevolent heart . . .'

As an example of committee prose, it is a horror. But the sentiments were sincere. Without Lord Cockburn, there would never have been an Edinburgh Academy.

And then, in the last week of July, 1854, Dr John Hannah informed the Directors that he was resigning. He had been appointed Warden of the recently-founded Trinity College, Glenalmond, in succession to its first Warden, Charles Wordsworth, the nephew of the poet. Glenalmond had been founded by the Scottish bishops as a school for the upper classes and a theological college for the training of divinity students for the Scottish Episcopal Church. Here was just what Dr Hannah wanted. He would be a headmaster, but he would be in charge of the ecclesiastical department too, and Pantonian Professor of Theology. He would also be installed as incumbent of the chapel, and pastor to any families in the parish who wished to use the college chapel.

The Directors of the Academy were shocked by his announcement, especially since he wanted to start at Glenalmond right away, leaving the Directors only two months in which to find a new Rector for the opening of the next session. They managed it, with twelve days to spare; but they directed the Secretary to put it on record in the Minutes that in future the Directors were determined to enforce the rule that six months' previous notice must be given before resigning. They also set down for posterity their regret at losing Dr Hannah, and paid tribute to his indefatigable energy, unwearied zeal, and 'extensive talents'.

Just how extensive those talents were, particularly in the field of business, they did not fully realise until reports began to filter through to them of what Dr Hannah was doing at Glenalmond. The first thing he did was to take ten boys with him from Edinburgh, bringing Glenalmond's total roll of forty-two up to fifty-two. For the next six years the school kept growing at a rate of ten a year until it reached 120. A deficit of £500 a year was turned into a balance of £5,000, and the school got a beautiful cricket field, a new entrance lodge and hall, and (during the rest of Dr Hannah's sixteen years there) a sanatorium, gas heating, and a new water supply.

He raised £8,500 in loans from the Council which ran the College; the largest individual loan was from Mr Gladstone, one of the Founders – who wryly remarked that Dr Hannah would have made an excellent Chancellor of the Exchequer.

The Rev. Professor Browne, in an article in the *Glenalmond Chronicle*, wrote that Dr Hannah 'had a special horror of financial embarrassments. From the first moment of entering upon office he set it before him, as a task of paramount necessity, to readjust the balance between income and expenditure . . . Wherever gratitude is felt to Dr Hannah for the restoration of the fortunes of Glenalmond, there should be gratitude felt to his wife, who doubled the eyes and hands of her husband in his long struggle to stop the leak'.

Canon Overton wrote: 'His success at Glenalmond was quite as great, and perhaps more striking than at Edinburgh. For at Edinburgh he found the academy in a fairly prosperous condition, and what he had to do was to take care that that prosperity should not be lost. At Glenalmond he had, as it were, to turn the tide, and float the school up to a higher level.'

And he did it all for a salary (at least at the beginning) less than half of what he had been earning at the Edinburgh Academy; his predecessor, Dr Charles Wordsworth, had an income of less than £200 a year. But that was Dr Hannah's way; he had accepted a decrease in his earnings to accept the challenge of the Academy.

Dr Hannah left Glenalmond in 1870, just after the death of his daughter there. He became Vicar of Brighton, and in 1876 he was appointed Archdeacon of Lewes. He died at Brighton in 1888. In his *Reminiscences*, Andrew Beatson Bell wrote: 'He has left with me the recollection that he was by far the ablest man under whom I was, either as a schoolmaster or professor. He left at what he thought the call of duty to assume the Wardenship of Glenalmond, and I always think that his removal was the most severe blow the Academy ever sustained.'

CHAPTER X

Master and Pupil: D.W.T. & R.L.S.

So I determined . . . that I would do as little as possible in the exercise of my stern duties to make of life a weariness to young children; and especially to such as should be backward in their Latin.

(D'Arcy Wentworth Thompson: *Day-Dreams of a Schoolmaster*)

D'ARCY WENTWORTH THOMPSON wasn't a Rector of the Edinburgh Academy – but he deserves a chapter as much as any Rector. He came to the Academy as a classics master in 1852 to replace Dr Robert MacLure, who had just been appointed Professor of Humanity at Marischal College, Aberdeen. And he would leave the Academy for a University chair himself after twelve uneasy years on the staff – he was appointed Professor of Greek at Queen's College, Galway, in 1864.

D'Arcy Thompson was a scholar of Pembroke College, Cambridge, a man of large humanity and gentleness of mind and spirit to whom teaching was a joy, a man who regarded the learning of languages as such an exciting business, such a source of pleasure and satisfaction, that he rebelled against the accepted system of cramming boys with daily doses of Latin and bullying them into disgorging it on command, on pain of the tawse or hundreds of lines. Perhaps it was the only way to get results (in terms of exam places) in classes of sixty boys and upwards, and exam results were what parents demanded; but D'Arcy Thompson, who had suffered much under an even more brutal version of the system at his English public school, wanted his own pupils to enjoy Latin and get pleasure out of Greek, rather than to say with Lord Kingsburgh (who left the Academy the year that D'Arcy Thompson arrived): 'Oh, those nonsensical *pœnas* – those orders to write out three or even five hundred lines; a punishment as practical as the old prison crank, which was abandoned as being a useless and therefore demoralising punishment . . . What senseless insult to a poet like Virgil, to make his beautiful lines an instrument of torture.' (Sir J. H. A. Macdonald, *Life Jottings*, pp. 137–8.)

D'Arcy Thompson believed he knew better. His ideas on teaching, on treating a boy as a potential adult; his views on corporal punishment, his concept of teaching as an art and a vocation, and of the teacher as someone with a right to a dignified place in society – all these were far ahead of his time.

After a few years of teaching at the Academy he wrote it all down in a delightful book called *Day-Dreams of a Schoolmaster*; and in it he painted a rather unflattering picture of the teaching methods of the time. He described the system prevailing at the Academy as a machine 'somewhat resembling a patent engine for the simultaneous polishing of many knives; ... and I was desired to take a firm grasp of its wooden handle, and to turn it with vigour and rapidity. And an implement of simple leather was put into my hands, by the dexterous application of which I was to quicken the apprehensions of such children as might be uninfluenced by the monotonous music of my gerund-stone'. (D'Arcy Thompson was rather fond of whimsical puns of this nature, substituting 'gerund' for 'grind'.)

At first he behaved like all the other teachers: 'And for many a day, obedient to tradition and to my orders, I turned rapidly the wooden handle, and flourished vigorously the simple implement to the very best of my ability. But, strange to say ... I could never turn the machine without its creaking painfully; and whenever I applied my leathern implement to a child's palm, I was immediately conscious of a thrill, as of electricity, that ran from my finger-tips to the very centre of my nervous system; and sometimes, after the performance of such an ordinary act of duty, I would find myself standing before my pupils with a heightened colour upon my face, and a tingling in my ears; and to a looker-on I should have appeared as one ashamed of having done some questionable deed.'

So he abandoned his 'gerund-stone', the mindless chore of making boys repeat rules of grammar over and over again: 'To supply the place of its simple mechanism I brought to bear upon my pupils all the moral and intellectual means at my disposal. I spared myself neither in the matter of time nor trouble in my endeavours to educe the dormant faculties of my charges; and enjoying as I did for many years a bodily health impervious to fatigue, and having a keen sympathy with boyhood, I succeeded more and more, until I almost ceased at length to regret the disappearance of my gerund-stone.'

Some parents regretted its disappearance very much, however: 'But the more I gave satisfaction to myself, the less I gave satisfaction to the majority of my so-called patrons: the guardians of my young pupils.

From time to time, when I was indulging in a dream of appreciated toil, I heard of complaints being circulated by such as were favourers of mechanism in instruction. Pupils, in whose progress I had begun to take a keen interest, were from time to time removed without a word of explanation, or the civility of a farewell. They were not "grounded", said these waggish but unmannerly guardians; meaning all the while, they were not "ground".'

Complaints were made to the Directors, and at their meetings 'the condition of Mr Thompson's class' kept coming up for discussion: 'The consideration of the matters regarding Mr Thompson was resumed and the meeting adjourned to enable the Directors to make further enquiries.' At the next meeting it was resolved 'after mature deliberation that no step should be taken for the present in reference to Mr Thompson's position in connection with the Academy; and it was remitted to Lord Neaves to see Mr Thompson and explain to him verbally the views of the Directors regarding him and the manner in which his classes are conducted'.

The Minutes do not record what passed between Lord Neaves, Director of the Academy and Senator of the College of Justice, and Mr D'Arcy Thompson. But Thompson wrote in his book: 'I had almost begun to despair of my system, and to think that I had mistaken my calling; and was casting about my eyes for some honest trade to which I might apprentice myself, when one afternoon my class was honoured with a lengthened visit from a gentleman of acknowledged rank and worth and judgement. After the lesson was over, I complained to this distinguished visitor that my system of conveying instruction, as being natural and philosophic, was popularly considered a more difficult one for the pupil than the ancient turning of a piece of mechanism. My visitor, who had a son under my charge, stated his firm conviction that my system was not only likely to produce better results, but was also in its operation far more easy and interesting for a young pupil to follow. From that moment I felt reassured, and determined never again to regret the absence of my gerund-stone.'

Whether the visitor was Lord Neaves, whose son Charles had left the Academy the year before, or some other distinguished father, the Directors seem to have been reassured that Mr Thompson was all right, and were even at pains to make the point known, because in the following year the Rector wrote in his *Report* for 1857: 'With a view to obtaining a more thorough acquaintance with the progress of the boys who will come up into the Rector's class next Session, I have instituted a Private Examination by myself of the *Fourth* Class, which, contrary to all precedent, has been larger this year than it was as the Third or Second. The result has been most gratifying to me in every way, and reflects the greatest credit both upon the boys and their Master, Mr D'Arcy Thompson. I found great accuracy, combined with a most creditable amount of work, and extending to an unusual proportion of boys, in one of the most orderly and attentive Classes I have met with . . .'

Yet D'Arcy Thompson hardly ever used the tawse – and then only 'with the view of stimulating over-dormant energies, and of repressing tendencies to chronic negligence or misconduct'. But although he was conscious that he used it with good intent, and although he was 'aware that it was similarly used by men who were my superiors in age, and certainly not my inferiors in kindliness and sympathy with boyhood, I was haunted with an idea that the use of it was founded on an error in our system of instruction . . .'

One day, acting on 'an unalterable rule', he had cause to strap 'a little, quiet, well-behaved and intelligent foreigner' – and a boy sitting next to him actually hissed.

'Bless the lad!' wrote D'Arcy Thompson. 'I thought how that little foreigner, returning to his own land, the ancient home of courtesy and good manners, would tell his friends of our rude, northern ways.' And knowing that the boy who had hissed 'was no vulgar and low-natured boy, I felt sure in my heart that there was at least something right in the impulse that had pushed him into danger and disobedience'.

So when a little boy walked behind him 'with his hands beneath imaginary coat-tails in imitation of my gait, I considered him as only joking with me . . . and I merely asked him to desist, as otherwise I should make fun of him in revenge; and he desisted'. And when a boy wrote D'Arcy Thompson's name on the desk, 'I was contented with showing him how he had mis-spelt it; and he rubbed it out at my request.' When a boy 'put his tongue into his cheek after an admonition, I showed his comrades what little control he had over that organ; knowing as I did that he intended to protrude it on the side that would have been invisible to me'.

But still he was afraid of 'allowing sentimentalism or impulsiveness on my part to take the place of duty however stern and unpalatable'; until one morning, just as he was leaving home for the Academy, his wife playfully slipped her hand into his overcoat pocket – and 'drew a something out; then thrust it back hurriedly, as though it had been a something venomous. And over a very gentle face passed a look of surprise not unmingled with reproof.' His wife died shortly afterwards, giving birth in 1860 to their only son (D'Arcy Wentworth Thompson the second), and Mr Thompson long remembered the unaccustomed look of reproof on her face when she found the leather tawse in his pocket. But the suffering of bereavement did not make him bitter; his grief merely turned to an even deeper compassion and love for all vulnerable creatures.

Meanwhile, there was a boy in a corner of his class who was very backward at Latin. He was a solitary, friendless child, and was continually absent on what seemed to be frivolous pretences, so that he often had to be kept behind when others were out at play, to make up for lost time. On one occasion D'Arcy Thompson was rather cross with him, and the boy said, 'You have no idea, Sir, how weak I am.'

'Why, my boy, you look stout enough,' replied Mr Thompson.

But the boy answered, 'I am really very weak, Sir; far weaker than I look!'

D'Arcy Thompson was touched by the boy's earnestness, and thereafter there was a curious bond of sympathy between them. So the master felt concerned when one of the boy's frequent absences lengthened into weeks. Yet he was afraid to make inquiries about him, 'thinking he might have been removed, as many boys had been, without a letter of explanation'.

Then one morning he received a letter with a broad, black edge, telling him that the boy had died the previous day of a 'virulent contagious fever'. Cholera was rife in Edinburgh at this time. The Academy Janitor, the popular one-armed 'Jenny', Adam Pinkerton, had died of cholera in 1854, for instance; it was during the holidays, and the school and all the books had to be fumigated, the woodwork had to be oil-painted and the drains overhauled before the start of term.

People were terrified of catching the fever, and as a parent, D'Arcy Thompson was fearful of passing any infection to his baby son. So he went to the dead boy's lodging (this child, no more than thirteen or fourteen, had lived and died in a boarding-house), intending only to leave his card at the door as a mark of sympathy. But the landlady urged him to come inside and pay his last respects in person; and as he stood by the bed, D'Arcy Thompson thought sadly of how dreary this child's life had been: 'I thought that the good woman of his lodging had perhaps been his only sympathising friend at hand . . . I felt thankful for the chord of sympathy that had united us, unseen, for a little while. But, in a strange and painful way, I stood rebuked before the calm and solemn and unrebuking face of the child on whom I had frowned for his being backward in his Latin.'

And that night, sitting alone at his fireside with his memories of his wife and musing over the boy who had died: 'So I determined; from the recollections of my own dreary boyhood; for the mild reproof that once had clouded momently very gentle eyes; for the love I bare my own little one; and for the calm and unrebuking face I had seen that afternoon; that I would do as little as possible in the exercise of my stern duties to make of life a weariness to young children; and especially to such as should be backward in their Latin.'

If for nothing else, the man deserves love for that compassionate credo.

Much as D'Arcy Thompson disliked using the tawse, he nonetheless considered it 'almost innocuous' compared with the cane- and birch-flogging that went on in English schools. He wrote: 'We have gone a great way already in Scotland in the way of civilised teaching, in for-bearing to use an instrument of acute pain and an instrument of in-decent brutality. Let us make a further advance, and if we can invent some intellectual and moral substitute for our ridiculous scourges, let us send the latter in bundles to the public schools of England, to be there adopted when their system is sufficiently ripened by a few extra centuries of Christianity.'

So the boys of the 'Tamson Class', as it was called, sailed through their schooldays in an atmosphere (at least in the Latin and Greek classes) of tolerance and sympathy uncharacteristic of their day, while their Class Master battled successfully with the Directors to be allowed to use his own *Latin Grammar for Elementary Schools* (1857) and com-piled his blueprint for a humane teaching system that was a hundred years ahead of its time:

In the minds of many people education is inseparably connected with the idea of difficulty and tediousness. They imagine that a great deal must be accomplished when painful efforts are being made.

The melancholy fact stands that the classics are taught in such a way as to benefit only those who, by superior talents or inordinately long continuance at school, eventually emerge from the darkness overhanging their elementary training.

With an easier and more interesting method, I assert that . . . the more intelligent [would do] far more, and the less intelligent a great deal more; at present, the more intelligent do very little, and the less intelligent next to nothing.

If genius is rare . . . your dunce is still more rare. I have never met with an undoubted specimen of the 'booby'. Perhaps a physically healthy 'booby' is as great a rarity as a live Dodo.

In general . . . parents dread new-fangled ways, and cling piously to old, scholastic superstitions.

It is a positive cruelty to pin a novice in Latin wholly down for a year to monotonous lessons of memory, or to worry him too soon with formal rules for parsing.

A vile system of literal translation of Greek and Latin idioms so corrupts the well of English undefiled, that a boy often loses as much English in his Latin room as he will pick up for the day in his English one.

I would advocate the use of familiar, everyday sentences, such as a boy might carry about with him as easily as his jacket . . . In fact I should treat Latin and Greek . . . as though they were simple, honest, straightforward languages, like the one spoken without conscious effort by our own street ragamuffins.

I love little children. And I care not whether they be blonde or brown; clean or dirty; lordlings or chimney sweepkins. I would rather they were not too good; or goody. Let us have a little naughtiness sprinkled in at intervals.

Teachers must take a pride in their profession. They must work and work to take the tedium out of lessons. They must outstrip their pupils in every branch of learning . . . If we could only work ourselves up to some such standard, we might gradually then dispense with that little leathern instrument.

A schoolmaster in Scotland has certainly need of any aid that can be rendered for the improvement of his social status . . . The Rectors of the two chief Edinburgh schools are exceptions to the ordinary rule. They enjoy a social rank befitting the dignity of their official duties. But how is it that the masters of classics, mathematics and modern languages, in these and similar institutions, take a lower place at feasts than a medical man of little practice, and an advocate of few briefs?

I am wholly at a loss to account for the fact that in England the teaching of classical languages should be considered as almost necessarily devolving upon the clergy. Why should it require Holy

Orders to fit a man to teach the heathen tongues of Athens and Rome?... There is some mystic Open Sesame that unbars the gates to all Head-Masterships; and the words are known only to the clergy.

Most of these sentiments were absolute heresy in mid-nineteenth-century Edinburgh, when the Rector of the Academy, like his pre-decessors, was an English clergyman; when most of the Directors and many of the parents were advocates or held other legal positions which D'Arcy Thompson clearly considered far too socially exalted in com-parison to that of a teacher; when 'Spare the rod and spoil the child' was the accepted dictum, and a 'thorough grounding' in Latin gram-mar was considered to be as essential a part of a middle-class child's upbringing as his daily Catechism or attendance at Church on Sundays.

So it was just as well that *Day-Dreams of a Schoolmaster*, in which he committed all his musings to print, was not published until 1864, the year he left the Academy. Or did it hasten his departure? Whether or not anyone in Edinburgh read his book, his views must have been well known. His philosophy must have been aired in the Masters' Lodge and pervaded the classroom. He certainly practised what he preached about the teaching of Latin and taking the drudgery out of lessons. The parents, as he said, did not like his new-fangled ways. Despite the Rector's glowing report in 1857, and the sympathetic testimony of Lord Neaves (if that was 'the gentleman of acknowledged rank, worth and judgement' who pronounced in favour of the Thompson system of teaching), the Directors began to be disturbed by the number of com-plaints they received from parents about his teaching methods and – much more alarming – the number of boys in his class who were being removed from the school.

A special meeting was held by the Directors on May 23, 1864, 'in consequence of the increased frequency with which complaints con-tinue to be made of Mr Thompson's mode of teaching his class. Statements were made by various Directors in regard to the removal of boys from Mr Thompson's class, and the threatened removal of others. After lengthened deliberation it was resolved to adjourn till ¼ before 12 o'clock tomorrow.'

Next day, after further 'lengthened deliberation', they agreed that Lord Neaves should write to Mr Thompson on behalf of the Directors, pointing out the diminishing state of his class and inviting him to explain. The letter of explanation must have been a real Thompson special, because the Directors, having considered it on May 31, unanimously resolved that if Mr Thompson were to tender his resignation they would be pleased to accept it. Four Directors, headed by Lord Neaves, were deputed to see Mr Thompson 'to accept his resignation and to take all necessary steps consequent thereon'. D'Arcy Thompson pleaded extenuating circumstances, saying that the state of his health during the previous session might have been to blame for the situation in his class, and the Directors decided to leave things as they stood until the new session in October. But in November, D'Arcy Thompson announced that he had been appointed Professor of Greek in Queen's College, Galway, and the Directors accepted his resignation with alacrity and without the usual three months' notice.

Their tribute to him in their 1865 *Report* was fulsome enough: 'He secured the esteem and admiration not only of his colleagues and of the Directors, but of the public generally; while ample testimony has been borne to his accurate and extensive scholarship by the number of his Pupils who have attained the very highest Classical distinctions at the English Universities. The Directors believe that in the new position which he now occupies, Mr Thompson will find a sphere peculiarly suited for his varied accomplishments and high scholarship.'

The phrase 'peculiarly suited' seems a left-handed compliment, and the Directors had given a more frank assessment of D'Arcy Thompson as a teacher in the Minutes of their meeting of June 8, 1864, when they 'thought it right to put on record that the small and diminishing number of pupils in Mr Thompson's class, together with the frequent complaints in regard to his method of teaching, which continue to reach them from the parents of his remaining pupils, have caused the Directors great anxiety. They cannot but attribute this state of things in great measure to peculiarities in Mr Thompson's mode of teaching, which, although they believe them to be adopted by him from conscientious motives, and with a full conviction of their propriety or necessity, are nevertheless inconsistent with the system which has hitherto been successfully followed in the Academy, and have manifestly not gained the approval of the public, but have even alienated the feelings of many friends and supporters of the Academy'.

Whether or not his talents were 'peculiarly suited' to his new post at the Queen's College, Galway, where he spent the last forty years of his life, he simply dropped out of sight of the scholarly and literary world. Hardly anything more came from his pen, except for a *Ladder to Latin* in 1866 and a collection of *Wayside Thoughts* in 1868. After that, he never took up his pen again: 'And all the poetry, the eloquence, and tenderness, and command of laughter and of tears that lay within him, were lost to the world. His dreams and self-communings by the sea took the place of work and glory and advancement. The spirit of that strange Celtic Connaught, with its stony fields, its beating ocean, its mists, its mountains, its terrible poverty, its mysticism, its moist and enervating climate, had taken possession of this Saxon's soul; and so he remained silent, obscure – he who ought to have added rich volumes to the literature of his country . . .' (Obituary reprinted in the *Chronicle*, March, 1902.)

But while D'Arcy Thompson senior sank into obscurity in that remote and poverty-stricken town in the west of Ireland, comforted by a second wife, beautiful and Irish, the son of that first tragic marriage, D'Arcy Wentworth the younger, was fulfilling all his father's hopes and dreams and potential by proxy, as it were. He was sent to the Academy in 1870, and became one of the most distinguished Academicals of all time (he died, laden with honours, in 1948 at the age of eighty-eight). At school he won the 1st Academical Club Prize in 1877 and excelled in classics, German, and mathematics, and went on to become a zoologist of international renown: Professor of Biology (later Natural History) at Dundee and then St Andrews University for sixty-four years; Scientific Member of the Fishery Board for Scotland for over forty years; knighted in 1937. With the father he had, it is not surprising that he should have been that rare combination, a brilliant scientist who was also a classicist and a stylist. His pioneering study *On Growth and Form*, his two Glossaries of *Greek Birds* and *Greek Fishes*, his translation of Aristotle's *Natural History* – these were all works of literature as well as science.

He was a true Renaissance man – and looked it. Like his father he was a tall, striking figure, with a magnificent head and a flowing beard. No Academy boy who attended the Exhibition of 1943 will ever forget his speech that July day, as Professor Sir D'Arcy Wentworth Thompson, C.B., LL.D., F.R.S., talked about his own days at school, seventy years earlier. All the austerity of the wartime years melted away – the black-out, the coupons, the rationing – as he recalled his morning walks to school wearing a Balmoral bonnet and swinging a bundle of books through an Edinburgh with no telephones, no motor-cars, no bicycles. He talked of his school-fellows – and what a class they were, that class of 1870–77! Four of them became University Professors and Fellows of the Royal Society – William Herdman, the naturalist (he went on the *Challenger* expedition), Diarmid Nöel Paton, the physiologist, John Scott Haldane, the physiologist, biologist and philosopher, and Thompson himself. They and others of like mind formed an unofficial Scientific Society in their class, the 'Eureka Club', and of course everyone else called them mad. Another class-mate, John Sinclair (later Baron Pentland of Lyth), became Secretary for Scotland; another, Edward Douglas Brown, won the V.C. in South Africa in 1900 as Colonel Browne-Synge-Hutchinson, while Henry Raeburn Macbeth won fame as an artist in London as Henry Macbeth-Raeburn.

This magnificent Renaissance man was one product of D'Arcy Wentworth Thompson, schoolmaster. What kind of men developed from the other boys who came under the influence of this teacher who was a hundred years ahead of his time? One of the boys he 'fostered' as a boarder in his house was Andrew Lang. But what of the 'Tamson Class' of 1861-8? Well, it produced the inevitable crop of Writers to the Signet, doctors, C.A.s and advocates, of course; but could it be that there was more than the usual proportion of men with romance in their souls and adventure in their sights? Four became sheep-farmers in New Zealand and Australia, and one was a cattle-rancher in Texas, Colorado, New Mexico, Wyoming, and Dakota. Two became tea-planters in Ceylon, and four in India.

One became a big-game hunter in South Africa. There were merchants and businessmen and civil servants in Hong Kong, Manila, San Francisco, Australia, Sierra Leone, the Falkland Islands, Java, New Zealand, the Seychelles. There were soldiers in every quarter of the globe, a missionary in the Philippines, and a cattle rancher on the Santa Fe frontier in the Argentine who, according to the *Register*, 'helped to convert the natives from the errors of their bandit ways'.

And there was a boy in D'Arcy Wentworth Thompson's class called Robert Louis Stevenson . . .

R.L.S.: THE 'STAMMERING LAUREATE'

> *The roll-book is closed in the room,*
> *The clacken is gone with the slate,*
> *We, who were seventy-two,*
> *Are now only seven or eight.*
> (Robert Louis Stevenson, E.A. 1861-3)

One of the Tamson Class in the Edinburgh Academy noticed a new boy in a sailor hat crying quietly in a corner of the Yards one day in the autumn of 1861. He was down in the school register as Robert Lewis Balfour Stevenson, and there were two other Lewis Balfours in the Tamson Class, so it's a wonder the boy in the sailor hat did not drop the 'Lewis' and called himself Robert. But then there were half a dozen Roberts in the class, so in the mysterious way in which boys sort these matters out, Robert Lewis Balfour Stevenson became known as 'Louie' Stevenson, and 'Robert Louis Stevenson' was how he signed himself when he became a celebrated writer.

As everyone knows, he was a delicate child at school. In fact, most people imagine from his wistful poems that he spent all his childhood either in bed or confined to the house. But 'Louie' went to no fewer than four schools in Edinburgh between 1858 and 1867. Three of them were obscure private schools, like Henderson's in India Street. He also had a private tutor in the evenings, Mr Peter Rutherford (later a United Presbyterian minister in Glasgow) to make up for the long absences caused by his ill-health.

In 1861 he was enrolled at the Academy in the Geits Class at the age of eleven. Perhaps his parents had heard that the gentle if unorthodox Mr D'Arcy Thompson was starting a new class that year, and felt it would be safe to expose their son to the rigours of a real boys' school under this man's care. What an influence his teaching and philosophy must have had on a boy with so much romance in his soul, and an ear already attuned to the magic of words and the excitement of story-telling. At this time the Stevensons were producing a little family magazine called *The Sunbeam*, and Louis used to write stories for it; occasionally he would do it in the Writing Class when he was supposed to be copying capitals and copper-plate curves for the Writing Master, John Maclean – he once drew a cartoon of the 'writing man', tawse in hand, rushing at young Louis, who was busy on a few verses for *The Sunbeam*.

How he must have enjoyed his English classes under Dr W. F.

Collier, who came to the Academy in 1859 from Madras College, St Andrews, and left in 1870 to found Park School for Girls in Glasgow. The man who wrote *The Loves of Rose-pink and Skyblue, Tales told to Children* in 1868 must have left an impression on the boy who was to write *The Child's Garden of Verses* in 1885. Certainly, Stevenson never forgot the poetry he learned at the Academy, even though he was only there for two years (and with many absences through illness). In one volume of his own poetry he recalled learning *Bingen on the Rhine, A Soldier of the Legion lay dying in Algiers*, and another that he loved reciting, *The Soldier's Funeral*. In later life he was to find Byron's *Isles of Greece* a bit lacking in merit, but he always enjoyed *The Address to the Ocean* and *The Dying Gladiator*, which he had to take his turn at rendering before the whole class in 1863. Dr Collier, who called him Robert, considered his voice 'not strong but impressive'. Another contemporary called it 'peculiar and vibrating'. He certainly made a considerable impression with his slim, dark, long-haired good looks, his great dark eyes and his brilliant smile.

Despite his weak constitution, he enjoyed games as long as they were not too vigorous and demanding; but with the imagination with which he was blessed he was always inventing his own games, and he loved play-acting. He had a toy theatre with a stage and little cardboard figures attached to pieces of tin, called 'spoons', with which he manipulated all the characters while he recited all the lines, having written the plays himself too. But he also loved games of imagination played in the open air after school and on summer evenings. How much does *Treasure Island*, or *The Master of Ballantrae*, or *Kidnapped*, owe to those wonderful, endless games of pirates played with his Academy friends among the sand-dunes to the west of North Berwick, and the exploration of old castles and ruins which were his special delight?

He had to leave the Academy in 1863 because his mother, who was also in poor health, was going to spend the winter in France, and Louis joined her there after a short spell at a school near London. When he returned to Edinburgh he took classes in engineering at the university, where he became friendly with the Professor of Engineering, Fleeming Jenkin, one of the stars of the Cumming Class of 1841–8 at the Academy. Stevenson, with his passion for drama and his fluency in French, was a real capture for the French comedies which Fleeming Jenkin and his wife put on annually in their house in Great Stuart Street. Stevenson took part in other plays staged by this enthusiastic group of amateurs, and in a production of *The Merchant of Venice* at the house of the Mair sisters (they were great-grand-daughters of Sarah Siddons, the actress) he played Antonio to the Shylock of another Academical, J. H. A. Macdonald (later Lord Kingsburgh):

'He and I walked home together that night,' wrote Lord Kingsburgh, 'and severely criticised some performances of others, as possibly others did of ours. I little thought then that I was side by side with one who was to carry forward the literary fame of Edinburgh into yet another generation. I never saw him again after that night.' (*Life Jottings*, p. 350.)

Stevenson gave up the study of engineering in 1874. Engineering was in the family – his grandfather had been the engineer of the Bell Rock Lighthouse, built on a submerged reef, his uncle Alan was the engineer of the Skerryvore Lighthouse, and another uncle, David, was the engineer of the North Unst Lighthouse, on the northernmost point of Britain. But engineering did not suit the youngest Stevenson; he took to law instead and passed the examination for the Bar in 1875, but his heart was not in that, either: 'He did nothing at the Bar,' as Lord Kingsburgh put it. He was always writing. In 1873 he had published his first important work, *Inland Voyage*. In 1881 he applied for the Chair of History at Edinburgh University, and when he was turned down he gave himself entirely to writing and travel – although there was little enough money in that until 1883, when *Treasure Island* turned the tide in his fortunes.

He always had a love-hate relationship with Edinburgh. He could not stand the climate, but neither could he forget the old familiar haunts and the happy scenes of his boyhood. In his *Ethical Studies*, written in sun-drenched Samoa, he declared: 'Happy the passengers who shake off the dust of Edinburgh, and have heard for the last time the cry of the east wind among her chimney-tops! And yet the place establishes an interest in people's hearts; go where they will, they take a pride in their old home.'

Go where he would, Stevenson never lost interest or pride in his old school. He was a founder-member of the Tamson Class Club, and attended its dinners whenever he was in Edinburgh. Once he was entrusted with the catering arrangements, and one of the members wrote, in a volume called *I can remember Robert Louis Stevenson*: 'Unfortunately, amongst his other good qualities he was not a judge of wine, and on this occasion the claret selected by him did not prove to be up to standard, as next day hardly any of those present were able to attend to their ordinary duties, for which they blessed R.L.S.'

Whether he was in Edinburgh or at the other side of the world,

Stevenson always tried to produce a few verses for the annual dinner. He called himself the 'stammering laureate' of the club. But there was nothing stammering about those delightful poems that recalled the golden days at the Academy. In January, 1875, he wrote to a friend, Mrs Sitwell: 'Well, I was at the annual dinner of my old Academy schoolfellows last night. We sat down ten, out of seventy-two! The others are scattered all over the places of the earth, some in San Francisco, some in New Zealand, some in India, one in the backwoods – it gave one a wide look over the world to hear them talk so. I read them some verses. It is great fun; I always read verses, and in the vinous enthusiasm of the moment they always propose to have them printed: *Ce qui n'arrive jamais du reste;* in the morning they are more calm.'

This is the poem he read that night:

> *Whether we like it, or don't,*
> *There's a sort of a bond in the fact*
> *That we all by one master were taught,*
> *By one master were bullied and whackt.*
> *And now all the more, when we see*
> *Our class in so shrunken a state,*
> *And we, who were seventy-two,*
> *Diminished to seven or eight.*
>
> *One has been married; and one*
> *Has taken to letters for bread;*
> *Several are over the seas;*
> *And some I imagine are dead.*
> *And that is the reason, you see,*
> *Why, as I have the honour to state,*
> *We, who were seventy-two,*
> *Are now only seven or eight.*
>
> *One took to heretical views,*
> *And one, they inform me, to drink;*
> *Some construct fortunes in trade,*
> *Some starve in professions, I think.*
> *But one way or other, alas!*
> *Through the culpable action of Fate,*
> *We, who were seventy-two,*
> *Are now only seven or eight.*

So, whether we like it or not,
Let us own there's a bond in the past,
And, since we were playmates at school,
Continue good friends to the last.
The roll-book is closed in the room,
The clacken is gone with the slate,
We, who were seventy-two,
Are now only seven or eight.

We shall never, our books on our back,
Trudge off in the morning again,
To the slide at the Janitor's door,
By the ambush of cads in the lane!
We shall never be sent for the tawse,
Nor lose places for coming in late;
We shall never be seventy-two,
Who now are but seven or eight.

We shall never have peeries for luck,
We shall never be strapped by Maclean,
We shall never take Lothian down,
Nor ever be schoolboys again.
But still for the sake of the past,
For the love of the days of lang syne,
The remnant of seventy-two
Shall rally together to dine.

Some of his Tamson Club poems *were* privately printed, as promised, and distributed as leaflets among club members. Some have since been published in various editions of Stevenson's works. The private copies were greatly treasured after Stevenson's death in Samoa in 1894; and in 1924 the Tamson Club gave the Academy £500 to endow a scholarship in memory of D'Arcy Thompson and Robert Louis Stevenson. £350 of the money came from the sale of those privately printed verses written by the club's poet laureate: master and pupil immortalised together in the D'Arcy W. Thompson-R. L. Stevenson Scholarship.

CHAPTER XI

'Goudie' Hodson: The Stormy Petrel
(1854-69)

The Directors must express their great regret that the position of the Rector, as well as of the Directors, should have been embarrassed, and the interests of the school imperilled and prejudiced by Dr Hodson's conduct in this matter.

(Directors' Meeting, July 23, 1864)

THE boys waiting expectantly in the Academy Hall on October 2, 1854, for their first glimpse of the new Rector were faced with a tall, commanding figure, elegantly and immaculately attired in black gown, high white choker (beautifully tied), and the inevitable lavender gloves. The Rev. James Stephen Hodson, of Balliol and Merton Colleges, Oxford, son of the Venerable George Hodson, Canon and Chancellor of Lichfield Cathedral, was seldom seen without his lavender kid gloves. He even wore them in the classroom.

They were not an affectation. There was nothing of the dandy about the man who took over the running of the Academy from Dr Hannah at such short notice. But lavender gloves were correct dress for a man of academic distinction in those days, as were his black frock-coat, tightly buttoned across the chest, and his narrow black trousers; and being correctly dressed was as important to Dr Hodson as a smart uniform is to a soldier. In fact, there was more than a little of the military style about his air of haughty dignity, his rapid stride, and the smart salute with which he would return the courtesy of a raised cap in the school Yards or on a summer evening on the old 'top walk' of Princes Street Gardens. He was soon nicknamed 'Goudie' – nobody quite knew why. Because he always shone like a new pin? Because he wore a gold watch chain? Anyway, the boys were not surprised to hear that 'Goudie' Hodson was the brother of 'Hodson of Hodson's Horse', a rather callous hero of the Indian Army, whose daring exploits on the North-West Frontier were eagerly discussed in the school Yards. Dr Hodson was intensely proud of his younger brother, the galloping major – even though he was deprived of his command in 1856 for 'irregularities in the regimental accounts and unjust treatment of the natives' (*Chambers's Biographical Dictionary*). At the head of the irregular troop of cavalry he raised during the Indian Mutiny of 1857-8 – 'Hodson's Horse' – the major was in at the fall of Delhi in 1857 and personally shot the sons of the Mogul, thus ending the ancient Mogul Empire. Three Academicals won V.C.s during the Indian Mutiny: two at Delhi – Lt. James Hill (E.A. 1843-7, later Lt.-General Sir James Hills-Johnes) and Lt. (afterwards Colonel) Thomas Cadell (E.A. 1845-8); and a third at Choopoorah, Lt. (afterwards Colonel) J. A. Tytler (E.A. 1838-40). Great was the rejoicing at the Edinburgh Academy when the news came through; cheers for the gallant Major Hodson were followed by cheers for the Rector when he announced a holiday for the school. The major's subsequent death at Lucknow was just one of numerous fatalities of the Indian Mutiny that affected the Academy, orphaning some who had not been orphaned by Sebastopol, Balaclava, or Inkerman, and cutting off the lives of young men who had been leap-frogging home across the Dean Water only a few years previously.

Very soon everybody at the Academy realised that Dr Hodson, in his own way, was every bit as formidable a character as his brother. He wielded neither pistol nor sword. He did not even have to use the tawse to command obedience – it was his proud boast that he never once resorted to corporal punishment in all his fifteen years as Rector of the Academy. Nor did he lose his temper, or thunder and rage at the boys. Dr Hodson's weapon was his tongue. He could wither with a word, slay with a sentence. His retorts were deadly, his sarcasm paralysing. Henry Montgomerie Bell, joint Dux of the School in 1869, recalled it nearly fifty years later: 'Which of us did not feel the lash of that terrible tongue? "What a silly answer!" was a favourite jibe, once addressed to myself, and rightly, too. "Why don't you bring the crib in one hand and the book in the other?" was said to the unhappy booby boy who was stammering through a line or two of Latin and slowly deciphering his pencil notes on the margin . . . But there was honey in every sting that he gave to us boys. "It wasn't the nasty things he said, 'twas the nasty way he said them." But his sarcasm was only skin deep, like beauty.' (*Chronicle*, December, 1915). Another former pupil, Dr A. S. Cumming (E.A. 1858-64), remembered him as 'cold and haughty, without emotions, so far as we knew. He rarely lost his temper with us. We old boys remember how, when any one of us, fresh from the lower school, indulged in any mild indecorum in his class, the Rector would simply raise his eyebrows languidly, and say quite coldly, "My good boy, do you think you are in a stable?" and that was the end of that boy for the rest of time.' Dr Cumming vowed that 'My *good* boy', in languid and tired accents, 'expressed more to us than much flourishing of leathery tawse.' He and his schoolmates believed the Rector to be absolutely fearless – 'just such another rather cold-hearted dare-devil' as his famous brother; and they pictured him in battle, marching up to the cannon's mouth, and 'giving a languid wave of his lavender kid glove to the jibbering Sepoys he would, we were quite sure, say "My good boys, do you think you are in a stable"?' (*Chronicle*, November, 1901.)

No one escaped Dr Hodson's tongue. Pupils, masters, or any parents brave enough to challenge him, usually wished they hadn't. Even the Directors – for the first time in the history of the Academy, the Directors found themselves at odds with a Rector; not because of his methods, but because of the occasional arrogance of his responses.

His methods, in fact, proved very good for the school. During his fifteen years' Rectorship (1854–69), the Academy rode the crest of the wave. By 1860 he was reporting a roll of 434, the highest for thirty years, and a hundred more than 'I found when I came to the Academy'. In the following year it was to reach a peak of 460. But it was only the crest before the trough, and in the 1860s the numbers began to slide alarmingly when other top-layer schools like Glenalmond, Merchiston and Loretto really began to get going and draw on the boy-material of which the Academy had virtually had a monopoly. But Dr Hodson was a far-sighted Rector – more far-sighted than the Directors themselves – and he was responsible for many significant changes that obviously went down well with parents, although he did not achieve everything he advocated.

He was always keenly interested in the development of sports, for instance. He was a passionate believer in 'Arnoldism', the theory that games were more than just a social occasion; they were an integral part of character-formation. In 1857, *Tom Brown's Schooldays* by Thomas Hughes had given a highly romanticised view of school games at Dr Arnold's Rugby as something that contributed to manliness, patriotism, moral character-building, stoicism, courage, team spirit and all the rest. In his 1857 *Report*, Dr Hodson attributed the high level of good health in the school 'to the successful establishment of the Academy Cricket Ground'; and he commended the example of one of the masters, Thomas Harvey (later to succeed Dr Hodson as Rector of the Academy), for superintending and participating in the cricket games, thus 'affording a proof that the most refined scholarship is not incompatible with the love of manly sports; a truth of which we have another example this year amongst ourselves, since the Dux of our whole School is also our best Cricketer and the Captain of our Eleven [*R. B. Ranken, Dux in 1856, who went on to gain a Cricket Blue at Oxford*].

He returned to the theme again in his *Report* for 1859: 'The marked benefit, both to health and character, which the boys have derived during the last two years from their spirited pursuit of Cricket and Foot-ball, makes me more than ever anxious to promote, in every way, their physical no less than their intellectual education. Far from suffering, both the discipline and the studies of the boys have been perceptibly advanced by their increased cultivation of manly games.'

Dr Hodson, fired by his brother's example, no doubt, wanted to take this development farther. He made repeated efforts to foster military drill, gymnastics and fencing in order to inculcate courage and patriotism: 'It would be very desirable to follow the example of military ardour, now being set us by all classes of our fellow-citizens, by establishing a regular system of drilling in the yards of the Academy during the winter months, when the Cricket-field is comparatively of little use.' (*Report*, 1859). And although he started a Drilling Class in October, 1859, which was attended by 130 boys, it proved a failure. Throughout his Rectorship he campaigned to form an Academy Cadet Corps; but despite the mass appeal of the Volunteer Movement that was sweeping Scotland in the 1860s, his efforts were firmly resisted by the Directors, and it was not to be until 1908 that the Academy eventually formed a contingent of the O.T.C. (Officers' Training Corps).

On the intellectual side, Dr Hodson was responsible for the introduction of a Modern side to the curriculum almost as soon as he arrived at the Academy. This was the first attempt to 'stream' the school into Classical and Modern Departments in order to stem the flow of boys who were being removed from the Academy, according to Dr Hodson, because their parents wanted them to spend less time on the Classics and more on subjects that would be useful to them in commerce, in the Civil Service and the Army. The Modern Side learned more English, French, German, and Maths, less Latin, and no Greek, apart from the Greek Testament for religious instruction. The Directors, in their *Report* for 1855, claimed that thereby the Academy was 'the first Public School in Scotland' to take active steps 'to meet the requirements of the day' – namely, an alternative system of education to suit

C.S.   N boys 'who are to enter into the Civil or Military service, or upon mercantile pursuits, where high classical attainments are not necessary'.

As it turned out, it was to be some years before the Modern Side became anything more than a dustbin for boys who were not very good at anything in particular – not until 1866, when the curriculum was properly reorganised into two separate schools, Classical and Modern, and Dr Hodson could claim in his *Report* for 1866, 'From the beginning of next session we shall, I believe, stand alone of all the Classical Schools in Great Britain in being able to say that every boy in the Academy without exception learns French, and everyone in the Rector's Classes German also.'

But that first step in 1855 showed that Dr Hodson saw clearly the direction in which education should be heading. It was revolutionary enough to meet with the disapproval of Dr Hannah, to whom the Directors sent the new plan for comment before seeking the approval of the Proprietors; but Archie Tait, who was then Dean of Carlisle, heartily approved of it, though his letter saying so was lost in the post and one of the Directors had to go to Carlisle to hear his views in person.

The Directors felt emboldened to sanction the change from the exclusively classical tradition by the publication in 1855 of the Report on the Indian Civil Service, which announced the first entrance examinations for both the civil and military departments, in which, as the Directors put it, 'while the elements of classical and practical education are combined, more prominence is given to the latter than the former.' In the event, the very poor showing of Scottish candidates in the first competitive examinations galvanised the 'Modern' movement in other Scottish schools. So the Directors felt that the Academy had 'good cause to congratulate itself on having in a great measure anticipated improvements in Education (to which the adoption of that Report must necessarily give rise throughout the country) and on having been the first Public School in Scotland, which has shown itself alive to the conviction, that the requirements of the day called for additional attention to the Modern and Practical branches of Education'.

Parents were enthusiastic, too; and the school roll began to rise. No, there was nothing wrong with Dr Hodson's ideas. It was simply the way he did things that began to annoy the Directors. For instance, he gave the school a holiday on Christmas Eve (unheard of in Presbyterian Edinburgh) so that he himself could get to England in time for Christmas Day. And when Mr Thomas Harvey, one of the Classical Masters, left in 1856 to become Headmaster of Merchiston, the Rector was discovered attending the meeting held by the Directors to decide on a replacement. He was told that the appointment was the sole responsibility of the Directors, and politely asked to leave. When there was difficulty on another occasion in finding a new English Master, Dr Hodson suggested dividing his work (and his salary) among the Classical Masters and himself. He told the Directors there was no need for them to confer with the masters on the matter; so the Directors put it on record that 'it must be understood to be the undoubted right of the Directors at all times to communicate directly with the ordinary Masters of the School'.

But Dr Hodson's most crashing indiscretion was at the Exhibition of 1859, when the young Prince of Wales (afterwards King Edward VII) was the Guest of Honour at the Rector's invitation. 'His Royal Highness's presence in the Hall,' wrote Dr Hodson in the following year's *Report*, 'and the interest he expressed in the proceedings of the day, will not soon be forgotten by any who witnessed them.'

He was right. But it was not the presence of Royalty that made the occasion so unforgettable, but what Dr Hodson himself said in his speech. He used expressions, according to a hastily-called Directors' meeting, 'calculated to produce injury to the Academy, and to convey an erroneous impression to the public as to the system which, at the commencement of the Institution, prevailed with regard to the discipline of the classes.'

It was in all the Edinburgh newspapers on the next day, July 28. The *Courant* reported: 'He knew there were some who recurred with pleasure, if not with pride, to the time when the Academy was in a much rougher state, when football was played to the considerable peril of the smaller boys, and when a reign of terror prevailed in some of the departments; and only yesterday a gentleman told him that when he was a boy at the Academy, a certain Classical Master used to begin at the top of a large Class, and administer corporal punishment from the top to the bottom of it. All this was now changed and, he thought, changed for the better.' The *Scotsman* added that Dr Hodson had said that the Classical Master in question had told the boys that 'nothing but weariness would make him desist'.

It was a tactless speech, certainly; but history suggests that Dr Hodson was probably right, by modern standards at least. There can be no doubt that there was a great deal of indiscriminate tawsing in the early (and not so early) years at the Academy; and the reminiscences of Academicals at Dinners down the years always took a perverse pride in the amount of 'beating' to which they were subjected in their own time at school, compared with the 'soft' conditions that set in after they left! But to the Directors, who had always laid so much stress on their policy of keeping corporal punishment at a minimum, the Rector's speech that day was unadulterated heresy. Immediately they had seen the Prince of Wales off the premises they held an emergency meeting in the Masters' Lodge and demanded an explanation from the Rector. The Chairman of the Directors, Lord Neaves, was particularly incensed, and said that if it had not been for the presence of the Prince of Wales he would have given Hodson the lie on the spot. Who was the traitorous and unprincipled Academical who had been opening his big mouth? The Rector gave his name, and the Directors promptly appointed a committee to investigate the whole matter, as was their wont in times of crisis. The committee discovered that the gentleman in question, a relative of John M. Balfour's, was away on a visit to Ayrshire, and sent a deputation, consisting of Balfour and the Secretary, Andrew Beatson Bell, to see him. He stuck to his story. They also sought out former classmates and wrote to masters who had taught the class. All said they had no knowledge of the kind of violence described by the Rector. Neither had that champion flogger, Dr Gloag. (According to the *Register*, the culprit was believed to be Mr George Ferguson, one of the original Classical Masters, who had left in 1847 and was by this time Professor of Humanity at King's College, Aberdeen.)

Letters were exchanged between Dr Hodson and the Directors, who decided not to make a public contradiction of his statement, but to wait until next session for 'further consideration of the present relations with the Rector'. By the following session Dr Hodson had 'expressed his regret', and the Directors contented themselves with placing it on record that 'no reign of terror ever did exist in the Academy', and that the Rector's statement was 'in a high degree rash and inconsiderate'.

The Directors really had no choice but to forgive, if not forget, for Dr Hodson was clearly a successful Rector as far as the fortunes of the school were concerned. He had just chalked up his 100th addition to the roll since his appointment. His former pupils were sweeping the board at the universities. The Marquis of Lorne, afterwards 9th Duke of Argyll, who had left in 1859, was now top of his form at Eton (he was later to write the version of the 121st Psalm, *Unto the Hills*, that is always sung at the Academy Exhibition). His own son, Hubert

Courtney Hodson (E.A. 1855–9) would soon win a scholarship to Cambridge from Uppingham. In the Oxford and Cambridge Boat Race there was an Academical in both crews. And the Academy could claim the Champion Rifle Shot of all England. The Rector was in a virtually unassailable position.

But then in the summer of 1864 a spectacular row blew up over an extraordinary episode that came to be known as the Affair of the Round-Crowned Hat; and relations between the Directors and the Rector plummeted to a new low.

It all began because a 16-year-old boy called George Graham Bell wore to school a round crowned hat which his father had chosen for him – a pork-pie hat, in effect. The Rector did not like it, and after some months he forbade the boy to wear it. The boy's father, a civil engineer and Colonel of the City of Edinburgh Artillery Volunteers, countermanded the Rector's instruction, and told the boy to keep on wearing it. The Rector warned the boy a second time, and when his ban was still ignored, he gave the boy 100 lines of Virgil to write out. Once again the father intervened, and sent the boy to school without doing the imposition. When the boy told Dr Hodson that his father had forbidden him to do it, the Rector kept him in after school for two hours, locked in the Library, and warned him that he had better write out the lines or change his cap – or else look for some other school where he could dress as he pleased.

Col. Bell now wrote to the Secretary of the Directors:

'Sir – Will you be so good as to inform me if there is any regulation as to the dress of boys attending the Edinburgh Academy? The Rector has punished my son Graham Bell for appearing in a round crowned hat which I consider respectable, and which I have no intention of causing him to change unless the rules of the Academy demand it.'

Having ascertained that no such rule existed, he now wrote to Dr Hodson, on July 12, 1864; he went over the events which had taken place, and ended on a placatory note: 'Summary as your proceedings have been, I have no desire that this matter should go further, and shall be glad to hear that after reconsideration you are willing to let it rest – Graham attending his classes as usual. Otherwise I have no course left me but to bring the affair before the Directors of the Academy.'

Dr Hodson's reply that same day was astoundingly tactless and imprudent: 'Sir – Your son ought to have been the last Boy in the School to set my wishes or my authority at defiance, as he has received more indulgences from me for habitual idleness and inattention than any boy in his Class as I really pitied him as believing him incapable from bad health or want of ability. Moreover he always cried when I found fault with him. He is the only Boy in the School who has not at once attended to my speaking to him about wearing a Cap of some sort which has been the *custom* of the Academy from the first, even if not a "rule". I spoke to him *three* times before I gave him an imposition, which for want of courtesy if not of obedience he fully deserved . . . If you choose him to do as the rest of the Boys in the Academy do, I shall say no more to him on the subject. If not, you can do as you threaten and complain to the Board of Directors.'

This arrogant letter infuriated Mr Bell: 'You turn round upon my Son for want of ability due, as you now discover, to habitual idleness but which at one time you attributed to bad health. You may remember that I called upon you at the Commencement of the Session and told you that owing to very severe illnesses he was behind boys of his standing, and I think it very unfair of you to place this on record as it is totally irrelevant to the matter in question. You surely do not wish to plead your neglect of punishing him if he was idle as a set-off against your having punished him for a fault of which he was not guilty . . . From the personal feeling which I find has arisen between you and my son – bad as it is in a boy but infinitely worse in a grown-up man holding the responsible position you do – I see that it will not be to my son's advantage to remain longer under your guidance. I will lay a copy of this correspondence before the Directors.'

Nothing horrified the Directors more than the removal of a boy from the Academy, and Dr Hodson was asked for an immediate explanation. His reply, on July 15, was characteristically off-hand and high-handed at the same time:

'I found in the Rules (or Customs) of the Academy ten years ago that all boys should wear Caps at School, the kind being left to themselves. This I have from time to time enforced and in several cases recently: no Boy having for a moment resisted my expressed wish except Bell, the last Boy in the Fifth Class. On the third occasion, after a week's interval I gave him an imposition as I told him I should, for Disobedience and then for him not bringing it and saying his Father would not let him do it. I locked him in the Library after Three to do it.

'Hinc illae Lachrymae. Of course I trust you to support the Rector's authority in such a matter, absurd as it seems. It is bad enough to have Masters setting such Rules at Defiance and appearing for a whole Session without gowns. But a parent's authority ceases at the gates of the Academy. This boy . . . was without a cap or made any excuse. He is not a bad boy but very idle and inattentive and from bad health or want of brains terribly ignorant.'

But Dr Hodson's trust that the Directors would support him was sadly misplaced. They hastily convened a meeting for Saturday, July 23; and one Director (George Dundas, afterwards Lord Manor) who could not attend and feared that a quorum would not be present wrote his views in a letter to the Secretary (Sheriff J. C. Thomson): 'You know my sentiments regarding the Rector's conduct in the matter of the *Hat*, and I cannot suppose that among the Directors there will be two opinions about it. He was wrong from the beginning, and put himself infinitely more wrong by his correspondence with Mr Bell. It is therefore impossible to give him any support and he must be told so plainly.'

And so he was, with all the plainness and clarity of a judgement from the Bench: 'The Directors have come to the resolution that anxious as they are at all times to support the Rector's authority, it is impossible for them to do so in this instance. There is no rule and no imperative custom in the Academy as to the dress of the boys and although it may have been common and may be reasonable that the Rector should state his suggestions or wishes on that subject he has no power or authority to enforce them. In particular where, as in this case, it must or ought to have appeared that the boy's dress was the deliberate choice of his parent, the Directors are of the opinion that whatever other course might have been taken it was wrong to punish the boy who was nowise to blame.

'In this respect the Directors are of the opinion that the Rector committed an error in judgement with regard to the nature and extent of his authority. But they regret to say that they view in a much more serious light the proceedings which followed. After Mr Bell in his letter to the Rector of July 12 had said that he had no desire that the matter should go further if the Rector was willing to let it rest . . . it was the plain duty of the Rector to consider well his position, and either to acquiesce in the father's proposal or to learn what were the Directors' views on the subject. Had that course been followed the dispute would have terminated without unpleasant results of grave importance; but instead of so acting the Rector addressed to Mr Bell his letter of July 12, which the Directors consider to be most unfortunate and improper in its terms and tone in so far as it throws out harsh and disparaging reflections upon the boy's conduct and abilities which were quite irrelevant to the question and were calculated to give great pain and just offence to any parent. The Directors cannot but see that it is this letter which has led to the boy's withdrawal from the School and has excited the strong feeling that Mr Bell obviously entertains as to what has taken place, and which they have no doubt will meet with a very general sympathy.

'The Directors feel it to be their duty to communicate to Mr Bell: 1st, That they consider the Rector to have exceeded his authority in the matter of his son's dress, but that they believe this to have arisen not from any personal feeling against the boy but from an error in judgement; 2nd, That they regret exceedingly that the Rector should have addressed to Mr Bell the letter of July 12, of the terms of which they highly disapprove.

'The Directors also desire to record their hope that the Rector on his part will see the propriety of apologising amply to Mr Bell for the terms of that letter.

'The Directors in conclusion must express their great regret that the position of the Rector, as well as of the Directors, should have been embarrassed, and the interest of the school imperilled and prejudiced by Dr Hodson's conduct in the matter.'

A copy of this Minute was sent to Dr Hodson, with the reminder that 'many complaints, similar to Mr Bell's original complaint, have reached them'.

Mr Bell at least seems to have been mollified, because although he did not send the boy back to school, he kept his younger son, Francis Graham Bell, there until 1866. But there was no comfort in it for the Rector.

It was an exceptionally severe reproof, and Dr Hodson's haughty pride must have found it bitter to swallow. Altogether it was a bad year for Dr Hodson. Dr Gloag retired after his forty years of service to the Academy. Mr D'Arcy Thompson was in trouble over his teaching methods. He himself had been seriously ill for a time, and came back to find his Class disorganised. And the numbers at school were sinking ominously from that peak of 460 in 1860–1, down to 433 in 1861–, to 393 in 1860–3, to 375 in 1863–4.

But his *Report* in 1864 was as spirited a counter-attack as any that his brother might have made. He launched into an attack on two of his bugbears – the size of the classes at the Academy, and the system of automatic promotion, whereby boys moved up the school without regard to their ability: 'In a School absolutely without endowment, and at the present scale of payment in Scotland for a first-rate Classical Education, large Classes must, I fear be looked upon as a necessary evil. But I can see no reason why this evil should be unnecessarily aggravated by retaining boys in the same Class without the slightest reference to their ability, industry, or attainments . . . In all other respects, we have secured most of the advantages and avoided many of the defects which the Royal Commissioners have recently reported in the chief English Public Schools. For example, we have anticipated by nine years the plan which they recommend of dividing the upper Classes of the School into Classical and Modern Sides . . . Again, we have succeeded in doing what the Commissioners only venture to recommend, making Modern Languages and Mathematics an integral and compulsory part of the work of the School; while we have for years solved the problem, which appears from the evidence appended to their Report to have been so puzzling to English Public Schools, of teaching French and German in all but the very youngest Class, without sacrificing discipline on the one hand, or, on the other, a pure pronunciation of these languages. These are surely points in our system on which we have a right to congratulate ourselves; nor am I less gratified at observing that the Commissioners unanimously maintain the supreme value of a classical as opposed to a general Education, though willing to combine with the study of the Ancient Languages an acquaintance with Modern Literature and accomplishments.'

By the following year, although the numbers had gone down slightly again (from 375 to 363), the Directors seemed to be edging farther his way on the matter of automatic promotion. They instituted 'a system of Periodical Examinations of the School, which are conducted in writing, without any previous special preparation, and the results of which, in the case of each boy, are communicated to his parent or guardian. The object of these Examinations is partly to test the progress of each Pupil in the general work of the School, and partly to accustom the boys to the system of Written Examinations, which is now so general as an introduction to the learned professions, and to many branches of the public service' (*Report*, 1865).

This had come about as the result of a suggestion put forward by Leonard Horner just before his death in 1864. He was concerned at the poor performance of Academy boys in the Civil Service exams. He advocated more spelling and handwriting instead of literature in the lower classes; also, although the Academy could turn out brilliant mathematicians at university level, ordinary pupils sitting public service exams must be better at simple arithmetic, especially mental arithmetic.

What pleased Dr Hodson about the new system of exams was that each boy would now be awarded a certificate, and he hoped that this certificate would be used to put an end to automatic promotion; for the Directors had agreed to abolish the system ('prevailing nowhere but in Scotland') of allowing boys to advance from class to class without examination. But the Directors jibbed at taking the last step; they were still afraid of offending parents who had always enjoyed the right to say which class their sons should be in, and so it was decided that 'it would not be expedient for some time, to refuse admission to a higher class to a boy not provided with a Certificate of competency; the responsibility, in that respect, might be left with the parents'.

Perhaps if Dr Hodson had not been such a contentious man and had not given the Directors so much trouble in other matters, they might have paid more heed to him on matters about which he was absolutely right – the dangers of automatic promotion, the unwieldy size of the classes (up to eighty or ninety), and the tendency for boys to leave too early. He realised that with the competition growing from new schools and the demands for a more controlled educational system throughout the country, hard times were ahead for the Academy unless they made a bold effort to change the weak points in their system.

At first Dr Hodson sulked a bit and refused to co-operate in the running of the new examinations, which he must have felt were a waste of time unless they were used to control promotion; but in 1866 he was helping the Directors to produce a scheme to strengthen the Modern Side along the lines recommended by Leonard Horner, involving an increase in the number of classes from seven to nine, two new masters, more German and Maths, French in the First Class – and a rise in fees to a maximum of £17 per annum. 'The Directors cannot entertain a doubt that such an increase will be cheerfully acquiesced in by parents and guardians, in consideration of the benefits likely to accrue to the whole School, from strengthening the Staff of Masters, and diminishing, in the higher Classes, the numbers under the superintendence of one Master' (*Report*, 1866).

For his part, the Rector, cheered by a jump in numbers from 363 to 393, welcomed the new system and hoped that it would attract those parents who had taken their boys away from the Academy, thus sacrificing 'the moral gains of our systematic discipline and punctuality, to say nothing of the sanitary advantages of the Academy rooms, and its playground and cricket-field'. And he returned with enthusiasm to his hobby-horse, physical education: 'Like her namesake in ancient Athens, which was a gymnasium long before it was the school of Plato, the Edinburgh Academy has of late years gained a renown in ἡ γυμναστική (physical education) little inferior to that which she has long enjoyed in ἡ γραμματική (learning), those twin sisters whom the Greeks never allowed to be separated in their schemes of ἡ μουσική, or a liberal education.'

But after this his relations with the Directors deteriorated rapidly. He was continually asking for a rise in salary, and as regularly being refused. By 1868, when the school numbers had dropped again to 337, his annual *Report* seemed to be defending his own record over the past fourteen years, making a list of his achievements: nine professorships, nine Fellowships, thirty-seven scholarships and exhibitions, twenty-two Oxford and Cambridge prizes, eighteen Glasgow prizes, eleven St Andrews prizes, two Aberdeen prizes, thirteen appointments to the Indian Civil Service with eleven medals, and twelve commissions from military colleges with four firsts. He himself had never resorted to corporal punishment, and even in the lower school the use of the tawse had become almost unknown.

He wanted longer holidays for the boys. The English public schoolboy worked 1,110 hours per year, while the Scottish schoolboy worked 1,980 hours per year, or nine hours a day for forty-four weeks. They were greatly overworked, he claimed. He also suggested changing school times to suit the family dinner hour, and once again he deplored 'the great blot on the Scottish system of higher education' – automatic promotion. He quoted his predecessor, Dr Hannah, who had said that the Academy policy of keeping boys together in the same class all the way up the school, irrespective of their abilities, 'tended to subordinate the interests of the higher to the interests of the lower . . . or sacrificing the class to its tail . . . It is deplorable to see clever boys wasting time and patience at the top, while the master, with the instinct which leads him to labour most where labour is most needed, is hammering at the heavy weights of the Class . . .' He also mourned, once again, the failure to get P.T. and drill going on a proper footing. He referred to 'the necessity of physical training for the completeness of real education. Any amount of literary distinction would be dearly purchased at the cost of *mens sana in corpore sano*'. He also regretted the fact that 'nothing has been done towards forming from among our boys a Cadet Company of the Volunteer Rifle Corps, and so enabling them to join the Annual Shooting Match of the Public Schools'. (It was not to be until 1911, forty-three years later, that the Academy took part in the competition for the Ashburton Shield at Bisley, and carried it off at the first attempt.)

But his warnings and exhortations went unheeded, both then and for several years thereafter. And in 1869, after a long quarrel between the Rector and the German Master which strained relations at the school to the breaking-point, the Directors arrived 'reluctantly but unanimously' at the conclusion that it was necessary 'to terminate the engagement of Dr Hodson as Rector of the Academy'.

The writer of the Historical Introduction to the *Register*, Professor John Hepburn Millar (Professor of Constitutional Law and Constitutional History at Edinburgh), made severe references to Dr Hodson's sarcasm, his 'hybristic' manner and speech, and his 'positive genius for calculated indiscretion'. He went on, 'But it cannot be seriously doubted that he was a great headmaster . . . the highest testimony to Dr Hodson's clearness of vision and soundness of judgement . . . is afforded by the fact that he foresaw the termination of the "halcyon days", and the advent of a period of storm and stress, when the Academy system would be tested to the uttermost . . . Had his warnings been heeded in time much trouble and anxiety might have been spared.'

Professor Millar, who was Dux of the School in 1881 and later served as Secretary to the Directors from 1896–1906 and then as a Director until his death in 1929, had entered the Academy five years after Dr Hodson left, and never knew him. And after the publication of the *Register*, Dr Hodson's former pupils sprang to his defence. Henry Montgomerie Bell wrote: 'I liked his face the day I entered the Academy gates in 1862. He had a pleasant way of eyeing the classes as they came walking and trotting into the Hall, and a pleasant way of reading prayers, rather melodiously, and quite free from *unction*.' Bell believed that 'the keystone of Dr Hodson's character was his love of truth. He never wearied of inculcating upon us boys in the Rector's classes the love of truth and the hatred of falsehood. I remember, as if it were yesterday, in the Fifth, when we were reading Saint Matthew's Gospel in the original Greek with the Rector – chapter v., verse 11 – he suddenly turned to the top boy and said: "Which is the emphatic word in that verse?" Two wrong answers were given, before he got the true answer, the word *falsely*. But it was the earnest, solicitous way he looked at us that impressed me for life, just as if he was examining us for confirmation . . . I know well, from my own personal experience of him, both in schooldays and after them, that he had as kind and true a heart as ever beat in a headmaster's breast . . . I do not know the derivation of the word "Goudie", but I made a point of never using it. I do know this, that "gowdie" means a jewel in good, broad Scots, and a jewel I found him as teacher, and friend, and counsellor.' (*Chronicle*, December, 1915.)

Another former pupil, Dr A. S. Cumming, had already written: 'He was, I do believe, a born teacher. As you left the lower school, where the drudgery of the classics was got over more or less painfully, you felt on entering the Rector's class that you were in another atmosphere. My recollection is that his turn of mind was less towards the construction of the ancient languages than towards history. He revelled in ancient classical history; with him we rehearsed all the delights of the old mythology and the stories of ancient Greece and Rome.

'Was Hodson popular? No, I suppose not. Perhaps we were too Scotch, and the Oxford-bred Englishman did not understand us, nor we him. I do not know.' (*Chronicle*, November, 1901.)

For a few months after his departure from the Academy in 1869, at the age of fifty-two, Dr Hodson took private pupils in Edinburgh, and then he was appointed Headmaster of St Andrew's College, Bradfield, where he remained for three years. The *History of Bradfield College*, edited by A. F. Leach, records that the numbers attending the school increased rapidly under Dr Hodson; but the fire seemed to have gone out of him, for he is described as 'a tall, pale, man of quiet, retiring habits, who seems to have made no very strong impression upon the School'. He was apparently noted for his absent-mindedness (not a quality that was very noticeable at the Academy) – 'When he took walks with his family he was given to walking out in front, thinking out problems to himself.' Once he wandered into a line of boys fishing from the river bank and got a fish-hook in his cheek; on another occasion he was knocked down on the platform at Reading Station and was 'barely rescued by a porter from being crushed to death'.

But he must still have had some fight in him, mainly directed against his superior, the Warden of Bradfield. When Dr Hodson returned to Oxford in 1872 and a friend asked him what he had been doing, he replied, 'I have been disputing daily in the School of one Tyrannus.' That sounds more like our Goudie; or as the Bradfield history puts it,

'The answer proves that he was certainly not without the saving sense of humour.'

He became Vicar of Steventon in Berkshire, and Rector of South Luffenham, Rutland, and in 1881 he was appointed Rector of Sanderstead, Surrey, where he remained until his death in 1890.

CHAPTER XII

Dr Harvey: Years of Decline (1869-88)

We are surrounded by schools which are backed up by large endowments and great
wealth. For my own part, I do not know that these are unmixed goods. With schools
as with individuals, poverty is a useful spur, but we should still have this useful
incentive even although we are raised out of debt.

(Rector Harvey, *Report to the Directors*, 1873)

IN 1867, the two Assistant Commissioners of the Argyll Commission
on Schools in Scotland had visited the Academy. In his *Report* for that
year, Dr Hodson had declared that he would leave it to the Commissioners 'to state their opinions as to the system of the Academy, its
practical working, its excellencies, or its defects. To their forthcoming
Report I look with the deepest interest, as I welcomed them to the
Academy with the sincerest pleasure, and gave them every facility in
my power for seeing its true condition, since I have long been driven
to the conclusion that Government Inspection is the best machinery
for ascertaining the real state of any School, as well as the only effectual
means of bringing about reform'.

In the event his confidence in their judgement was fully justified; the
Commission's Report, published in 1868, criticised the size of the
classes and the system of automatic promotion, as he himself had done
so often, but affirmed that: 'The Academy is probably, taken as a
whole, second to none in Scotland, and will stand comparison with the
English Public Schools in point of scholarship and spirit.'

Not that he had very much to fear: Dr Hodson knew better than
most the quality of the school he had been nursing for more than a
decade – and besides, as he pointed out in his 1867 *Report* with engaging candour, the two Assistant Commissioners detailed by the Argyll
Commission in 1866 to investigate education in the burgh and middle-
class schools in Scotland were 'gentlemen not only admirably fitted
for it by varied experience in examining Schools, but most kindly
disposed to the Academy . . .'

In fact one of them was himself an Academical, Alexander Craig
Sellar (E.A. 1844–50, advocate and later M.P., son of the notorious

Patrick Sellar who played such an infamous part in the Highland
Clearances), brother of the brilliant William Young Sellar (E.A. 1832–
9), Dux of the School in 1839 and later Professor of Humanity at
Edinburgh University from 1863–90.

The other was Thomas Harvey, who had been a Classical Master at
the Academy from 1847–56, and who had been commended by Dr
Hodson for playing cricket with the boys at Raeburn Place. He had
been headmaster of Merchiston for an unmemorable spell, from 1856–
1863: the *Merchiston Castle School Register, 1833–1962* was less than
fulsome about him – '. . . It must be admitted that he was not exactly
suited to the particular climate of Merchiston. He was a brilliant classical scholar, but appears to have been less able to inspire respect and
friendship among his pupils than the first two headmasters.'

It was this man, Dr Thomas Harvey, who was appointed as the
fourth Rector of the Edinburgh Academy to succeed Dr Hodson in
1869. He was forty-six years of age. He had been born and brought up
in Glasgow, and had had a distinguished academic career at Glasgow
University and as a Snell Exhibitioner at Balliol College, Oxford,
before joining the staff of the Edinburgh Academy. As a teacher he was
remembered at the Academy for his sound scholarship ('An accurate
and elegant, if scarcely a profound, scholar,' according to the *Edinburgh
Academy Register*) and for an exceptional ability to translate Latin and
Greek fluently and accurately at sight. In the *Chronicle* of November,
1932, an elderly Academical who was then in his nineties, Colonel
Robert d'Esterre Spottiswoode (E.A. 1851–4), who had been a member
of Harvey's Class, remembered him as 'a young and hot-tempered
Oxford man', and recalled that 'I have repeatedly seen Harvey, when
he had . . . the Third Class, tell Finlay, the Dux, to go to Mr Trotter,
whose tawse was known to be especially severe, "to give my compli-
ments to Mr Trotter, and ask for the use of his tawse," and having got
them [*sic*], would lay them well on the legs of two benches of boys,
"to wake them up".' (Finlay was R. B. Finlay, Dux of the School in
1858, later Viscount Finlay of Nairn, the Lord Chancellor.)

His superintendence and sharing of the cricket games at Raeburn
Place, at a time when it was rare for a master to do so, was a reflection
of his personal conversion to 'Arnoldism' at Balliol, just like his predecessor, Dr Hodson. At Balliol he had formed a lifelong friendship
with the great Greek scholar, Benjamin Jowett (later to be Master of
Balliol from 1870–93), and with William Young Sellar; but it was
another student at Balliol who was, indirectly, to have a greater effect

on his career – Hely Hutchison Almond. Almond was a member of the all-conquering Balliol boat, and became the great apostle of 'muscular Christianity' in Scotland. He was a member of the teaching staff at Merchiston during Harvey's headmastership there, but by the time Dr Harvey took over the Academy, Dr Almond had begun his long and distinguished career as Headmaster of Loretto. Loretto had only fourteen pupils when he took it over in 1862; but when Dr Harvey became Rector of the Academy in 1869, the numbers at Loretto had risen to nearly fifty, and by 1878 they reached three figures.

It was Dr Harvey's misfortune to be Rector of the Academy at a period when the school was running out of steam during a time of severe competition from other schools; it seems clear that one of the reasons for his appointment was the Directors' gratitude for his kind remarks about the Academy as an Assistant Commissioner for the Argyll Commission, but hindsight suggests that he was quite the wrong man for the job at that particular time. His nineteen years in office (1869–88) were little short of disastrous for the Academy, and under his care the numbers fell to the lowest point in the school's history (211 in 1888). He inherited from Dr Hodson a school in which he found much to praise in his first *Report* in 1870: 'The discipline of the School has been excellent . . . I attribute this in a great degree to my predecessor, Dr Hodson . . . punctuality, exact order, and good conduct are legacies which I find he had left to the Academy.' When he left, he bequeathed a school which needed a miracle-maker to save it – and was fortunate enough to find one.

Yet Dr Harvey was by no means an inconsiderable figure. Although he had not been highly thought of at Merchiston, he had laid a solid foundation for the future academic standards of the school under greater successors like Dr Rogerson. He had introduced written examinations and broadened the curriculum on Academy lines, using a mainly Scottish staff. As far as sporting activities were concerned, he had instituted the first recorded inter-school Rugby matches in 1858 (against the High School and the Edinburgh Academy), and had built the first school swimming-pool in Scotland.

Ironically, it was Dr Harvey himself, as an Assistant Commissioner for the Argyll Commission, who had helped to sow the seeds that brought about the competitive situation that nearly killed off the Academy. The Commission had been highly critical of the management of the well-endowed Hospital schools for the children of impoverished merchants. The ensuing Endowed Institutions (Scotland)

Act of 1869 gave the governors of these loveless, residential institutions the right to make better use of their endowments, by converting themselves into elementary and secondary schools open to all at greatly reduced fees.

The effect was electrifying. George Watson's Hospital, one of the Merchant Company institutions, had eighty-three boys before it was converted in 1870 – and then the Headmaster was inundated with 1,000 applications for places in the new school. The maximum fees for senior boys at George Watson's College were £6, compared with £17 at the Academy. Overall, the number of pupils at Hospital schools in Edinburgh leapt from about 400 to over 4,000. Many of the smaller private schools were almost immediately forced out of existence as George Watson's (boys and girls), Daniel Stewart's, and the others started scooping up pupils by the hundreds.

Two factors saved the Academy from extinction at this point. One was the fact that the Governors of the George Heriot's Trust, who also wanted to rechannel their funds and extend their use in 1870, were prevented from doing so on a series of legal technicalities until 1886, when Heriot's opened as a secondary school for boys. Had it happened fifteen years earlier, the extra weight of competition might have forced the Academy to succumb.

The second fortuitous factor during this difficult period was the fact that Fettes College, which opened in 1870 as a fee-paying boarding-school modelled on the English public schools, did not become a day school. The building of the school, which cost £230,000, was thought in many quarters to run counter to the new directions established by the Argyll Commission, and there were people who wanted to see it thrown open as an endowed secondary school like George Watson's College. Fettes took a few day-boys (and quite a number of boarders, too) who might otherwise have been expected to go to the Academy; but if Fettes were now to be compelled to take in great numbers of day-boys, at reduced fees, the combined competition from the south side of the city (Watson's) and the north side (Fettes) would undoubtedly have been too much for the Academy to cope with. A Commission was appointed to consider the proposal, under the Educational Endowments (Scotland) Act of 1882, and the hearing took place in 1885. The proposal was opposed by the Fettes Authorities and by the Edinburgh Academy, which was represented by one of the Directors, Andrew Beatson Bell, and eventually the proposal was turned down by the Commissioners in their *Report* of 1886. One bizarre suggestion which was put forward by one of the Commissioners was that the Academy should be amalgamated with Fettes, to which Beatson Bell replied, unexpectedly, 'I should not oppose that at all'!

So Thomas Harvey was in charge at the Edinburgh Academy at a time when the educational system in Edinburgh and elsewhere was undergoing revolutionary changes. It was clear that changes would have to take place at the Academy, too, if the school was merely to keep pace, never mind outdo the mushrooming crop of schools in Edinburgh in the scramble for pupils. Yet Dr Harvey seemed curiously unmoved; in the face of the threat from Fettes, Loretto and Merchiston on the one hand, and George Watson's and Daniel Stewart's on the other, Dr Harvey declared that the 'competition which surrounds us now on every side' was 'not calculated to do us any injury, but the reverse. More and more Edinburgh is becoming the school of Scotland, and attracts to herself scholars from every quarter. The Academy, if it continues to deserve it, will receive a full share of those who come from a distance, and can depend on the support of its friends in Edinburgh itself'. (*Report*, 1871.)

His response to the challenge was to tinker with the Academy system, rather than to try to revolutionise it. In his first year he decreed that German should start in the Fourth Class instead of the Fifth, and he gave the Sixth Class two hours of English dictation and essays every week, to 'help to remove a reproach which is sometimes made against Classical Schools, that with much Latin and Greek the boys are not infrequently unable to spell correctly and to express themselves with ease and propriety in their own language'. (*Report*, 1870.)

He also put his foot down on a tradition as old as schooling itself – the system of tutorial assistance to schoolboys: 'I do not think that tutors were employed as extensively a few years ago as they are now. At present in all the classes a large proportion of the boys have the advantage, or disadvantage, of this extraneous aid. Now, were all tutors judicious and faithful in the discharge of their duties, and did they render to their pupils only such assistance as a boy may require after he has done his best to solve the difficulties of his lessons, I should not be disposed to say anything on the subject. But I conceive that the system from small beginnings has become a great evil, and that it must be, if not repressed, at all events regulated as far as possible. The parents have a right to insist on it, that our lessons shall be so ordered, and difficulties so cleared away, that the expense, save in exceptional circumstances, shall not be required. Not infrequently it is money thrown away; for the tutor, to save himself trouble, explains all the pupil's difficulties, crams him, in fact, for his daily lessons, and leaves nothing for the boy to do himself. There are cases, certainly, for which the aid of a tutor may be absolutely required. For such cases I would suggest that there should be a certain number of recognised tutors connected with the school, whose names should be entered with myself and with the other Masters, and that the scale of their charges should be regulated by us. Parents and others who desire such aid for their boys should apply to us, and should employ only those tutors whose fitness we guarantee, and whose terms are reasonable . . . If this reform is effected, an objection that is sometimes made against the Academy on the score of expense will be removed.' (*Report*, 1870.)

He gave his full support to the system of periodical exams that Dr Hodson had found rather pointless, and urged the Directors to rid themselves of the fear that if parents received a succession of bad reports they would remove their sons from the Academy: 'It is best to know the truth, and parents are just the very persons to appreciate it, and when a report of progress is unsatisfactory, to co-operate with the Masters in working a cure.' (For the first time, examination results were being taken into consideration in giving the boys class positions at the end of the session and determining class prizes.)

But strangely enough, for an Assistant Commissioner who had criticised the size of classes at the Academy in 1868, Dr Harvey now strenuously denied the charge. Only the three youngest of the nine classes had more than forty pupils, he claimed, and 'present no difficulty to a teacher of experience and skill'. (The numbers were sixty-seven, sixty-four, and sixty-seven respectively in the First, Second and Third Classes.) The remainder were all under forty: 'A class of from thirty to forty boys is acknowledged by all teachers of experience to be one which a good Master can deal with successfully. It is not too large for individual examination of the boys every day, and it is large enough to supply good material to work upon, and to keep up wholesome emulation and rivalry.' (*Report*, 1870.)

During his Rectorship, the teaching of elementary physics was introduced, or re-introduced, into the Modern Side, and a workshop was opened to teach carpentry. The Academy also installed 'the most improved system of hot water pipes', and after complaints by the police the school's entire drainage system was renewed at great cost. This was a sign of the times, as health authorities began to get down to the cause of plague epidemics in the city, but there was no official obligation to take action, apart from laying a new pipe to connect with the main sewer being laid by the Burgh Engineer. The Academy asked the Sanitary Inspection Society to examine the other drains, and the Directors were advised to separate the drinking supply from the W.C. supply.

INNOVATIONS

Brown Soup, Roast Beef, and Bolster Pudding.
(Miss Elliot's *Cookery Book*)

To Dr Harvey fell the triumph of bringing the Academy back to the Scottish method of pronouncing Latin, which Cockburn and Horner had wanted from the beginning, and whose disappearance Lord Cockburn had mourned shortly before his death. Although the Directors had agreed on a compromise of a 'softened' version of the Scots pronunciation for the lower classes, while the English version was taught in the senior classes, the English method had taken over throughout the whole school by 1844. But classical scholars at Oxford and Cambridge had been discussing for some time the need to reform their own way of pronouncing Latin, and in 1871 the Oxford Committee decided to do away with 'the application to Latin of the modern English vowel system' which 'makes Latin in an English mouth unintelligible to all other Latin-reading nations'. A circular sent to the public schools from Oxford declared: 'The course which reform should take is obvious, as there is no controversy about the pronunciation of the vowels in ancient Rome, and, with insignificant exceptions, a uniform pronunciation of them prevails over the continent of Europe.'

Cockburn and the others could have told them that a long time ago. As Dr Harvey pointed out to the Directors in his *Report* for 1871, 'The proposal made in the circular is substantially that the vowel sounds, such as we have them in Scotland, should be adopted . . . I am of the opinion we should now resort to the original plan of the Academy.' The 'Scottish mode' was re-introduced into the First Classes in 1871–2.

The Academy performed its first play, the *Antigone* of Sophocles, in 1881, produced by Mr Islay Ferrier Burns, who was briefly a Classical Master from 1880–2: the first time that a Greek play had ever been presented in Scotland in the original Greek. It was not followed up until the reign of Harvey's successor, R. J. Mackenzie, who was to launch the great Academy tradition of dramatic productions and musical performances that have been such a feature of school life ever since. But this was to be the fate of many of Dr Harvey's ideas and innovations – his successors would gain the credit for actually putting them into practice.

For instance, it was during Dr Harvey's Rectorship that at long last the Directors were persuaded to agree to put an end to the system of automatic promotion – but it was not until Mackenzie's Rectorship that it actually came about. Dr Harvey had prodded away at the Directors for a long time; as early as 1872 he had told them in his *Report*: 'There is indeed one question which I should like you to consider with a view to future action, and which I believe ultimately will have to be faced, namely the comparative merits of promotion by routine, of each class in a body, and promotion by merit . . .' It is difficult nowadays to understand the extraordinary stubbornness with which the Directors clung to the old system, even though the High School had long since started to use exams to establish the fitness of boys to move up a class. It was rooted in a reluctance to offend parents who still demanded the right to say which class their sons should start in, and to have them move up with that class year after year whether or not they could keep up with the work. It was an attitude peculiar to Scotland, and stemmed from the Scot's deeply-founded sense of his 'rights' in the matter of education. Education was every Scot's right. Nobody could stop him moving up to the next class, even though it meant 'sitting it out' year after year and never catching up. The Education Department that was set up in London in 1856 with jurisdiction over Scotland found itself up against the same attitude when it wanted to award school grants, as in England, for elementary education. The grants were to be given on a capitation basis dependent on each pupil proving his proficiency in the three Rs. The Scots objected strongly to grants being tied to exam results: every Scot had the right to move up the school and go to university whether he could pass some English-type exam or not. As a result of the protests the Revised Code of grants was suspended in 1864, and although examination by inspectors was made compulsory, grants to Scottish schools did not depend on exam results. With the setting up of the Scotch Education Department through the Education (Scotland) Act of 1872, the government began to take a closer grip on school standards. Still, it was not until 1886 that 'The Directors resolved that promotion from Class to Class shall in future be by merit, and not by time alone; and that the

School shall be placed under (voluntary) Government inspection'. In the following session a first tentative beginning was made to adopt this innovation, based on examinations during the year conducted by the Rector, while in July, 1887, Academy boys sat the S.E.D. Examinations for the first time. Dr Harvey had eventually won his point, but it would be left to others to put it into effective practice.

In just the same way, it was Dr Harvey who put up the suggestion that the Academy needed a Preparatory Department. He had been to Glasgow and seen the flourishing junior department run by Glasgow Academy; and in his *Report* for 1881 he urged the Directors to start planning an elementary department taking boys of five and six, with women teachers in charge. But the Preparatory School, which was to prove of such inestimable benefit to the Academy, was not opened until October, 1888 – the term after Dr Harvey had left the school.

But there *was* one innovation which Dr Harvey not only suggested but also saw come to fruition: he started School dinners. He had been to Glasgow to study the way in which Glasgow Academy organised its school meals, and came back afire with enthusiasm. Until then, the only sustenance available to Academy boys in the middle of the day were the 'baps' and 'cookies', or the rye-rolls and 'half-alberts', available at the window of the Janitor's Lodge from the 'Mrs Jenny' of the day. But in 1881 a Dining Room was fitted out in one of the classrooms behind the Hall, and the ladies of the Edinburgh School of Cookery 'kindly gave their valuable assistance' to provide 'a good hot dinner of two courses' for one shilling, or a lunch of soup or coffee, with potatoes and bread, for sixpence. Part at least of the credit for the success of this innovation must go to the cook, a Northumberland farmer's daughter, Miss Ann Hall Elliot, who worked for the Academy for twenty years. Her brief from Dr Harvey was simply that she should 'do things nicely and at the same time economically . . . not . . to make any money; only that it should be self-supporting'. (In 1909, Miss Elliot published a booklet containing full details of the menus and recipes she used in that first year, under the title *Cookery Book*, 'with instructions for ingredients suitable to be taken into the stomach at the same time, which have been tried and found seasonable, nourishing, and agreeable to nearly three hundred persons at one meal in the Edinburgh Academy'. The staple menu remains instantly recognisable to every Academy boy who ever took School dinner – Brown Soup, Roast Beef, and Bolster Pudding, better known, perhaps, as Currant Stodge.)

There have been some notable cooks since Miss Elliot's day –
especially Mrs Isa Urquhart, who retired in 1957 after forty-six and a
half years slaving over a hot stove. She was there through two wars and
five Rectorships; and it would require a Dr Gloag to calculate just how
many thousands of school dinners, New Field teas, cricket lunches and
Denham Green meals she prepared in her time.

The original idea of School dinners, however, was very much Dr
Harvey's own brainchild, and the Directors recognised at the time
that without his 'unwearied efforts' it would have been a failure.
Nevertheless, despite the original altruism of a non-profit-making
scheme, after Dr Harvey left the Academy the Directors reckoned that
the declared profits from the school dinners were not as high as they
ought to be, and they wrote to Dr Harvey asking him to make up a
deficiency of £130!

SPORTING RECORDS

Mens sana in corpore sano (Juvenal, *Satires*)

Under Dr Harvey's Rectorship the Academy had mixed fortunes in
sport. He was Rector when the first Football International was played
on the Academy Field at Raeburn Place on March 27, 1871, with seven
Academicals playing in the Scottish XX and one in the English XX.
The School XX of 1873–4 was an extremely powerful one, and was
considered the first great school combination in the game. It included
Ninian Finlay (the brother of Viscount Finlay), W. E. Maclagan and
P. W. Smeaton, all of whom played for Scotland – Finlay, indeed, was
the first of four Academy boys who were 'capped' while still at school.
In the 1880s, Fettes, Loretto and Merchiston, with growing numbers
and a tendency for boys to stay on at school longer, beat the Academy
in practically every game; but in 1881 the Academy achieved the
distinction of being the only school to have had two of its boys playing
in a Rugby International – on opposing sides. The Academy captain,
Charles Reid, played as a forward for Scotland; he was a big strong
boy, barely seventeen years old, known as 'Hippo' because one day in
class he had failed to give the meaning of the Greek word for horse
(*hippos*). One of the Academy quarters, Frank Wright, a Manchester
boy, was drafted into the English team at the last moment to take the
place of a player who had missed the 'night mail' to Edinburgh;
according to the pundits of the day, he 'saved England repeatedly' as

the match ended in a draw. On the following morning (the game was played on a Tuesday) the Rector was forced to abandon Prayers in the Hall, so prolonged was the cheering for the two boys when they entered with their class.

Dr Harvey, as an 'Arnoldist', greatly approved of sports, and in his *Report* of 1874 he included 'the lists of our Football Twenty and of the Cricket Eleven all the more willingly that among them is a fair proportion of prize-takers in the ordinary work of the classes'. Yet he did not think to make sports a compulsory part of the school curriculum – that was left to his successor, Mackenzie, in 1891 (thereby making the Academy the first day school in Scotland to take this step).

But paradoxically he disapproved of the Inter-Scholastic Games which had been a feature of the athletics season at Raeburn Place since 1866. He felt that through them a disproportionate amount of honour was given to 'the gladiators', and he tried to prevent the Games being held at Raeburn Place. In 1872 there were tremendous ructions within the Academical Cricket Club (which ran the field on behalf of the school and the Academicals), when the committee decided not to make Raeburn Place available for the Games; several committee members resigned, and a new committee overturned the decision. The Rector objected strongly to this reversal; it seems that his objections may have been concerned with the growth of betting and drunkenness at popular spectator sports like pedestrianism and horse-racing. Perhaps he feared that boys might be tempted to take part in sports for pecuniary gain, which would corrupt the whole idea of 'Arnoldism'. Whatever the reason, the Inter-Scholastic Games were not held at Raeburn Place in 1874; and Dr Harvey, the sportsman who played cricket with the boys as a master, is remembered chiefly for his opposition to the Games as Rector.

STAFF: THE CLYDE DYNASTY BEGINS

> And he has justified it.   (Dr. Clyde)

Apart from James Carmichael, three men stand out from the Academy staff during Dr Harvey's Rectorship, for different reasons: two classicists, and a mathematician.

Henry Weir ('Puggy') was a Berwickshire man, who first came to the Academy as one of the Classical Masters in 1853, when Harvey himself was a teacher there. He stayed for twenty-eight years, and was long remembered as one of the most truly *popular* of all the Classical

Masters at the Academy in the nineteenth century. He was educated at
Edinburgh University and Caius College, Cambridge, where he
graduated with honours in both classics and mathematics. He was headmaster of Berwick Grammar School when he was appointed to the
Edinburgh Academy at the age of thirty-seven.

George Crabbie, a Director of the Academy, wrote a brief but
touching obituary in the *Chronicle* of December, 1904, when his old
master died: 'At school he was beloved, there is no other word to
express it, and when he retired (in 1881), this love took a very tangible
form, a handsome sum being subscribed to provide him with an
annuity which he enjoyed for many years. His personality was delightful, full of quaint humour and real humanity; his little stories never
palled, although oft repeated, his joy in telling them being infectious,
and his listeners were always prodigal in their applause. The teaching
hours passed pleasantly and profitably, both master and pupils understanding each other and rejoicing in their intimacy. He wore no mask,
and hence his popularity. In school and out of it our friend and master
was always the same, essentially human, treating parents and boys
alike with a consideration born only of a large, warm Christian heart.
"Magister nascitur non fit".'

The Weir Class Club Essay prize, founded in his memory, was for a
long time a coveted award, where juniors in the Fifth Classes could
take on their seniors in open competition.

John Sturgeon ('Mucky') Mackay, who came to the Academy as
Assistant Mathematical Master in 1866, shortly after Dr Gloag retired,
and stayed as Head Mathematical Master until he retired thirty-eight
years later, in 1904, was a very different kind of man – different from
Mr Weir, and different from Dr Gloag. A Perth man, he had studied
at St Andrews and Edinburgh Universities, and made his name for his
work in pure geometry, with a string of textbooks ranging from
Chambers's *Standard Arithmetical Exercises* to *The Elements of Euclid*. But
Dr Mackay had a most extraordinarily versatile intellect, for he was
also a fine linguist and classicist. In the 1870s he was the victim of one
of those poignant blows that fate can sometimes deal scholars. He was a
renowned authority on Greek Mathematics, and for years he spent all
his vacations in libraries in London and on the Continent studying the
manuscripts of the only great Alexandrine geometer who had never
been published, Pappus. At long last he completed the work, and the
whole book lay complete on his desk in his fine handwriting, with a
wealth of drawings. One morning soon after he had finished it he

walked into Williams and Norgate's foreign bookshop in Frederick Street, where the manager, a Mr Wheatley, said to him, 'I've something for you today that will interest you.' And from the shelves he took down the first volume of a newly published edition of Pappus by the German scholar Hultsch. Dr Mackay took the book home with him to study it. One can imagine his feelings of despair as he realised that Hultsch had collated precisely the same manuscripts as he had, arrived at precisely the same interpretations, and noted all the same difficulties down to the smallest detail. All those years of labour wasted! But he was never heard to complain; the work had been done, and well done, the needs of his few fellow-scholars of Greek mathematics were sufficiently met, and what was lost was a matter for him alone. It takes a great man to get over a bitter disappointment of that nature; but 'Mucky' Mackay remained unfailingly modest and magnanimous, wearing his enormous erudition lightly and with dignity. Towards the end of his long career at the Academy his sight began to fail him, and he was unequal to the task of keeping discipline in a large class. On a dull day it was possible for a hardy sinner even to smoke a cigarette in the back seats, unobserved by 'Mucky' Mackay's eyes and undetected by his nose, for Dr Mackay was an inveterate snuff-taker. Boys selected for punishment by him would push notebooks up their sleeves and pull the sleeves well down over their wrists; the resulting blow from the tawse made more than the usual amount of noise, and the victim would scream in affected agony until old 'Mucky's' soft heart would melt, and the tawsing would end in a welter of profound apologies.

He was the last of the sterling nineteenth-century dominies of the Academy staff, although one other master who retired at the same time, in 1904, matched him for sheer length of service. This was Alexander ('Gillie') Gilmour, who joined the staff as Assistant Writing and Arithmetic Master for three years in 1851, when Dr Hannah was Rector, and returned in 1868 as Head Writing and Arithmetic Master, just before Dr Harvey began his Rectorship. 'Gillie' and 'Mucky' were boon companions in their old age, the one half-blind and the other half-deaf, and were known as David and Jonathan. 'Gillie' never quite mastered the technique of using a tawse effectively, either; or perhaps he was just too kind-hearted. Instead of laying on with the whole instrument, he would flip at the victim's palm with one thong only.

But the third outstanding master of Dr Harvey's Rectorship probably has the greatest claim to fame of them all – Dr James Clyde. Not only was he a scholar with a European reputation, but he was the progenitor of one of the most remarkable families in Academy history.

Dr Clyde came to the Academy in 1861 from Dollar Academy in succession to Mr Trotter, and stayed for seventeen years until 1878. He had already written several text-books before he arrived – *Romaic and Modern Greek*, *Greek Syntax* (which ran to six editions), *Elementary Geography* (which ran to twenty-five editions), and *School Geography* (which ran to twenty-six). At the Academy he wrote *Edinburgh Academy Rudiments of the Greek Language* (which went to fifteen editions), and *Rudiments of the Latin Language for the Use of the Edinburgh Academy*, which came out in 1879, the year after he resigned from the Academy to concentrate on his writing. He was hardly gone before he was asked to return because his successor was too ill to take up the post; but the Directors made the proviso that he must give up all his literary work if he came back, and this Dr Clyde would not accept.

He was an excellent teacher, although never as popular as Mr Weir or Mr Carmichael – he was too forbidding and stern a man for that. There was something of the Roman and the Stoic in him, with an unbending sense of duty and propriety and rectitude. But some very distinguished men emerged from the Clyde Class – D'Arcy Wentworth Thompson, the Haldanes, Professor Herdman, Professor Nöel Paton. But his most distinguished product was never in his class at all – his only child, James Avon Clyde, on whose education he lavished all his leisure time (in later years he was heard to say quietly, 'And he has justified it').

James Avon Clyde entered the Academy in 1873, and was successively Dux of every single Class, including Dux of the School in 1880 (as well as being best in French, German, English, and Latin and Greek Composition). An awesomely clever boy; and he grew into an awesomely brilliant and indefatigable man – Advocate, K.C., Solicitor-General for Scotland, Unionist M.P. for West Edinburgh, Dean of the Faculty of Advocates, Lord Advocate, and as Lord Clyde, Lord Justice-General and Lord President of the Court of Session. He was considered the greatest advocate of his time, a perfect pleader and examiner of witnesses, and rapidly acquired a practice which has probably never been equalled in quantity or quality; he was certainly one of the most distinguished men the Academy has ever produced. And he never forgot his debt to the Academy. In 1905, he founded the Clyde and Millar Greek Prizes with his close friend, Professor John Hepburn Millar, who succeeded him as Dux of the Academy in 1881 and later as Secretary to the Directors in 1896. Clyde served as Secretary to the Directors from 1889–96, forming a marvellously creative partnership with Rector Mackenzie. He was then appointed to the Board of Directors, and served as a Director until 1936, and an Honorary Director until his death in 1944.

He was followed as a Director by his elder son, James L. M. Clyde, who served on the Board from 1955–61. His career paralleled that of his father to an uncanny extent. He, too, was Dux of the Academy, in 1916, and like his father he became successively an advocate, K.C., M.P., Solicitor General, Lord Advocate and, as Lord Clyde, Lord Justice-General and Lord President of the Court of Session. He is a founder-member and President of the Quinze Club, which was formed at Oxford in 1920 and consisted originally of fifteen members, all of whom had studied Classics at the Academy and left school between 1916 and 1919. They meet for dinner once a year, wearing quince-coloured waistcoats as a result of an undergraduate pun on the word 'quinze'.

And now a fourth-generation Clyde, James J. Clyde, son of James L. M. and grandson of James Avon, is bidding fair to follow in the same steps. He was Dux of the Academy in 1951, is a Q.C., has been a Director of the Academy, and has already stood as a Parliamentary candidate. And a fifth generation is now at the Academy, too . . .

Yes, a remarkable Academy family, the Clydes.

THE ACADEMY JUBILEE: 1874

> I believe the Academy has abundantly fulfilled its mission.
> (Principal Shairp)

To Dr Harvey fell the honour of leading the Academy in its jubilee year, 1874. He recognised the opportunity to use the 50th anniversary of the school to rally support for the next half century. In his *Report* of 1873, he urged the Directors: '[In 1874] the Academy will then have to commemorate its Jubilee. Advantage will be taken of that occasion, I trust, to wipe off the debt of the School, and, it may be, to raise funds to form the nucleus of a permanent Endowment for the masters, and of Scholarships for the pupils. Although it has attained a goodly age, many of those who were the Academy's pupils in the year of its foundation are still in the vigour of life, and there must be thousands in our own country and abroad who, I am convinced, will be willing . . . to assist in setting the Academy on even a more secure and solid basis than before. We are surrounded by schools which are backed up by large endowments and great wealth. For my own part, I do not know that these are unmixed goods. With schools as with individuals, poverty is a useful spur, but we should still have this useful incentive even though we were raised out of debt.'

The Academy debt stood at £1,631. This was more than cleared by the Jubilee Appeal Fund, which ultimately brought in £1,970 14s., and a great company of about 170 Academicals gathered in the Douglas Hotel in St Andrew Square on October 16, 1874, to sing the praises of the School and the men who had created it.

His Grace the Archbishop of Canterbury, Archibald Campbell Tait, Dux of the Academy in 1826 and 1827, was in the chair. Proposing the toast of 'Floreat Academia' (*May the Academy Flourish*) he recalled the boys who had sat beside him in the Hall on that first day on October 1, 1824: Alexander Wood, the first Dux, whom 'it pleased God to afflict with weak health and almost a total loss of eyesight', yet he won regard and esteem as a Sheriff; and Walter Mackenzie, who was drowned in the Solway in the second year of the Academy. He praised Leonard Horner and Lord Cockburn – 'those Scotchmen who loved Scotland and loved the system of education which had made Scotland great', but who, to prevent Scots sending their sons to England, 'desired that there should be abundant opportunity for receiving a full and thorough education such as England afforded, within the walls of the old capital'; and Archdeacon Williams, the first Rector, who 'taught us in a way that none but a very able man indeed can teach'.

Had the founders of the Academy succeeded in their aims? – 'I am bound to say that somehow or another they did manage to surround this new institution with associations almost as hallowed as those which naturally attach to an institution which has lasted for a hundred years.' He went on: 'When others shall meet together, perhaps some fifty years hence . . . I believe they will look back over the hundred years as we now look back over the fifty years, with much thankfulness, with much gratitude to those who founded this institution.'

Principal John Campbell Shairp of St Andrews University (later Professor of Poetry at Oxford), who had been at the Academy from 1829 to 1832, recalled Sir Walter Scott's hope at the Opening that the Academy might do something to wipe away Dr Johnson's reproach that 'in learning, Scotland was like a beseiged city, where every man had a mouthful but none a bellyful'. He said: 'We must in candour admit that as far as deep scholarship goes we are like a beseiged city still. We all know that the Academy has trained during the last fifty years not a few very eminent Greek Scholars; but they, with the sure instinct of our race for the main chance, have for the most part carried their wares to southern and more lucrative markets. Scotland has been, when it was a poor country – it continues now when it has become a rich one – a land in which scholars are few. But to produce great scholars is not the only or even the chief work of a large school – rather to train boys so that they shall become upright, honourable, intelligent, industrious men in all walks of life. Tried by this test, I believe the Academy has abundantly fulfilled its mission.'

Dr Harvey spoke of the competition which was facing the Academy at this time – and showed how little he appreciated the gravity of the threat: 'The school has no endowment, and, speaking for myself, I have to say that . . . it does not greatly desire endowment. All the more fortunate . . . that it is not the least likely to get it. But really if a school like the Academy ceases to be able to maintain itself unless bolstered up by grants of money from the public purse or from private purses, the sooner it dies the better. I trust that no call for further help need be made.'

(It makes strange reading compared with the infinitely more realistic approach of his successor, R. J. Mackenzie, in the last year of his Rectorship at a Reunion Dinner on July 5, 1901: 'This School has to confront, almost unarmed, a fierce conflict of competition. It is like a little David with his sling and stone going forth to meet giants in their panoply. On the one hand, there is the famous and ancient High School of Edinburgh, backed by the limitless resources of the rate; and George Watson's College with its numberless bursaries and bottom-less endowment. On the other hand, there is Fettes College with its numerous Foundationerships, Scholarships, and Exhibitions. And lastly, there are the Public Schools of England with their great accumul-ations and even greater prestige. To meet such adversaries my col-leagues and I had to place this School in the forefront of organisation and equipment. It has cost brains and labour to do so. It has also cost money . . . Gentlemen, you must take better care . . . of my successor. You must lift from his shoulders the load of debt, and put him in com-mand of an endowment which will enable him to face serenely the chances and changes of the School. There is no body of old boys so devoted as old Academy boys to the memory of their School' (*cheers*) 'yet up to the present there is no body of old boys whose affection has taken a less pecuniary form.')

The Directors, too, were lulled into a false sense of security in that Jubilee year of 1874: '. . . The Directors confidently maintain that the present position of the School challenges favourable comparison with any in Scotland. Unassisted by any endowment, and surrounded on all sides by keen competition, the Academy more than holds its ground.'

But the years that followed the triumphant celebration of the Jubilee were to be the worst period in the history of the Academy. By 1886 there were only 247 boys at the Academy. By 1888 the figure was down to 211. Discipline was poor, morale low. With so little money coming in, staff had to be reduced. Once again the English Master was sacrificed – his classes were chaotic anyway – and his work divided among the Classical Masters; the French and German departments were combined under one master and the German Master was dismissed. The two senior Classical Masters, Dr Clyde and Mr Weir, had left the Academy halfway through Dr Harvey's Rectorship, and it proved difficult to recreate continuity; there had been dissatisfaction over discipline in Mr Elliott's and Mr Islay Ferrier Burns's classical classes, and both soon left, and the Directors refused a testimonial to Mr Burns when he applied for a professorship at Dundee (he became a tutor at Westminster College in Cambridge instead). After having been promised a pension of £100 a year after his twenty-nine years' service, Mr Weir could only be given an annuity of £70, with no prospect of receiving anything else in future.

Dr Harvey blamed the falling-off in numbers on the failure of the English department; on the trend among preparatory schools to keep boys on for two years longer and start them in Latin before releasing them to the Academy; on the introduction of an entrance examination to the Scottish universities, with the proviso that if a student spent a year in a junior class at the university he need not sit the entrance exam, which encouraged parents to remove their boys from school a year earlier and send them to university instead. The Academy was being squeezed on every side.

As for discipline, Dr Harvey tried to continue Dr Hodson's achievement of sparing the rod, and at the end of his first year he had reported that the discipline of the school had been excellent and 'my duties in enforcing it almost a sinecure'. But Dr Harvey did not have Dr Hodson's whiplash tongue to take the place of the tawse (he was also the first Academy Rector to have to exercise control without the sanction of a dog-collar). By the following year, the diligence and progress of the classes were 'on the whole satisfactory'. Next year diligence was only 'fair', and Dr Harvey, champion of 'manly sports' though he was, had to admit: 'I am not sure . . . with the attraction of games, and the high value attached to excellence in all sports of strength or skill, that work has quite so fair a chance as it used to have. The best boys will always study with a will and need no spurring; the idle, however, have lighted on times exceptionally favourable to them. Now, too, that the spirit of the age has pronounced decidedly against severe punishments in all circumstances, and that corporal chastisement is absolutely disused though not formally forbidden in all the Rector's Classes, masters have to depend more than ever on themselves. One result of this undoubtedly is that they do not get so much out of the incorrigibly idle as they otherwise might, but, on the other hand, they establish much more friendly relations with all the boys, and if a master is discreet and zealous, if he gains the respect and faith of his scholars, he will always get a fair and reasonable amount of work done.' (*Report*, 1872.)

He was so right. He really knew all the answers, in theory. He could have written a magnificent thesis on how to run a successful school. But when he resigned in 1888 to live in retirement in Tain and Montrose (where he died in January, 1901), the Academy was in desperate straits. He had simply happened along at a time when the Academy needed much more than just a good teacher who was a good headmaster. It needed a new kind of man in charge, a new species of Rector; not a head teacher; not a man of the classroom, but a man behind an office desk; an administrator; a man of vision, power, dedication, and driving personality.

The Directors did not know it, but what they wanted was a nineteenth-century whizz-kid to take them into the twentieth century. And they got one . . .

CHAPTER XIII

R. J. Mackenzie: Into the 20th Century
(1888-1901)

This is my work, my blessing, not my doom;
Of all who live, I am the one by whom
This work can best be done in my own way.
(Quoted in the *Chronicle*, December, 1912)

THE man who was to lift the Edinburgh Academy out of the doldrums and launch it into the twentieth century was Robert Jamieson Mackenzie, son of Donald Mackenzie (later Lord Mackenzie), one of the Senators of the College of Justice. He was born in 1857, and really began training for his life's work on the day he became a pupil at Loretto in 1866; because there he came under the enduring influence of a man he revered for the rest of his days and whose biography he would eventually write – the great Dr H. H. Almond, Headmaster of Loretto. Almond was then in the first phase of establishing at the little school in Musselburgh an educational system based on fostering 'character, physique, intelligence, manners and information' – in that order. The first phase involved training a number of senior boys to carry out his regimen of vigorous physical exercise, compulsory games, strict discipline, toughness, manliness, and high moral standards of honesty, fair play, and the honour of the school.

Bob Mackenzie became the most trusted of those specially trained senior boys – the Head Boy. At this point in Loretto's development the Head Boy was senior to every master in the school except Dr Almond himself. Young Mackenzie was consulted by the Head on all school matters, and was once left in complete charge of the school for a fortnight when the Head was away. There were only about fifty boys at Loretto at this time, but it is a measure of Dr Almond's system of character training that he could place so much trust in a lad in his teens; and it also helps to explain the sort of man who emerged from that training – the man of confidence, sureness of decision, power of personality and certainty of policy who swept Directors, masters, parents and boys along with him in the Academy's triumphal march forward a dozen years later.

Mr Mackenzie absorbed everything that Dr Almond had to teach about training a boy's body as well as his mind – and keeping both in step with his soul. He trained on a diet of moral dissertations, delivered in Dr Almond's celebrated sermons, such as: 'Why, oh why, cannot there be a holy alliance between the athlete and the Christian; an alliance against the common enemies of both, against intemperance and indolence, and dissipation, and effeminacy, and aesthetic voluptuousness, and heartless cynicism, and all the unnatural and demoralising elements in our social life?'

It is unlikely that this kind of heart-cry, aimed at the corruption which Dr Almond and other reformers perceived in the English public schools, would mean very much in the down-to-earth, Presbyterian, day-school atmosphere of the Edinburgh Academy; but the principles of strict discipline, moral rectitude, and cleanliness of soul were dear to the heart of every Victorian parent, and when the time came for him to take the helm at the Academy, Mr Mackenzie the Scot had the sense to take just enough of what he believed best in Dr Almond's English-boarding-school vision and apply it to what he considered the more wholesome 'Home School' system at the Academy.

Loretto's rigid (and some might say ridiculous) regimen of cold baths, physical endurance, and games, games and more games, was not only unnecessary but intolerable and impossible to put into practice in a school where the majority of the boys spent half of every day, all week-end and every night in their own homes. Mr Mackenzie realised this. He appreciated that while a boarding school headmaster could run his menage pretty well as he wished, with very little interference from parents, the head of a school like the Academy not only has parents constantly breathing down his neck but must have their whole-hearted co-operation in everything, because the home is part of the school and the two must work together.

Nevertheless, as Head Boy at Loretto, and then (after being Senior Scholar at Keble College, Oxford) as a teacher at Loretto for six months in 1881 and as Assistant Master at Clifton College from 1881-8, Mr Mackenzie became convinced that there were certain basic essentials in the running of any great school, which were applicable to both day schools and boarding schools. He also had a keen perception of what was required in educational reform and reorganisation to meet the demands of the next century. It was this irresistible combination of high principle and hard practicality that persuaded the Directors into a breathtaking programme of expansion and expense which they would have been horrified even to contemplate before this time. As Mr Mackenzie himself put it at the end of his thirteen-year Rectorship (1888–1901): '£16,000 was the sum expended in the original foundation of the Academy. During the years of my Rectorship, nearer £17,000 has been spent on its reconstruction.'

Even a bare summary of what he achieved during those thirteen years of reconstruction is staggering:

He successfully launched the Preparatory School.

He built a science laboratory and made science compulsory.

He built several new classrooms, and expanded the staff.

He established an Upper Seventh, and encouraged pupils to enter the Academy earlier and leave it later.

He enforced the system of promotion by merit, reducing the size of classes, and reorganised them into A and B levels.

He started the school Boarding Houses.

He made sports a compulsory part of the curriculum.

He bought a new school playing-field, New Field.

He built a gymnasium, and started gymnastic displays.

He introduced a system of school prefects, and called them by a Greek name, *Ephors*.

He created a new sense of discipline inside and outside the school – parents had to conform to it, too.

He insisted on an official school head-dress.

He started a school choir and sang leading roles in it himself.

He started a school orchestra.

He composed the music for the school song, *Floreat Academia*.

He launched *The Edinburgh Academy Chronicle*.

He revived the school library.

He started a school museum and established a fund to maintain it.

He established regular productions of Greek plays in Greek.

He started regular Academical Reunions involving the school.

He fostered enthusiasm and loyalty amongst Academicals, helped revive the Academical Club, and urged the establishment of an Endowment Fund which was eventually started in 1904 . . .

And he did it all with a blend of determination, charm, enthusiasm and sheer hard work that inspired an extraordinary degree of loyalty and devotion in everyone connected with the school. He brought the number of boys attending the Academy soaring from its nadir of 211 in 1888 to a new peak of 493 in 1895. But it was only achieved at a high cost; in his thirteen years at the Academy, Mr Mackenzie ruined his health through overwork.

The Directors, of course, had to give their approval to all his reforms, and it says much for the man's charisma, his magnetism and ability to put his ideas across, that he had very little difficulty in persuading these cautious and rather conservative men to sanction his ambitious schemes and financial outlays.

And of course he did not do it all by himself. He built up a team of new teachers to supplement the Old Guard, young men from the English public schools and universities, who supported him in all his schemes and cheerfully gave up their leisure time to undertake all the extra-curricular duties that his revolutionary all-round programme of classwork, games, and cultural activities entailed.

He also had James Avon Clyde – another shining example in the Academy's history of the moment producing the man. Mr Clyde was the Secretary to the Directors during the crucial early years of Mr Mackenzie's Rectorship (1889–96), and as such he was the intermediary between him and the Directors. Mr Mackenzie had the ideas; Mr Clyde was the man who translated them into practical form, reduced them to cash terms, and backed up Mr Mackenzie's idealism with facts and figures which the Directors could understand and appreciate.

But when Mr Mackenzie came to the Academy in 1888 he was alone, a thirty-one-year-old bachelor, in charge of a school in which morale was low, discipline ragged, debts high, and prospects poor. Immediately he swept in and took command, with what the Directors described in their 1889 *Report* as 'all the energy and organising power which his reputation led the Directors to expect would distinguish him'. Mr Mackenzie's own first *Report* in 1889 in turn apologised for his long list of changes and new regulations, but insisted that they were being introduced 'not a moment too soon'.

Perhaps the first thing he had to do was to re-establish the authority of the school itself. To this end, he immediately started enforcing the system of promotion or detention strictly according to attainments. The new syllabus also clearly laid down rules about punctuality, attendance, and the prevention of infection. He enforced the old founders' rule against boys leaving the premises during school hours. He came down heavily on parents who had been in the habit of keeping their sons off school at odd times to run messages or meet trains. Boys must attend from the first day to the last, and family holidays must fit in with school holidays. He also insisted on an official school head-dress (perhaps he had been reading about the unfortunate Dr Hodson and the Affair of the Round-Crowned Hat in the archives). At first it was a glengarry with the badge of Homer's head, or a straw boater in summer with ribbon of the blue-and-white colours of the Academy football jerseys (later, in 1902, a blue cap with a laurel wreath encircling the letters E.A., worked in white, was introduced as an alternative to the glengarry).

Gone now was the former apologetic attitude to parents; it was a case of obeying the rules – or 'it shall be in the discretion of the Rector to refuse to admit such boys . . .' Later the Directors took cold feet and replaced the word 'must' in their rules for attendance with 'par-ticularly requested'; but it soon became apparent that the more difficult it was to join the Academy, the more wanted to join, and 'particular requests' had the force of 'unquestioned rules' in no time at all. Even during that first session of Mr Mackenzie's Rectorship, the school roll rose from 213 to 235 . . .

Another innovation during that first session was to abandon entirely the principle of large classes that the Argyll Commission had criticised. More than fifty boys had enrolled in the Geits that autumn, so at Christmas this class was divided into an A and B division according to merit, and year by year this double division would move up the school until all but the most senior classes were divided in this way.

THE PREPARATORY SCHOOL

. . . An Elementary or Preparatory Department, for the education of boys from the age of five or six till they are fit to pass into the Upper School and begin Latin . . .
(Directors' *Report*, 1888)

One of Dr Harvey's last acts before he resigned the Rectorship was to urge the Directors to establish a Prep School that would take boys from the age of six or seven to that of nine or ten, with a playground and schoolrooms entirely separate from those of the Upper School, to be taught by ladies. Eventually the Directors agreed, and the detached building to the north-west of the grounds containing the old Writing and Mathematical Block was taken over, and the north-west corner of the Yards was walled off. Three lady teachers were engaged: Miss

Wood, Miss Hardie, and Miss Clark, each with a salary of £80 rising to £100, compared with the minimum salary for men of £250.

On October 1, 1888, about forty small boys gathered apprehensively for their first day's schooling. Their fees ranged from two guineas to three guineas per term. In the course of the first session the numbers at the Prep rose to sixty-one, and during the Easter holidays the Rector started a beginners' class to prepare boys for the entrance exam to the Prep. Within three years the numbers at the Prep had doubled, to 130.

Of the three Prep school mistresses who started in 1888, one soon showed herself to be an outstanding teacher: Miss Isabella Wood. She became Senior Mistress in 1893, and was to remain at the Prep for thirty-two years and become an outstanding figure in the annals of the Prep – 'at once the embodiment of its traditions and the prime mover in their creation,' as the Rector of the time (Dr R. H. Ferard) said of her when she retired in 1920. She had come to the Academy from teaching at the Clergy Daughters' School at Casterton, Westmorland, where Charlotte Brontë had been a pupil and which was the prototype of 'Lowood School' in *Jane Eyre*, and Miss Wood was always extremely proud of the fact. In the classroom she was a formidable disciplinarian; absolute silence reigned in her class – 'Woe betide the offender who did not on every occasion come up to her high standard of neatness and accuracy; he received such a torrent of rebuke as many an older person would have flinched under.' (*Chronicle*, November, 1920.) She died only a few months after she retired, and was sincerely missed by generations of small boys who had been trained under her eagle eye. To this day there are Academicals who remember her with affectionate respect, and can still vividly recall the model of the Temple of Jerusalem which always stood in her classroom.

Another Prep long-timer of the early days was Miss Elizabeth Clark – 'Clarkie' – who joined the staff in 1893 and stayed for over thirty years until she retired in 1924 (she died in 1944). She is remembered for her lucid teaching and exceptionally vigorous piano accompaniments at musical occasions. 'Dull indeed must the boy have been who was proof against her determination that he should understand his lesson and master it,' as the Rector (Dr Ferard) wrote when she retired. Then there was Miss Mabel Fuller, who joined the staff in 1895 and stayed for thirty-seven years until 1932; for the last eight years she was Senior Mistress. Until her death in 1953 there was nothing she enjoyed more than a good gossip about her boys. In 1911, the charming Miss Sophia

J. Tullo joined the staff, and stayed for thirty years until she retired in 1940. She continued to take a lively interest in the Academy and her former pupils after she retired, and was a regular and welcome attender at Staff social functions until shortly before her death in 1973 at the age of ninety-three.

After the First World War, the numbers at the Prep remained steady at just over the 200-mark. Nostalgia casts a wistful glow over these inter-war years, and the stalwarts who ran the Prep in those days with Miss Clark, Miss Fuller and Miss Tullo; ladies like Miss Vera F. Smith, for instance, who joined the staff in 1919 and taught in the Prep for thirty-three years before she retired in 1952. She is indelibly associated with the Fourth Classes – a hurdle in life to be approached with trepidation, like Becher's, only to find it much more exhilarating and rewarding than one had feared possible. She was always firm, and looked it; but in her class, boys discovered how kind she was, too. When war broke out in 1939 and the Prep was temporarily closed for a term, Miss Smith was one of the three mistresses who kept classes going at Mackenzie House (one of the Boarding Houses). She became Senior Mistress in 1945 and took charge of Class V, but after a breakdown in health she gave up her class and undertook general teaching throughout the Prep until she retired.

Then there was Miss Alison M. Ogilvie, yet another long-timer, who joined the staff in 1932 and served for thirty-four years before retiring in 1966. She started with Class I, and ended as Senior Mistress. Academicals remember her obsessive insistence on keeping pencils razor-sharp (it meant sharpening your pencils almost down to stumps the night before in a desperate attempt to get the points right), and also the happy moments when her natural history demonstrations came to their climax, and a butterfly, lovingly cherished from a caterpillar, was released in the Yards.

But the champion of them all, when it comes to long service, is Miss Helen F. McTavish, who was appointed in 1923; she was to spend forty-two years of unbroken service with the Academy before she retired as Head of the Prep in 1965, and not one of the thousand and more boys who passed through her classes will ever forget her kindly, understanding attitude. For a long time she was Class Mistress of Prep VA, and during the war she taught senior English in the Upper School with conspicuous success. She more than anyone else bridged the pre-war and post-war generations; and when she retired in 1965, an era ended, for she was last lady Head in the history of the Prep.

Dear 'Tabby'! She was that rare presence in school, an institution who never became ossified.

The post-war years have seen tremendous developments in the Prep. They started almost before the war had ended. In the summer of 1944, the Directors of the Academy were offered the gift of a substantial house, Denham Green, set in three acres of ground in Trinity, half a mile from New Field. The gift came from a distinguished Academical, Major Noel Salvesen (E.A. 1898–1911) of the Edinburgh whaling and shipping firm. Major Salvesen, who was Dux of the Academy in both 1910 and 1911 and a fine all-round athlete, presented his Edinburgh house when he left Edinburgh to make his home in Ross-shire – just one of many generous benefactions that he and his brothers made to the Academy. An anonymous gift of £2,000 covered the cost of fitting the house out as a Junior Department of the Prep, and Denham Green was opened on October 3, 1945, for a hundred pupils. The Senior Mistress in charge was another Prep school stalwart, Miss Elizabeth H. Millar, who had joined the Prep away back in 1910. She extended her career in order to get Denham Green off the ground, before retiring in 1947 after thirty-six years service. Miss Millar died in 1966 at the age of eighty.

She was succeeded as Senior Mistress by Miss Rosina B. Hagart, one of the most popular mistresses the Prep has ever known. She joined the staff in 1922, and stayed for thirty-seven years before retiring in 1959. Her particular form of war service was to keep a small part of the Prep School alive by migrating with fourteen small Academy boys and two colleagues to a house near Grantown-on-Spey called Tullochgribban for two years. In a decade as Senior Mistress of Denham Green she made it into a very gay and active little school, with its own music concerts which Miss Hagart instituted. The present Mistress in Charge is Miss A. M. Taylor, who joined the staff in 1947.

In June, 1971, Denham Green House was seriously damaged by fire after vandals broke in. For several months, classes were continued in the Old Sanatorium at Fettes College, which sprang to the assistance within twenty-four hours of the blaze – a splendid gesture. But in the summer of 1973, Denham Green rose again like a phoenix – a transformed and modernised phoenix. At the start of the 1973-4 session there were 134 pupils at Denham Green. (The Old Sanatorium at Fettes was transformed as well – it has now been converted into Fettes Junior School, taking day-boys from eleven to thirteen years of age.)

The opening of Denham Green in 1945 obviously took some of the pressure off the accommodation at Henderson Row as numbers began to rise rapidly after the war. But by December, 1946, the Rector (Mr C. M. E. Seaman) was pointing out to the Directors that the Upper School urgently needed new accommodation if it was not to fall behind what was required of a modern up-to-date school. The Directors made inquiries about the possibility of expanding Denham Green to take another 150 pupils – all but the two upper classes of the Prep; but the cost was prohibitive, and so the Directors agreed in July, 1950, to launch an Appeal Fund to build a new Prep School at Inverleith Place, on a 13½-acre site close to New Field. The idea was to start with a Prep School, with the prospect of eventually moving the whole school to the new site and abandoning Henderson Row: the tail wagging the dog with a vengeance! The Appeal was launched in 1951, with a target total of £100,000, but it was clumsily handled and the money was slow in coming in. By the summer of 1953, only £51,645 had been raised. The original grandiose scheme had to be reduced considerably – just as William Burn had had to reduce his original scheme for the Edinburgh Academy in 1823. The scheme was now for a Prep school only of fifteen classes, to hold 400 boys; but the estimated cost was still substantially in excess of £100,000. Site-clearing started in August, 1957. By April, 1958, with the fund standing at £89,449, the Directors tried to get the building started; but the lowest tender was £142,314, and further reductions had to be made in the plans. School fees were raised to try to help the financial problem, and eventually the work on the building began.

At long last, the new Prep School was opened on Friday, October 7, 1960. It was now designed to hold 250 boys in nine classes.

It was Miss McTavish who was Head of the Prep during all the difficulties of moving from Henderson Row and settling into the new school at Inverleith Place. When she retired in 1965, her successor was a man – the first Headmaster of the Prep in its history, Mr James D. Britton, who came from the Dragon School, Oxford. A versatile teacher – Latin, Maths, Science, French, and above all English – he made a notable mark with his stage productions, in which he not only wrote many of the plays but helped to build and paint the scenery. Mr Britton left in 1973; the present Headmaster, Mr James J. Burnet, is himself an Academical (1936–49), who distinguished himself at school as a piper and middle-distance runner (he gained a full Blue for Athletics at Cambridge).

No school stands still. The Prep at Inverleith has already expanded, and at the start of the 1973-4 session had 322 pupils in 14 classes. Together, Denham Green and the Prep make up more than a third of the numbers of the Edinburgh Academy. The little group of forty boys who started in 1888 has grown prodigiously, like the acorn that Miss Ogilvie gave to a small Academy boy during the war and which now flourishes as a young oak in the grounds of Denham Green.

ENTER THE EPHORS

1889-90 . . . probably the busiest session which had been seen at the Academy since that of 1824-5, when the School was founded.   (*Chronicle*, March, 1893)

In December, 1889, Rector Mackenzie presented to the Directors his proposals for the changes he wanted in his second session. The breadth and scope of his schemes must have taken their breath away. It called for a new chemical laboratory, a military and engineering department to stop boys leaving school early for Military School before going into the Army, additional modern language teaching, and a class for teaching business methods. He wanted five new masters, and two gymnastic instructors, and an extra mistress for the Prep, whose numbers had already risen to eighty-six. He had the whole scheme worked out: the building work involved would cost exactly £1,077, from £320 for a brick laboratory to £6 for a path to a new urinal.

To pay the salaries of the new masters required, 'I propose,' he told the Directors, 'to amend the fees as follows . . .' There was nothing of the style of previous Rectors, who always 'begged to suggest' in long Victorian circumlocutions. Mr Mackenzie had no time for flowery language. In his new scheme, to which he appended a map of Edinburgh, plotting 'the paying power of parents', he urged the Directors to raise the fees by at least £3 per boy, insisting that 'We shall have to hammer into parents the fact that . . .'; and where the Directors apologised in their *Report* for the hold-up in a building project due to 'unforeseen circumstances in the construction industry', Mr Mackenzie stated bluntly in his *Report* – 'The builders went on strike'.

His plan, drawn up with the help of J. A. Clyde, covered everything – how to keep the masters happy, pay for stationery, even how to pay off the School debt. The Directors gave their approval, with only a few modifications – and Mr Mackenzie spent his holidays visiting laboratories in England for ideas on building and equipment. That was the sort of thing he did: when new classrooms were required, he designed them, ordered the furniture, and dashed down to Oxford to look at designs for oak tables and benches.

In fact, his enthusiasm and energy and optimism were so infectious at the meeting where his plans for expansion were passed that the Directors went even farther than he had suggested: the Lord Justice-Clerk proposed the building of a new gymnasium in the Yards, and a Boarding House on the ground to the west of the playing-field at Raeburn Place. The Boarding-house scheme was shelved meantime, but the Directors decided to build a gymnasium beside the new laboratory at a cost of £600, helped by a loan of £300 from the Lord Justice-Clerk.

The whole reconstruction scheme, as finally passed in July, 1890, involved building a gymnasium and a laboratory at the north-east corner of the playground. They decided to engage the five new masters, and two gymnastic instructors, and to have two hours of compulsory gymnastics for all boys every week. They fixed the maximum size of classes in the Prep School at twenty-five, and in the Upper School at thirty. They introduced a course of elementary science in the first three Classes (the Junior division). And they raised the school fees by an average of £3 in the Prep School and £5 in the Upper School; the highest fees in the Senior division of the Upper School were now twenty-four guineas per annum (and thirty-six guineas for the special Army side). These increases had no effect on the upward march of the numbers at the Academy; during the session 1889–90 they rose to 253, the following session they rose to 277.

Within the School itself, Mr Mackenzie now introduced a prefectorial system of a kind he had got to know well at Loretto, where Dr Almond had invested senior prefects with almost the same authority as masters – including the right to inflict corporal punishment; he believed that this would reduce the amount of schoolboy tyranny and bullying that disfigured so many English public schools, as well as teach the boys a sense of responsibility. Dr Almond's delegation of authority and his close, informal relations with senior boys had much to do with his success at Loretto, and Mr Mackenzie wanted the same kind of thing. But the system he introduced at the Academy was different in many respects. In the first place, the prefects were elected by the boys themselves, not appointed by the Rector. There were eight of them, chosen by members of the Rector's classes and the cricket and football teams from a list of twelve names submitted by the Rector. And he called them *Ephors*, a term borrowed from ancient Sparta because 'the method of appointment was different from any other school prefectorial system, and it seemed better to adopt some title as yet unappropriated'. Perhaps recalling his own happy experiences at Loretto, Mr Mackenzie wrote in his *Report* of 1890 that the boys had been 'of the greatest service to me and to the school in a great variety of ways; a good deal of the school management falls to their share; I consult them in all plans affecting the general life of the boys, and I think that, under the new system, their functions are likely to be still further developed'.

(Many years later, during the Rectorship of Mr P. H. B. Lyon (1926–31), the present custom of appointing Ephors by the Rector began to creep in – a regrettable development, to many people's minds. However, after the War a subsidiary system of Division Ephors, now called Junior Ephors, was instituted by Mr Seaman, and these, at least, are still elected by the senior classes on something like the original basis, and the Senior Ephors are now appointed from among their number.)

When the Ephors were first introduced, Mr Mackenzie wanted to give them the authority to punish younger boys by corporal punishment; but this was one thing that the Directors were not prepared to countenance, and they said an emphatic 'No'. In 1903, however, Mr Mackenzie's successor, Mr Carter, persuaded the Directors to change their minds and allow the Ephors to inflict corporal punishment 'in the case of serious offences, subject to safeguards similar to those suggested by the late Rector, Mr Mackenzie, in the report presented by him to the Board on 17th December, 1890'. After 'a full discussion, in which the meeting had fully in view Mr Mackenzie's said report', the Directors agreed that the Ephors should be empowered (1) to impose such minor penalty for slight offences as the Rector should approve of, and (2) in serious cases, to inflict corporal punishment on the offender in such manner as the Rector should approve of; subject always to the following safeguards, viz.; (1) that no boy should have corporal punishment inflicted on him by the Ephors except as the result of a meeting and careful deliberation of the whole Ephors; (2) that every boy on whom the Ephors thus propose to inflict corporal punishment should have a right of appeal to the Rector; (3) that when corporal punishment has thus been inflicted, the senior Ephor should immediately report the matter to the Rector.

This decision led to the unseemly (some would say barbaric) practice of 'Ephors' beatings'. The instrument used was not the cane, as in other public schools, but the flat-faced clacken. The Ephors would summon the trembling miscreant to their room after school, where he was 'tried' and then solemnly sentenced to two, four, or six wallops. Unless the boy exercised his right of appeal to the Rector (which did not happen often), he was required to place his head under the edge of the large table in the Ephor's Room, with his hands on top, whereupon the Ephors, in turn, would deal him a stinging blow on the buttocks with a clacken (left-handed Ephors were considered a great asset).

After the Second World War, with views on corporal punishment changing, there was much discussion on whether the practice should be discontinued. The Ephors feared that their authority might be undermined if they did not have the ultimate deterrent of the clacken, others wanted to see them exercise leadership by example rather than by sanctions. There has been no formal edict; but in recent years, during the present Rectorship of Dr H. H. Mills, the custom of beating by the Ephors has lapsed. Theoretically, the Ephors still have the power to inflict corporal punishment, but only after application to the Rector, and on the rare occasions when application has been made, it has been refused. Older Academicals may regret the passing of this particular Academy tradition; but one Academical at least sees it as a welcome change. In today's climate of opinion, allowing 'beating' by the Ephors to lapse by general consensus has been a credit to the humanity and good sense of Rector and senior boys alike.

1890–91: THE NEW WAVE OF MASTERS

A very large part of the progress recently made by the Academy is due to their un-wearied exertions.   (Rector's speech, 1893 Exhibition)

Something drastic happened to the beautiful School Hall in October, 1890. It had always been an amphitheatre, the pride and joy of the Directors at the annual Exhibition. But now it was floored flat on the level of the present lower gallery, warmed by under-floor hot pipes, and converted into a dining hall. The number of boys taking school dinners had increased dramatically from sixty in 1888 to 130 in 1890 (and was to increase even further once the hall came into use), and this seemed the only solution. The floor was later removed, in 1913, when a new dining hall was built in the Prep Yards; only the Rectorial dais at the far end is left as a reminder of that period.

With the rapid increase in numbers the Hall was soon considered to be too small to hold even the annual Exhibition, and in 1893 this ceremony, the high-point of the school year, was moved away from the Academy to the U.P. Synod Hall in Castle Terrace. Fortunately, this arrangement only lasted for ten years.

To compensate, the Rector held the first of his celebrated Gymnastic Displays in the Academy Yards in June, 1901, attended by nearly 700 parents and friends in glorious weather. These became a spectacular feature of the Academy calendar, with well over a thousand people coming to see the display and then take tea in various classrooms. It was all part of Mr Mackenzie's plan to involve parents and Academicals more closely in the activities of the School – and advertise what was going on in it. (His constant efforts to strengthen the Academical arm of the Academy came to fruition in June, 1900, when the original Academical Club, the Cricket Club and the Football Club were incorporated into a reconstituted and much more effective Academical Club.)

But 'the great feature of the session', as the first *Chronicle* of March, 1893, put it, was the new wave of staff who were moving into the Academy; young men with new energies, a new intellectual vigour, and a predisposition to accept the 'public-school' ideas of the Rector. Many of them stayed on at the Academy for a great number of years, to become legends in their own lifetime to succeeding generations of Academy boys.

The first of the newcomers was Henry ('Mummy') Johnstone, of Radley and Keble College ,Oxford, who arrived in 1888 from Loretto to take over the newly-formed B class of the Geits, and was promoted to special History Master in 1891. He was called 'Mummy' for the simple reason that schoolboys thought he looked like one with his wizened, cheerful face. He was an engaging man, extremely popular with the boys, whom he always used to address by their Christian names in class – a most unusual, indeed revolutionary habit for those times in a School where surnames are still almost *de rigueur*. Perhaps that is why he was suspected of not being able to keep very good order in class. He resigned from the Academy in 1908, but for many years thereafter, particularly in the 1920s, he would come back for long spells to fill temporary vacancies. He died in 1940.

While he was at the Academy in his early days, he took over the Library, which the Rector revived with the help of £100 subscribed by parents and friends of the school. It was further revitalised in 1900,

when a handsome new Library building was donated by George
Crabbie (E.A. 1860–4), a well-to-do Leith merchant who had previously
presented two Fives Courts to his old school in 1898. It was opened in
July, 1900, by Andrew Lang, who had been in the Trotter Class of
1854–61. Lang was now at the peak of his career, the busiest and most
versatile journalist in London, a prolific novelist, poet, philosopher and
historian. He took a leading part in the celebrated controversy with
Professor Friedrich Max Muller and his school about the interpretation
of myths and folk-tales. He was the first Clifford Lecturer at St
Andrews University. He wrote fairy stories, books on Joan of Arc, Sir
Walter Scott, John Knox, Tennyson, Prince Charlie, and Mary Queen
of Scots; he translated Theocritus and Homer, wrote *Ballads and
Lyrics of Old France*, and several studies of the philosophy and religion
of primitive man. His speech at the opening gives a hint of his racy,
popular style; he said that it was a mistake to suppose, as he had supposed while at school, that the object of education was simply to give
annoyance – the object was to teach one to endure annoyance! And he
announced that he was giving a prize to the boy who wrote the best
essay on 'The Character of Mary Queen of Scots', of whom he said, 'A
short and sufficient account of Queen Mary would be, that though she
was a regular bad lot, all the same she was a ripping good sort'. And
as befitted a celebrated writer on cricket and the brother of T. W.
Lang (E.A. 1866–70), the Oxford and Gloucestershire cricketer, he
offered to give cricket bats to the boys who were most successful in
batting and bowling against Merchiston the following day.

It was 'Mummy' Johnstone who was also responsible for the launching of the *Chronicle* in March, 1893, 'to record the life of Academy
boys both past and present.' Mr Johnstone was editor for the first eight
years, and the Rector was delighted to find 'a large amount of information concerning the doings of old boys continually coming in', and
that boys were contributing 'articles of considerable literary merit and
interest . . . and some poetry well worthy of a magazine of more
literary merit'. The first number, which contained a short history of the
early years of Mr Mackenzie's Rectorship, was sent free to all Academicals who could be contacted. The editorial committee was made
up of masters and boys, and three issues of the magazine were published between March and July. Originally it was published six times a
year, at a cost of 6d. per number (annual cost 3s., 'including postage to
any part of the world, 3s. 3d.'). It has been published ever since, at
varying times in the year, sometimes as often as nine times a year; now

it comes out three times a year, at the beginning of each term so as to give a full account of the preceding term's activities, priced 15p. The price, however, is irrelevant because all Academy boys and Academical Club members get it free, even overseas. The eighty-one volumes of the *Chronicle* tell their own history of the Academy in the first-hand memories, annals, anecdotes and nostalgic recollections of Academicals down the years. Its regular features recollecting 25, 50, 75, 100, 125, and now 150 years ago; its articles celebrating retirements and anniversaries of people and events; its Births, Marriages and Deaths; its School and Academical Notes; its records of School and Academical matches, reunions, money-raising efforts; its pictures of every aspect of school and Academical life – all these have helped to keep the sense of Academy continuity alive, and feelings of pride and loyalty and old-school bonhomie thriving in a way that nothing else could. Once again Mr Mackenzie knew exactly what to do – and did it.

'Mummy' Johnstone has one other major claim to Academy fame: he wrote the school song, *Carmen Academiae Edinensis Novae* – the familiar *Floreat Academia* – which is sung at major Academy occasions and reunions. The music was composed by the Rector himself, who was an accomplished singer; but perhaps he overestimated the virtuosity of the average Academical, for it requires the singer to be able to range from bass to soprano, thereby leading to some interesting switches of register at the start and middle of the chorus. It was first sung at an 'Academy Commemoration' in 1896:

FLOREAT ACADEMIA

The Text	*The 'Crib'*

1. Floreat Academia,
    Mater alma, mater pia:
      Huic paremus, hanc amamus,
      Ergo fortiter canamus
        'Floreat Academia'.
	1. Floreat Academia,
	    Mater alma, mater pia:
	      Love and homage we are bringing,
	      Eager to be loudly singing: –
	        'Floreat Academia'.

2. Domi suboles est nota,
    Atque loca per remota:
      Hic et illic gloriantur
      Quia nostri nominantur.
	2. Sons afar her fame are telling,
	    Sons at home her glory swelling;
	      Each one proud that he was reckoned
	      As a 'geit' or as a 'second'.

3. Utriusque togae decus,
    Sunt qui Dei pascunt pecus,
    Sunt qui legi roborandae
    Opus dant et illustrandae.
	3. Of her sons, some earn their dinner
	    Toiling to convince the sinner;
	      While some abet the Law's excesses
	      As advocates or W.S.-es.

C.S.

4. Hi complexi sunt honorem
   Pacis imponentes morem,
   Indulgentes hi virtuti
   Signa Martis sunt secuti.

4. Some cut quite respected figures,
   Dealing law to conquered niggers;
   Some, whose cry for glory's louder,
   Yield themselves as food for powder.

5. Hi sciendis rebus nati
   Sunt Naturam percontati,
   Illi freti medecina
   Aegros eximunt ruina.

5. Some set Nature at defiance
   Dabbling in the things of science:
   Some are chemical decoctors,
   Others fashionable doctors,

6. Artis exsecuti normas
   Hi venustas fingunt formas,
   Illi vias humanarum
   Munivere litterarum.

6. Some are painters, some are etchers,
   Some are merely canvas-stretchers;
   Others pass a life infernal,
   Writing for some weary journal.

7. Floruit, florebit usque
   Artibus virtutibusque,
   Arbor ferax et natura
   Rite fruges repensura.

7. Like a stately tree she'll flourish,
   Generations yet to nourish;
   While her sons, in all directions,
   Gather fruit from her perfections.

8. Venit vox a Solis ortu,
   Redit a cadentis portu,
   'Nos te, Mater, salutamus':
   Ergo fortiter canamus
   'Floreat Academia'

8. Hark! from regions near and distant,
   East and west, a cry insistent: –
   'We salute thee, gracious Mother!'
   Loud then brother sing with brother –
   'Floreat Academia'

The 'Crib' was supplied by an Academical, the publisher and historian Dr Walter B. Blaikie (E.A. 1858–64), for the benefit of fellow-Academicals whose classical learning had become a little rusty. Like so many anthems, some of the sentiments expressed (verse 4, for instance) are too embarrassing to be sung nowadays, like the central verse of 'God Save the Queen' with its unflattering reference to the Scots. One can only hope the Latin of 'Mummy' Johnstone is more distinguished than the English of Walter Blaikie!

('Mummy' Johnstone, incidentally, was one of several Academy people expected to write a History of the school. He had an elegant pen, as can be seen from his *Short History of Ancient Greece* (1900), but alas he never got round to doing even a Short History of the Academy.)

Mr Mackenzie's next appointment, in 1889, was a man who achieved a record of long service in the Upper School that will probably never be surpassed – Frank Hardy, known to generations of Academy boys as 'Twank' because some junior member of his family was unable to pronounce his name properly. Frank Hardy taught at the Academy for forty-two years – a remarkable achievement; he retired in 1931, and died in 1944. He went to school at Clifton College, where, he used to say, he had been fag to Douglas Haig (later the 1st Earl Haig of Bemersyde); from there he went to Keble College, Oxford, where he had been a fine all-round athlete and oarsman, and the Academy was his first and only teaching post. He taught Classics, English Literature and English History, but he made just as much a mark with his extra-curricular work as in the classroom. He had an excellent tenor voice which was always at the school's disposal for musical evenings. He was fanatically keen on horse-riding; at the Riding School in Pitt Street, which he helped to direct for twelve years, more than 200 boys learned to ride on the fifteen horses that were kept there before the First World War. He crossed the Atlantic three times – quite a record for those days – and enjoyed nothing better than to reminisce about the cattle ranches he had visited in Canada; indeed, he would carry his reminiscences into the classroom, and delight the boys by demonstrating how to rope a steer, using the master's high stool-chair as the target. His former pupils remember him with enormous affection for the enthusiasm he brought to his teaching, even of Greek irregular verbs. He must have been quite a man.

After 'Twank' Hardy, the newcomers came thick and fast. Arthur 'Beaky' Druitt was one of the 1890 intake. He came from Marl-borough and New College, Oxford, to teach Classics and French, and stayed for thirty-eight years before retiring in 1928. Later he served as a Director of the Academy from 1931–42; he died in 1943, aged 79. He was a stately man of great presence, with a piercing eye and the aquiline features that gave rise to his nickname, and a bristling mous-tache. A ruthless disciplinarian, too; for a time he would test homework by setting a brief paper of ten questions, which members of the class corrected for each other. Failure to get six right out of ten led to summary punishment – the tawse. No one ever forgot his method of introducing French: he would march into his classroom amid the usual dead silence, and scrawl on the blackboard the words *un bon vin blanc*. Then he would pronounce them carefully, to demonstrate the subtlety of the difference between French vowel sounds. The only snag with this admirable intention was that no one could detect the slightest difference between them, the way they were pronounced by 'Beaky' Druitt. Very English, was 'Beaky'. Every Monday morning, too, he would hold a private form of Responses with a selected deskful of boys: *N'oubliez jamais*, he would intone, and the selected boy would repeat it after him; *Souvenez vous toujours*, he would say to the next boy for the next Response, *que vous êtes* (Response) *des élèves de l'Académie* (final Response). They never did forget it, either.

Two other long-serving masters joined the staff with 'Beaky' Druitt in 1890. One was A. J. Pressland, who had studied at St John's College, Oxford, and taught at Christ College, Brecon, before joining the Academy staff. He stayed for thirty-five years before he retired in 1925, a fine mathematician but curiously ineffectual when faced by large classes despite his luxuriant beard; he left boys of his generation with the indelible impression of always wearing at least two pairs of spectacles simultaneously. He came as a Mathematics Master in charge of the new Military side of the school. Before he knew what had hit him, he had been set to work by Mr Mackenzie compiling the *Edinburgh Academy Army List*, the first official record of Academical military achievements and honours round the world since the school was founded. It was first published in February, 1894, as a Supplement to the *Chronicle*, and must have stirred old Academy pulses in various outposts of Empire. The 500 names included five V.C.s, two D.S.O.s, and two Iron Crosses of the German Army – 'the highest Order of that Empire for valour and services.' More than fifty Academicals had risen to be General Officers, and eight had been knighted. Many of the early Academicals had fought in the Afghan Wars (1832–42). In the Crimean Wars there were more than forty Academicals in the trenches before Sebastopol, and another was in command of the Heavy Brigade. There were seventy involved in the Indian Mutiny, and several were murdered by their regiments in the initial uprising.

The *Army List* must also have served to boost the Military Side at school, and the arduous toil involved in collecting seventy years of Service records shows the kind of enthusiasm that Mr Mackenzie could generate in his staff. 'Pressy' Pressland also spent part of his summer holidays taking boys to Germany to continue their Army studies; and he started a School Holiday House at Inverness in 1896 for summer coaching and outdoor studies with another master, Dr H. J. Spenser (1896–1901), who became Rector of Glasgow High School in 1901 and Headmaster of University College School of London in 1903. During the Boer War, 'Pressy' went to inordinate trouble to make up composite news-sheets from many newspapers referring to matters likely to interest Academicals serving in the field; he would send each sheet to an Academical, with a request to send it on, when read, to some other serving school-fellow. He was a prolific author as well, writing several text-books like *Geometrical Drawing* (1892), *Elementary Trigonometry* (1899), and *Murray's School Arithmetic* (1907); he also had a particular interest in the educational system of

Switzerland, and published several books about it. He died in 1934.

The third long-timer of the 1890 batch was J. Tudor Cundall, who came from Clifton College and London University as the first special Science Master to be appointed, to organise the new Laboratory and a course of Science studies. He was only twenty-five years old when he joined the staff, and would undoubtedly have rivalled his colleagues for length of service had he not died of cancer of the throat in 1913 at the early age of forty-eight. Like his contemporaries, he was not content to confine his work to the classroom. In 1896, encouraged by the Rector, he founded the Scientific Society, which was restricted at first to the Upper Fifth and higher classes and limited to thirty members. At the monthly meetings, papers were presented by distinguished scientists (including five members of the original 'Eureka Club' of 1870–77), and Mr Cundall would take the boys on visits to factories, power-stations and other establishments of scientific interest. Under Mr Cundall, the Academy science department received such a 'very favourable report' from the Inspectors of the Board of the Royal Colleges of Physicians and Surgeons in Edinburgh that in 1897 it recognised the Academy as 'a Teaching Institution . . . in which the study of Chemistry, Practical Chemistry and Physics will be held to qualify for admission to their Examinations'. This meant that boys wanting to be doctors could stay an extra year at the Academy (always Rector Mackenzie's dearest wish) for purely Medical studies. In 1899 an article on 'The Schools of Men of Science' in the magazine *The School World* placed the Edinburgh Academy, with nine distinguished names, second in Britain only to the High School of Edinburgh, which had ten. Mr Cundall had sixty boys attending his classes, and in 1908 he supervised the design of the new Laboratory and Lecture Theatre that was built to cope with the continuing rise in science pupils (there were 150 by then). As a teacher, Mr Cundall had a reputation for having eyes everywhere in his head, with a disconcerting ability of knowing what was happening everywhere in the lab as experiments were being conducted – especially experiments in misdemeanour. On such occasions his tongue, like Dr Hodson's, rendered the use of the tawse superfluous.

There were many others: G. B. ('Buckie') Green, for instance, Classical Master of the Seventh, who joined the staff in 1891 and remained for thirty-four years before he retired in 1925, even though he never became totally enamoured of Scotland or the Scots. And L. G. ('Tommy') Thomas, all-round athlete, who taught Modern Languages, especially German. Immensely likeable, with an open, outgoing nature, he was the catalyst in the Masters' Lodge that prevented too much tension developing between the new men and the old. He was educated at Clifton College and Keble College, Oxford; he joined the staff in 1893, and died in harness in 1930. Senior boys automatically turned to 'Tommy' for advice on school affairs; and his own children did him proud, too. One son, L.G., known as 'Buz' (E.A. 1907–21), was Head Ephor and captain of the champion XI of 1920-1, and won the Sword of Honour at Woolwich. His other son, E.W. (E.A. 1906–15), was captain of the XI and XV and the Shooting VIII at Clifton; and his two daughters were Head Girls of Lansdowne House and St George's in Edinburgh.

Then there were the masters that Mr Mackenzie 'inherited' – men like James Taylor, the Mathematics Master, known to all and sundry as 'Jas. T' because that was the way he always signed chits for school books and stationery. He had joined the staff in 1886, and was to stay for just over forty years until he retired in 1926 (it is said that he stayed an extra month at his own request, in order to beat the Mathematics Department long-service record established by Dr Gloag!).

Like Mr Cundall, 'Jas. T' also appeared to have eyes at the back of his head, as many a defaulter found to his cost; when facing the blackboard, and without ever turning round, he could pick out the slightest hint of inattention anywhere in the class, and call the offender out by name. So uncanny was the accuracy with which he could pinpoint nefarious activity behind his back that it fostered the suspicion that his spectacles had been doctored, like a card-sharper's, to act as reflectors of a peculiarly powerful nature. According to the late Sheriff T. B. Simpson (E.A. 1900–11), who wrote up some reminiscences of his schooldays for the Academy archives, 'Jas. T' ranked high as an original; he recalled occasions when Taylor deputised for the Rector at morning Prayers in Hall: 'I can still hear his staccato Scots voice say, as he bent over the Bible, "And the Lord said unto Moses, Give me a light, Janitor, I can't read a word".' But he was always a very 'personal' master and was particularly good with the Geits Class coming up fresh from the Prep. (One of his sons, Sir James Braid Taylor, was Dux of the Academy in 1909, a brilliant scholar in classics and history, and became Governor of the Reserve Bank of India; he died in the same year as his father, in 1943.)

And there was the redoubtable C. G. ('Caleb') Cash, who sported an enormous square black beard, which made his tall and erect presence even more commanding. He joined the Academy staff as an Assistant

Master teaching Analysis and English Composition in 1886, and was appointed special Geography and Music Master by Mr Mackenzie in 1891, which he stayed almost until his death in 1917. According to Sheriff Simpson, 'Caleb' Cash was everybody's prize museum piece (or freak). Like every schoolmaster ever born, he had his own particular fads and foibles; he had a mania for punctuality, and he invariably interrupted his luncheon in order to go into the Yards and check his timepiece and the one o'clock gun in the Castle against each other. If the gun dared to differ from his watch, so much the worse for the *goon*, as he pronounced it. He also had a mania for method, and clarity of articulation, and all his words were 'broken up into easy stages', like his lessons on Analysis. He pronounced 'classes' to rhyme with 'masses', and called the Himalayas the 'Himahliahs', and always insisted on the pronunciation of the first 'c' in 'Arctic' (he once thrashed the entire class because one member of it had missed out the letter 'c' and spelt the word 'Artic'). But he was a fine teacher of young minds: 'He moved among the Geits as the tutelary genius of the tribe, exacting a punctilious obedience, and requiting it with a not less punctilious devotion,' a later Rector (Dr Ferard) said of him. When Mr Mackenzie introduced singing into the curriculum of the First and Second Classes in 1890, it was 'Caleb' who was put in charge of it, and he did much to help the Rector found the musical tradition which flourishes so strongly at the Academy today. 'Caleb' Cash had no University degree, but he turned himself into a respected scholar, and later in his life he co-edited *A Contribution to the Bibliography of Scottish Topography* for the Scottish History Society. But he also wrote 'pop' books on exploration – *The Story of the North-East Passage* (1899), *Ansen's Voyage Round the World* (1909), and so on; and his topical geography lessons were fascinating for the boys. The exploits of the Norwegian explorer Fridtjof Nansen, who reached the highest latitude (86° 14N) that man had yet attained when he tried to get to the North Pole by letting his ship, the *Fram*, freeze into the ice north of Siberia and drift with a current setting towards Greenland, were carefully mapped by the boys in Caleb's class. This was geography and history in the making, just as the first American moon-landings were to be for schoolboys in the 1960s. It was an age of discovery in science and geography and mathematics, and these departments flourished as never before in the Academy as the boys warmed to the feeling of being involved in the great things that were happening in the outside world.

Such were the men of the New Wave who followed in Mr Mackenzie's wake as he forged ahead with his schemes to bring the Academy up to date. There was, it must be said, a good deal of prejudice against them from the Old Guard in the Masters' Lodge to begin with; but thanks to men like 'Tommy' Thomas, soon they were all working together cheerfully towards the Rector's avowed goal – to make the Academy the leading school in Scotland once again.

COMPULSORY GAMES: ANOTHER FIRST

If I were asked what was the most dangerous occupation for a boy's hours of leisure, I should at once name loafing.   (Rector's *Report*, 1889)

Mr Mackenzie was an 'Almondist' through and through. He talked about the importance of sport in every one of his thirteen annual *Reports* to the Directors.

'Vigorous exercise of some kind is, I think, a necessity for boys, and it would be difficult to find more wholesome and recreative forms of it than the School games afford. They develop physique, endurance, presence of mind, qualities of the highest value in practical life. Moreover they afford an education in public spirit, and if . . . school life should yield a training in good citizenship, we cannot afford to neglect this . . . If I were asked what was the most dangerous occupation for a boy's hours of leisure, I should at once name loafing. As an outlet for manly energies, and an education in manly virtues and public spirit, I commend the school games to the cordial support of the parents.' (*Report*, 1889.)

In 1891, Mr Mackenzie produced yet another innovation – the introduction of compulsory exercise on three afternoons a week for every boy excepting those with medical certificates or special exemption from the Rector. They had a choice between playing cricket and football, or taking 'a carefully arranged course of Drill, Gymnastics, Singlestick, etc., which will be conducted by Sergeant Barker' (the new Gymnastics instructor) – but this would be in addition to the compulsory two hours of gymnastics a week that was already in force. Attendance at School matches on Saturdays was left optional; and the Games sessions of the Senior division at Raeburn Place were to be managed by the Ephors, while one of the new masters took the Juniors.

The Academy was the first Scottish day school to take this step, and Mr Mackenzie was immediately delighted with the results: 'It has proved entirely successful. I am convinced that the present neglect in most Day Schools of efficient arrangements for physical education is in glaring opposition to common sense . . .' (*Report*, 1892.)

Almost the whole of the Upper School opted to play cricket and football (rugby is always called 'football' at the Academy, because it was adopted there before Association football was codified in 1866) rather than take the special course in gymnastics, and almost at once the Academy football teams began to hold their own again against the formidable opposition of the games-orientated Boarding Schools. In 1892–3, the football team 'broke the long spell of defeat at the hands of the Boarding Schools' with victories over Merchiston and Loretto (four of that team later played for Scotland). In the following year, the XV 'for the first time in nearly twenty years raised the football of the School to a level of that of Boarding Schools'. The victory over Fettes was the first for nearly twenty years. Mr Mackenzie waxed enthusiastic in his *Report* for 1894: 'I think it worthwhile to dwell upon these results, as it is in the physical department that Day Schools all over the country almost uniformly fail. Any reference to published lists of successes won by examination shows that in this sphere the Day Schools more than hold their own with the Boarding Schools. In all forms of manly exercises, however, it is commonly admitted that they are inferior. The tradition at the Academy has been different, and the successes which our boys have won in the field are, I think, worthy matter for congratulation.'

With the XV back on its feet, Mr Mackenzie turned his attention to the cricket team; he added an extra professional, G. Wharmby, and his cup of happiness overflowed when he was able to announce, in his last *Report* in 1901, that the Academy XI, under G. L. D. ('Gibbie') Hole, had won the 'Schools Championship'.

He also tried to persuade the Directors to build a swimming pool in 1893. The cost would have been £2,750 – only £2,750; but the Directors were then in the thick of yet another major reconstruction scheme urged by Mr Mackenzie, and shrank from adding this 'optional extra' to the overall costs. It was a regrettable decision; to this day, the Academy is still without its own swimming pool.

As early as 1891, he was putting forward to the Directors a case for buying further playing field accommodation, in view of the increasing numbers. In his 1895 *Report* he was 'happy to announce to parents and friends of the School' the final purchase of the new field: 'During the last seven years the numbers attending the Academy have increased from 213 to 493, with the result that the field accommodation, which in 1888 was not more than sufficient, is now utterly inadequate . . . the new Field covers a space of nearly nine acres of easily levelled ground. It is beautifully situated immediately to the north of Inverleith Park . . .' The ground was purchased from the Fettes Trust for £6,000, which was financed by means of a loan from George Heriot's Trust (from which the Academy's site at Henderson Row is still feued), using the field itself as security. It was being used as turnip and nursery land, and had a considerable hog's-back towards the north, but all winter and spring a gang of fifty navvies laboured to level it, and in July, 1897, it was officially opened.

'It is pleasant to think that generations of Academy boys yet unborn, distant descendants no doubt of the present boys, will disport themselves on this favoured spot,' wrote Mr Mackenzie. Once again his vision was unerring; it always was.

It was Mr Mackenzie, too, who presumably introduced to the Academy a modified form of cricket that used to be a favourite summer pastime in the Front Yards; it was a kind of tip-and-run 'small cricket' played with a thick round stick called a 'porringer' (derivation unknown), usually shortened to 'porrie'. It was played on concrete pitches that used to run down towards the old bicycle sheds under the front wall, with a wide wooden baulk at one end serving as a wicket. The pitches have disappeared into the asphalt that now covers the Yards, and the timber wickets have been replaced by concrete uprights; and the porringer itself has almost vanished from the scene. It was a cross between a sawn-off broomstick and a baseball bat, tapered at one end for a handle. The game apparently came from Loretto, where it was called 'puddex'. H. B. Tristram described it in *Loretto School* (1911): ' "Puddex", often shortened into "dex", is the Loretto name for small cricket . . . It is played with a tennis ball (this does *not* mean a lawn-tennis ball) and a porringer, *alias* broomstick. There have been many varieties of the game at different times, such as "shotty" and "squash-ball", but puddex proper is practically single-wicket cricket, with the above limitations of bat and ball. A degenerate age has introduced further modifications and has robbed the bowling of much of its skill, by rejecting anything short of a full pitch, but to prevent scores being too long under such conditions, the laws order that a batsman shall retire on making twenty-five . . .' *The Encyclopaedia of Sport* (1898) noted: 'In the summer [at Loretto] a modification of cricket called puddex is played at odd times. A hard tennis ball and a thick round stick are used . . . The pitch must be fourteen yards long, the wicket at least a foot wide. No hit behind the wicket counts. Every batsman retires when he has made twenty-five; only slow underhand is allowed. The other rules are the same as in single-wicket cricket.' The name *puddex* was apparently invented by Andrew Lang, who spent a year at Loretto as a private pupil of the Headmaster at about the age of twenty before he went to Oxford.

EXPANSION AND EXPENSE: THE RECKONING

These projects involve the provision of a considerable amount of capital . . .
(*Chronicle*, March, 1893)

To accommodate the growing number of boys, expansion was urgent. A new block of seven classrooms was built along the west wall up from the Janitor's Lodge (the first three were complete by 1893), and another block was projected to run along the east wall up from the Masters' Lodge. Plans were made for the enlargement of the Hall by including in it the History and Geography rooms; for the creation of a Preparatory Hall, for the creation of a new playground, and so on. But it was all going to cost an enormous amount of money. Mr Mackenzie tackled the problem with his customary energy and persuasiveness.

He now had a secretary, or clerk, to help him with the clerical work, and he put him to good use. This was James H. Jamieson, who was appointed Rector's Clerk in 1893 and served four successive Rectors loyally and efficiently for thirty-seven years until he retired in 1930. Mr Mackenzie's methods were always slick, businesslike and up-to-date. The laboriously handwritten Minutes of the Directors' meetings began to be interspersed by typed reports and memoranda submitted by the Rector and the Secretary, Mr Clyde. A remarkable memorandum presented to the Directors by Mr Mackenzie on June 24, 1895, was printed in leaflet form, setting out a carefully-argued clutch of proposals for dealing with the need for expansion and all its implications. It illustrates vividly his meticulous attention to detail, his way of seeing every argument and every side to a question, of weighing up the difficulties, discussing the alternatives, foreseeing the likely results of a move; and it illustrates, too, the conviction that he was not just an employee of the Directors making a few suggestions for the smoother running of the school, but the man at the helm, the leader, telling them what they must do to achieve the kind of great school that he envisaged.

On the Financial Position of the School:

'The existing debt is £2,000. The new field is to cost £6,000. A further sum of £2,000 will be required in connection with enclosing, levelling, drainage, and the erection of a pavilion. The total present or prospective indebtedness of the School therefore . . . amounts to £10,000 . . .'

Remember, this is not an accountant speaking, or the School Treasurer. This is the Rector, who is also grappling with the new Higher and Lower Leaving Certificate Examinations, the Indian Civil Service Examination, Army entrance requirements, Oxford and Cambridge entrances, the Gymnastic Display for parents, changes in the curriculum, and a full teaching stint, including a daily Bible lecture given to the entire Upper School every morning at Prayers – 'day after day, without masters present, to an audience of 270 boys varying in age from nine to nineteen', was how he described it in one of his *Reports*.

This is the man telling the Directors how to sort out the school's expansion and financial problems, with particular reference to the question of salaries:

'. . . It seems clear that provision made in past estimates for the rise of Salaries will prove quite inadequate. Next Session we shall be most seriously straitened for room, and as one new School Room will be required for every twenty new boys, it is probable that five new School Rooms must be built in the course of the next five years. The North Preparatory Room . . . is not satisfactory . . . The number of boys who take Science can even now be scarcely accommodated in the present Laboratory. A Scientific Lecture Room must therefore shortly be erected. The housing of the School Library in one of the ordinary Class-rooms is a source of serious inconvenience and intellectual loss to the School. The erection of an adequate Library is a matter of urgent necessity. By the year 1900, therefore, six School-rooms, one Scientific Lecture Room, and a Library must, in all probability, be erected . . . The cost of erecting, painting, and furnishing a School-room of the smallest size hitherto admitted may be set down at not less than £300. The Library and Scientific Lecture Room must, however, be of a considerably larger size. Not less than £3,000, therefore, without making allowance for any of those unforeseen necessities which may at any time demand increased accommodation, will probably be required under this head in the course of the next five years.'

Allowing £1,000 for unforeseen expenses, all this added up to £14,000. And now Mr Mackenzie proceeded to the matter of how to

pay it off. He reckoned that the £3,000 loan raised on the security of
the new field could be regarded as a permanent debt, reducing the
amount to be dealt with by the Sinking Fund to £11,000:

'I think the Directors will agree with me that an existing and prospective debt of £11,000 cannot, without serious injury to the school,
be liquidated out of the existing fees. The requirements of a school are
continually changing, and money is continually being required in
order to provide for new developments . . . Although, unless the
School shifts its locality altogether, no decade is likely to approach the
scale of expenditure undertaken between 1889–99, the Directors would
certainly be mistaken if they were to conclude that capital expenditure
will ever wholly cease.'

Now hear this classical scholar, games enthusiast, Bible lecturer and
choirmaster breaking down the financial situation:

'I am informed . . . that in the circumstances it would not be safe to
extend the liquidation of the £11,000 . . . over a longer period than
fifteen years. This would demand an annual payment upon the part of
the School towards interest (including interest on the £3,000 above
referred to) and sinking fund, of £1,150. The extra 100 boys on whose
behalf much of this expenditure has been, or will be, incurred, will
bring in under the head of existing fees £2,000. It will cost £1,000 to
teach them. The total surplus upon these 100 boys will therefore be
£1,000.'

Allowing £150 for additional expenses the surplus from 100 boys
would be £850, or £170 from each annual increase of twenty boys.
Taking twenty as the probable annual increase, Mr Mackenzie calculated the probable surpluses for the next five years as: 1895–6,
£1,020; 1896–7, £1,190; 1897–8, £1,360; 1898–9, £1,530; 1899–
1900, £1,700. He reckoned that by 1900 the school roll would have
risen from 498 to 600 – the absolute limit of the existing premises.
From these surpluses the annual payment of £1,150 for interest on
debt and sinking fund would have to be deducted.

On the face of it, these figures looked encouraging: expansion could
be paid for by rising numbers. But now came the rub:

'Taking the figures as they stand, I consider the effect upon the
salary fund disastrous . . . I may say generally that in order to avoid
serious and imminently threatened loss to the School a sum of not less
than £350 is urgently required for distribution among the more indispensable members of the teaching staff. The Treasurer's salary is
admittedly inadequate. The salary of the Rector's clerk must be raised.

Something must be reckoned for raising the salaries of men who, though scarcely indispensable, are yet most valuable and efficient masters. A total sum of not less than £250 should be set down under these three heads.'

Then he came to the Rector's salary – 'a matter which I have not pressed, and which I here consider apart from the individual circumstances of the present Rector.' He considered the Rector's salary of £800 'wholly inadequate for the position which the Directors would no doubt desire that he should occupy.'

(£800 sounds a lot for 1895, when women teachers were being employed in the Academy Prep at £80 a year, and the cook got £70 per annum and her rent paid – but only on condition that she boarded free 'all the servants required for the service of the dinner . . . and is allowed for their use the broken meat which is left over each day.')

But princely as £800 seems in comparison with these, Mr Mackenzie declared: 'As compared with the salaries of other Scottish Headmasters, which I happen to know, it is less than half of the smallest . . . and several hundreds a year less than the income of one at least of the Fettes College Housemasters. I think I can safely say that any successful Rector of the Academy could at any time obtain elsewhere an income double of that now attached to the post, and, so long as this is the case, I consider the prosperity of the School insecure. In the event of a vacancy in the Rectorship few first-rate men will stand. Successful Rectors will leave; unsuccessful Rectors will stay.

'In view of what can be got elsewhere I look upon £1,200 as the minimum salary which the Directors should contemplate for the Rectorship . . .

'If we add it to the £350 and £250 mentioned above, we see that not less than £1,000 should be spent in the raising of salaries . . .'

And now, at last, how to pay for it all:

'The existing fees can be drawn on to a certain extent, and a new fee can be imposed, part of which will go to the maintenance of the new field, part to the assistance of the existing field fee and the abolition of the slump fund, and the remainder to the liquidation of the debt upon the school. I should propose 10s. 6d. per term as the fee for the Preparatory School, and £1 1s. per term as that for the Upper School . . . This will yield £160 from the Preparatory and £1,260 from the Upper School, total, say £1,400. About £900 or £1,000 of this would be left free for the liquidation of the debt.'

Then he advised the Directors to appeal to former pupils for subscriptions to the capital fund of the school (a theme he was to return to over and over again): 'The old boys are a very numerous body; a large proportion of them are devoted to the School; some of them are extremely wealthy, and many of them are substantial men. In straitened circumstances, and as the result of exceptional labours upon the part of the staff, the School has in seven years been raised from a position bordering upon failure into one of high prosperity and success. It seems to me a most natural thing that, when in the further development of the School the Directors are confronted with pecuniary claims, which ordinary resources do not enable them to meet, they should . . . appeal to the old boys for their friendly aid. I think that if the subscription was properly managed, a very considerable sum of money might be raised. The Directors . . . should aim at the creation of a Capital Fund. Apart from the claims of the Staff, I consider it dangerous to allow a School which is subjected to such keen competition from richer rivals to remain longer than can be avoided in a position of pecuniary helplessness.'

It took the Directors some time to recover their breath from this deluge of realistic facts and figures and appoint a committee (as usual) to go into the ramifications of Mr Mackenzie's Memorandum, which was just one of many with which he bombarded them from time to time. They did put the salaries up at once, however, including that of the Rector to £900, that of Miss Wood, the Senior Mistress of the Prep, from £115 to £125, the cook's to £80, and the Janitor's to £70. The fees were also raised as the Rector had suggested.

In the event, Mr Mackenzie's basic premise on which his calculations had been founded – a forecast of steady expansion of numbers – was proved wrong, for the high point had already been reached (493), and from now on until the end of his Rectorship there was to be not a steady rise in numbers to 600 but a steady dwindling of numbers down to 374 in 1900; and this would leave the school once again in a difficult financial position. But the long-term seeds had already been sown – the tapping of Academical resources. George Crabbie, a Director of the Academy from 1899–1925, would present the new Library before the decade was out, and one of the early Duxes of his Rectorship, W. J. ('Pussy') Stuart, who was Dux in both 1890 and 1891, also took his old Rector's exhortations to heart; as President of the Royal College of Surgeons, and an Academy Director from 1920–49, he became one of the Academy's most generous benefactors (the Stuart room in the School Library is named after him). When he died in 1959, he be-

queathed to the School £5,000 'towards an Endowment fund', and
his unique collection of the eleven medals he won at school.

Even despite the 'straitened circumstances' of the school in the 1890s,
there was one other major – and expensive – expansion that Rector
Mackenzie succeeded in launching; and it did not cost the Directors of
the Academy a penny. He built the first School Boarding Houses.

THE HOUSES: BOARDING THE BOYS

I consider the existence of these Boarding houses a matter of the highest importance
to the school.   (*Rector's Memorandum*, June 24, 1895)

Academy boys who had no homes in Edinburgh had traditionally
boarded with the Rector or masters in Buckingham Terrace, Great
King Street, Warriston Crescent, and other streets in the New Town.
In 1895 there were two official Academy boarding-houses run by
members of staff: 'Twank' Hardy took in boys at 23 Buckingham
Terrace, and 'Gillie' Gilmour at 5 Mary (now Mary's) Place; while
'Beaky' Druitt was about to take in boys at 14 Great King Street. Mr
Mackenzie fully recognised their importance – 'in the first place as
adding numbers, and in the second place, as [providing] for those
highly efficient masters, who produce the prosperity of the school,
modest but sufficient incomes.' But not enough boys were being sent
to the masters' houses, and the main reason, he felt, was 'that the houses
are in the streets and have not been built for the purpose. I believe it
would be infinitely easier to fill Boarding Houses, situated in their own
grounds, in close connection with one of our cricket fields'.

At this time, the Directors were about to take over the nine-acre
site known today as New Field. Mr Mackenzie now proposed: 'As
soon as the new field is acquired, I should propose that an adequate
amount of ground overlooking it should be obtained from the Fettes
Governors, with a view to the erection of Houses for the accommodation of our Boarders. The financial responsibilities of the School are
already too heavy to induce me to recommend the Directors to become
the proprietors of such Houses. I think, however, that as good rents
could be paid for the Houses in question, it would not be difficult to
form a private Company, who would subscribe the funds necessary for
the project.'

He pointed out that 'the value of an Academy Boarding House of
twenty boys at existing rents and fees may be held to be equivalent to

top: The Houses, across New Field

bottom: The Field, looking south

top left: R. H. Ferard

bottom left: C. M. E. Seaman

top right: P. H. B. Ly

bottom right: R. C. Watt

an income of not less than £300 a year'. Then he went on to deal with the objections which, 'after long consideration, I think are outweighed by the advantages I have mentioned before.

'The first is that the Academy would be injured as a Day School, by the increase in the proportion of Boarders to Day boys . . . I think that this would be a serious objection if the intention was to create large Boarding Houses. The maximum number, however, which I propose to allow in a House is twenty, and, if possible, I should like the number restricted to fifteen. It will be seen that Houses of this size are equivalent to large families. We have already sufficient experience to judge of their working, and we find that there is practically no distinction between our Boarders and our Day boys. On the other hand, if at any time the number of Boarders threatened to become too large, the Directors could limit it.

'The second objection to the proposal is that it involves a challenge to the Boarding Schools, and more particularly Fettes College. In the first place, however, it must be remembered that there were Boarding Houses in connection with the Academy forty years before Fettes College was built. We are surely, therefore, at liberty, if we think proper, to provide for the better accommodation of our Boarders. In the second place, I am far from proposing to make a great Boarding School of the Academy. Our competition would be a comparatively small affair. The field, from which Fettes and the other Scottish Boarding Schools draw, is by no means confined even to Scotland. On the other hand, if we have Boarders, (and there is no proposal to abolish the existing Houses), we ought to provide them with better accommodation in better surroundings.

'It has further been suggested that an increase in the Boarding side of the Academy might lead Fettes to take Day Boys. But the presence of say fifty Boarders at the Academy ten years hence would not, I think, have much weight in inducing the Fettes Governors to take such a step. It is a step which is always open to them, and, in the event of their taking it, we should be much better able to maintain the standard of the School, if we were not wholly dependent upon Day boys.'

It was a subtle and persuasive argument; and the Directors agreed. Towards the end of 1896, Mr Mackenzie secured a strip of two and a half acres of ground, with a frontage of 250 yards, running along the northern boundary of the New Field: 'The land is within a quarter of an hour's walk of the Academy and is situated in a district which is largely composed of parks and pleasure grounds, and can never be spoilt by the erection of tenements. The feus command a splendid view of Edinburgh to the south, extending from the Calton Hill to the Pentlands – a view of which they can never be deprived, as the new Academy Field of nine acres lies immediately to the south, and, beyond that, the large Public Park of Inverleith and the Arboretum and Botanical Gardens.'

The Directors of the Academy had no financial responsibility for the new Houses. Mr Mackenzie raised the capital by forming a company called 'The Edinburgh Academy Boarding House Company Ltd' with thirty-seven members, mostly Academicals. The Rector was one of the six directors. Among the shareholders were the Attorney General for England – Sir Robert (later Viscount) Finlay (E.A. 1851–8) – Professor Marcus Dods, the famous divine and theological writer (E.A. 1843–8), and Dr Joseph Bell (E.A. 1847–54), the celebrated Edinburgh surgeon on whom Conan Doyle based his character of Sherlock Holmes.

And so Bob Mackenzie, as he was known to his many friends in Edinburgh, built his dream Houses, which he described as being of red Dumfriesshire stone, three stories in height, each with a House-master's wing, dining-room, study, music-room, sick room, matron's room, and a dark-room for photography. Each house could hold twenty-eight boys in rooms ranging from single bedrooms to dormi-tories sleeping seven, and the average cubic air space assigned to each boy in the bedrooms was 'above 800 feet, which is the amount recom-mended by Dr Dukes of Rugby in his well-known book upon School Hygiene'. Mr Mackenzie was also plainly proud of the claim that 'considerations of health and eyesight determined the adoption of the electric light, which had proved a great success'. (The school itself was not fully lit by electricity until 1927.)

The terms for the boarders at the two new Houses were (exclusive of school fees) £70 per annum, or £23 6s. 8d. per term, with no extra charges, except for Church Sittings, Washing (one guinea per term), bicycle accommodation (5s. per year) and for medical attendance.

In the summer term of 1899 the two new Boarding Houses came into occupation, and 'Twank' Hardy moved in with his boarders from Buckingham Terrace and 'Beaky' Druitt from Great King Street ('Gillie' Gilmour kept on his own house at 5 Mary Place, which was 'under the inspection of the Sanitary Association, and warranted to be in a thoroughly healthy condition'). The official opening was per-formed on July 13 by Sir John Gilmour of Montrave (E.A. 1860–4), who had himself been a boarder in the home of the Rector of the time, Dr Hodson.

One of the Houses was named Scott House, in honour of Sir Walter Scott, who had made the Opening speech in 1824; the other was named Jeffrey House, after Lord Jeffrey, who had been one of the original Proprietors of the Academy.

Two more Houses were to be added after Mr Mackenzie's time. Originally, Mr Mackenzie had reserved the name 'Cockburn' for a house he intended to build for himself to the west of the Boarding Houses, and had left room for another two Houses to be built, 'so that the total number of boarders contemplated under the scheme is about one hundred, or one in five of the probable numbers of the school' (not even this visionary could have been expected to foresee that by the 1970s the total number of boys at the Academy would exceed 1,000). But he never built his 'Cockburn Lodge'; and soon after Mr Mackenzie left the Academy it became apparent that another Boarding House would be required, for the particular use of junior members of the school. The 'Edinburgh Academy Boarding House Company Ltd' were prepared to build, but the required feus were held by Mr Mackenzie himself, and the Directors eventually bought them for £1,675. Mackenzie House, named in his honour, was opened in May, 1910, as a Junior Boarding House; and in 1922 the Directors bought the fourth Boarding House (No. 2 Kinnear Road, just across from the other Houses). It was named Dundas House after two prominent Academical benefactors – W. J. Dundas (E.A. 1859–65), a Director for fifteen years, who left the Academy £1,000 when he died in 1922, and his brother Lord Dundas (E.A. 1864–71). Dundas House started as a Senior House, then became the Intermediate House, and is now the Junior House, where the youngest Prep boarders are.

The Directors gradually took over full control from the individual Housemasters, to whom they had previously rented the Houses to be run as private enterprises; now they are simply paid a Housemaster's salary. And in 1951 the 'Edinburgh Academy Boarding House Company Ltd' started by Mr Mackenzie was liquidated, and its assets transferred to the school for £5,600.

Today the Houses have all been renovated and modernised, as one would expect, and hold about 160 boarders. They come from all over the world. To take a random example: at the end of the summer term in 1967, the Housemaster of Dundas House (which was still the Intermediate House then) had £2,000-worth of air-tickets to hand out to his charges as they returned home for the holidays. The destinations of the sixteen boys were: Whitburn, Lanark, Brechin, Broadford (Isle of Skye), Carlisle, London, Malta, Cyprus, Calcutta, Nairobi, Kuala Lumpur, Teheran, Singapore, Borneo, and Hong Kong (2). Quite a scatter for the 'Home-School' that Mr Mackenzie had envisaged, at which boarders could also be at home.

CULTURAL ACTIVITIES

Much value is attached by the Directors to Music as a cultivating and refining agency, and the Choir and Orchestra are leading features of the School.

(*Academy Prospectus*, 1896)

The Houses were the culmination of ten years of persuading and hard work for Bob Mackenzie, years in which he involved himself deeply in every single aspect of school life. In 1890 he started an Upper Seventh Class for boys who were staying on until eighteen and nineteen years of age; he was also trying to extend the length of stay at school, and in 1893 he was rewarded when that year's Dux, George Rainy (later Sir George Rainy of the Indian Civil Service, and a Director of the Academy from 1937 to his death in 1946) became the first Academy boy ever to win a scholarship to Oxford direct from the Academy (he was awarded a Classical Exhibition at Merton College). In the session of 1893–4 Mr Mackenzie expanded the Mathematics and Science sides to make it possible for boys to specialise for awards at Oxford and Cambridge, and was immediately rewarded by a Maths Exhibition to Cambridge in 1895, followed by a Maths Scholarship in 1898, and a Natural Science Exhibition in 1900.

As a further advertisement for the Academy, he followed up the publication of the *Edinburgh Academy Army List* in 1894 with the publication of the *Edinburgh Academy Bar List* in 1895. It demonstrated the extraordinary achievements in the legal world of Academy boys from the school that had been founded by legal men. The *List* was compiled by a future Director, himself a distinguished legal figure, John Hepburn Millar (later to be Professor of Constitutional Law and History at Edinburgh University), who had been Dux of the Academy in 1881. It listed over 130 names, which included one Lord of Appeal in Ordinary, four Deans of the Faculty of Advocates, three Lords Advocate, one Lord Justice-Clerk, six judges of the Court of Session, seven university professors, ten Members of Parliament, a large number of Sheriffs of Counties and innumerable Sheriff-Substitutes. The literary traditions of the Bar were upheld by Robert Louis Stevenson and Professor William Aytoun of the Chair of Rhetoric and Belles Lettres at Edinburgh University. By 1900, the *Bar List* also included the Lord Justice-General of Scotland and Lord President of the Court of Session (John Blair Balfour, later Lord Kinross, Dux of the Academy in 1855) and the Attorney-General for England (Robert Finlay, later Lord Finlay, Dux of the Academy in 1858). Of the thirteen members of the Scottish Bench, five were Academicals in 1896, seven in 1905, and six in 1910 (of whom three had been in the same Weir Class of 1864–71: Lord Dundas, the Dux of 1871, Lord Skerrington, and Lord Ormidale). In 1903, out of twenty-eight K.C.s at the Scottish Bar, no fewer than eleven were Academicals.

When the Bar List was published, an Academical was Under-Secretary for Scotland at Dover House in London, and five other Academicals were working there at the time. To commemorate this fact they offered to endow a prize for the school. But at this time Mr Mackenzie was more concerned with collecting a picture-gallery of Academical fame for the Hall and building up the Gardiner Collection of classical works of art started by the Classical Master, G. B. Gardiner (1883–96), and he asked the Dover House Academicals to donate their portraits to the school instead. So industrious was he in his collecting that after he left the Academy, the Directors were forced to refuse any further offers for the time being – the walls of the Hall were crammed. Mr Mackenzie also had the names of all the Duxes of the School painted on the walls – a constant incentive to younger boys to try to achieve the same giddy, golden heights.

Mackenzie also threw his energies into fostering a musical and dramatic tradition at the Academy. In 1895, the *Antigone* of Sophocles was performed again in the original Greek in the School Hall, with music for the choruses composed by Mendelssohn. Mr W. Cecil Laming, one of the new Classical Masters (1891–1900), was in charge of the production and played the part of Creon, and 'Beaky' Druitt, 'with his resonant voice and venerable presence, was a very effective Coryphaeus'. The Rector himself was a leading tenor in one of the two Choruses. Tickets for admission cost 3s. In 1898 Mr Laming repeated his triumph with the *Alkestis* of Euripides; the cast consisted of sixteen Academy boys, six Academicals, nine masters, and seven ladies. In the *Chronicle*, the Rector stoutly defended the eyebrow-raising idea of having female parts taken by ladies – at a boys' school: 'What could be more natural for a school, where home life bulked largely, than that it should upon such occasions invoke the aid of the sisters of the boys?' That particular innovation never became a tradition, alas; but members of the Academy staff have a long and noble history of lending their stiff burdouns to the choirs in Academy musical performances down to the present day.

But it was the musical side of these activities that engaged Mr Mackenzie's personal interest most. He himself was an accomplished musician, with a fine tenor voice. After starting music for the First and Second Classes under 'Caleb' Cash, he founded a school choir – the first in the history of the Academy. It consisted of about thirty members, and met in the drawing-room of the Rector's House at 12 Great Stuart Street.

One of the boys who came to the first choir practice just after Christmas in the 1891–2 session was a treble called Ernest Torrance Thomson, who achieved considerable distinction at school as a solo singer and pianist (he played two piano solos at the Exhibition of 1895). When he left school he studied at the Stuttgart Conservatorium and the Royal Academy of Music in London, where he carried off the prizes for piano-playing and operatic singing. Then he developed lung trouble, and emigrated to California for his health; there he took up acting, and became celebrated as a silent movie star called 'Ernest Torrence'. Another Academy boy of that era who found fame in Hollywood was John Murray Anderson (E.A. 1901–3), who became known as the 'Revue King' for his musicals on Broadway, and created and directed the 'first all-colour musical motion picture' – a film called *The King of Jazz*.

The school choir went from strength to strength, and made its first public appearance in March, 1893, in the Music Hall in Edinburgh, under the sponsorship of the 'People's Entertainment Society'.

Meanwhile, Mr Mackenzie encouraged another master, Mr M. W. Keatinge, who taught Modern Languages (1894–7) to start the first Academy orchestra; it was known at first as 'Mr Keatinge's string band'. Orchestra and choir became a popular feature of Exhibitions and At Homes, and always there was the Rector, singing solos, singing in quartets, singing in the chorus, conducting the choir. In 1899 the Choir undertook the ambitious task of singing the Serenata of Handel's *Acis and Galatea*, and Acis was sung by none other than the Rector. By the time Mr Mackenzie left in 1901, music was firmly established at the Academy.

END OF A REIGN: 1901

This ravished brow, this emaciated form, this defective respiratory power which I
carry with me so shortly to a sunnier clime, bear witness in my case to the severity of
the struggle. Gentlemen, you must take better care of the locks and lungs of my
successor.   (The Rector, *Academical Reunion*, July 5, 1901)

Besides all these manifold activities (he also revived the old Academy
clacken-and-ball game of Hailes and organised a competition for a
Silver Clacken presented by the Carmichael Class Club) – besides all
this, there was a war on at the end of Mr Mackenzie's Rectorship, the
Boer War of 1899–1902. It was like the Indian Mutiny all over again;
the whole school followed the glorious exploits of more than a hundred
Academicals in the field, and patriotism was kept at boiling-point by
the presence of returning heroes at school lunches where they recounted
their feats in battle. After ten Academicals in the Imperial Yeomanry
Mounted Sharpshooters had come to lunch, the Rector reported 'such
enthusiasm among the boys that a number made efforts to enrol themselves'. They were discovered to be too young, and had to be content
with subscribing to the Lord Provost's Fund for the relief of widows,
orphans and other dependants of soldiers killed in the war; while the
Prep boys sent newspapers to Academicals serving in South Africa,
and the Prep staff sent comforts to the troops, provided a hospital bed
in South Africa, and collected for the Red Cross.

But many of the heroes did not return; and one in particular strikes a
chord of memory – Lewis Balfour Bradbury (E.A. 1888–95). He was
one of those golden boys of athletics – beautifully built and handsome
as Adonis – a member of the XV and the XI, a marvellous sprinter
who won the 100 yards and the 440 yards, both at school, at Sandhurst
and at Aldershot; a boy who, in the prime of his youth, as a 2nd Lt.
in the Gordon Highlanders, was killed in action at Elandslaagte in
October, 1899, aged twenty-two. There must have been something
intensely magnetic and likeable about his personality; for his classmates
all subscribed for the Bradbury Shield that is still awarded annually to
the best all-round athlete in the school.

By the end of the Boer War, Mr Mackenzie was worn out, and so ill
from chronic chest trouble that he was having to stay away from school
more and more often, leaving the school to be run by his deputy, Mr
Alexander Macbean. Macbean was an Aberdonian who had had experience as a headmaster of Paisley Grammar School before he came

to the Academy in 1883 (he retired in 1905); he was one of those excellent seconds-in-command, always ready and able to step in and run things when required, but never expecting, and never being asked, to take over permanently in his own right. He was in charge from the middle of November, 1899, until May, 1900, while the Rector recuperated in Egypt and Italy. Mr Mackenzie was no sooner back than his doctor was telling him that he could not spend another winter in Edinburgh. The Directors granted him leave of absence again to spend the winter of 1900 abroad, and the loyal Mr Macbean agreed to take over again. But the writing was on the wall. The school was missing Mr Mackenzie desperately. Mr Laming left to become Rector of Kelvinside Academy, Dr H. J. Spenser left to become Rector of the Glasgow High School. The numbers at school had been slipping ominously, and difficult times were clearly ahead once more.

The Directors wrote to Mr Mackenzie in his sunny climes asking him to come back and tell them how to reduce the staff to meet the fall in the number of school fees. Instead they received a letter from him resigning the Rectorship. He knew what was best for the Academy, and he could no longer give it. He was only forty-four, but his health was ruined. He had given all he had.

In his final *Report* in 1901 he wrote, 'The Academy is for the most part a Day School, and the effective endeavours of Day Schools have too commonly been limited to the class-room. I have tried to produce not scholars merely, but men; my desire has been to train the physical and spiritual, no less than the intellectual capacities of the boys . . . Amid the stress of competition we have kept steadily before us that the school is a preparation not for examinations but for life.'

To the Academical Reunion of July 5, 1901 – the sort of reunion that he himself had been so instrumental in bringing about – he summed up his thirteen momentous years as Rector:

'The work I have done at the Academy has owed little to the stern motive of duty. It has been a labour of love, an affair of the heart. To carry on the noble intellectual traditions of this place; to improve and make available for all Academy boys that culture of the physical virtues which, by their lease of the old field, Dr Hodson [sic] and the members of the old Academical Club first introduced into Scottish education; to make the moral standard of the School as sound as that of the homes from which it draws; and from the height and union of all these to create, if it might be, a new type of Home-School – these things formed the substance of my dream. It is the romance of the

Home-School, if I may so call it – the romance of the Home-School that has made these years so pleasant to me.'

Then he added, in typical light-hearted fashion, although the seriousness was hardly concealed: 'Like all men who make pleasure their aim, I have had a hard time of it . . . This ravished brow – this emaciated form, this defective respiratory power, which I carry with me so shortly to a sunnier clime, bear witness in my case to the severity of the struggle. Gentlemen, you must take better care of the locks and lungs of my successor. You must lift from his shoulders the load of debt, and put him in command of an endowment which will enable him to face serenely the chances and changes of the School.'

During his travels and long sojourns in sanatoria, he wrote books, including a *History of Dulwich College* and a biography of his beloved *Almond of Loretto*; he wrote songs, he studied harmony, and he learned to play the viola. In 1911 he gave a lecture to the Academy on his experiences in America, and the following year he died, still a bachelor, in London.

Edinburgh flocked to his funeral in St Mary's Cathedral, and he was buried not far from the Academy in the Dean Cemetery. Many were the tributes to his cheerful good nature, his vitality and optimism, his versatility and breadth of outlook; they recalled his high ideal of devotion to duty and the honour of the school, his firm contention that the most dangerous pastime for a boy was 'loafing'; they remembered him singing with gusto, for all his weak chest, the difficult solo part in his choir's triumphant production of *Acis and Galatea*; they remembered the wonderful musical evenings at his mother's house.

The Directors of the Academy wrote in the 1913 *Report*: 'It is doubtful whether any other man could have successfully accomplished the work that he achieved . . . He was a born Headmaster, gifted alike with imagination and foresight and with a genius for the practical work of organisation.'

That year, in its newly decorated Hall, the Academy installed 'the Mackenzie organ', in memory of the man who established musical education at the school and did more than any other to re-establish the school itself. It was one of his School Duxes, Sir Patrick Ford (Dux in 1897 and 1898, and E.A. Director 1909–44) who paid for the reconstruction and redecoration of the Hall and donated the organ. On the lowest panel was engraved the Homeric motto from the sixth book of the *Iliad* – *AIEN APIΣTEYEIN* – 'Always strive to excel'.

CHAPTER XIV

'Reggie' Carter: Years of Consolidation
(1901-10)

... A Rector who gave himself wholeheartedly to every School interest, whether its work or its games, its music or its art, for he was himself an all-round man, not only scholar and athlete, but also artist and musician ... (*Chronicle*, November, 1936)

BOB MACKENZIE, who was the first Academy Rector (apart from the unfortunate Sheepshanks) to remain plain 'Mr', left the school with its feet firmly braced against the onset of the twentieth century. It was the year Queen Victoria died. It was the year after the great Paris International Exhibition, to which the Academy had sent photographs and illustrations of the school and won a Collective Grand Prize Diploma. An Academical, John Henry Lorimer the portrait painter (E.A. 1867–1871, the elder brother of Sir Robert Lorimer, the architect of the Thistle Chapel), was one of the five British artists who won a Gold Medal at the Exhibition, and two of his paintings were bought by the French Government for the Louvre.

It was a year filled with honours for the school's old boys. An Academical was appointed Vice-Chancellor of Calcutta University. Another was made Military Governor of Mafeking, with an old schoolfellow in charge at Johannesburg. The Chief Justice of Northern Nigeria was an Academical. So was the Assistant Commissioner to the Punjaub Commission, the Principal of the Heriot-Watt College in Edinburgh (the college that Leonard Horner had founded in 1821), and the senior president of the Royal Medical Society, Edinburgh – the fourth Academical in succession to hold the office.

That year the presidents and vice-presidents of both the Royal College of Physicians and the Royal College of Surgeons in Edinburgh were old boys of the Edinburgh Academy. There were two Academical honorary surgeons to the new King Edward VII, and one Gentleman-at-Arms. Professor Peter Guthrie Tait, that brilliant mathematician and contemporary of James Clerk Maxwell, who had learned his first mathematics under old Dr Gloag in the Cumming Class of 1841–8, retired at the age of seventy after thirty years as Professor of Natural Philosophy at Edinburgh, and was given the degree of LL.D. by Glasgow University, along with the Dux of 1857, Sheriff Sir John Cheyne, and Professor John Chiene, a brilliant surgeon who had been one of the stars of 'Old Trot's' Class of 1854–61. (Professor Tait died that same year, not long after his son, Freddie Tait, the British Amateur Golf Champion of 1896 and 1898, who was at the Academy from 1879–83, was killed in the Boer War.)

The Academy honours list also collected an LL.D. from Edinburgh University that year through the Attorney-General, Sir Robert (later Lord) Finlay (Dux of the Academy in 1858), and also a D.D. conferred on Professor Marcus Dods (E.A. 1843–8) by the University of Chicago. This was only the second honorary degree ever conferred by Chicago University; the first went to the President of the United States.

Throughout that year the Directors of the Academy were busy trying to find a new Rector. Before advertising the post, they had to decide on the salary to offer the new man. Mr Mackenzie was invited to join the discussions, and said that their ultimate aim should be £1,200 plus a house, and that the Rector should not take boarders. The Directors had before them a committee report of 1899 which declared that Mr Mackenzie's salary of £800 plus a bonus of £80 was 'much too low' and gave a list of salaries paid to headmasters of similar schools (excluding the more prosperous English public schools):

Merchiston – £1,000 plus board and lodging worth £300.

Glenalmond – £1,300 plus house, coal, light, etc., worth £200–£300.

Fettes College – about £1,500 plus house and extras.

City of London School – £1,250, without a house, but with a good pension.

Westminster – £1,000 plus capitation grant of £400 plus house.

St Paul's – £1,500 and a house.

The report concluded that 'the post of Rector of the Academy offers little to attract a really first-rate man, especially in view of the fact that a House-mastership at a public school is considerably more lucrative than any of the Headmasterships referred to'. (This was precisely what Mr Mackenzie had said in his Memorandum of June, 1895.) But after a long and anxious look at the financial situation and the school numbers, which had slumped from their peak of 493 to 374, the Directors decided that a fixed salary of £800 was 'the full risk which it would be advisable to run', plus a capitation grant of £5 for every fee in the Upper School beyond 280 (the average number of boys in the Upper School over the previous four years). The new Rector would need to add forty new pupils over the next four years to average £1,000 a year.

But thanks to Mr Mackenzie the new Rector would have more power to run the school himself than any previous Rector. The Directors took the opportunity of the new appointment to draw up a new list of the 'terms and conditions of the Masters' tenure of office', recognising that under Mr Mackenzie 'the old system underwent a revolution'. With a master no longer following his class from the bottom to the top of the school, the system had become much more elastic and complex, and the Directors were finding it impossible to keep in personal contact with the staff as in the old days.

The Directors now decided: 'In the altered conditions of the School, it is impossible for the Board to know what changes it may be desirable to make in the time-table and in the duties of the Masters. This is the work of an expert, not of a layman, and as the Rector is responsible to the Board for the success of the school . . . he should be given as free a hand as possible . . .' So they decreed: 'Subject to the approval of the Board, the Rector shall have under his control the choice of books, the methods of teaching, the arrangement of Classes in school hours, the arrangements for Games and all forms of physical exercise, and generally the whole organisation, management and discipline of the school.'

He would also have the power of appointing and dismissing all masters, but all such appointments and dismissals must be reported to the Board, to which masters would have a right of appeal.

In effect, it was merely formalising the situation and power that Mr Mackenzie had created for himself; and thus ended, officially, the personal involvement of the Directors in the day-to-day running of the school. It was a function they must have relinquished with some relief – an unpaid, frequently thankless task that successive Boards had undertaken at considerable sacrifice of their time and other interests. They had patiently nursed the Academy through the often difficult decades of the nineteenth century; now the school was ready to receive its first twentieth-century Rector.

The man who was appointed from a short-leet of four was Mr C. E. M. Hawkesworth, an Assistant Master at Rugby. He was thirty-three years old and had all the right qualifications – educated at Clifton College, senior scholar at Queen's College, Oxford, a teacher at Bradfield College for a year and then, since 1894, on the staff at Rugby; a fine scholar and athlete, a typical first-class English public school product; but he was destined to have an even shorter career as Rector of the Academy than the unhappy Mr Sheepshanks. He was appointed on July 11, but on August 15, the Secretary to the Directors received a letter intimating his resignation, apparently over the difficulty of finding a house in Edinburgh. A busy exchange of letters and telegrams ensued in an effort to make him change his mind; and for a time, apparently, he *did* change his mind, because on September 23 he arrived in Edinburgh 'with a view to entering upon his duties'. The Secretary, John Hepburn Millar, had an interview with him the following day, at which he was handed a letter that Mr Hawkesworth had prepared the previous Sunday; but this letter, coupled with the interview, satisfied Mr Millar 'that he would no longer be justified in withholding Mr Hawkesworth's resignation from the Board'. The Board agreed, and unanimously accepted Mr Hawkesworth's resignation at a meeting on September 26. Mr Hawkesworth himself remained on the staff at Rugby and became a House master: he retired in 1924. He was a J.P. for Warwickshire, and died in 1945. It was a curious little episode, the brief Rectorship of Mr Hawkesworth; it seems likely that the difficulty arose over the lack of a Rector's house owned and provided by the school itself. It was to crop up again frequently in the future; in 1926, during the search for a successor to Dr Ferard, a candidate who was invited to apply for the Rectorship turned it down because of the lack of a house. It was not until after the 1939–45 War, when the school acquired 50 Inverleith Place as a Rector's residence, that the problem was finally resolved.

Meanwhile the Directors issued a carefully-worded notice about his resignation: 'His reasons for doing so are entirely personal; and, while the Directors express no opinion as to their sufficiency, they have thought it right to release him from his engagement to the School.' It meant that the new school session of 1901–2 had to start without a Rector, and with the faithful Mr Macbean in charge again as Acting Rector with a bonus payment of £100 for the term (or £10 per week for as much of the term as his services were required). In October they met again to choose a new Rector, and the Secretary was instructed to write to another man who had been on the short-leet and invite him to re-apply for the Rectorship 'on the same terms and on the same conditions as were attached to the post when it was vacant in summer', on the understanding that he would be appointed if he did so. And on

October 26, 1901, they announced their second choice 'in room of Mr Hawkesworth'.

This was Mr Reginald Carter, Fellow and Classical Tutor of Lincoln College, Oxford. He, too, had been educated at Clifton College, where he had been a near-contemporary of Hawkesworth; he had gone up to Balliol and now, in addition to his Fellowship at Lincoln he was Secretary to the Delegates for the Training of Teachers, and Principal of the Oxford University Day Training College. He turned out to be an inspired choice, not at all a second-best; his nine-year Rectorship (1901–10) was a highly successful one, and he is remembered with real and enduring affection.

(Come to think of it, Clifton College has proved a fine nursery for Edinburgh Academy staff. Apart from Mr Carter, Mr Mackenzie had taught at Clifton, and three of his 'New Wave' were Old Cliftonians – Mr Hardy, Mr Cundall, and Mr Thomas. The present Rector's predecessor, Mr Watt, had taught at Clifton, and the present Headmaster of the Prep, Mr Burnet also taught at Clifton College Prep School. There is, to be sure, a certain affinity between the two schools, because although Clifton College is a boarding-school is takes a very large number of day-boys. But it is an extraordinary coincidence that the two Rectorial appointments of 1901 should both have been Old Cliftonians.)

Mr Carter was unable to take up his duties until after Christmas. The schoolboys assembled in Hall for Prayers on the first morning of the Easter term in 1902 saw a burly thirty-two-year-old with a broad face, a square chin, a booming voice, and a ready chuckling smile behind which, they were soon to learn, lurked a strong will. But it was a strength laced with kindliness and a simple, natural charm that soon endeared him to boys, teachers, parents and Directors alike. This was no educational whizz-kid like the whirlwind Mackenzie with his blazing missionary zeal, his bachelor devotion to an ideal, his preoccupation with school affairs to the exclusion of everything else; Mr Carter was a pipe-smoking family man, with three young sons, Dick, Malcolm, and Jack, all of whom became pupils at the Academy, and a daughter, Margaret. His wife threw herself wholeheartedly into the business of being the Rector's lady, and the parents of the Academy boys warmed readily to the family atmosphere and the feeling that here was a Rector who understood a parent's problems. Of course, it was easier for 'Reggie' Carter, as the boys soon christened him, to be popular with parents than it had been for his predecessor, who had come to the Academy when discipline was at its lowest and had had to whip the parents into line over uniform, attendance, punctuality and the like; parents had by now become accustomed to toeing the line as far as school rules were concerned, and Carter's firm but sympathetic dealings with parents seemed to keep everybody happy. Somehow he had the knack of treading a path between tradition and change without stepping too hard on anyone's toes. He got on well with the Directors, too, and the *Chronicle* recorded after his death that 'both masters and boys loved him'.

All this might suggest that he was content just to jog along, changing nothing and offending nobody, reaping the benefit of his predecessor's efforts. But that was far from being the case. It has to be remembered that during the last period of his Rectorship, Mr Mackenzie had been a very sick man. He was physically incapable of doing all the things that had to be done. Numbers at the school were still going down. It was far from being a soft situation in which the new Rector found himself, and the Directors' *Report* for 1901–2 described that year as 'one of unusual and almost unprecedented anxiety'.

Mr Carter had his own very definite ideas about how to deal with the situation, and less than six months after taking up his appointment he delivered to the Directors his first *Memorandum by the Rector* (June 5, 1902). It was not a professionally printed missive like some of Mackenzie's. It was not even typed by the Rector's Clerk. It was painstakingly written in pen and ink in his own rather schoolboyish hand on four sheets of quarto-sized school 'block'-paper, and it stated:

'After a careful examination into the practical working of the Academy, it appears to me that there are two main questions which require to be dealt with as soon as possible:

A. How can the standard of work be raised?

B. Is it not desirable to arrange the salaries of the staff on some definite system?'

(Clearly he felt that the standard of scholarship at the Academy was not as high as it ought to be, particularly with regard to English and History; indeed, the only reproach ever uttered against Mr Mackenzie's reign is that he may have sacrificed intellectual standards in his pursuit of all-round education.)

Under the first heading, Carter proposed:

1. That boys shall start reading authors in various languages and studying Science at an earlier stage than heretofore.

2. That a course of History and English Literature shall be carried systematically up through the School.

3. That the Modern (non-Latin) Classes shall be given a more definite scheme of work.

4. That the Upper Classes in the Preparatory School shall have short elementary lessons in Latin.

5. That the 'non-singing' periods in the Upper School shall be used for a definite purpose . . .

Although Mr Carter was a talented musician, like his predecessor, and played in the school orchestra, he thought that the time spent on singing was wasted on many boys ('Boys who do not sing had better learn to draw, or, if their writing is bad, to write properly'), and that there was too much time spent on another of Mr Mackenzie's pet subjects, gymnastics ('In order to bring in a course of English Literature, less time than heretofore will be given to singing and gymnastics; and it may possibly be reasonable to make some reduction in Sergeant Sheen's salary'). Mr Carter, the son of an artist, was an accomplished artist himself, and wanted to build up the Art side of the Academy. He wanted the Directors to introduce additional art lessons by taking on a new Drawing Master and Assistant in addition to Mr George Paterson, who had been holding voluntary drawing classes at the Academy since 1891 – the fifth Drawing Master since the subject was introduced into the curriculum in 1851. (Mr Paterson drew the picture of the Academy that was on the cover of all the early *Chronicle* issues, and was also the Edinburgh representative of the *Graphic* and *Daily Graphic*.) The Directors thought it a good idea and agreed to the new appointments, and also to the appointment of an extra Science master ('if these new instructors are in the opinion of the Rector essential to the efficiency of the school, their remuneration must be provided'), but in the event no new Drawing Masters were taken on, and when Mr Paterson resigned through ill-health in 1906 (he died the same year), a single visiting Drawing Master, Mr A. H. Jenkins, was taken on in his place.

Under the second heading, the Directors also approved the Rector's proposals for increases in salary for the existing staff, satisfied that 'the increment is in every case thoroughly well deserved, and indeed represents no more than what faithful and zealous service during more than a decade is justly entitled'.

As regards his carefully worked-out long-range plan for a systematic salary scale, however, the Directors were less definite; they were 'not prepared to pledge themselves to a definite scheme in all its details

Rector A. L. F. Smith

top left: Lord Kingsburgh   *top right:* Lord Clyde (E.A. 1873-8
ottom left: Lord Cameron   *bottom right:* Rae Tod (Chairman 197

when the possibility of its being carried into execution must necessarily depend upon the financial results of each year. But if they understand him aright, the Rector has no wish that the Board should at one plunge commit itself to any such hard and fast scheme of automatic increase in salary. What he desires is that the Board should keep steadily before them some such proposal as that which he puts forward, and endeavour, so far as may be practicable, to carry it out'.

Briefly, the principle on which Mr Carter's scheme was based was that new masters should start with an annual salary of £180, advancing by triennial rises of £20 to £260. The Directors approved it 'as embodying the ideal of policy which ought to be kept steadily in view', but added in a nice piece of double-speak: 'Nothing should be disclosed to the existing Staff with regard to the likelihood of a rise in salary, but . . . the Rector might be authorised, in the engagement of new Masters, while abstaining from binding the Directors in the matter, to hold out prospect of a triennial rise in the event of his services proving satisfactory.'

They also agreed with Mr Carter's view (seeing ahead to the 'responsibility payments' in today's schools) that the Board should aim at 'having several highly paid appointments on the Staff, which would not only act as objects of ambition to Masters whose emoluments are smaller, but would also facilitate the departmental organisation of the school. The curriculum is so complex at the present day that the creation of recognised "heads of departments", as they might be called, will probably become a necessity in the not very remote future.' They also observed that 'in the event of an Endowment Scheme being set on foot, with a reasonable amount of success', they might find themselves in a position to 'adopt en bloc a comprehensive scheme for adjusting the salaries of the staff on a gradually ascending scale until a given maximum should be reached'.

The idea of an Endowment Fund, long urged by Mr Mackenzie, had been sanctioned by the Directors in 1899 but laid aside during the troublesome times of Mr Mackenzie's illness and resignation and the search for a new Rector. Now the Directors once again started sounding out Academicals and preparing a circular which would be sent out to work up support for the scheme, but things moved very slowly, and it was not until Mr Carter had had time to gain the confidence and support of Academicals that the Endowment Scheme finally got under way in 1906.

Money problems bulked large in the first years of Mr Carter's

Rectorship. He knew there was no hope of adding to the cramped Science quarters in 1902, but he suggested a temporary method of reorganising and refitting the existing rooms at a cost of £32–£35, to allow Science to be taught at an earlier stage in the school; and he assured the Directors that 'the numbers of boys in the Senior Division will almost certainly be increased, and probably there will be an increase of something like £60 in the income from this part of the School'. And like Mr Mackenzie before him, he mobilised outside resources to inject new interests and incentives into the school. He got Academicals interested in his efforts to raise the standard of English studies, and in his first year persuaded the Weir Class Club to endow a prize for an English Essay; the following year the ever-generous George Crabbie presented a Spelling Prize. The Rector also sponsored more lectures on non-classroom subjects; he invited Mr Mackenzie, much improved in health after a trip to America, to come and give the school a lecture on his travels, and he encouraged members of the staff to do the same: 'Pressy' Pressland on 'The Holiday Colonies of Switzerland and Elsewhere'; 'Mummy' Johnstone on Darwin; 'Twank' Hardy on 'What we owe to the Greeks'; 'Buckie' Green on 'What was Greece?'.

The number of boys attending school *did* go up that first year, to hover for a time just over the 400-mark, and the Directors felt financially secure enough to put a new lead roof on the main building and have the trees pruned. They also felt sufficiently confident of the future to give their secretary, John Hepburn Millar, the man who had compiled the *Edinburgh Academy Bar List*, permission to use the seventy-eight years of Directors' Minutes in order to prepare a history of the Academy, which 'he hoped shortly to be able to undertake'. (That hope never came to fruition; in his historical Introduction to the *Register* he was still hoping: he described himself as 'the *vates sacer*, whose constitutional habit of procrastination still delays the appearance of a full-dress history of the Academy, but who hopes before long to mend his ways.')

In that first year, Mr Carter sent a second *Memorandum to the Directors*. This time it was printed and marked Private and Confidential. It outlined a scheme for Free Scholarships to the Academy 'in order to raise our standard and increase our numbers'. Six scholarships, provided simply by remitting fees to the value of £28, would be awarded on the results of a yearly examination in Latin, English, Mathematics, and either Greek or Elementary Science. Candidates would be required to present a character certificate and a statement of parentage, with an assurance from parent or guardian that a scholarship would be necessary for their maintenance at the Academy.

'The presence of three or four hard-working boys in each of the important classes of the Upper School,' wrote the Rector, 'will be a great help to Masters in raising the standard of work. Scholars are very often good at games; they will remain in the Academy up to the age of eighteen and a half on average; and this will undoubtedly tend to strengthen the school both in work and in games. In fact, to put it shortly, the adoption of such a scheme would mean the addition of from twenty-five to thirty hard-working boys to our numbers without any increase of expenditure, for, as far as I can see, the present staff could quite well undertake the work.' He also believed that the Boarding House masters would each be prepared to board one boy at a lower charge to help the scheme.

It was an excellent idea for injecting new vigour into the school, and the Directors agreed. Unfortunately, they then spoilt it; in trying to be fair to all, they stipulated that boys already at the Academy should be allowed to compete for them, and that there should be no parental means-test. No one foresaw that this would frustrate the whole purpose of the scheme. The first Scholarship Examination was held in May, 1904, 'open to candidates from the Academy and elsewhere between the ages of twelve and fifteen'. The first two scholarships were won by Academy boys – J. S. C. Reid (later Lord Reid of Drem, a Lord of Appeal in Ordinary) and J. B. Taylor (later Sir James Braid Taylor, the son of 'Jas. T'). And from then on, Academy boys went on winning the scholarships year after year, and the scheme was abandoned in 1910 because it was merely depriving the Academy of fees it would otherwise have got.

PENSIONS AND ALLOWANCES

Well done, thou good and faithful servant.
(*Gospel of St Matthew*, xxv 21)

Between them, the Rector and Directors were working steadily towards a more stable and rational system of salaries with built-in increments. But the question of pensions for retired teachers had never been satisfactorily tackled, and many members of staff had left the Academy in former years with less to comfort their declining years than either they or the Directors would have liked.

The matter came to a head over old 'Gillie' Gilmour. He was well over seventy by now, and was getting very frail, and was continually having to be absent because of illness. He was an immensely nice old man, just a plain teacher of two or three Rs, without any of the degrees or special qualifications of the new breed of younger men, highly talented all-rounders mainly from the English public schools and universities, who were replacing the older generation of dominies. But his associations with the Academy went back a very long way; in 1901, his new colleagues had presented him with a handsome Rose Bowl to mark his Jubilee as a teacher (he had come to the Academy in 1851 for a short spell as Assistant Writing and Arithmetic Master). He was an enthusiastic organiser of the Games, and he was well-liked in the Masters' Lodge and by the boys who boarded with him at 5 Mary Place; when he eventually retired, 525 of his former pupils subscribed to a cheque for £70 for him. (The Rose Bowl was later presented to the Academy by members of the family and became the Gilmour Challenge Trophy for the Mile.)

The Directors were well aware of his services to the Academy; in spite of all his long absences they paid him a full salary and even paid for a replacement (in former days he would have had to pay the substitute out of his own pocket). But at the end of the 1902–3 session, Mr Carter suggested that next year, Mr Gilmour's work should be reduced 'in view of his advancing years', and his salary reduced from £300 to £200. The Directors – and Mr Gilmour – agreed to this arrangement, and a master was engaged to do the arithmetic side of Mr Gilmour's work at a salary of £40–£50. In 1904, Mr Gilmour was asked to retire, and agreed; he was seventy-six years old, and in view of his long and loyal service to the school, he was awarded a pension of £150 – half-pay – which was extremely generous in the light of many previous awards when the school finances had been particularly perilous. The Rector thought that the other remaining long-service member of the staff, Dr John Sturgeon Mackay, should also retire; he had been there for thirty-eight years, and now Dr Mackay, too, was asked to leave 'in the interests of the Mathematical Department'. Dr Mackay, that proud and upright man, agreed immediately; when the matter of his pension arose, he merely stated his financial position to the Directors and left it to them to determine the amount. The Directors awarded him £200 a year for five years, after which it would 'probably be reduced'.

At the same time the Directors consulted one of their colleagues,

James Avon Clyde, K.C., as to whether the School Charter allowed them to pay pensions, because 'the Directors think that it may be in the interests of the Academy that they should be able to grant retiring allowances to Masters who resign on account of advancing years, bad health or for any similar innocent reason'. Counsel's opinion was that the Directors were free to grant retiring allowances or to establish a pension fund under the terms of the Charter, and it was obvious that some such scheme was going to have to be tackled very soon. Mr Macbean's health had now broken down, too; the doctors had ordered six months complete rest, and he was on half-salary. He was unable to return to work after his six months' absence, and in 1905 he retired with a £200 pension 'for five years'. He died in 1911.

Eventually, a Pension Fund for Masters, under a system of Endowment Assurance, was started in 1908. Much of the credit for getting it started belongs to Mr Carter; it was through his efforts that his successor would be able to look forward to a pension of £1,000 a year if he stayed on and retired at sixty-five. But Mr Carter himself was not to stay that long; when he resigned in 1910 to become Headmaster of Bedford School, however, the Directors showed their gratitude for the 'much time and trouble' he had devoted to devising and introducing the pension scheme by giving him his policy free – 'without asking repayment of the premiums paid by the school on his behalf, which amounted to £33 15s. 3d.'

THE NEW SCIENCE BLOCK: 1909

Science is no longer regarded in this country (or even in England) as a subject to be apologised for . . .   (Sir George Thomson, 1961 Academy Exhibition)

While these complex financial matters exercised the ingenuity of the Directors, the school itself was moving serenely through the first decade of the twentieth century. Numbers rose steadily until in the session of 1908-9 they topped the magic figure of 500 (355 in the Upper School, 151 in the Prep, 506 in all). The Academy continued to turn out Duxes who were to reach positions of high distinction – H. H. Monteath in 1903 (later Professor of Conveyancing at Edinburgh University), P. R. Laird in 1906 (later Sir Patrick Laird, Secretary of the Department of Agriculture for Scotland), Charles Mackintosh in 1907 (later Lord Mackintosh, and a Chairman of the Directors of the Academy), A. H. Kyd in 1908 (a brilliant classical scholar who died in his twenties – the Alastair Hope Kyd Prizes were founded in his memory), J. B. Taylor in 1909 (the son of 'Jas. T'), and N. G. Salvesen in both 1910 and 1911 (scholar and athlete combined, who later presented Denham Green House to the school).

The extra-mural activities started by Mr Mackenzie flourished even more vigorously under Mr Carter. The choir and orchestra tackled important musical pieces, an annual 'Free and Easy' concert was instituted, plays were performed in French and Greek and German. The school XV went from strength to strength, and in 1906–7 was unbeaten in school matches (one game with Loretto was drawn); the following year it contained three future Scottish internationals and a future English international – yet lost more school matches than it won!

By now the Academy had an official Games Master, 'Tommy' Thomas. Previously the Rector himself had supervised games and practices at New Field; he was an athletic man as well as being an artist and a musician, and he would dash up and down the touchlines, exhorting the forwards to get their heads down in remarkably robust language. In 1904, however, he told the Directors that he was finding the field duties too onerous, and Mr Thomas, who was special German Master, was appointed to supervise games for an extra £30 per annum.

Mr Carter also instituted a covered wagonette service (the first school bus) to bring Murrayfield boys to school for 12s. a term, and arranged for cabs to take younger boys home from Games.

And as the last of the Old Guard of masters retired, new ones came in who would themselves form the Old Guard of the future.

Mr Robert McEwan came in 1904 after a brilliant university career at Glasgow and Oriel College, Oxford. He was a Paisley man, and was instantly nicknamed 'Boab' as a result. It was a nickname that stuck with him for thirty-five years, until he retired in 1939 as Senior Master. (He also came back to help out during the War.) He took over Mr Macbean's work, and was Class Master of VIA for many, many years: a quiet, myopic man who enjoyed his teaching with restrained gusto.

That same summer a young man called Bertram Lennox Peel arrived to fill a temporary vacancy – and stayed to become an institution. 'Billy' Peel, he was always called, from his initials; a fine cricketer and all-round sportsman who was so severely wounded in the lungs during the First World War that his health remained indifferent for the rest of his life (he died in the same year as 'Boab' McEwan, in 1945). He was for a long time Housemaster of Mackenzie House. He loved nothing better than an argument; there was nothing he liked more than a boy who would stand up to him. 'Just state your view – and then apologise!' Like all masters, he had his own favourite ploy for revitalising a lesson – he would ask what he called a tricky question, and if a boy got it right, he was given a 'penny for a bun' at the Tuckshop. His ears stuck out in a way that delighted schoolboy caricaturists, and memory no doubt exaggerates the pitch of his squeaky voice. He was not a man you could forget; and when the Second World War broke out, he too stayed on after retiral age to help out for a couple of years.

Then there was W. G. Sherriff, who arrived in 1907 to help Mr Carter raise the standard in the English and Mathematics side. Later he concentrated on Modern Languages, for he had exceptionally diverse qualifications – he graduated from Cambridge with distinction in both Classics and Mathematics, and studied French at the Sorbonne and German in Leipzig. He enjoyed telling the story of his first visit to Edinburgh, when he went to the Rector's house to be interviewed for the job. In those days, garden gates were often operated mechanically by remote control, by a handle in the porch or a pedal in the ground beside the gate; but Mr Sherriff was unfamiliar with this contraption. After his interview he walked down the path, but the gate, operated from the porch, had swung shut before he reached it. There was nothing in Mr Sherriff's extensive academic training to equip him to cope with a problem of a gate locked in this mysterious way; baffled by the situation, unaware of the function of the foot-pedal under its hatch near the gate, and reluctant to go back to the door and admit his inability to solve the problem, he rapidly climbed the gate, which had spikes on it – and tore his best trousers.

He was always known as 'The Moot', the result of an obscure academic pun, for 'sheriff' derives from the Anglo-Saxon office of 'shire-reive', who was in charge of the 'moot', or assembly. He was a tall, dignified, white-haired man, who would come sweeping into the classroom uttering the words 'La dictée!' – and the boys fairly grabbed for their paper to be ready at once: a strict disciplinarian, but always considered scrupulously fair. Small boys quaked before him, for he always looked so stern; but he had an exceptional and dry sense of humour, much enhanced by the fact that he always kept his face straight. It just took a bit of getting used to. 'The Moot' retired in 1945 after thirty-eight years on the staff; he died in 1969, aged ninety-two.

But what exercised Mr Carter's mind most in those years was to develop the Science side. Ever since the temporary improvements to the Science quarters in 1902, he had been pressing the Directors for more accommodation. The Directors kept telling him to wait for the outcome of the Endowment Scheme. When the Fund got under way, it attracted £8,270 in its first year, so in 1907 the Rector presented a *Memorandum for the Consideration of the Directors*. In it he outlined the probable future requirements of the School, and set out a detailed scheme for building a Science Lecture Theatre and installing electrical power in the laboratory, building a new gymnasium and workshop, and providing extra rooms by purchasing the house at 42 Henderson Row, next to the Masters' Lodge.

The Directors bought No. 42 almost immediately, and used it as offices for the Rector, Rector's Clerk and private tutors, as Mr Carter had suggested, in order to relieve the pressure on rooms in the main building. And in 1908 they announced their decision to build a Science Lecture Theatre and 'add to the scientific equipment of the school by the introduction of motive power'. The new building, to the south of the existing science laboratory, cost £1,800, which was raised by means of a £1,600 loan from the Endowment Fund Trust (constituted by the Directors under a Declaration of Trust on May 30, 1908). The opening ceremony on January 12, 1909, was performed by the Secretary of State for War, R. B. (later Viscount) Haldane, who had been a member of Dr Clyde's Class from 1866–72. It was a great occasion for the Academy; it was also a triumph for Mr J. Tudor Cundall, the Cardiff man who had started the Academy's Science Department in 1890. There had been no Science course at all before then, although the discovery of three or four odd pieces of apparatus in a dusty cupboard hinted at some obscure experiment or demonstration, perhaps for the benefit of scientifically-minded boys like Clerk Maxwell or P. G. Tait, or else a relic from the 'Eureka Club' of 1870–7.

It was Mr Cundall who had designed and equipped the first laboratory, a building measuring 30 ft. by 50 ft., to which was attached a small Preparation and Masters' Room. The Science course he organised covered four years of practical and theoretical chemistry, preceded by a first year of Elementary General Properties of Matter and Heat. The laboratory had been built to accommodate sixty-eight boys, twenty-eight of whom could be taught at one time. By 1908, 150 boys were taking Science, the preliminary course of Elementary Physics had been extended to two years, and advanced courses of Physics had been added to meet the needs of Scholarship and Army candidates.

An Assistant Science Master joined the staff in 1903, who would become another Academy institution – Mr M. McCallum Fairgrieve. He stayed until 1935, two years before his death, having reached the position of Senior Science Master. His two sons and two grandsons also attended the Academy. He was naturally nicknamed 'Fairy', and his mannerisms have become enshrined in the Valhalla of Academy masters' lore, like so many others. He spoke with a pronounced aspirated 'burr': 'Foh this exphiment we need a cohk – not a cohk cohk but a hubber cohk,' he would say, and the recollection of it can still convulse older Academicals. Or he would say, 'This exphiment prhoduces gas which is fatal to any *nohmal* man' – and leaning over the beaker he would take three or four deep and prolonged sniffs and triumphantly exclaim, 'Yes, it's coming off now!' In his younger days he was a great favourite at the 'Free and Easy' concerts with his hilarious party-piece, 'When Father laid the Carpet on the Stairs'.

Once again, it was Mr Cundall who prepared the specifications for the new Science building in 1908. The whole of the old Laboratory was converted into a new lab, with additional benches and cupboards to accommodate 170 boys, with a class of fifty working at one time. A fine new Lecture Theatre was built as well, 42 ft. by 30 ft., in which sixty boys could write and 200 listen to a lecture, the desks arranged in rising tiers so that everyone could see. A permanent electric lantern was fitted. Between the Laboratory and the Lecture Theatre there was a Masters' Room, a Balance Room, and a Preparation and Store Room.

Well in advance of the main school building, which was still lit by gas and would remain so until 1927, the new Science buildings were connected to Edinburgh's electricity mains for their lighting and for the power for a 4 h.p. motor to drive a dynamo for experiments. Mr Cundall also took the opportunity to lay a cable to the school Hall to supply current for an electric lantern and for an emergency lighting supply.

Mr Cundall's laboratories were extended farther northwards in 1928–9, and the Biology Lab was re-equipped in 1950–1. It was to be 1956 before there was any extensive development of the Science Building, however. In that year, thanks to the financial support of the Industrial Fund for the Advancement of Scientific Education, work was started on a complete reconstruction of Mr Cundall's laboratories. With the opening of the new Prep School at Inverleith in 1960, the way was clear to rebuild part of the main building at Henderson Row for Science use, with a Physics Lab in 1960, a Maths Lab in 1960–1, and a new Biology Lab in 1962–3. The completed Science set-up gave more lab-space per boy than any other school in the country – a far cry from the somewhat basic 'Stinks' of prewar days. At a special ceremony before the annual Exhibition of 1961, on July 31, Sir George Thomson, F.R.S., the Master of Corpus Christi College, Cambridge, unveiled a plaque dedicating the Advanced Physics Laboratory to the memory of the most distinguished scientist the Academy has ever produced – James Clerk Maxwell.

'James Clerk Maxwell is the greatest figure in Scottish science and one of the three or four greatest Scots,' said Sir George. 'The Academy may well claim much of the credit, for he came here as a young day boy of nine, living with relatives, and found the Academy well fitted to cope with an unusual genius . . . It is hard to name with certainty the dramatist who is nearest after Shakespeare, and equally hard to name the physicist next after Newton, and perhaps it is foolish to try; but if such a competition were voted on by physicists, James Clerk Maxwell would stand as good a chance as any.'

From the unveiling ceremony at the Advanced Physics Laboratory, Sir George Thomson went straight in to the Exhibition in the Hall, where he was the Guest of Honour:

'A few minutes ago,' he said, 'I had the great honour of unveiling a plaque in memory of James Clerk Maxwell, the greatest of the many distinguished men that this Academy has produced. Apart from this connection, Maxwell's work and its consequences have an interest and an application today. Science is no longer regarded in this country (or even in England) as a subject to be apologised for, something definitely "non-U".'

He was speaking only a few yards from the spot where 'Dafty' Maxwell had the clothes half torn from his back on his first day at the Academy in 1841 . . .

WAR DRUMS: THE O.T.C.

We thought that if we could get the boys to begin sufficiently early to take a serious view of their future as citizens, to take a serious view of the duty that might some time be incumbent on them, to fight and if necessary to die for the Empire, then we would make a step forward . . .

(R. B. Haldane, Speech at the Academy, January 12, 1909)

Sir George Thomson's speech on that day in 1961 was all about science. When Mr R. B. Haldane (E.A. 1866–73), the Secretary of State for War, opened Mr Cundall's new Science Buildings in 1909, 'he made no formal remarks'. The event was somewhat overshadowed by another ceremony that he performed that January afternoon – the first official review of the Edinburgh Academy Contingent of the O.T.C. (Officers' Training Corps). It had been formed in October, 1908, with Lieut. H. F. Thompson in command. This is what Dr Hodson had tried and failed to start at the Academy fifty years previously. Mr Carter, in his turn, had been urging it strongly. So had the Academical Club, and two years earlier two anonymous Academicals had provided the school with a miniature rifle range to whet young martial appetites. The Academy O.T.C. – it was not a Cadet Corps – came about under a War Office scheme to build a reserve of Army officers from the public schools and universities; Mr Haldane had launched it the previous year as part of his campaign to establish a great Territorial Army in Britain.

Science took a back seat that day. After inspecting the members of the O.T.C., 'which had previously gone through with success some rather complicated evolutions, some of them previously quite unrehearsed', Mr Haldane made a rousing speech which was punctuated loud and often by patriotic applause. He complimented the boys on their smart new kilts of Mackenzie (Seaforth) tartan, chosen in honour of their former Rector, and launched into some reminiscences of his own school-days at the Academy. ('In those days, the only drinking-water we had was to be got in a trough which was the centre of a mass of boys fighting to get their luncheon. You dipped down as well as you could and got a jugful of water – and crumbs.') But the main burden of his speech was about the O.T.C. and the decision of the War Office 'to look to the young brains of the nation' for a reserve of officers:

'We thought that if we could get the boys to begin sufficiently early to take a serious view of their future as citizens, to take a serious view of the duty that might some time be incumbent upon them, to fight and if necessary to die for the Empire, then we should make a step forward, then we should have given them a piece of idealism, and we at the same time should have given to the nation a reserve of Officers.'

There were plenty of boys listening in the Hall that day who in five or six years time would go straight from the Academy in their smart Seaforth Highlander kilts to fight and die for the Empire. Some would be in the undefeated cricket XI of 1913-14, of whom seven were killed in the war and the other four wounded. Some would be in the triumphant Academy O.T.C. shooting team which won the coveted Ashburton Shield at the first attempt in 1911, and received the kind of adulation accorded nowadays to Cup-winning football teams.

But Reginald Carter was not there to witness that particular triumph. Having established the O.T.C. in 1908 and started the Debating Society, and having seen Mackenzie House on to the stocks, Mr Carter applied for the Headmastership of Bedford School because 'for family reasons' he wanted to return to the south. He left the Academy at the end of the Easter term, 1910, after eight years during which he had brought the school roll up from 374 to 539, the highest in the school's history.

The Directors passed a resolution declaring that he had been 'a conspicuously successful Headmaster . . . possessed of sound judgement and great strength of character'. They praised him for raising the general standard of work and for maintaining discipline 'with firmness and vigour', and paid special tribute to his efforts in establishing the Endowment Fund, the Staff Pension Scheme, and the O.T.C. They believed that he had 'shown himself in thorough sympathy with the peculiar traditions of the school, and in developing it so as to meet modern requirements and changing conditions, has sacrificed none of its characteristic and cherished features'. The Directors wanted it placed on record that 'their personal relations with him have uniformly been of the pleasantest and most satisfactory description'.

It was rather ironic that the Directors' meeting at which Mr Carter announced his intention of leaving the Academy also approved a committee report recommending the raising of the Rector's salary. Mr Carter knew that the rise was on the way and it made no difference to his decision to leave Edinburgh, but it meant that the Directors, in advertising for a new Rector, were able to offer £1,000 a year plus a capitation grant of £5 for every fee in the Upper School over 320 and up to 360, and £1 for every fee above 360. The average number of Upper School boys for the past three years had been 327; that year's number of fees was 356. Actually, this 'rise' in the Rector's salary was rather a piece of sleight-of-hand. Mr Carter's salary was £800 plus a capitation grant of £5 for every fee over 280; therefore, as long as the number of fees was over 320, he would be earning precisely the same amount as the new man, who simply had his *minimum* guaranteed at £1,000 (he would not be affected by any fall in fees below 320). Between 320 and 360 fees, both Mr Carter and the new man would earn exactly the same; but if and when the numbers rose *above* 360, the new man would actually earn less than Mr Carter would have done under the old system, for there was no limit on the number of £5 capitation grants in Mr Carter's contract, whereas the new man would only be getting £1 a head for every fee over 360!

Mr Carter said goodbye to the assembled school on the last day of the Easter term, 1910. The boys presented him with a silver watch, and at the time of his death in 1936 it was reported in the *Chronicle* that he wore the watch 'to the very last'. He returned to Edinburgh for the Academy Centenary Dinner in 1924, and his old pupils nearly lifted the roof off the Music Hall in George Street with their cheering when his name was mentioned. One of his former pupils wrote in the *Chronicle*: 'It was typical of him that he had all records of his great ovation deleted from the accounts of the Dinner.'

But not quite all. The *Chronicle* of July, 1924, describing the Centenary Dinner, records the fact that 'In answer to persistent calls, Mr Carter said a few words expressing his deep gratitude for the privilege of having worked at the Edinburgh Academy, where everyone . . . had been so good to him. The company joined in singing "He's a jolly good fellow" when Mr Carter resumed his seat'.

He seems to have been a genuinely likeable man: big, warm, good-humoured, a strong man in every sense of the term, benevolent and imperturbable. When he retired from Bedford School in 1928 to live in Tavistock, he devoted the rest of his life to helping the unemployed at Devonport; he founded a Social Centre there, and used to visit the convicts at Dartmoor. When he died in 1936, his friend, Bishop Walter Carey, wrote: 'What an epitaph to a man's memory it was to say that he had lived for God and his fellowmen and not for himself! Of few men could that be more truly said than of Reginald Carter.'

The man the Directors chose to succeed 'Reggie' Carter was Mr R. H. Ferard, one of His Majesty's Inspectors of Secondary Schools in England. He had been educated at Eton and Exeter College, Oxford, and was a Tutor at Keble College, Oxford, for twelve years (three of them as Dean). Under him the Academy would go on to even greater things, with that Ashburton Shield triumph, victorious football and cricket teams, four classical scholarships to Oxford in one year; the start of the school Pipe Band, the annual athletics matches with Merchiston, and the biennial Gilbert and Sullivan performances; the Centenary celebrations of the Foundation of the school, and the highest enrolments of pupils since the school began.

But Mr Ferard's Rectorship (1910–26) was also marked by the Academy's involvement in the bloodiest war the world had yet known. The figures alone make appalling reading; 1,539 Academicals are known to have fought in it, and 298 died – many of them boys just out of school. It was a high price paid in maintaining the military tradition that had been building up since Mr Roland gave his first fencing lessons at the Academy in 1831.

CHAPTER XV

Arms and the Schoolboy

No more our pestered mothers shall bats but bayonets see:
This year young Geits, birds-nesting, will tumble from the tree;
And in the field at Raeburn Place the balls must roam at will,
Among the feet of little muffs, whose brothers are at drill.
(R. H. Moncrieff, *Chronicle*, November, 1916)

WHEN the Academy O.T.C. was started in October, 1908, there was a chorus of Academical 'Hear-Hears' that echoed round the world. Almost since the day of its inception there had been pressure on the Academy from friends and supporters to establish some kind of military training in the school; and although Academy boys had been winning honour and glory on the battlefield to an extent that made the publication of the *Edinburgh Academy Army List* in 1894 a mammoth task, the Directors had always strongly resisted attempts to start an official school Cadet Corps.

According to an unpublished thesis by Ian Thomson on *Almond of Loretto and the Development of Physical Education in Scotland during the Nineteenth Century* (Edinburgh University, 1969), three months before the Academy was due to open there was an article in the *Edinburgh Magazine* appealing to the Directors of the Edinburgh Academy to introduce fencing and gymnastics into their curriculum. A few days later the Directors appointed a committee to consider the propriety of introducing gymnastic exercises at the Academy. The committee visited the Scottish Naval and Military Academy in Edinburgh in December, 1824, and came away convinced that the military aspects of the exercises, using swords and muskets, was unsuitable for the Academy, but recommended the gymnastic exercises as having considerable value for the health of schoolboys. At the same time they warned against the possibility of opposition from parents and public, and suggested confining gymnastics to the older boys at first.

But it was two years before anything further was done, and then the Directors decided it would not be advisable to introduce gymnastic exercises 'to the extent to which they have been adopted in other public seminaries, but that it would be better to confine them to the instructions to be derived from a drill sergeant'. A Sergeant Ralston was appointed and enrolled nearly 200 boys, but enthusiasm waned, and in two years Sergeant Ralston stopped holding his drill classes. In his place the Directors arranged that Mr George Roland, the fencing master at the Military Academy, should hold classes in a room which he rented from the school, with the boys paying their fees directly to him.

Mr Roland, whose two sons also went to the Academy and later became Fencing Masters with their father (George Roland, E.A. 1828–32, and Henry Roland, E.A. 1836–40), was one of the most colourful characters in the history of the Academy. He and his sons ran their little school for nearly sixty years, and turned out a stream of skilled swordsmen and enthusiastic militarists who slashed and cut their way across Africa and India and the Crimea, practising on distant battlefields the lunges and thrusts and parries they had learned in the Roland's little room in the basement of the Writing and Arithmetic Block at the Edinburgh Academy. But it wasn't part of their Academy training. Attendance at the Rolands' classes was always optional; the Rolands were never members of the Academy staff, and the Directors had no influence over what was taught at their classes.

When Dr Hodson, brother of one of the heroes of the Indian Mutiny, became Rector in 1854 he started a campaign, which he kept up to the end of his fiery Rectorship, to foster military drill, gymnastics, and patriotic fervour at the Academy. But the Directors, reflecting as always what they believed to be the general feeling of parents, resisted his repeated requests for a school Cadet Corps. All Dr Hodson could do, when a drilling class that was begun in 1859 withered away, was to persuade the Rolands to put more emphasis on military drilling, and by 1864 two afternoon classes for fencing and gymnastics were being supplemented by two classes for military drill conducted by the Rolands' military assistant, Sergeant Kearney. But the boys preferred cricket and football to after-school drilling, and in 1865, the Directors were drawing attention to the fact that 'attendance at the classes for Drawing and Fortification, and Fencing and Gymnastics, has of late years unaccountably diminished'. In 1868, Dr Hodson once again regretted 'the falling-off in the attendance in the Fencing and Gymnastic Classes . . . and the fact that nothing has been done towards forming from among our boys a Cadet Corps of the Volunteer Rifle Corps . . .'

But in fact something *had* been done, albeit unofficially: in 1859 an unofficial Academy Corps of Volunteer Rifles had been formed when Napoleon III was making war-like noises and the British were rushing to arms, with volunteer companies springing up all over the country, with men and boys drilling and marching in makeshift uniforms and a flurry of patriotism.

Robert Hope Moncrieff, who wrote more than 200 story-books like *The World As It Is* and *Adventures in America* and *Bonnie Scotland* (he also used the pseudonyms A. R. Hope and Ascott R. Hope) was at the Academy at the time (E.A. 1856–62), and became a member of the Corps. Many years later, as 'Septuagenarius', he described its activities in an article in the *Chronicle* in November, 1916: 'Certain vapouring threats of French officers threw our country into a fit of invasion fever, when we for once became aware of our army as much too small to meet such a force as might be thrown upon our shores, now that steam raised a new question as to Britannia ruling the waves. Men of all ages and classes rushed into awkward arms, and everywhere sprang up Volunteer corps after half a century's disbandment.

'The movement spread to beardless boys; then at the Academy it behoved us to raise a cadet company that might do its part in confounding the politics and frustrating the knavish tricks of any hostile power. I enlisted at the outset, but the *Edinburgh Academy Register* quite erroneously puts on me an undeserved honour as "organiser and first captain" of this corps. Our organiser, one takes it, must have been Mr Roland, a portly old gentleman, who struck me as the type of Dickens' "Mr Turveydrop", when he had retired from active service as our fencing and gymnastic master, most of the work being done then by his son. Our headquarters were their room below the separate building used as writing and arithmetic class-rooms; we drilled under Messrs. Rolands' auspices; and we were commonly known as the "Roland Volunteers". I rather think myself responsible for this name, my rank in the company being as its minstrel or trumpeter, when I made a first appearance in print by some verses entitled "The Roland Volunteers", which were inserted in the *Scotsman* . . .'

The weapons of the Roland Volunteers were discarded army carbines from which they were allowed to fire nothing more deadly than percussion caps; but they had a uniform, specially designed by a tailor on the Bridges. It consisted of a pepper-and-salt tunic and trousers, but it was seldom worn, because drilling after school hours 'soon began to look too much like being kept in'. The boys much preferred the sword exercise and singlestick, at which Mr Roland's son was their instructor. It was no game for softies; Moncrieff recalled a contest with a boy who later became Major-General R. H. D. Lorn Campbell (E.A. 1857–61) and a hero of the Chinese Boxer uprising: 'At school he was dubbed "Ben", since after he and I had slashed at each other for a stricken hour, he showed so many black and blue stripes all down one side as to be likened to a Bengal tiger.'

Moncrieff described that first volunteer corps as 'rather a damp squib, fizzling out after a year or so. In vain, as its Tyrtæus, did I strive to galvanize a flickering ardour. Too falsely I prophesied, piping after the tune of Macaulay:

> 'No more our pestered mothers shall bats but bayonets see;
> This year young Geits, birds-nesting, will tumble from the tree;
> And in the field at Raeburn Place the balls must roam at will,
> Among the feet of little muffs, whose brothers are at drill.'

The drill sergeant's opinion of the schoolboy officers of the corps was illustrated by his crushing rebuke to a lad who was playing the fool: 'Mr So-and-so, I wish you would fall to the rear and become an officer or something, then we should get on better.'

The Edinburgh Academy Volunteer Rifles only lasted three years. As Moncrieff put it, 'Me duce, we melted away under the sun of the cricket season; and next year my tunic was made down into a first attempt at a tail-coat.'

And still the Academy Directors declined to establish an official Cadet Corps. The Directors of Glasgow Academy, too, turned down an invitation to form a Cadet Corps, in their case in connection with the 1st Regiment of the Lanarkshire Rifle Volunteers, though the English public schools had set the fashion in 1860 by introducing military drill in Rugby, Harrow, Eton, Westminster, and other schools. The first Scottish School Cadet Corps was not formed until 1875, at Glenalmond.

The pressure on the Academy Directors to be the first Scottish School in the field must have been strong, especially from Academicals who were in the forefront of the Volunteer movement during the time of alarms and national emergencies in the early 1860's and during the Franco-Prussian War of 1870–1. It was a time of intense patriotic fervour, and spare-time soldiering became almost a national sport. One of the keenest enthusiasts was John Hay Athole Macdonald (later Lord

Kingsburgh), Lord Justice-Clerk of Scotland. He was a most remarkable man, who started at the Academy in Dr Cumming's Class in 1845 and left school in 1852, the year that Napoleon III became Emperor of France: and in 1915, at the age of nearly eighty, he published his delightful volume of reminiscences, *Life Jottings of an Old Edinburgh Citizen*.

Lord Kingsburgh never took part in a battle or served on any war front in his life: 'Anything I have done in the military line was a matter of hobby,' he said when he presided at the Academical Reunion Dinner of 1911. Yet as a lifelong volunteer he rose to the rank of Brigadier-General, the first Volunteer Brigadier to command a Brigade. It consisted of the three battalions of his own Queen's Brigade (formerly the Edinburgh Volunteers) and the 5th, 6th, and 8th Volunteer battalions of the Royal Scots, and it was called the Forth Brigade. Lord Kingsburgh was given the command in 1888 when he had just left Parliament as Lord Advocate to take a seat on the Scottish bench as Lord Justice-Clerk. During the Boer War he took his Brigade to training camp, and regularly 'saw my lads off from the station' when they left for South Africa to serve with the Royal Scots.

But Lord Kingsburgh, who was then sixty-three years old, continued to serve as a judge – 'it was *toga* in the morning and *arma* in the afternoon' – and enjoyed what was 'probably a unique experience' of drawing his Brigadier-General's pay and allowance and his salary as a judge at the same time.

He marched past Queen Victoria at the great Review of 1860, when 21,514 Scots Volunteers assembled in the Queen's Park to shake their fists at what Lord Kingsburgh called 'truculent utterances of certain French colonels'. On that occasion in Edinburgh, he wrote, 'the Queen saw in one *coup d'œil* a larger number of her loyal subjects than she ever saw in all the rest of her long reign . . . Arthur's Seat being a natural amphitheatre, made it possible to see the whole assemblage at one view.' He was also on parade nearly twenty-one years later, when almost twice as many Volunteers were reviewed by Queen Victoria in Edinburgh; but this time she saw very little because of the rain. It was the famous Wet Review, and as Lord Kingsburgh wrote later: 'No ordinary words can describe that downpour . . . There had been nothing seen in the Queen's Park to compare with it in the memory of man . . . There were, it was reported, two hundred deaths traceable to what was gone through on that day, and I know myself a gentleman who contracted evil in consequence, which has at times troubled him up to this hour, after more than thirty years have passed away.' The Queen's servant, John Brown, was said to have raided the quarters of the royal Maids of Honour and carried off thirteen umbrellas, which he took with him in the rumble of the Queen's carriage. Whenever an umbrella began to leak under the weight of the torrent he handed the Queen a dry one over the back of the carriage. 'I have no doubt the whole thirteen were used and that he wished he had brought more,' wrote Lord Kingsburgh.

Lord Kingsburgh himself apparently suffered no ill effects from his soaking. He became a Director of the Academy that same year, 1881, and remained on the Board until 1919. He was Lord Advocate from 1885–9; M.P. for the Universities of Edinburgh and St Andrews from 1885–8. He was captain of the Royal and Ancient Golf Club, President and Steward of the Royal Automobile Club, and Arbiter in the great dispute over the laws between the four Rugby Unions. (After the settlement of 'The Dispute', in 1890, he was presented with a handsome silver bowl by the grateful Unions; it was bequeathed to the Academy after his death in 1919 as the Kingsburgh Cup.) He was Adjutant-General and Ensign-General of the Royal Company of Archers; Vice-President of the National Rifle Association; President of the Royal Scottish Society of Arts; a Member of the Road Board, a Commissioner of Lighthouses, and chairman of the Royal Commission on Boundaries of Glasgow.

As well as all this he won medals for inventing life-saving gadgets, military aids, and electrical contrivances. He invented, according to the *Edinburgh Academy Register*, 'a holophote course indicator for preventing collisions at sea,' a military field telegraph, and a barathermotele meter; and it was 'through his exertions' with the Post Master General and the Government that postcards were introduced into the postal service in Great Britain.

He published a stream of books and pamphlets, ranging from *Hints on Drill for Volunteers* and *Electricity in the Household* to his *Life Jottings*. He was finishing this book when the First World War broke out in 1914, and at the age of nearly eighty he wrote that he was drilling an emergency company of volunteers three nights a week and 'I have been grinding them as I did when I trained my company fifty-five years ago.'

At the Reunion Dinner of 1911, Lord Kingsburgh was in the chair as Sir Thomas Raleigh, Fellow of All Souls College, Oxford (E.A. 1862–7) sang the praises of the Academy O.T.C., whose achievements in shooting 'are the envy and wonder of the shooting world'. They were about to win the Ashburton Shield at Bisley that summer, and the trophies they had already won since the start of the Corps in 1908 were on display in the School Hall that evening.

But Colonel J. C. Campbell of the Royal Engineers, who had been in Mr Carmichael's Class of 1863–70, replying to the toast of 'The Imperial Forces' reminded the company that the sharpshooters of the O.T.C. were not the first Academy boys to take up arms. He referred to the first School Rifle Club, which practised on Hunter's Bog (the shooting ground for all the Edinburgh Volunteers) in 1870, the year of the Franco-Prussian War; and he recalled an incident when one of the boys ('now a very distinguished officer') accidentally shot a sheep. When the account of his speech had appeared in the *Chronicle* another Academical, signing himself 'The Slayer of the Sheep', wrote from Aldershot describing the sheep incident in detail.

The boys had been led by the Mathematics Master, Mr John Shand, who left the Academy that same year to become Professor of Mathematics at the University of Otago, New Zealand: 'Johnny Shand got Enfield rifles and ammunition for us somehow,' wrote the sheep-slayer. 'Schoolboys nowadays may be surprised to hear that we had muzzle-loading Enfields, and that we went on to the range without any preliminary drill, as far as I can remember. The cartridges supplied to us were of stiff paper, greased at one end. We had to bite off the paper at the other end, pour the powder, which was then revealed to view, down the bore of the rifle, and then, placing the greased bullet in the bore, ram it down on top of the powder. These were the greased cartridges which caused so much trouble in the Indian Mutiny and they were still in use with us in 1870. The rifle was a long weapon and heavy; and I remember it kicked most abominably after the first shot or two, especially on a rainy day.'

There were sheep grazing all over the range, most of them dark grey, like the rocks and boulders on the hillside. On his third shot, when his shoulder was aching from the kick of the rifle, he missed – and 'a grey rock shot up into the air and fell with four hitherto-unseen legs kicking spasmodically . . . In reviewing the career of the Rifle Club shortly afterwards before the whole school, the Rector alluded with ill-concealed amusement to the "casual and incidental circumstances which sometimes attended rifle practice".'

The Rector was Dr Harvey, and the sheep-slayer got his revenge shortly afterwards when he took part in a shoot with the Rector at a country house, and had the satisfaction of seeing Dr Harvey, whose 'skill as a shot was execrable', blasting away at the game and managing to shoot only – *horribile dictu* – a fox.

A more serious approach to the business of shooting was taken with the opening of the first Academy Rifle Range, east of the Fives Courts, in 1906, and shooting matches were held with Fettes and Merchiston. As war noises increased in Europe the calls for a school Cadet Corps were raised more frequently at Academical gatherings. By 1908 the Rector, Mr Carter, was also urging the Directors to start a Cadet Corps as soon as possible under War Secretary Haldane's scheme (announced in March, 1908) for forming Officers' Training Corps, comprising a Senior Division from the Universities and a Junior Division from the Public Schools. Certificates gained would entitle cadets to exemption from, or reduction of, training for Army Commissions.

At last, in the annual *Report* of 1908, the Directors announced the formation of a School Cadet Corps, and expressed themselves as confident that it would be 'a valuable addition to the life of the School'. It was also a strict necessity now, if the Academy was to continue to keep pace with the English public schools. The Academy had already introduced an Army side into its course of studies in order to compete with schools putting forward candidates for Army entrance exams. Now the Directors were obliged to take a step they had resisted since the school was founded: no parent with Army ambitions for his son would now contemplate a school that did not provide the officer training recognised by the War Office as qualification for an Army Commission.

The War Office scheme was a clever one. The Academy's old boy at the War Office, the Rt. Hon. Richard Burdon Haldane, had his old school firmly by the scruff of the neck. He offered it £1 capitation fee for every efficient cadet, and £10 for every cadet who gained a certificate and got a Commission in the Special Reserve or Territorial Force. There would also be a small capital grant towards the initial cost of starting the Corps. According to Merchiston Castle School, which already had a Corps, the cost of running one would work out at about £280 a year. Uniforms at £3 each – Mackenzie kilt, tunic, etc. – were bought by the school for 100 boys, to be handed on to others as boys left school, though parents could buy uniforms if they wished.

Service in the Corps would be a compulsory part of the regular physical training of boys above a certain age, and Sergeant Sheen, who had been giving gymnastic lessons at the Academy for some years, was dismissed to make way for full-time military instructors. Mr H. F. Thompson, the Mathematics Master who replaced Dr John Sturgeon Mackay in 1904, was appointed Commanding Officer.

The Directors made their announcement briefly, merely explaining that 'this step has been rendered necessary by the recent Army Orders . . .' But Mr Carter, in his *Report*, declared: 'I regard this as a most important departure in the history of the School, and I hope not only that the Corps will reach and maintain a high standard of efficiency, but that our boys, when they leave School, if they are not serving as Officers in the Army or in the Special Reserve, will make a point of joining the Territorial Force. It is the duty of every Briton to be trained for the defence of his country, and Schools in the position of the Edinburgh Academy should spare no efforts to set a good example in this matter. Military training should be an essential part of a school education.'

At the first examination for the coveted War Office Certificate 'A' in 1911 all the Academy entrants failed, but the number of passes increased each year and when the Great War started in November, 1914, nineteen boys had just won their certificates which were a passport to a quick commission in the Army and an early passage to the mud of Flanders. Eleven of those nineteen were the members of the undefeated cricket XI of 1913–14, of whom seven were to be killed in the war and the other four wounded. Several masters left to join up; Captain H. B. Cummins, who had joined the staff in 1908, was killed in 1916 and 'Billy' Peel was severely wounded in the lungs; and the school drill sergeants were soon all in real uniform. But the O.T.C. continued to operate during term-time and in the holidays, when the boys attended special Army courses. In 1917 the Directors noted 'the tendency of boys to leave school as they approach the age of eighteen in order to qualify for military duties': at the beginning of the summer term in 1917 there was not a single boy in the school aged eighteen.

As the annual list increased of medals and decorations for gallantry won by Academicals, so did the toll of war dead, until it had reached 298 by the end of the war – 298 out of 1,539. The Honours List included two V.C.s – Lieut. (afterwards Lieut.-Colonel) W. L. Brodie (E.A. 1892–9) at Becelaere in 1914, and Lieut. (afterwards Captain) A. E. Ker (E.A. 1890–9) at St Quentin in 1918 – one K.C.M.G., fifteen C.M.G.S.s, six K.C.B.s, sixty-eight D.S.O.s, and 160 M.C.s.

And then came the prizes, the endowed scholarships, and the gifts of school equipment in memory of sons and brothers killed in the war. The clock over the entrance to the Library was presented in memory of Capt. R. D. Stevenson (E.A. 1905–14), a member of that victorious XI of 1913–14, killed in action in 1916. The Archibald Douglas English Prize commemorates Lt. A. H. Douglas, Dux of the School in 1914 and Captain of the XV, who fell at Armentières in September, 1916. The Mill English Prize commemorates 2nd Lt. William Henry Mill (E.A. 1904–13), killed in action at Gallipoli in 1915. The Nelson Mathematics Prize was instituted in memory of T. A. Nelson (E.A. 1887–95), one of the Nelson publishing family and a rugby International, killed in action in 1917. The Sloan Cup for Pipe-Playing commemorates 2nd Lt. T. I. T. Sloan (E.A. 1906–15), who had won the Piper's Prize in 1912, and was killed in action in 1917. The Stewart Prize for Modern History commemorates two brothers who fell – Capt. C. E. Stewart (E.A. 1897–1904), who died in 1917, and Lt. F. A. Stewart (E.A. 1903–9), who died in 1916. The Aitken Prize for the Dux of Class VI commemorates 2nd Lt. J. M. Aitken (E.A. 1913–17), who had barely time to leave school before he was killed in 1918. The gong in the Dining Hall is a mounted shell-case sent from France by Capt. G. D. Ferguson (E.A. 1901–8), who was killed in action in 1917.

By 1920, £10,000 had been subscribed to the Academy War Memorial, which took the form of the fine gymnasium behind the main building. It was completed and opened in 1923.

The O.T.C. went from strength to strength after the war, gradually settling down from its role as a spearhead in a possible war situation to being a regular part of school life, with competitions for shooting, piping, and the best platoon as the aim, rather than ultimate glory on the field of battle. The Shooting VIII never quite managed to recapture the first fine rapture of 1911 at Bisley, although they came close on occasion; but between the wars they were, along with Glenalmond, the outstanding school team in Scotland and won the Brock Challenge Shield for competition among the Scottish schools several times, and they were the first team to win the Strathcona Challenge Shield on the miniature range. The Academy Pipe Band, which was formed in 1909–10, frequently won the East of Scotland Schools O.T.C. Pipe Band Competition. In 1930, the Rector (Mr P. H. B. Lyon) reported that the Corps had 'covered itself with glory' at the annual camp competition at Elie, winning all the competitions for guard-mounting, band, team and individual dancing, and individual piping: they had been officially reported 'the best contingent in camp'. Next year forty-three boys passed the exam for the War Office Certificate 'A', the highest number from the Academy since the start of the scheme; by 1935 the number had risen to fifty-six.

In 1938, when the hounds of war were baying again, the Academy O.T.C. became officially affiliated to the Royal Scots, and appeared in the Army List as such. The last War Office report on the Edinburgh Academy O.T.C. before the outbreak of war read: 'One of the best. Should make suitable officers. Will be glad of the training they have received when they are called up for Militia Training.'

An Air Force section of the O.T.C. was formed in 1940, and combined with other Edinburgh schools to form a squadron, and the Army Corps acquired a Bren gun. Of the three most important appointments in the Royal Navy at the start of the war, two were held by Academicals – Admiral Sir Percy Noble (E.A. 1893) in command of the China Station, and later C.-in-C. Western Approaches; and Admiral Sir Andrew (later Viscount) Cunningham (E.A. 1892–4), C.-in-C. Mediterranean. Air Vice-Marshal (later Sir) Patrick H. L. Playfair (E.A. 1898–1901) commanded the Advance Air Striking Force in France; Lieutenant-General Sir James H. Marshall Cornwall (1894–6) was G.O.C. in C. of the British troops in Egypt; and following British victories in East Africa, both Ethiopia and Italian Somaliland were put under the military jurisdiction of Lt.-General (later Sir) Alan G. Cunningham (1897–9), the younger brother of Admiral Cunningham.

Admiral of the Fleet Lord Cunningham finished the war as First Sea Lord and Chief of the Naval Staff; Lt.-General Sir Philip Christison (1902–12) represented Admiral Mountbatten at the signing of the Japanese surrender of Singapore in 1945.

Of the 1,700 Academicals who served in the Armed Forces, 179 lost their lives and ninety-one were wounded. There were seventy-three prisoners of war, and an Academical Dinner held at the German prison camp, Oflag VIIC, on September 23, 1941, was attended by twenty Accies.

Academicals won 321 war decorations, including one V.C. (Commander A. C. C. Miers (E.A. 1915–16), later Rear-Admiral Sir Anthony Miers, who commanded the submarine *Torbay* in a daring raid on enemy shipping in the Corfu Roads in 1942), twenty-nine M.B.E.s, twenty-three D.S.O.s, thirteen D.S.C.s, forty-five M.C.s, ten D.F.C.s, seven Mentions in Despatches, and 110 Commendations. Sir Anthony Miers brought the Academical tally of V.C.s since the Victoria Cross was instituted in 1856, to nine.

The Edinburgh Academy itself was listed as a 'military objective' by the Germans during the war. A German military map of Edinburgh dated 1941 showed the Academy outlined in red as being of military importance – one of the three *Kasernen* (Barracks) in the city, along with Redford and Leith Fort!

And after the war – once again the sad list of donations and prizes to commemorate the fallen. The Hamish Robb Trophy for the best cadet of the year was endowed in memory of Lt. H. W. Robb (E.A. 1934–9) of the Lothians and Border Horse, killed in action at Cassino in May, 1944. Another name now on the Academy prize-list is that of James Michael Blair (E.A. 1928–40). He was a fine all-rounder: Dux of the School in 1939, Captain of the XV, Head Ephor, winner of a Scholarship in Classics to Corpus Christi College, Oxford. At Oxford he won his rugby Blue before joining the Services. Murrayfield saw him playing scrum-half for Scotland in the Services International in February, 1944; five months later he was dead from wounds sustained in action in Normandy as a Lieutenant in the Reconnaissance Corps. He was twenty-one years old. The James Michael Blair prizes for Classics, French, Mathematics, and English Essay are his personal memorial.

Twenty years and more after the war was over, another Blair who died in the war – Lt. William Blair of the Seaforth Highlanders (E.A. 1926–32), who was killed in the Western Desert in 1942 – had his name immortalised, when the school received a most generous donation to set up a Field Centre in the Highlands. The words which accompanied the gift declared: 'It is to be for the School to establish a centre in the hills of Scotland where boys may stay and find facilities to walk, climb, fish and study nature in rough but friendly conditions, and where they may learn to appreciate the beauty, isolation and peace of the hills.' To that end, in 1969, the School acquired a small house at Glen Doll, at the head of Glen Clova in Angus, which had once served as a hostel for workers with the Forestry Commission. It had accommodation for thirty boys, and was named Blair House. It was done up largely by Academy boys themselves, and since then Blair House in Glen Doll has fully lived up to the hopes of the donor and the memory of the young man in whose name it was gifted. In the summer of 1974, to celebrate the 150th Anniversary of the school, parties of Academy climbers scaled 150 'Munros', in one weekend, from Ben Hope in the north to Ben Lomond in the south, and from Mount Keen in the east to Sgur na Banachdich in the west. The climbers included the Rector (Dr Mills) and several members of the Prep – an epic and historic enterprise.

But just after the war in Europe had ended, the rush of prize money in memory of fallen sons was becoming a slight embarrassment; and the Prize List had to be revised because the presentation of prizes was taking up too much time at the Exhibition.

In June, 1945, a War Memorial Appeal was launched. The response was considered disappointing at first – only £4,600 had been sub-scribed by the end of August – but by 1948 it had reached nearly £18,000. This time the War Memorial was used to provide grants to assist the education at the Academy of the sons of Academicals who had been killed in the war or had suffered financially or otherwise as a result of the War. Part of the Fund was also spent on reconstructing and reconditioning the Pavilion and Squash Courts at Raeburn Place. Five Academical brothers Carmichael – A. M. (E.A. 1927–37), D. D. (E.A. 1927–36), G. C. (E.A. 1930–9), I. R. (E.A. 1936–47) and J. R. (E.A. 1927–32) – met the entire cost of restoring and improving the Raeburn Place field, which had been dug up to grow vegetables during the war. It was during this restoration that the celebrated 'Mound' at Raeburn Place was levelled at long last – after the Inspector of Ancient Monu-ments had stated that it had no archaeological significance. Earlier Academical antiquarians had opined that it was an ancient butt for archery, but trial excavation after the war revealed it to be a natural mound of boulder clay topped by nineteenth-century debris. It was only common-sense to level it, to create more room for pitches; but older Academicals will always mourn it, as a fine vantage point for watching matches (prone during the cricket season) and as a nostalgic landmark.

In the immediate post-war years, the Corps saw many changes. One of them was the departure of a man who had become as much a fixture at the Academy as the School clock itself – Sergeant-Major S. J. Atkinson, 'The Bud'. He was on the Academy staff for forty years, 1910–50. He was a Londoner born and bred, who had enlisted in the Royal Scots Greys in 1903. When he came to the Academy as Assistant Gymnastic and Drill Instructor, the senior Instructor was a Sergeant Reid, who had been christened 'The Buddy' from his peculiar method of intoning the order: 'Buddy tweesting – first poseetion – commence!' So naturally the new Assistant inherited the nickname as 'The Wee Buddy', later shortened to 'The Buddy' and finally, simply, 'The Bud'. In August, 1914, 'The Bud' was at camp with the O.T.C. at Barry; before the end of the month he had been mobilised, shipped to France and wounded in action. By October he was back at the Academy on sick leave, and his missing fingertips were objects of awed interest to generations of Academy boys as he taught them gym. Such were the stories of his prowess in battle and apparent immortality that a member of VB once wrote in a General Knowledge test: 'Sgt.-Major Atkinson was wounded at the Battle of Plassey.' As a gymnastic instructor he was unsurpassed; he was a short, stalwart man, but his suppleness and agility were legendary, and other gym teachers used to come along in droves to watch him at work. He drilled literally thousands of boys in the O.T.C., he taught boxing, and as an egger-on of recalcitrants he helped that most elegant of fencing masters, M. Léon Crosnier, to train such skilled swordsmen as L. G. Morrison (E.A. 1920–32), Scotland's foremost foil and epée exponent for many years, and Sir Bruce Seton (E.A. 1920–7), who later earned celebrity in films and on television as 'Fabian of the Yard'. But the most familiar memory of 'The Bud' is of him standing in white singlet or sweater on a platform before the portico steps conducting the 10-minute mass P.T. sessions at eleven o'clock that were introduced for the Upper School in the 1920s. The sight of hundreds of boys bending and swinging and jumping, morning after morning, year after year, made Sgt.-Major Atkinson so renowned that he was often called on to lead mass displays of P.T., including one at Murrayfield on the occasion of the Coronation celebrations in 1937. Alas – in later years the Schools Inspectors found mass P.T. in the Yards a faintly ridiculous spectacle as a modern form of physical exercise, and yet another noble Academy tradition bit the dust. Sgt.-Major Atkinson died in 1969, at the age of 83.

Peace-time saw many changes in the Corps. Soon the Army and Air Force units were formed into one Combined Cadet Force, the C.C.F.; and a master who had served with the Royal Scots, winning the Military Cross, returned to the Academy in 1945 after an early release because of wounds, and took charge of the Corps. This was Mr Maurice H. Cooke, who joined the Academy staff in 1931 and retired in 1969 after thirty-eight years' service (he was Senior Master for the last three). After getting the C.C.F. into shape, he retired to introduce the Duke of Edinburgh's Award Scheme; the Academy was one of the first Scottish schools to take part in it, and Mr Cooke himself, as a member of Sir John Hunt's Committee, had much to do with the shaping and development of the Scheme. Here he could give his life-long love of the outdoors free rein; he is a skilled and experienced mountaineer, and he personally supervised innumerable expeditions at all levels. Recently, he has devoted an enormous amount of time and energy to the monumental task of editing the *Edinburgh Academy List, 1824–1974*, a roll-call of all pupils and members of staff of the Academy since its foundation, to celebrate the 150th anniversary. But then, Maurice Cooke has never been averse to hard labour; when a boy in school was asked one day, 'What is meant by the working classes?', he replied without hesitation, 'Mr Atkinson's and Mr Cooke's.'

Today the C.C.F., with a Naval Unit that was added in 1964, does things never dreamed of before the war. As well as drilling and shooting and piping, today's cadets go orienteering in the hills, flying in Chipmunks with the R.A.F., sailing in coastal minesweepers, taking part in assault courses, climbing in the Alps and visiting rocket-launching bases in Germany.

In 1966 two dozen boys were allowed to opt out of the C.C.F. after nine terms' service, and instead of attending parades on Monday afternoons they started doing social work – visiting Old Age Pensioners, helping the handicapped at the Simon Square Centre, and organising games and sports at Donaldson's School for the Deaf. In October, 1971, the Court of Directors (as they had now become) 'endorsed the Rector's view regarding participation in the C.C.F. as part of the compulsory school activities'; but they also agreed to a rewording of the Prospectus to highlight the change of emphasis within the C.C.F. and 'the non-military character of this activity in its present form'.

It's a far cry from that first Academy O.T.C. contingent who showed off their 'rather complicated evolutions' in front of the Secretary of State for War in January, 1909.

CHAPTER XVI

Dr Ferard (1910-26): 100 Not Out

He knows every boy by name, and knows all about him . . .
(*Chronicle*, July, 1926)

On the face of it, the choice of Reginald Herbert Ferard as Rector to succeed the extrovert Mr Carter was a curious one. He was small, bespectacled, rather reserved and austere, even severe-looking, in the eyes of younger boys. Mr Carter was forty-two when he resigned; Mr Ferard was forty-four when he came and sixty when he left, and to the boys he was always an elderly, balding, formal gentleman who never deviated from his dark suit, hard white collar, and bowler hat. Also, he had never had any experience of actual teaching in a school. He had been to Eton and Exeter College, Oxford, and had been a Tutor of Keble College, Oxford; but since 1905 his experience of schools had been as an administrator and observer – he was one of H.M. Inspectors of Secondary Schools in the Midlands of England. Perhaps it was this very lack of schoolmastering experience that made him take extra pains to get to know the boys individually, establish a sound relationship with the staff, and win the confidence of the Directors. Be that as it may, he certainly applied himself to the job with the same business-like thoroughness that must have made him an excellent Schools Inspector. The *Chronicle* of July, 1926, summed up his career: 'Dr Ferard is a first-rate business man . . . and his business abilities are based upon the only sure foundation, viz. common sense. He piloted the Academy with a firm hand through the time of the War, and has raised the School to a pitch of prosperity unknown in recent times.' The boys at the Academy called him 'Little Dick'.

He also had an exceptionally keen brain. There is a tribute to his sharpness of mind and skill as a debater in J. G. Lockhart's biography of *Cosmo Gordon Lang*, Archbishop of Canterbury from 1928–42. Ferard and Lang were contemporaries at Oxford, and fellow-members of the Canning Club. Lockhart quotes another member describing Lang's powers of oratory in club debates: 'He dominated us all by his eloquence. When he had delivered his address, we all felt that nothing more was to be said. None of us was able to stand up against him except Ferard, afterwards Rector of the Academy at Edinburgh. In a little thin voice he used to pick holes in what we thought an unanswerable argument, and in a few minutes we saw the whole bubble collapse, to our intense relief.'

He had an unerring knack of being able to judge a boy's capabilities. If he said a boy would win a scholarship, that boy usually did, and whether his confidence was inspiring or prophetic, the Academy turned out a stream of scholastic successes during his time as Rector, despite the War and the tendency for boys to leave early in order to join the Forces. The Academy roll rose steadily, up and up, until it reached a record 671 in its Centenary session (1923–4). All this was a source of intense satisfaction to Dr Ferard, because for him the success of the Academy represented the success of a system of education which he believed to be the best there was. As an Inspector of Schools in England he had become a convinced supporter of the Day School system, and it was the fact that the Academy was a day school that prompted him to apply for the Rectorship. He was a family man himself, and he believed that the every-day contact between home and school was more beneficial to a boy than the artificial segregation of the boarding school; but he also had a special word to say about the Academy Boarding Houses, which 'amply justified the aims of those who founded them. In a special degree they meet the needs of those who, while compelled to live abroad, wish to send their sons to their old school'.

The school that this administrator with the human touch inherited was having an *annus mirabilis*, a kind of last glow before the holocaust of the First World War. The school roll was its highest yet – 553. The Dux of the School Noel G. Salvesen, (for the second time) won an Open Classical Scholarship at University College, Oxford. The Shooting VIII, captained by Harry F. W. W. Buchan, went to Bisley for the first time and won the Ashburton Shield. The Football XV, also captained by Buchan, won all the eighteen matches played, scoring 409 points to fifty-four. The Cricket XI, captained by W. M. Wallace, lost only one school match, against Fettes, and were equal School Champions. At the Academical Reunion Dinner of June, 1911 (the fifth gathering of its kind), the 215 Academicals present were able to heap congratulations on their old school and bask in its spectacular success. Activity and prosperity were the keynote of that first year of

Mr Ferard's Rectorship. A large building programme was put under way on the north side of the Prep Yards; this new block contained a Dining Hall and kitchen, three new classrooms, and a new shooting range, all designed by an Academical, A. F. Balfour Paul (E.A. 1885–1892). A pavilion was built at New Field, designed by another Academical, R. S. Reid (E.A. 1893–1901), and donated to the School by William Ewing Gilmour, a director of the United Turkey Red Company, who had been at the Academy from 1868–72 and won the Medal for Fencing at 'Roland's Assault' of 1871. Mr Ferard also ventured 'with confidence to submit' to the Directors that now that a new Dining Hall was being built, it was high time that something was done about redecorating the school Hall itself: 'In general design it is fully worthy of such treatment as would make it adequately reflect the traditions of the school. Oak panelling might take the place of the painted wood which now surrounds the walls, and the names of the Ephors might be inscribed thereon from year to year.'

It was 1913 before the Hall was partially reconstructed and redecorated, and the false flooring removed; but the Rector's suggestion of oak panelling was not taken up. Instead, the walls were plastered, and the Ephors never got to see their names immortalised. But the names of the School Duxes were painted in blue round the front of the upper gallery (the colour was changed to gold during the next redecoration in 1936). Later the names were all painted over, regrettably, and they are now recorded on two ill-sited panels near the main entrance to the Hall. Electric lighting was installed, and the 'Mackenzie Organ' gifted by Sir Patrick Ford was played for the first time by the newly-appointed School Organist, Mr A. W. Nalborough, who had been singing teacher and music coach at the School since 1893. (Mr Nalborough died in 1915, and was succeeded by the redoubtable 'Daddy' (later 'Pop') Whalley; and the organ, after fifty years of strenuous service, was totally reconstructed in 1962.)

While the Hall was being renovated, the Exhibition was held in the Dining Hall; when it was re-opened, it fell to the Prep to have the honour of hanselling it, for the Prep had just started holding its own separate Exhibition – which left a lot more room in the Hall for the Upper School Exhibition.

The Hall was being smartened up – and so were the boys. The School colours had been blue and white for as long as anyone could remember – 'The colours of the young Gargantua,' the *Register* had enthused, 'the white signifying gladness, pleasure, delight and rejoicing, and the blue, celestial things.' And now, in 1911, the familiar 'Academy-blue' blazer was introduced for summer wear, when it was decided that 'the ordinary "blazer" of the School should be an all-blue blazer of Academy blue, with the School crest, and the blue-and-white blazer at present in general use throughout the school should be confined to the first three XVs and the first three XIs'. (The blue-and-white striped blazer had been adopted for cricket as long ago as 1866; it was later confined to those who won their caps for the 1st and 2nd XVs and XIs.) A note was inserted in the annual Prospectus instructing parents that 'the School colours may be obtained at various outfitters in Edinburgh. Care should be taken to secure that they conform to the standard pattern and material, as supplied by Messrs Gulland & Kennedy, 35A George Street'. Soon afterwards, in 1913, the Rector announced changes in the school cap, too: 'Some confusion has been caused during recent years by the great variety of pattern in the School Cap and its resemblance to those worn by other Schools in the district. A new badge has therefore been designed in which the letters E.A. are kept distinct within the wreath, so that the Cap may be more easily recognisable.' (*Report*, 1913.) The Academy cap has remained largely unchanged since then, apart from the addition in 1927 of silver braid round the peak and the lower rim. But there have been changes of custom and usage; today the cap is no longer required to be worn by boys above the Second Classes – as the hair-styles of senior boys grew inexorably longer, despite a stiff rearguard action by the School authorities, the cap was beginning to look a little absurd on them. Straw boaters with an Academy ribbon are still optional headgear for summer, but the taste for them fluctuates from year to year. The regulation winter wear is now a tweed jacket of 'Academy tweed' and grey flannels, with a dark worsted suit for formal occasions. Boys up to and including the Fourth Classes wear grey shirts, Fifths and above may wear white shirts; the school tie of blue and white is obligatory with school dress. School Ephors now have a special tie of their own as a badge of office (in design, it is the obverse of the Academical Club tie). The Academicals too have their own range of loyal accoutrements, including tie, scarf and cuff-links. It is reported (*Chronicle*, 1965) that in 1965 a London shop in Sicilian Avenue which specialises in Accie and other club gear received an order from the Foreign Office Secret Service Dept., under a coded name, for an Academical pair of solid gold cuff-links – no expense to be spared. (There is no record of a Bond, J., in the *Edinburgh Academy List*.)

On the educational front, Mr Ferard soon announced some changes in the curriculum. In future, boys who studied Greek were also to be taught some Science: 'In an age when scientific methods and conceptions have entered so largely into the life and thought of the nation it seems no longer desirable that a boy should pass through his School life without any instruction in the elements of Natural Science. Two periods a week will accordingly be set aside for the purpose for boys taking Greek in the Third and Fourth Classes.' At the same time, boys taking Science would get more English. He also announced that 'in future the history of Great Britain will take precedence of that of ancient times, and the history of Scotland will receive special attention'.

And as the scientific age surged on, one of its more humble victims was the slate. The slate, that ever-present symbol of education at the Academy for nearly a century, disappeared from the Prep at last – because 'modern practice condemns them as a frequent source of infection'. (*Report*, 1912.) Ah well, they still had the clacken . . .

Science meant the inevitable start of a Radio Club at school. It also meant a waiting-list for membership of the Scientific Society. A large audience packed the Hall for a lecture on 'Friend or Foe – the Microbe' (no friend to the poor old slate, anyway), and there were talks on 'My Ideal Motor Car' and 'The Development of Electric Lamps'. Since the Hall had been renovated, there was room for more portraits, and the collection started growing again. In his first session, the Rector added the portrait of R. M. Ballantyne, the writer of adventure stories for boys. Ballantyne had been a pupil in Mr Ferguson's Class of 1835–42 for a couple of years; so now the Hall sported the portraits of the authors of both *Coral Island* and *Treasure Island*.

These were good years for Academicals, too. In 1912, Viscount Haldane of Cloan had become the first Academical to ascend the Woolsack as Lord Chancellor (the second was Viscount Finlay of Nairn, in 1916). The List of Academical Honours and Appointments that year also included the Governor of the Straits Settlements, the Surgeon-General of the Madras Presidency, the Lord Lieutenant of Kinross-shire, the Professor of Philosophy at Leeds University, an LL.D. at Edinburgh and another at Aberdeen, the Gill Memorial Prize of the Royal Geographical Society (for work in Tibet and the valley of the Yangtse), the Murchison grant of the Royal Geographical Society (for Survey work in Uganda), a first prize-winner in the entrance exams for the R.A.M.C., three Gold Medals for Medicine at Edinburgh

University, and a clutch of scholarships and medals for classics and law.

Mr Ferard's educational policy at school was to try to avoid too much specialisation. He used the word for the first time in his *Report* of 1912; commenting on the difficulties of arranging the timetable to meet the varying needs of the boys, he stated a principle that the Academy still tries to follow in the face of extreme specialisation, particularly in English schools: 'Some degree of specialisation is inevitable,' he wrote, 'but there is always the danger lest it should be carried too far. A boy should take an Examination, as it were, in his stride with the least possible derangement of his ordinary work. Requests are occasionally received, that a boy may be allowed to concentrate on one or two subjects required for an examination to the exclusion of the rest. Even if this were possible, it could only be done by the sacrifice of the future to the passing requirements; that this is alien to the policy of the Edinburgh Academy is proved by the long list of distinctions gained by Academicals, which this year is headed by the honoured name of the Lord Chancellor.'

In the following year, however, he was reporting a record number of three Classical Scholarships and one Classical Exhibition to Oxford – and sounding the same warning: 'The number of Scholarships gained . . . gives proof that the classical tradition which the original founders of the School sought to impress upon it is in no danger of losing its vitality . . . But no School at the present day can afford to give such prominence to Latin and Greek as will exclude other branches of knowledge, such as Mathematics, Science, English and Modern Languages, from an adequate place in the curriculum.' (*Report*, 1913.)

In 1914, he was rewarded by the first-fruits of the provision he had made in his first session for boys wanting to pay special attention to the study of History, with an Open History Scholarship and a History Exhibition to Oxford.

(Despite the Academy's policy of providing an all-round education, specialisation is here to stay, of course; and it is worth noting now, in view of Mr Ferard's difficulty in arranging the timetable to suit the demands of five 'extra' courses of study – French, German, Maths, History and Science sets—that the present Rector, Dr Mills, reported in 1969: '. . . In the middle of the School, where eighty-odd boys are grouped into four classes, there are thirty-three different teaching sets, covering eleven subjects; in the Fifth there are thirty-eight different sets, and in the Sixth and Seventh there are nearly fifty sets covering seventeen examination subjects.')

THE ACADEMY AT WAR – I

In spite of adverse circumstances arising out of the War, the exceptional success
which has attended the School in recent years shows no sign of abatement. The large
number of pupils has been fully maintained, and the available accommodation has
been taxed to the utmost.

(Directors' *Report*, 1918)

Unlike the Second World War, which was almost to bring the
Academy to its knees, the First World War had little effect on the
School's march forward. There were 595 pupils when it started, and
612 when it ended; and in between, the numbers had reached a record
641. Of course, compared with the '39–'45 war, there was no fear of
large-scale bombing, and no evacuation of cities and schools; but it
seems extraordinary today that the '14–'18 war made so little difference
to the day-to-day working of the school, apart from the fact that boys
were leaving earlier to join up.

The main problem was staffing. Even before the war, Mr Ferard
had been concerned about the demands being made on the staff by
the new courses he was setting, and he had got them all a rise in 1911.
Now, when two masters went off to the war in 1914, he persuaded
the Directors to make up the difference between their school salary
and officer's pay. The Directors agreed, provided that the sum they
had to pay was not more than half the usual salary. The same terms
were arranged for Sgt.-Major Brazier and the other gymnastics
instructor, Corp. S. J. Atkinson ('The Bud'), when they joined the
colours.

The Rector was finding himself torn between feelings of patriotism
and the difficulty of running a school as more and more teachers went
off to the war. The War Office had stated that schoolmasters were 'not
desired to join the colours', but Mr Ferard, after consultation with the
Lord Justice-Clerk, Lord Kingsburgh (that octogenarian stalwart of
the Volunteers), advised masters of military age in 1915 that it was
their duty to 'come forward and be attested', and allow the appropriate
tribunal to decide whether or not they were indispensable to the
school. The Rector considered that they *were* indispensable, and told
the Directors that any further drain on the resources of the staff would
seriously impair the efficiency of the Academy. There were five teachers
on active service by then – W. Petty (1909–18), H. B. Cummins
(1908–16, killed in action), A. D. B. Wauton (1913–19), H. W. Pierce
(1912–28), and 'Billy' Peel, who was seriously wounded; a sixth

master who had been due to join the staff in October 1914 was also serving, and another had applied for a job as an Army interpreter in the East. When S. H. Osborne went off to the war, his wife was given charge of Mackenzie House, where he had been Housemaster. ('Osser', an Old Fettesian who had played rugby for England, did a fine job coaching the school football team, and was in charge of the all-conquering XV of 1910–11. He left the Academy in 1922 and eventually became Headmaster of Dreghorn Castle Prep School in Edinburgh, which closed just before the Second War and never reopened.)

For the rest, it was a matter of making do. The number of candidates for the Army and Navy exams was increasing yearly, but the remaining staff coped. The Seventh Class went down to two members. There were no At Homes or Concerts, but the choir and orchestra continued to practise – 'national songs being selected as specially appropriate to this time' – and eight hymns to use during the war were added to the school hymnary. (Later, the rehearsals were suspended because of lighting restrictions). Dinner and boarding fees had to be raised to meet the increased price of food and services, and parents were asked for voluntary contributions in the event of a 'sudden further increase in the price of provisions'. A strip of the field at Raeburn Place was ploughed up and planted with potatoes, and the proceeds from their sale went to War Charities. The Academical Club raised £1,170 to provide two Field Ambulances for the Red Cross. The School met the cost of endowing a bed in Rouen Military Hospital. The Prep had various collections, including one for providing 'plum puddings for the minesweepers of the Forth'.

Extra French and English lessons were given in the Fourth Classes as an alternative to German, though the Rector was at pains to point out that 'it would be a short-sighted policy indeed if we ceased to learn German through disapproval of German policy. There is little doubt that German will be of more rather than of less value after the War'. However, some boys were finding both French and German in addition to Latin too big a burden.

And still the roll of distinguished Duxes went on: 1915 – Eric Malcolm Fraser, later of I.C.I., who was Director-General of Aircraft Production for a time in the next war, and who bequeathed 3,000 books to the School Library when he died in 1960; 1916 – J. L. M. Clyde, later Lord Clyde, the Lord Justice-General; 1917 – John Cameron, later Lord Cameron, Senator of the College of Justice, and a Chairman of the Court of Directors of the Academy; 1918 – W.

W. Dalziel, who won a Classical Scholarship to Corpus Christi College, Oxford, and achieved high office in the Indian Civil Service.

In fact, the main 'war casualties' at the Academy were due to an epidemic of influenza in Scotland in July, 1918, when the authorities ordered all schools in Edinburgh 'falling under the provisions of the Scotch Education Code' to close for a month. The Directors of the Academy decided that since the Academy did not come under the Scotch Education Code, the Magistrates of Edinburgh 'had no power to enforce their recommendation at law' (the Academy was never short on legal advice!). The exams were on at the time and the Directors were loth to close the School, so the Rector was instructed to consult 'an eminent practitioner' as to the advisability of staying open. On his advice they decided to stay open, but a week later the number of cases of influenza at the Academy had increased, and the Directors decided to close. The Exhibition was cancelled for the first time in the School's history; but not altogether abandoned. On July 19, after the session had been closed, the parents of the Dux, W. W. Dalziel, and a handful of other people met in the echoingly empty Hall for the ceremony of handing over the Dux Medal.

'Flu raged again in November of that year, and once again the authorities advised all schools to close for a month. Once again the School's medical adviser agreed to keeping the School open. The health of the Academy boys was high – certainly above average – and in his opinion they would be better off in the well-aired Academy classrooms, with 'fresh air intervals between the classes, regular bodily and mental occupation, and no loafing, with plenty of exercise in the football field in the afternoons'. The Academy stayed open, and the number of absences from influenza steadily decreased.

After the war, the School fees were increased for the 1918–19 session for the first time in twenty-three years. The new scale ranged from 12 guineas a year in the lowest classes of the Prep to 33 guineas a year at the top of the Upper School. The reasons were given as war costs, taxes, and increased expenses of all kinds. One of these expenses was the increased cost of teachers' salaries. In a circular to parents the Directors stated: 'The future education of the country depends on an adequate supply of well-qualified teachers, and . . . these will not be forthcoming unless the prospects which the profession holds out are improved.' Mr Hardy, after twenty-seven years as a Classical Master, had his prospects improved to the tune of £15 a year, bringing his salary up to £280. The most junior Prep mistress was brought up to £95 a year.

The Pensions Scheme was also giving the Directors headaches as teachers retired or returned from the war incapacitated. Clearly a much more ambitious scheme of pensions was badly needed, and the Academy asked the Scottish Education Department to recognise the School for inclusion in its Superannuation Scheme of 1919, on the ground that 'the Academy is contributing efficiently to the higher education of the country'. The Education Department made certain conditions, one of them being a specific number of passes in the Scottish Leaving Certificate examinations. After consultation with the Headmasters of Loretto, Fettes, Merchiston and Glenalmond, the Directors agreed to accept the Education Department's conditions with two provisos: (1) The rule stipulating passes in the Leaving Certificate exam should add 'or any other examination approved of by the Department'; (2) The requirements of the Scottish and English Education Departments should be co-ordinated in the matter of training teachers to avoid difficulties in the engagement of teachers from England.

The Department announced in October, 1920, that it was prepared to recognise service in the Edinburgh Academy for the purposes of the Superannuation Scheme. The staff were now eligible for Government pensions, but the Directors decided to continue their own staff pension scheme as a supplement, and it was not abandoned until 1926. (In 1922, under the Government scheme, the retiring age for teachers would be made 60 for both men and women, instead of 65 for men and 55 for women.) But the better conditions came too late for Miss Wood, who retired in 1920 after thirty-two years with the Prep and died a few months later. She had been paid £50 of the £660 that had accumulated towards her pension, and in accordance with the rules of the scheme the balance of £510 went back into the Pension Reserve Fund. 'Caleb' Cash, the Geography Master for thirty-one years, had died in harness in 1917 without benefiting at all from the pensions scheme.

And still the salaries rose. In 1920, after the Rector had informed the Directors of the salaries paid at the Edinburgh Merchant Company schools, and the scale recommended by the Burnham Report of October, 1920, Academy salaries were raised again, working from a new starting base-line of £300 for the Upper School and £180 for the Prep. The new scales were: Heads of Departments, £600 rising to £700; other masters, £300 rising to £525 by fifteen annual increments of £15; ex-Servicemen masters to get £15 for each year of military service; Prep School, £180 rising to £355, with a maximum for the Senior Mistress of £400.

All this added another £1,087 to the salary bill, and to pay for it the fees went up again in the following session to £45 a year for senior Upper School boys (£144 for Boarders). They were to stay at that level for a very long time (perhaps too long), until the 1940s, when the aftermath of a second war once again sent fees spiralling upwards to keep pace with rising costs. But despite the increases in fees in the early 1920s, the number of boys attending the Academy went on increasing, and in the 1921–2 session the figure rose to another all-time record of 653; the Rector had to open a waiting-list for entrants, and the application form now contained the significant question, 'Are there any Academy connections?' An overflow class was started in the Prep. The Boarding Houses, too, were overflowing, so in 1922 the house at No. 2 Kinnear Road was bought and Dundas House came into being.

The double raising of the school fees, always a hazardous exercise, had worked. In 1921 the Directors reported that 'as a result of the increased revenue from the higher rate of fees the finances of the School are now in a more satisfactory position than was the case last year. Expenditure, however, has been higher this year even than last, chiefly owing to some further additions to the salaries of the Staff, and the finances of the School continue to call for the exercise of the strictest economy and care.' By the following year, with the additional rise in numbers, the gamble had clearly paid off: 'The Directors are gratified that . . . the debt which for many years has been resting on the School has now been cleared off. This successful result has been brought about by the fact that in spite of the recent rise in the Fees, there has been no diminution in the number of boys attending the School.' (*Report*, 1922)

So the Edinburgh Academy ended the war and entered the 1920s, the decade of the General Strike, in a stronger position than ever before, and – wonder of wonders – free of debt. There were some little local difficulties. The prolonged coal strike did not make the provisions of dinners for 475 boys any easier for the superintendent, Miss Paterson, and while the miners were on strike the Shooting VIII lost a month's practise for Bisley because the authorities had removed all the rifles to safety, and the Academy did comparatively poorly that year. But elsewhere, Academicals were getting their share of glory. The Academy provided its second President of the Oxford Union Society in C. B. Ramage (E.A. 1902–13), a former member of the School Debating Society which had been founded in 1908 and was now flourishing to such an extent that the number of members reached the record total of 166 in 1920–1. (The first Academical to be President of the Oxford Union was Sir Thomas Raleigh, Dux of the School in 1867.) Also in 1921 A. T. Sloan, a member of the all-conquering School XV of 1910–11, captained Scotland against France, five Academicals played in the team against Ireland, and 'Gibbie' Hole played cricket for Scotland against the Australians and Ireland; and that remarkable all-rounder, Leslie Balfour-Melville (E.A. 1864–71), who had played cricket and rugby for Scotland, been lawn tennis champion of Scotland, and also Amateur Golf Champion in 1895 – Balfour-Melville won the Silver Medal of the Honourable Company of Edinburgh Golfers at the sprightly age of 67.

At this time Academicals were holding the posts of Lord Justice-General and Lord President of the Court of Session (Lord Clyde); Solicitor-General for Scotland (C. D. Murray, E.A. 1875–82, later Lord Murray); Lord-Justice in the Court of Appeal (Robert Younger, E.A. 1875–9, later Lord Blanesburgh); and, oddly enough, the Greek Consul in Japan. And Sir Iain Colquhoun of Luss (E.A. 1896–1904) had been made Lord Lieutenant of Dunbartonshire.

To round off the chapter of the Academy at War, the stately War Memorial, designed by the same Academical, R. S. Reid, who had designed the pavilion at New Field, was dedicated on June 24, 1923. It took the form of a handsome new gymnasium on the upper floor, with Metal and Carpentry Workshops, an Armoury, and Craft Instructors' Rooms on the lower floors, and it cost £10,000. Meanwhile, the old gymnasium was being converted into laboratories at a cost of nearly £3,000. Bronze panels recorded the names of the 298 Academicals who had fallen in the war. The speeches were made by Lord Clyde and General Sir James Aylmer Haldane (E.A. 1873–8), veteran of many campaigns, including the Russo-Japanese War, and holder of a clutch of decorations including the Japanese Order of the Secret Treasure (3rd Class). General Haldane was one of a score of boys who have attended the Academy bearing this celebrated name. He was a pupil in 1873 when there were two other Haldanes at the Academy – R. B. (later Viscount) Haldane, who rose to be Minister of State for War and Lord Chancellor, and was shortly to be appointed Minister of Labour in 1924; and John Scott Haldane, physiologist and father of the author

Naomi Mitchison and the brilliant J. B. S. Haldane, biologist and geneticist, who died in 1964.

Bronze plaques bearing the names of the fallen were unveiled beside the entrance portals. Later, one of the names was removed, leaving a space which curious visitors to the Academy occasionally notice. It came about in this way: one of the Academicals listed as 'Missing' in the *War Supplement* was T. Davidson (E.A. 1900–4), and his name was subsequently included on the bronze panel. Just before the Second World War, however, the present Academy Registrar, Bruce Stenhouse, was processing the School records when he noticed that an eight-year-old boy called William George Davidson (E.A. 1938–9) who had just entered school had a father with the same name and dates as the 'Missing' Thomas Davidson. It turned out that he had been a Prisoner of War and that after repatriation he had never got in touch with the School again – until he applied for a place for his son. Davidson, who had no idea that he was on the Academy Roll of Honour, died in 1970.

NEW FACES

All young men, straight from the University, who fought for their country during the late war . . .

(Rector's *Report*, 1921)

The early twenties saw a big influx of new masters who were to set the 'tone' of the Academy staff during the inter-war years and through the next war into the fifties. But there was one man there already who would become the doyen of the 'War generation' as the years passed: Reginald T. Dawson, known invariably as 'Ronnie Daw'. He joined the staff as a Science master in 1913 and stayed for thirty-six years, undertaking all sorts of classes from the Geits to the Sixths, and he was Housemaster of Jeffrey House from 1928–41. When he retired in 1949 as Senior Master, he was appointed a Director of the Academy – only the second member of the staff, after 'Beaky' Druitt, to achieve this honour; but his health was broken, and he died two years later in 1951. With his neat centre-parting and quizzical eyebrows he became a familiar and well-liked figure to generations of science students, especially those reading Higher Science. He had few eccentricities, apart from a tendency to hurl chalk at pupils in class to wake them up; a plain, honest-to-goodness teacher, a family man who understood boys and treated them like a firm but affectionate father.

The first of the new post-war men was J. B. Lockhart in 1920, who came straight from Edinburgh University, where his career had been interrupted by war service in Egypt and at Gallipoli. He was the most brilliant mathematician of his year, and although he was offered a post at the princely salary of £750 per annum, he wanted above all to be a teacher, and came to the Academy instead for a good deal less than half that salary. For thirty-one years he taught mathematics throughout the Upper School, ending as Senior Mathematical Master. 'Fushy' Lockhart (a shortened form of his less decorous nickname, 'Fish-face') was always an immensely meticulous teacher, and expected his pupils to be the same; his favourite (or best remembered) expression was 'forty minutes' conscientious wurk', which he expected to be put into homework or free periods, thereby placing the pupil on trust, for he would accept any boy's word of honour about the time he had put into his work. After the war he took on a job that required all his mathematical genius – organising the Upper School timetable. When he retired in 1951 the Rector (C. M. E. Seaman) paid tribute to his work in his speech at the Exhibition that year: 'I cannot begin to describe to you the complexities of this vital operation. It is an intricate matter for any school, and here there are factors which make it even more intricate. For example, the Upper School shares with the Preparatory School the Gymnasium and certain specialist members of the staff, and on the other hand the hours of the Upper School are, and must be, different in time and length from those of the Prep . . . We come back at the beginning of the session and take it all for granted. We find the right number of double periods for Science and the right number of single periods for French, all spaced out through the week; nor do we find ourselves down to do gym when we have our Corps boots on. All this is a heavy labour accomplished during the summer holidays. If you add to this the fact that Mr Lockhart knows more than any of us about the mysterious regulations of Examining Bodies and Universities, and that he has put this knowledge at the disposal of any individual boy that he could help, you will see how much the school owes him.' If anyone offered to help him with this remarkable jigsaw puzzle that he constructed during the summer, he would invariably reply, 'I like doing it.' After he retired in 1951, he gave invaluable help in the Appeal to raise funds for the new Prep School. He died in 1969, aged 82.

Another young man, direct from university, arrived in 1921 – E. R. Hempson. He had gone straight to Flanders from school at Tonbridge, then up to Emmanuel College, Cambridge, for an Honours Degree in Mathematics and Geography, and from there to the Academy. From then on he stayed with the Academy for the rest of his career, before he retired in 1958. He spent much of his time in Scott House, as House Tutor from 1921-30, and Housemaster from 1931-9. During the twenties he was also Games Master in charge of the organisation of football, cricket and athletics, he was in charge of First Practice for a time and coached the Under 15½ Football Practice for several years, and helped run the Boxing Competitions. During the war he ran a little Academy in exile – the evacuated section of the Academy in a converted prep school in Hartree House, near Biggar – from 1939 until it was closed down in July, 1944, and the exiles returned to the fold at Henderson Row. A perpetually cheerful, infectiously gay man, no one will forget his peculiarly jaunty walk. Perhaps his most memorable contribution to the Academy was to its musical and dramatic life. He plunged in right away, and in July, 1922, he sang the part of the Defendant in a performance of *Trial by Jury* – the first Gilbert and Sullivan opera in the history of the Academy. It was produced by another of the new post-war crop, Mr H. ff. Ozanne, the French Master, who had come straight from Oxford in 1920 with an M.A. and an M.C. This was the start of the Academy's G & S tradition; in the following year he produced a full-scale *Mikado* in 1923, with Mr Hempson singing Nanki-Poo and helping the tenor chorus behind the scenes. Then came a Centenary production of *The Gondoliers* in 1924, with Mr Hempson as Marco ('better than ever'). This was followed by *H.M.S. Pinafore* in 1925, with Mr Hempson as Ralph Rackstraw.

By the time the Academy did *The Mikado* again in 1927, the piano accompaniment by Mrs Ozanne had been replaced by 'Mr Watt Jupp's String Orchestra', and Mr Hempson had retired to the chorus, leaving all the principal parts to be sung by boys. The tradition was well and truly founded. When Mr Ozanne left in 1928 to be Headmaster of a Prep School in England, there were those who feared the 'tradition' had been still-born; but 'Hemp' thought otherwise. He co-opted the delectable Aileen Davies, who had been a D'Oyly Carte principal singer and was now the wife of the distinguished international cricketer D. S. Weir (E.A. 1909-18, who died in 1959). Together 'Hemp' and Mrs Weir produced *The Gondoliers* in 1929, and for over twenty years thereafter Mrs Weir coached and inspired the biennial Gilbert and Sullivan opera production at the Academy until 1951, with *Patience*. And for all these years every Academy boy who took part in these productions fell helplessly but secretly in love with her. (In recent years Gilbert and Sullivan productions have been leavened with other fare, like Purcell's *King Arthur* in 1969, Vaughan Williams's *The Poisoned Kiss* in 1971, and Smetana's *Bartered Bride* in 1973.)

But it was a triumvirate, really; and the third member was 'Pop' Whalley. Mr Horner Whalley was Organist and Choirmaster for thirty years until he retired in 1945 (he died the following year). It was his job to din some sort of musical sense and voice production into his latest batch of trebles and altos. They were all 'strangled sparrers' when they came to him; but after a few weeks of his ripe Lancashire accent and devoted coaching, they would be singing like larks. He had a great enjoyment of music which was infectious; and morning after morning the Hall would resound with his spirited playing of the 'Mackenzie Organ' at Prayers.

On the Science side, Dr W. P. D. Wightman arrived at the Academy in 1923 bursting with degrees and erudition from the Royal College of Science and London University. He succeeded 'Fairy' Fairgrieve as Head of the Science Department in 1935, and for the next fifteen years, until he left to take up an appointment as the first Lecturer in the History and Philosophy of Scientific Research at Aberdeen University, he poured his unbounded energy and wealth of learning into building up a dynamic tradition of success. He was a throwback to the days when Academy masters were prolific writers of scholarly books; the last book he published before he left the Academy was *The Growth of Scientific Ideas*. He was also a great fencing enthusiast, and was master in charge from the time of its introduction to the Academy under M. Léon Crosnier in 1927; and it was M. Crosnier too who taught him much about the vintage wines of France, and was surely responsible for the small blue beret that Dr Wightman was wont to wear.

Some men almost automatically become legends in their own lifetime; certainly Mr B. G. W. Atkinson – 'The Bag' – did. He had several nicknames: 'Bagwash', of course, from his initials, shortened to 'The Bag'; 'Atco', or just plain 'Atty'. He came to the Academy in 1925 with a formidable reputation as a cricketer and rugby player; he left it thirty-seven years later with an even more formidable reputation. He had been an outstanding athlete in his youth: a tall man with a long raking stride as a centre three-quarter, and a spectacularly hard-hitting batsman for Middlesex. For twenty-two years he was in charge of First Practice for both cricket and football; and he did it four afternoons a week, winter and summer, dealing out praise and reproach alike in laconic asides (to one young enthusiast who could not get the hang of putting his head *behind* his opponent's knees instead of in front of them, it was merely 'If you keep on tackling like that, you'll break your neck' – and nearly fifty years later he hasn't forgotten it). In the classroom, Mr Atkinson built up an equally formidable reputation for being the most fearsome wielder of the tawse the world had ever seen, which obviated the necessity for its use except on rare occasions; and even when the prospect arose, he had a quixotic, even chivalrous attitude to it that endeared him to his boys (one palpitating wretch in the Fourths was let off a well-deserved tanking one Monday morning for the sublimely logical reason that his elder brother had scored a maiden century on the Saturday). He taught Latin, History and English with the same terse economy that he brought to his coaching, his gown, grown green with age, hugged round his elbows. When he retired, he edited the *Edinburgh Academy List, 1888–1964*, a truly massive task. He died in 1966, but not before his former pupils had had a chance of showing him what they thought of him by making him the first Academy master to be President of their Football Club and of their Cricket Club. A great man, 'Atty'.

A considerable number of the men whom Mr Ferard selected for the staff became Academy 'fixtures' – men like Mr Selwyn ('Beanie') Read (1924–62), whose teaching played a large part in scholarship successes in Mathematics, and who eventually became Senior Master; and Mr H. R. Scott, who was unflatteringly known as 'Scabby' simply on the principle that *all* people called Scott are known as 'Scabby'. He came in 1926 and retired in 1959. Much as he liked living in Scotland, he always had an Englishman's horror of the Edinburgh weather, and once suggested that the Winter, Spring and Summer terms should be renamed Winter I, Winter II and Winter III. (Today, winter doesn't exist in the Academy calendar at all – the first term is now known as the Autumn term.) When Mr Scott retired, he became the first non-Academical to be elected Captain of the Academical Golf Club.

The last of the new faces of the early and mid-twenties was Mr E. P. West, a red-haired Irishman who was naturally called 'Paddy' by the boys but 'Teddy' or even 'Strawberry' in the Masters' Lodge. He stayed for forty years in the Mathematics department, of which he became Head until he became Senior Master in succession to 'Beanie' Read; he retired in 1966. At school he had a somewhat sardonic and cynical exterior which merely concealed a splendid sense of humour, as befits a Cork man; and he had his own foibles – at the stroke of noon every day, for instance, when a works whistle blew near the Academy, both teacher and class would slump into relaxed postures with arms on desk and head bowed for thirty seconds before the lesson was resumed. Mr West was the last Games Master at the Academy to look after every single sport in the curriculum; when he relinquished the task, the sports were shared out amongst separate Games Masters.

These men all bridged the inter-war years and the Second World War. But there is one corporate person who bridges the whole 150-year history of the Academy: the Janitor, or 'Jenny'. And it was during Mr Ferard's Rectorship that the most celebrated of all the Academy Janitors retired: William Bell.

JANITORS ALL

> Very neat in his tailed coat of brown cloth, with brass livery buttons.
> (*Chronicles of the Cumming Club*)

To schoolboys, Janitors are simply *there*. They don't have names or private lives. Generations of nineteenth-century boys at the Academy called the Janitor 'Jenny' for some obscure reason, and called his wife 'Mrs Jenny'; it was she who dispensed tuck from a window of the Janitor's Lodge for a hundred years until the opening of the Tuck Shop itself at the new Dining Hall in 1924.

So they tend to be somewhat anonymous men, and the School records do little to invest them with personality. But most of them had something memorable about them to schoolboy eyes – a ruddy face, a missing hand, a blind eye – something that remained sharp in the memory until ageing Academicals wrote their reminiscences of their schooldays.

The first Academy Janitor, John Howell, only stayed for two years before he resigned in 1826. He was an unusual man to find as a Janitor; he had clearly been well educated, and had had a bookbinder's business at 30 Thistle Street. The subject of ancient war galleys with their multiple banks of oars had become a passion with him since reading the *Life of Themistocles* at school, he said in his *Essay on the War Galleys of the Ancients*. He wrote that this was what gave him his first taste for mechanics, and he waited 'patiently for an opportunity to embody the ideas I had formed of the galley, and reconcile them to the fixed laws of mechanism by actual experiment, and taking the ancient authors for my only guide . . . Cheered by the harmony I discovered between my model and the authors, and its fitness for every purpose they mention, I finished my undertaking with a feeling I cannot express – but it was worthy of an age of toil.' (Quoted in the *Chronicle*, November, 1920.)

While he was at the Academy he constructed 'some very ingenious models' which the Directors purchased, including a model of a Hexireme; he also made a model of a Quadrireme which he presented to the Museum of the Society of Scottish Antiquaries in Queen Street in 1827. It looks as if he took the post of Janitor at the Academy in order to earn leisure to get on with his studies of the ancient authors and his model-making. He had started a vogue in military memoirs by publishing 'ghosted' biographies of down-and-out servicemen (there were a lot of them about after Waterloo): *Journal of a Soldier of the 71st Regiment, 1806–15*, was originally a 4,000-page diary which he spent a year reducing to two volumes of 300 pages each, and *The Life and Adventures of John Nicol, Mariner* was the story of an old sailor in Edinburgh whose yarns he wrote up and published in the hope of making enough profit to provide the old man with a pension, which he did. After he left the Academy he published *The Life of Alexander Selkirk* (the original of Robinson Crusoe) in 1828, and a *Life of Alexander Alexander* in 1830. The *Scotsman* of December 3, 1828, wrote of him: 'Bred originally as a bookbinder, the child of poverty, toil and hardships, his active and inquisitive mind was nevertheless continually on the alert to gain information . . . John is an antiquary, a biographer, a mechanic, a humorist, and a man of *virtu*; and it is no uncommon thing to see him surrounded by some of the most celebrated literary men of the day.' He ran a curiosity and antique shop, and died in 1863. On his death-certificate he was described as a 'polyartist'.

Of his immediate successors – Thomas Hogg (1826–33), Daniel Ross (1833–7), and William Ross (1837–8) – practically nothing is known. But the fifth Academy Janitor, Adam Pinkerton (1838–54), is known from Academical reminiscences:

'The Janitor was a small man and old, kindly and obliging, very neat in his tailed coat of brown cloth, with brass livery buttons. Mr Pinkerton had the misfortune to lose a hand – off at the wrist. Into a wooden stump he screwed a formidable hook of steel, polished till it flashed again in the sunlight. On this he used to carry the ponderous keys of the class-rooms, and with its aid – a loop having been tied in the rope for the purpose – he rang the big school-bell that summoned all to their various duties.

'In every instance of hemorrhage from the nose – a case of daily occurrence – the first step, if ordinary styptics failed, was to call in the "Jenny", who would thrust his cold "cleek" down the patient's back; then, if that were not effective, a couple of the class-room keys. It was held desirable to chill the sufferer to the bone.

'When sudden frost came, the "Jenny" invariably flooded the flag-stones in front of his Lodge overnight, to be ready for a slide by next morning, a singular piece of unselfishness, seeing the slide passed almost over his own doorstep.' (*Cumming Club*, pp. 10–11.)

Robert Louis Stevenson never forgot 'the slide by the Janitor's gate' either (cf. p. 189). And later Janitors, equally obliging, would pour water over the concrete cricket pitches that used to adorn the front side of the Yards. But, alas, it proved too dangerous to have boys careering down them full-tilt, to crash into the upright timber baulks (the wicket) and the bicycle sheds at the far end, and the practice had to be forbidden. Lord Cockburn would definitely not have approved of the ban, with his fabled fondness for a snowball 'bicker'.

Pinkerton died during a cholera epidemic in September, 1854. He was succeeded by his son, who died the following year, and he in turn was followed by Hugh Graham, in 1855, who stayed for thirty-three years until he retired in 1888 (he died in 1889):

'The one-eyed janitor who kept the gate and graced the whole establishment with his brown swallow-tailed coat, brass buttons, and tile hat with gold band must not be forgotten in even the thinnest outline of Academy recollections – though the only name by which he ever was known, to us anyway, was "Jenny" . . . We used to purchase our lunch at his window, which was thrown open at 12 daily. His wife, the female "Jenny", suffered chiefly during the lunch time, though the man in gold buttons had often to come to her assistance when the tumult became extreme. It was "Jenny, a rye roll" and "Jenny, a biscuit" and "Jenny, two cookies" or "Jenny, a tart" from 200 young hungry ruffians all scrambling and sprawling over the top of each other to get at the window, till the good woman's soul was torn and her life became not worth living.' (*Chronicle*, June, 1922.)

Now came the Janitor who was the outstanding figure in this post – *the* outstanding Janitor of the School's 150-year history. His name was William Bell. He came to the Academy in 1888 as a man of 44: a big man of tremendous physique, who had been a Leading Stoker Mechanic in the Royal Navy and had sailed in H.M.S. *Challenger* on her epic expedition round the world in 1872–6. He stayed at the Academy until he retired in July, 1923, in his eightieth year – 'still as fine a figure of broad, solid, manly strength as one could wish to see' (*Chronicle*, July, 1923). 'Closely allied to that is his natural dignity in all his relations with masters, boys and visitors; he has never forgotten what was due to each of them and to himself . . . Absolute trustworthiness, sincerity, and uprightness are conspicuous marks of his character; these qualities, with his natural courtesy and kindliness, have won him the esteem and respect of all who have known him, and the affection of those who know him best.'

It was the sort of tribute that the *Chronicle* reserved for retiring Rectors, not Janitors; and when William Bell died in 1933, in his ninetieth year, it was a former Rector, 'Reggie' Carter, who wrote a tribute to him in the *Chronicle*: 'To work for the Academy in all matters great and small, to have everything shipshape and ready, so that others could do their work, to spare no effort by night or day, in summer or winter, that all things should be done decently and in order, was the rule of his life. So fires were stoked, boilers tended with the care of an expert . . . and pipes unfrozen – he would keep the middle watch, or any other, to see to that in hard weather – rooms were cleaned, the regulating bell was punctually rung, lists and notices made up, and all kinds of casual details – confusing to a less robust brain – dealt with faithfully as a matter of course . . . A man of magnificent physique, with a natural dignity of presence, of strong character moreover, with a seaman's forthrightness and sense of discipline, he had a great influence over many generations of boys, and restrained or guided with fatherly firmness the exuberance of seniors . . . or the effervescence of Geits.' Mr Carter recalled the Janitor's patience with him and kindliness to him in the early years of his Rectorship: 'I was young and inexperienced . . . In emergencies he was never in a hurry, never at a loss, and I owe more than I can say to his steadiness and sturdy common-sense.' After a day's work, the two would sometimes get together, and over a glass and a pipe, ex-Leading Stoker Mechanic William Bell would tell yarns of his voyages. 'At these times of relaxation matters of business were seldom mentioned; if they ever cropped up, he never told tales out of School. He was a man above all meanness, to be trusted to the uttermost.' (*Chronicle*, February, 1934).

It's a remarkable picture, the young Rector and the wise, upright old Janitor sharing a pipe and a glass; and it is a measure of how remarkable William Bell must have been, for a Rector to have written of him like that. (It is also a measure of Mr Carter, come to that.)

William Bell was succeeded in 1923 by Sgt.-Major Willie Vass, who had been Musketry Instructor since 1920 (he was succeeded as that by Sgt.-Major Hector Macpherson, who retired in 1946). For twenty-seven years Willie Vass was a genial but commanding presence in the Yards, the guide, philosopher and friend to countless little boys who regarded him with affectionate respect. And if anyone *did* step out of line, there was always that stentorian Sgt.-Major's voice to fall back on.

When Willie Vass retired in 1946 his place was taken by C.Q.M.S. Peter McKeich, who had worked as an office boy at the Academy before the war, and now came back to Academy service after seeing action with the Royal Scots. He has already passed the twenty-five-year mark, keeping up the tradition of long service that has meant only four Janitors at the Academy in the 120 years since the appointment of Hugh Graham.

He is one of the most changeless institutions at the Academy, the Janitor. Although the 'brown swallow-tailed coat' of Hugh Graham's day has disappeared, the Janitor still appears on formal occasions in a dark blue swallow-tailed coat adorned with silver buttons monogrammed with the Academy badge; and, of course, a top hat.

THE CENTENARY CELEBRATIONS: 1824–1924

You might as well hope to make a religion without a mystery as you might hope to forge a great educational instrument without tradition. It is in the power of its jealously guarded traditions that the genius of an institution like the Edinburgh Academy resides, it is in them that you hold your present pride and your promise for the future.

(Lord Clyde, Centenary Dinner speech, July, 1924)

The Edinburgh Academy completed its hundredth year in July, 1924, a milestone which was celebrated for three days in a blaze of nostalgia and euphoria. A host of committees and sub-committees had been sitting for months, organising the programme of events and arranging accommodation for the hundreds of Academicals who would be pouring in from their various outposts all over the world.

The Rector, who had been made an honorary Doctor of Laws of Edinburgh University in 1922 and was now Dr Ferard, set the whole tone of the celebrations the previous year when he reviewed the state of the School at the end of its ninety-ninth session in 1923. Numbers had gone up to their highest point once again (659, with 443 in the Upper School and 216 in the Prep); three Open Classical Scholarships had been won to Oxford; there was an air of enthusiasm and drive about the School, the Debating Society had just held its 100th Meeting and had overwhelmingly voted in favour of the motion 'That it is better to have loved and lost than never to have loved at all' (always a useful pointer to the mood of an assembly, that one). And in his *Report* for 1923, Dr Ferard wrote: 'As the ninety-ninth session of the School draws to its close, it is but natural to look backward to its Foundation and forward to its Future. We believe that if its Founders could revisit the Academy they would not feel that it had betrayed their hopes. Much there might be that would perplex them, but they would soon recognise the old landmarks, and reassure themselves that their work had not been in vain and that its end was not yet.'

The Centenary Number of the *Chronicle* (July, 1924) tried to assess the changes that had taken place over the hundred years: 'In their original conception the Academy was to be before all things a classical school, in which special attention was to be paid to Greek, although, in accordance with the sound tradition of Scotland, mathematics were not to be neglected. But that chemistry or physics should be taught, or that football or music should become important elements in the School life, was not then in contemplation. Masters took boarders from the first, and there was an early proposal to erect boarding houses in Saxe-Coburg Place, but nothing came of this; and though the generation of Edinburgh men who had reached middle age in 1824 had furnished abundance of zealous volunteers in their earlier days, the conception of uniformed school-boys drilling, marching and shooting – to say nothing of winning a trophy in a distant part of England – was remote from the Founders' minds.'

Physically the School had changed, but not out of all recognition. The core was still the dignified and handsome structure of the Hall with its pillared portico, and classrooms leading off from it. But the School Yards had gradually become almost a built-up area, starting early with the new Writing and Arithmetic Block in the north-west corner; now, with the War Memorial gymnasium, the classrooms up the west wall, the Science developments and Library up the east wall, and the new Dining Hall and classrooms at the north end, there was scarcely room for any further expansion on the Henderson Row site.

The Academicals who came pouring back to school for the start of the celebrations on July 10 had every reason to feel pleased with the way the old School was getting on. The debt, that former bugbear of previous generations of Directors, was gone. The School numbers were still rising and had reached 671 for this Centenary session. There were two Open Scholarships in the bank, one to Oxford in Classics and one to Cambridge in Natural Science. 'This, the hundredth year of its existence,' wrote the Directors in their *Report*, 'finds the Academy in a state of abundant vitality, and taking a part of ever-increasing importance among the educational institutions of Scotland.'

There is no record of precisely how many Academicals attended the three-day celebrations; but as the *Chronicle* reported, 'One wondered how certain of His Majesty's dominions were progressing in the absence of so many of their administrators.' On the Thursday there was an afternoon reception at the School, a performance of *The Gondoliers* in the Hall, followed by a Ball in the Assembly Rooms in George Street. Next day there was a cricket match between the Academy and a team composed of former Academy captains – the oldest was the evergreen 70-year-old L. M. Balfour-Melville, who 'gave a marvellous display behind the wickets, stumping two and catching one', although the Academy won in the end by 22 runs. That evening came the highlight of the celebrations – the Centenary Dinner in the Music Hall in George Street.

It was attended by about 500 Academicals, and also the Rector, the staff, the Senior Ephors, the previous Rector (Mr Carter), and 'Mummy' Johnstone, who had written the words of *Floreat Academia* nearly thirty years previously. The members of the old Class Clubs were seated at their own separate tables, and the five oldest clubs ('Tamson' 1861-8, Weir 1864-71, Banks/Merry 1865-72, Clyde 1866-73, Carmichael 1867-74) shared a special dais with the High Table suggesting, according to the *Chronicle* report, 'a sort of Valhalla only to be reached by longevity or eminence'. The average age of the twenty-four Academicals seated at the High Table was 74. Not present at that particular Dinner, but celebrating the Centenary with fellow-Accies in Simla, was a man destined to hold the record for Academical longevity, Lt.-Col. J. C. Coldstream. He was born on July 16, 1872, and attended the Academy from 1882-8, during the last years of Dr Harvey's Rectorship. He spent all his active career abroad, in India, and then returned to Britain when he eventually retired. He died at a Taunton nursing home on January 26, 1972, aged 99 – only seven months short of his own centenary. Until then, the longest-living Academicals on record had been two members of Mr Mitchell's Class of 1826-33: J. A. Ker, who was born in September, 1818, died in 1915 aged 96 and nine months, just beating his classmate, the Hon.

Francis Charteris, afterwards the 10th Earl of Wemyss, who died in 1914 aged 95 and ten months.

The oldest Academical present at the Centenary Dinner in Edinburgh was the chairman of the evening and President of the Academical Club, Viscount Finlay of Nairn, who was celebrating his 82nd birthday that very day. There were twenty-one Academy Duxes at the Dinner, nineteen cricket captains, and fourteen football captains, including G. C. H. Dunlop, by then a Liverpool stockbroker, who had been captain of both cricket and football in 1863.

Viscount Finlay of Nairn was then, with Viscount Haldane, the most distinguished living Academical in public life. He had been Dux of the School in 1858, a K.C. at the English Bar, Unionist M.P. for Inverness Burghs and Edinburgh University, Solicitor-General, Attorney-General, Lord Chancellor in 1916–19, and a member of the Hague Permanent Court of Arbitration. At the age of 82 he was still one of the Judges of the International Court of Justice, and at ten o'clock the following morning he was leaving Edinburgh to travel back to the Hague. He made a brilliant and witty speech recalling the history of the School, his own proudest moment of sitting beside the School's founder, Lord Cockburn, when he was invited as Dux of the Geits to the Directors' sumptuous breakfast in 1852; his memories of Rector Harvey, Dr Hodson (whom he defended), and the delightful Classical Master D'Arcy Wentworth Thompson, whose son, Professor D'Arcy Thompson, was one of the guests that evening. Viscount Finlay announced the endowment by the D'Arcy Thompson Class Club of a scholarship commemorating their old master and his pupil, Robert Louis Stevenson; and he held up a magnificent silver cup which had been presented by the Fifth Class to the first Rector, Dr Williams, when he left school (only temporarily, as it turned out) in 1828; his grandson, Sir Ellis Cunliffe, had now returned the cup to the Academy as a Centenary gift.

Greetings were read from Academicals who were holding their own celebrations that night in places like Johannesburg and Kuala Lumpur. (A later account in the *Chronicle* of the dinner held at the Adyar Club in Madras described a table massed with blue and white flowers – 'blue flowers being scarce in Madras, the butler had risen to the occasion with a packet of Reckitt's' – and a hilarious after-dinner clacken-and-ball race round the club, using limes instead of balls, and clackens 'which were not quite the same pattern as those used in the Prep Yards or Ephors' Room, but then, of course, the native of India can hardly be expected to understand the niceties of clacken manufacture'. It sounds like a pretty typical Accie evening . . .)

Replying to the Toast of The School, Dr Ferard told the company: 'The School is in a very real sense alive . . . And not only is the School alive, but it is solvent, though solvency is not a state in which the School has always been. If to be in debt is a mark, as I have been told by business men, of the prosperity of an institution or a business, then the School has manifested that symptom abundantly. If in this Centenary year it is temporarily out of debt it is only enjoying a brief rest before plunging into it again . . .

'We wish to feel that every year there goes out from this School of ours into the life of Edinburgh, of Scotland, and of the Empire, an invigorating stream of energy inspired by high purposes and imbued with the thoroughness and respect for good work that are necessary to give effect to them.'

He also looked ahead briefly: 'I believe that if we could see the School a hundred years hence we should feel that, whatever changes there may have been in the last hundred years, they were as nothing to the changes between 1924 and 2024. I will not embark upon the dangerous task of prophesying, but there are forces at work in this country which bid fair to produce radical reforms in our schools.'

The Celebrations ended the following day with a Thanksgiving Service in St. Giles', attended by Academicals, parents and boys and the O.T.C., which marched to church behind the Pipe Band. Another Centenary event was the founding of Lodge Edinburgh Academy Centenary, No. 1327; it was the first 'School Lodge' to which a charter had been granted by the Grand Lodge of Scotland. The first Right Worshipful Master was Lord Clyde, the Lord Justice-General.

And in honour of the Centenary, that noble and ancient game, Hailes, was revived. It was still played in the Prep every day, but the rules were of the loosest and it had become somewhat simplified – a loose mêlée of small boys rushing about hitting the ball with their new clackens (a clacken was white when new, and only gradually acquired a darkening patina, 'colouring beautifully, like a good pipe', as an Academical once put it, 'and finally, as it approached perfection, getting broken'). But as an Upper School game, Hailes had long since died out. Rector Mackenzie had tried to revive it in 1890, when he persuaded the Carmichael Class Club of 1879–86 to present a Silver Clacken for competition by teams of boys distributed into Town divisions according to residence (a forerunner of the Division system that was introduced in 1905). For that occasion, a special booklet was printed with the *Rules of the Game of Hailes*:

Note: In the following Rules the word 'maul' shall be understood to mean that some of the Players on each side shall line-up five yards apart, when the Referee shall throw the ball between them.

Number of Side

1. There shall be Twelve Players in each team, and each Player shall carry a clacken.

Commencing Game

2. The game shall be started by the teams lining up ten yards apart, and the Referee throwing the ball between them in the centre of the yards. The game shall be restarted in the same way after a Haile has been scored.

Duration of Game

3. Each game shall be played for not less than forty minutes, and not more than seventy minutes, and the teams shall change ends at half-time.

Ball

4. The ball to be played with must be a *'hollow india-rubber ball with a hole in it'*, and shall not be more than three inches in diameter.

Referee

5. There shall be no Umpires. The Referee shall decide when appealed to, and shall use a whistle.

6. A Present Pupil shall not be eligible as a Referee.

Appeals

7. No Player may appeal for an infringement of the Rules committed by one of his own side.

Scoring

8. A Haile can only be scored under 'The Sheds', and the ball must be either kicked, thrown from the clacken, or rebound direct from one of the attacking side against the Hailes wall.

Touch

9. The ball shall be considered in touch when it enters – (a) the porch in front of the School; (b) Henderson Row; (c) other yards; (d) a covered place (e.g. Rector's Lodge), and shall be thrown out at right angles to the touch line.

10. If the ball be not thrown out straight, a maul shall be formed at ten yards parallel with the Hailes line.

Off-Side

11. A Player shall be off-side when the ball has been kicked or touched by one of his own side behind him (i.e. between himself and his own Hailes line).

12. A Player being off-side is put on-side when the ball has been touched by or strikes any Player on the opposite side, or when one of his own side runs in front of him, either with the ball on his clacken or having kicked it when behind him.

13. If any Player play the ball when off-side, a maul shall be formed where the ball was last played.

Handling the Ball

14. A Player may not at any time pass the ball with his hand.

15. A Player may not lift the ball off the ground with his hand, but he may catch it before it stots or on the first bound.

16. A Player having caught the ball must at once put it on his clacken; if he does not do so, a maul shall be formed where he caught the ball.

17. A Player may not hold the ball on his clacken with his hand, or take it into his hand to pass an opponent; if he does so, a maul shall be formed where he first got the ball on his clacken.

Running

18. A Player running with the ball on his clacken may throw it off his clacken over or past an opponent, and then catch it in his hand, but he must immediately return it again to his clacken.

Holding, Tripping

19. A Player deliberately holding or tripping one of his opponents, whether running with the ball or not, a maul shall be formed five yards from the Hailes line of the offending Player's side.

Slogging

20. There shall be no hard hitting (slogging). The Referee shall decide when there is a slog, and a maul shall be formed where the ball was 'slogged'.

21. If a Player kick or hit the ball on to the top of the School, and it stays there, or over the sheds at either end of the yards, a maul shall be formed five yards from the Hailes line of the offending Player's side.

Charging

22. A Player may charge another Player at any time except when off-side.

23. If the ball hit any person not taking part in the game, a maul shall be formed where such occurred.

24. If the ball enter the 'Waste-paper Gates', a maul shall be formed five yards from the 'Gate'.

That was how Hailes *ought* to be played, rather than the scramble into which it had degenerated. But it required a lot of room, and as the school numbers rose, it became squeezed out.

By the time of the Centenary, the attempt by the Carmichael Class Club to revive Hailes had failed, and the Silver Clacken was presented to the School. So now the only function of the clacken in the Upper School was as an instrument of corporal punishment in the Ephors' Room, and in the clacken-and-ball races at the annual Games. On July 21, 1924, however, the clacken got a new lease of life, when the Seventh took on the Ephors at a challenge game of Hailes. This has now become an annual end-of-season event, the contest of Brains *v.* Brawn, in which the Ephors are usually heavily outnumbered (they now have to take the Seventh on in relays). The game is played across the breadth of the Front Yards, from wall to wall, as in the good old days; and to score a Haile the ball must be played by the clacken against the wall defended by your opponents. It frequently ends up as a cross between the Eton Wall Game and shinty, and no quarter is given, or expected; the printed code of rules of 1890 is conveniently disregarded. The Ephors *v.* Seventh match is now the only occasion on which Hailes is played at the Academy. It was played at the new Prep School at Inverleith for a few years, but rising numbers made it difficult to continue because of the problem of space – several games of Hailes going on simultaneously take a lot of room; and so it was reluctantly abandoned as being too dangerous.

With the Centenary Celebrations over, the School got down to work again. The Masters' Lodge had been destroyed by fire in January, 1924, when a smouldering beam under the fireplace caused the gas meter to explode; some classical books a hundred years old had been destroyed, along with irreplaceable old photographs, and all the masters' gowns and degree robes. The Directors took the opportunity of rebuilding the whole block, at a cost of nearly £3,000, to provide better accommodation for the greatly increased staff, as well as a new Ephors' Room and a bookshop. It was brought into use at the start of the 1925–6 session.

And there was the Centenary Fund Appeal, which had been launched earlier with a target of £15,000. Despite the fact that Academicals had newly subscribed £10,000 for the War Memorial, the Fund had raised £9,823 by the end of July, 1824. The purposes of the Fund were threefold: (1) to extend New Field by four acres, to cope with the ever-increasing numbers, at a cost of £7,000; (2) to provide Exhibitions for boys going to the Universities, at a cost of £4,000; and (3) to provide Exhibitions tenable at the School itself, costing another £4,000. The Fund reached £10,500 by the beginning of 1925 and then petered out, and work began on the extension of New Field (the limit of the four acres of the western 'Centenary Extension' are marked by the line of trees and the small pavilion). The short-fall in cash would be met from the annual surpluses of income from fees.

The General Strike of 1926 seemed to pass the Academy by as it continued on its serene, successful way. The Rector noted that it had been 'embarrassing' in the summer term, 'but did not seriously interfere with the School routine. Boys at a distance contrived to come to School with praiseworthy regularity. Many of the Staff enrolled themselves as special constables for duty after School hours, and leave of absence was given to three or four boys who were in a position to give help of a special kind. It did not seem advisable to encourage the registration of boys as special constables when other volunteers were so numerous. The best way of helping was to carry on as usual, if only to counter the general disorganisation on which the promoters of the Strike had calculated.' (*Report*, 1926.) It was a typically cool response from this cool and unflappable man.

But now Dr Ferard's sixteen-year Rectorship was drawing to a close. He had had a serious heart attack in 1921, which had entailed two terms' leave of absence, during which time 'Beaky' Druitt had been Acting Rector and had presented the annual *Report*; and in December, 1925, he informed the Directors that he could carry on no longer; he would retire at the end of the 1925–6 session. The Directors asked him to reconsider, because the headmastership of George Watson's College was vacant and they were afraid that two vacancies in the same city would restrict the choice of a new Rector. But the Rector argued that the two appointments were essentially different and would not overlap, and he would not change his mind. So the Directors set about the task of finding a successor, having put it on record that the years of Dr Ferard's Rectorship 'have witnessed a great growth in numbers and a corresponding development in material equipment, all of which has been to a large extent due to his wise foresight and capable administration' (*Report*, 1926).

Dr Ferard retired to Oxford, the scene of his old academic associations, and he died there in July, 1934.

He left the Academy at the start of its second century in very good shape, with its numbers moving steadily up towards the 700-mark and a record in 1925 of eleven boys going straight from school to Oxford – four of them with Open Classical Scholarships. And he left behind, in his final *Report*, a paean of praise for the Day School:

'I applied for the office because I had come to the conclusion that the Day School is a higher, as it is certainly a more natural, type of institution than the Boarding School. Ever since the time of Doctor Arnold at Rugby the tide of fashion has set so strongly in the direction of the Boarding School that any one who declares himself a convinced adherent of the Day School is in danger of being written down a faddist. Yet experience and observation have only confirmed me in the prejudice, and that for the very reasons which are usually urged in favour of the Boarding School.

'The Public Boarding Schools of the country have done and are doing admirable work . . . But the artificial segregation involved in the system is apt to beget a code of conduct and attitude to life less in contact with reality than will be found where the life of the School is carried on in intimate union with that of the home. The boy at the Day School is in enjoyment of far more liberty than falls to the lot of his Public School cousin. He has not to attend roll calls at frequent intervals, or confine himself to a limited quarter of the city, or play endless games as the most obvious way of keeping himself out of mischief. He seldom abuses his liberty because there is so little incentive to do so. An interest in study is not stigmatised as the hall-mark of un-regeneration. He can think for himself and follow his own bent rather than that dictated by athletic eminence. The result is that instead of being less self-reliant, as is usually thought, he can adapt himself easily to a difficult or unusual situation. If in outward semblance he pays less homage to the pattern which fashion prescribes, yet where good sense and initiative are called for he will not be found wanting.

'The point seems worth emphasising, because there is a danger lest parents, with good Schools at their doors, should feel it their duty to seek them further afield and thereby to deprive their children of the humanising influences of the home.'

It is a notable declaration of faith, not only in the ideals of the Academy as a Home-School but in boys as a whole. It seems strange that it should come from a man whom many of his pupils thought to be cold and distant, just a desiccated calculating machine, to use a phrase made familiar in another context. Yet this unswerving faith in the Academy system had informed all his attitudes and decisions throughout the years of his administration; and in the event, he knew the boys better than they knew him.

Shortly before he left, Dr Ferard reprinted a pamphlet of Notes for the use of members of the staff, marked *Confidential*, which included some 'suggestions' for newcomers to the staff:

'He ought to refrain from personalia, sarcasm, or roughness of any kind in dealing with his boys. E.g. to call a boy a fool, or a duffer, or to shout at him, or in fact to do anything (beyond such quiet reproof or correction as circumstances may require) which we would not allow him to do to us, is unfairly to presume on our relation to him . . .

'How to secure diligence and interest from all the members of the class, even those who are naturally lazy or apathetic, is the chief problem with which the teacher is confronted in the Class-room. Certainly he will not do so by frequent recourse to such weapons as sarcasm, imposition, or the "tawse". It is no exaggeration to say that really good teachers very seldom resort to such means or have any need to do so . . .

'The main thing is to be keenly interested in one's subject and eager to communicate it to others. Boys are very responsive to those who are themselves interested and who can handle their subject in an interesting form. Further, they respond generously to personal interest on the master's part . . .

'The public is apt to think teaching a dull, pedantic business, but it is very far from being so if pursued in the right spirit. Boys are immensely interesting; each has his own individuality. How to get at this and to bring out the best efforts of each is the difficult but inspiring problem before us . . .'

There was no doubt whose side Dr Ferard was on.

CHAPTER XVII

P. H. B. Lyon: The Unfinished Rectorship (1926-31)

Nothing revolutionary or strikingly original is contemplated.
(Rector's *Report*, 1927)

LEANING casually against one of the pillars supporting the organ, Hugh Lyon looked absurdly young to be a Rector. Perhaps it was just the contrast with the retiring Rector, Dr Ferard; Dr Ferard was 60 now, Hugh Lyon was 33. Dr Ferard, who introduced him to the assembled school, was wearing his habitual black suit that made him look even more elderly; the Rector-elect was wearing a light-coloured suit, which made him look even younger. The boys in the School Hall that day early in the summer term of 1926 were frankly amazed that this breezy young man chatting to them from the platform so informally was actually going to be their new *Rector*.

Not that he was all that young for an Academy Rector. Dr Hannah had been 29; Mr Sheepshanks, 30; Bob Mackenzie, 31; Dr Williams, 32; Reginald Carter, 33. In fact, only Dr Hodson, Dr Harvey and Dr Ferard had been older than he when they were appointed. It was really the contrast that did it; after the rather prim, ultra-correct years of Dr Ferard's Rectorship, this relaxed young man who often rode to School on a bicycle felt like a gust of fresh air in a musty room.

Percy Hugh Beverley Lyon was a Rugbeian. He had been Head of his House at Rugby and gained an Exhibition to Oriel College, Oxford, where he won the Newdigate Prize for English Verse and a First in Classics. He was awarded the M.C. during the war as adjutant of the 6th Battalion Durham Light Infantry. Since the war he had been a master at Cheltenham College. Great things were expected of him when he came to the Edinburgh Academy, and he did many good things as Rector, laying the foundations for even better things. His Rectorship might have blossomed into a truly memorable one; but he was always a Rugbeian at heart, and after only five years he left the Academy to become Headmaster of his old school at the age of 39.

It was a great disappointment to the Academy; and Mr Lyon's term of office is now remembered as the unfinished Rectorship.

When Mr Lyon came to the Academy the General Strike was over, but it was still a time of depression and industrial unrest. Women in Britain over 30 years of age had been given the vote in 1918, but they were still clamouring for equal franchise with men – and got it in 1928. The American slump and the Wall Street crash came in 1929. Any idea of large-scale developments at the Academy during those years was inhibited by the general sense of financial insecurity. Unemployment, poverty and parish relief were the order of the day among the less fortunate inhabitants of the Stockbridge area in which the Academy stood.

In the dim and distant past, the only contact between Academy boys and the 'keelies' of Stockbridge had been the battles with fists and clackens in 'Stinky Lane' or Church Lane on the way home from school – 'the ambush of cads in the lane', as Robert Louis Stevenson had called it. But now Rector Lyon suggested that the Academy should follow the example of other public schools and start a social club for boys in the district. This was one of the first of the new Rector's schemes, and when the Directors heard of it in February, 1927, they 'expressed their hearty approval of the movement'. It took time to get off the ground, however; in his *Report* of 1928 the Rector castigated the parents and Academicals to whom he had appealed for funds in vain:

'It is indeed something of a disgrace that, in spite of four separate appeals, the [Boys'] Club Committee have not as yet received enough money to turn this proposal into a fact. There are few schools of the Academy's standing which have not long ago made this obvious contribution both to the welfare of their country and the education in humanity, sympathy and citizenship of their own members.'

Eventually, on February 12, 1929, the Edinburgh Academy Stockbridge Club was inaugurated 'for work among the boys of the poorer classes'. The Rector, who had thrown himself heart and soul into the project, was delighted: 'The most important event of the session' he called it in his *Report* for 1929; 'It is indeed with a thankful heart that I record the auspicious beginning of this far-reaching influence on Academy life and thought . . . The chief value of the Club to the Academy lies in the object lesson it gives to the older boys of the need and opportunities awaiting them for social service, whether at the Club or elsewhere.'

The Directors advanced £1,500 at five per cent interest from the Endowment Fund Trust towards the purchase of premises at 38 Raeburn Place. This was in character; throughout the hundred years of the Academy's history, when one law for the rich and another for the poor was an accepted fact of life, when there were no pension rights for workers, when a Janitor was expected to keep a wife and family on a few shillings a week and leave them completely unprovided for when he died, the Academy Directors had shown a social conscience and compassion in advance of the social legislation of the times. They had introduced their staff pensions scheme long before the Education Department got round to providing one; and out of their ever-meagre resources they had always managed to squeeze some provision for old servants or their dependants – £20 towards an orphan's schooling, 10s a week for a widow, free lodging in one of the Boarding Houses for a pupil who had to be taken from school and had to take a job.

With the Rector as its driving force, the Boys' Club was soon in full swing, administered by a joint committee of Directors, Academical Club, and School. A manager was appointed, Club leaders recruited, and as many as seventy or eighty local boys congregated there twice a week and met senior Academy boys for boxing, swimming, football and athletics. There were summer camps with climbing expeditions in the Selkirkshire hills, and pantomimes and concerts in the winter, with the boys and their families joining with Academy boys and their parents to sell tickets, make costumes and scenery, and raise money. A large number of people worked extremely hard and selflessly to make the Club a success; but none more so than Sgt.-Major Atkinson, who was known by the Stockbridge boys not as 'The Bud' but as 'Sarge'.

The Stockbridge Boys' Club had its ups and downs over the years as enthusiasm fluctuated both among the boys and among the senior Academy boys and Academicals, who frequently had to be chivvied to give up their time to help run the Club and, later, its additional branches at Portsburgh and Granton. It finally petered out in the post-war flush of national youth schemes, youth clubs, and social welfare; with housing redevelopment, Stockbridge no longer needed the Academy Boys' Club, and it was closed in 1956. But it had served the needs of its time and helped to break down the 'them and us' attitude of generations of snooty Academy boys to the 'cads in the lane'. As an exercise in social education, it was probably the most important innovation of Mr Lyon's Rectorship.

Compared with some of his more flamboyant predecessors, like Dr Williams or Mr Mackenzie, Mr Lyon's annual *Reports* tended to be low-key: 'The work of the School has proceeded steadily and calls for little comment', 'Nothing revolutionary or strikingly original is contemplated'. The School had settled into a comfortable rhythm of progress, undisturbed by either catastrophe or history-making triumph. And yet, in the first year of Mr Lyon's Rectorship, his Head Ephor was one of the most remarkable games players the Academy has ever produced – the legendary Ben Tod (E.A. 1919–27).

Ben Ross Tod (the brother of the present Chairman of the Directors of the Academy, Rae Tod) was the complete all-rounder. At cricket he scored the staggering total of 3,568 runs for the 1st XI at an average of 40.55 runs per innings, and took 224 wickets at an average of 12.50. At football he played for the Scottish Schoolboys XV. At athletics he won the hurdles, weight putt, high jump, long leap, and throwing the cricket ball. He won the Fives Challenge Cup and the Addis Golf Cup. He won fifteen cricket caps for Scotland (three as captain), and no one except the selectors of the time knows why he was never capped for rugby. He was captain of the Academical XV and the Academical XI . . . You name it, Ben Tod was brilliant at it. His spectacular career started in May, 1922, when he marched to the wicket for his first game in the 1st XI at the age of 13. He was a small, ginger-haired boy, and he scored 20 not out: 'Tod made a promising *début*, especially in batting,' said the *Chronicle*. It was the first of ninety-seven innings he was to make for the Academy. He did not win his 1st XI colours that year, but next year he did, after making a century against Merchiston when he was still only 14 (he made seven centuries for the Academy in all). This was the first of his five full seasons in the XI, of which he was captain for the last two seasons. In his last season he scored centuries against Merchiston and Fettes, and 824 runs in all, and took 75 wickets at an average of 11.76. He played in the 1st XV for four years (captain for the last two seasons), an outstanding fly-half, a fine tackler, and a deadly kicker (in one School match he converted all seven of the tries scored). And quite apart from being an outstanding games player and all-round athlete, he was a fine singer and actor (his Ko-Ko in *The Mikado* of 1927 was by all accounts unforgettable) and a thoroughly attractive personality. Five years after he left school, where he had been an admirable Head Ephor, he was described as 'probably the most popular Academical of his generation'. He died in 1967 at the age of 58.

To have a senior boy with such effortless gifts of leadership is a boon to any Rector; school discipline and morale seem to look after themselves. The mood at the Academy was buoyant. The numbers rose steadily – 709 in 1926–7, 721 in 1927–8, 727 in 1928–9, 735 in 1929–30; by which time Mr Lyon was expressing doubts as to whether the numbers 'should be allowed to pass beyond the present total, in the interests of efficient education'.

Mr Lyon's main contribution to all this was consolidation: 'nothing revolutionary or strikingly original', as he had called it. He remained friendly and open, easy of manner and much more accessible to the boys themselves than Dr Ferard had ever been. He delighted the School one morning when a large chauffeur-driven car slid up to the gates to decant a pupil from one of the wealthier families – to be followed by the Rector himself on a bicycle! To the boys in the School he was known, familiarly but not to his face, of course, as 'Percy'. But all the time he was quietly starting things up here and there that have become accepted factors in School life today.

According to the Directors' *Minutes*, the very first suggestion he made to the Directors as Rector of the Academy, in October, 1926, was to submit new patterns for the school cap, adding silver braid round the peak and lower rim of the existing cap – and this after only a month in the saddle. He arranged for tea to be served to boys staying behind after school for music lessons, he persuaded the Directors to buy a school radio for £33, and to allocate £20 a year for a musical recital by a professional musician, and to give 'Pop' Whalley an extra £35 a year to undertake the responsibility for the production of concerts and Gilbert and Sullivan operas. He also persuaded the Directors to install electric lighting throughout the School in 1927 at a cost of £482; up to then, most of the classrooms were lit by gas, somewhat inadequately, and the line of classrooms on the west side of the Yards, up from the Janitor's Lodge, had no lighting of any kind.

He introduced, in 1927, an annual School Roll Book containing the names of all boys and staff in the School, which helped to give the boys a feeling of corporate identity. He superintended an extension to the Science laboratory and the building of new school lavatories 'down the hill', at a total cost of £2,646, and the provision of additional dressing-rooms at the rear of the Pavilion at New Field. In 1930, a long-needed extension to the Crabbie Library building was added – a wing to the north to provide a special classroom for the VIIth, and a wing to the south as a Reading Room for the Library. It cost about £3,500. The

Library, which by then was 'slowly sinking into chaos', in the Rector's words, was completely reorganised, reclassified and recatalogued by one of the masters, Mr Robert Pugh Jones of the Mathematical Department, who had joined the staff in 1916 and retired as Head of the Department in succession to 'Jas. T' in 1939. At the same time, the Crabbie benefactions continued, when his widow, Mrs George Crabbie, and Courtenay Shiells (father of J. T. L. Shiells, E.A. 1905–19, who had recently been killed in a flying accident) presented two Squash Courts for Raeburn Place. George Crabbie, who died in 1929, had been one of the Academy's most loyal benefactors; he had been a member of 'Puggy' Weir's Class of 1860–7, and in addition to the Library and the Fives Courts he had endowed two scholarships to the Academy and given a succession of prizes for athletics. He was President of the Academical Football Club and Honorary President of the Scottish Amateur Athletic Association, and was a Director of the Academy from 1899–1925. He had three sons at the Academy who all shone at sports: J. E. (E.A. 1890–8) won his Rugby Blue four times at Oxford and was capped for Scotland; G.E. (E.A. 1891–1901) captained the School XV in 1900–1 and won the Bradbury Shield as the best all-rounder, and was capped for Scotland at rugby; W.M. (E.A. 1900–11) was a formidable middle-distance runner and won the Burma Cup twice as the best athlete. He ran for Scotland and became Honorary President of the S.A.A.A., like his father; and, like his father, he also became a Director of the Academy (1945–61).

Mr Lyon was also instrumental in making 'provision for the more suitable employment of older boys who are not cricketers' by the construction of five hard tennis courts to the west of Jeffrey House at New Field; and tennis at the Academy quickly became extremely popular under the enthusiastic leadership of 'Paddy' West (his worst threat to someone slacking on court was, 'You'll have to go back to cricket!').

He reintroduced fencing in 1927–8, with Dr Wightman as master in charge and instruction given 'in person' by Professor Léon Crosnier, and a trophy called the 'Crosnier Foil' presented by Sheriff John G. Jameson (E.A. 1888–95), a noted athlete in his time (fencing champion at Edinburgh University and a boxing, swimming and water-polo star at Oxford).

He also gave attention to sports in the Prep. Soccer had been introduced there in place of football (rugby) to make life easier for the mistresses who took Prep games. The Rector appealed in vain for

Academicals to come and help; so in 1930 the leader of the Stockbridge Boys' Club, Mr T. E. P. McCandlish, agreed to come and coach the Prep and run their games, 'as the mistresses are not able to do it properly'.

Off the field, Mr Lyon was delighted with the success of another 'new feature of Academy life' which he introduced in January, 1927. This was a series of short School Services in the Hall on the last Sunday of each month in term-time, attended by boys, parents and Academicals. It quickly became a part of the Academy tradition, and attracted many fine speakers, mainly Edinburgh ministers, but sometimes an Academical clergyman, or a headmaster of Loretto, or even the Archbishop of York. One of the young ministers who preached in the Hall in 1928 was the Rev. George Macleod (later Moderator of the General Assembly of the Church of Scotland and now Lord Macleod of Fuinary). From the start, the services were conducted by the Rev. Alexander Fiddes, who was Chaplain to the School for forty years. In recent years the Sunday Services have been replaced by Upper School Services, for staff and boys only, held once a month on weekdays during school hours.

Mr Lyon also put on the first Shakespeare production at the Academy. The Rectorial dais in the Hall was now fitted with a front curtain, and in July, 1928, 'The Academy Players' put on two performances of *Hamlet*. The cast was drawn entirely from the Fourth and Fifth Classes, and the acting version, 'stripped to its essentials', was prepared by the Rector. The Rector was the producer as well, and the fencing fight between Hamlet and Laertes was arranged by Dr Wightman. The title role was taken by Basil Douglas (E.A. 1920–32, later a BBC radio music producer in London and now a concert impresario), who turned in 'a very fine and finished rendering of the part'. Douglas also played leading roles in the Gilbert and Sullivan operas (the Duchess in *The Gondoliers* of 1929, and the Lord Chancellor in the *Iolanthe* of 1931); and he was once again the lead in the second of the Rector's major dramatic productions, as Lincoln in John Drinkwater's exquisitely tedious play, *Abraham Lincoln*, in 1930. After Mr Lyon left the Academy, a new member of staff, Mr J. E. G. Quick (1934–47) formed a proper Dramatic Society which produced some good performances before the war, and was revived by Mr Quick after the war with a production of Bridie's *What Say They?* in 1946. After Mr Quick left to become Rector of Morrison's Academy, Shakespearian productions were revived by his successor as English master, Mr W. H. Hook

(1947–74), with a production of *Romeo and Juliet* in 1948; this was a curtain-raiser to his towering production of *King Lear* in 1950, followed by *Julius Caesar* in 1952. His co-producer, Mr Peter Ford, who joined the staff in 1949, now took on the mantle of producer and has been responsible for the drama and opera productions since then. Mr Ford started with the Comedies, producing *Twelfth Night* in 1954, and *The Merry Wives of Windsor* in 1956, and then put on two fine productions from the Tragedies – *Hamlet* in 1958, to celebrate the thirtieth anniversary of Mr Lyon's first Shakespearian production, and *Macbeth* in 1960. The *Chronicle's* guest critic, the eminent Scottish playwright Robert Kemp, whose three sons all went to the Academy, commended in particular the 'sense of communal enthusiasm and team-work' which 'supplies the fundamental charm of these school performances'. (He also, wisely, advised schoolboy players not to get too carried away by dreams of stardom.) *Macbeth* was the last production to be given in the School Hall; from 1961 onwards, starting with Mr Ford's memorable version of *The Yeomen of the Guard*, all school productions have been given in the new Prep Hall, with its much ampler stage and backstage facilities. The Shakespeare productions in the Prep Hall have been *The Merchant of Venice* (1962), *Henry VIII* (1964), *The Tempest* (1966), *The Winter's Tale* (1968), and *Troilus and Cressida* (1972). There was no biennial Shakespeare production in 1974; instead there was a return to Gilbert and Sullivan, and Mr Ford celebrated the 150th anniversary and his own last Academy production with *The Yeomen of the Guard*.

Inside the classroom, Mr Lyon's policy was one of revision rather than revolution: a matter of consolidation more than anything else. After his first session he announced 'certain alterations' in the scheme of classes and the system of promotion. One bizarre side-product of this revision meant that the top Geits' Class became Lower IIB, and remained so for many years to the bewilderment of Geits and parents alike. But there was a more significant alteration under way: 'In the Upper School a movement is to be made towards more definite specialisation, and the new features include a Classical "side", as well as courses intended to equip more fully those intending to take up engineering and agriculture.' And with that, the Academy finally ceased to be what its founders had envisaged – a strictly Classical Academy. The VIIth Class was now widened to admit what had previously been the Special Class (which covered the Modern side), and was no longer the exclusive preserve of the classicists. But the Classical VIIth was still to retain its pre-eminence, and the Dux of the School was to be chosen from its number as before. (It was not until 1946, in Mr Seaman's first session as Rector, that the first non-classical member of the VIIth was awarded the Dux Medal – scientist S. R. Martin).

Mr Lyon also added a notice to the Prospectus informing parents that boys were expected to reach certain classes by a certain age: 'Boys are expected to reach Class Upper IIB by the time they are thirteen, and one of the Vth Classes by the time they are sixteen years of age; it is a question whether boys who do not attain this general standard of achievement would not profit more from a more individual tuition than a large school can give. In such cases, therefore, the Rector may exercise his right of declining to allow a boy to continue his career at the School, though every consideration will be given to individual cases as they arise.' This was strong stuff compared with the days when parents dictated which class their boys should enter and insisted on automatic promotion up the School whether or not the boy could cope with the work. But with the roll in 1928 at a record 727, the days were gone when the Directors felt they had to prune academic standards for fear of boys being removed from school in protest.

In that 1927–8 session too, Rector Lyon introduced the Academy to the Oxford and Cambridge School Certificate examination; it was taken that year by the Vth Classes 'by way of a preliminary canter for the Leaving Certificate the following year'.

The Academy also went into business on its own account in a small way. As early as December, 1926, the Rector had put forward a scheme whereby the Academy would take over from Mr Keddie, a local stationer in Howe Street, the business of supplying school books and exchanging second-hand books, the profits to go to the School. In May, 1928, the School Bookshop opened. Three years later the Academy went into business in a larger way when the Academy Clothing Shop opened in July, 1931, in the basement below the Rector's room. The Academy took over the stock of uniforms held by the official outfitters, Messrs Christie and Messrs Gulland & Kennedy, and arranged with a wholesaler in Leeds to provide future supplies direct from the factory. The idea behind the scheme was threefold: (1) To secure uniformity of design and colour in articles of school clothing, such as caps and blazers; (2) To keep down the costs for parents; (3) To make some profit for the School. By the end of its first year it had made a 'sturdy profit', and parents were benefiting by being charged prices lower than in the city centre. The Edinburgh Chamber of Commerce protested strongly that the Academy was being unfair to local tradesmen, and the Scottish Drapers' Federation complained too. But the shop continued, and prospered, with Sgt.-Major Hector Macpherson in charge and a woman hired to do alterations and fittings at 1s an hour. Parents were not obliged to buy at the School Shop, but prices were keen, and the advantages of 'Buying Academy' were trumpeted in issues of the *Chronicle*. The School Shop was eventually closed in 1947, owing to the difficulty of getting supplies of school uniforms after the war. (The room in which the School Shop functioned is now the Bursar's Office.)

And the ebb and flow of faces in the Masters' Lodge went on. In Mr Lyon's first session, 'Jas. T' Taylor retired from the Mathematical Department, having beaten Dr Gloag's long-standing record of forty sessions' service; and Mr A. C. Dodds, who had been a part-time Art Master at the Academy since 1911, now became a regular member of the staff (he retired in 1953). Next year 'Beaky' Druitt retired, soon to become the first member of staff to be appointed a Director of the Academy. The session of 1928–9 saw the arrival of Mr A. C. Munro, who came straight to the Academy from Oxford. His appointment was due to start in October 1928, but to fill a vacancy caused by illness he taught for a month in the preceding term. He taught Latin and French, and after the war he was Housemaster of Mackenzie House; an energetic and thorough teacher known to his friends (and most of his pupils) as 'Tony'. In 1965, when it was decided to increase the age range at the new Prep School and to appoint a Headmaster of the Prep for the first time, Mr Munro volunteered to go there as Senior Master and thus strengthen the link between the Prep and the Upper School. He retired in 1970 after forty-two years and one month on the staff. That extra month at the beginning would appear to have given him the record for long service previously held by 'Twank' Hardy and Miss McTavish, who both achieved exactly forty-two years; but purists in these statistical matters point to Mr Munro's five years with the Prep, and Miss McTavish's nine years in the Upper School, and argue that the record still properly belongs to 'Twank' Hardy. But there is no general agreement; perhaps it would be best to call it a triple tie, and congratulate all three on a magnificent record of service to the Academy.

'Twank' Hardy himself retired in July, 1930; the following session Mr Cooke arrived, and Mr H. C. Ferguson. 'Fergie', an Ulsterman, was to stay for twenty-seven years until he retired in 1957 (he died in 1972), teaching French but doing an enormous amount of extra-curricular work as well. He was editor of the *Chronicle* for thirteen years, which included the war, he was the School Librarian for a time, and he was in charge of selecting and purchasing books for School Prizes. But he was probably happiest working with his hands; he was a skilled woodworker, and was responsible for erecting the stage in the Hall for drama and opera productions. He was also a farmer at heart and was in charge of the war-time farming operations at the New Field Extension, producing splendid crops of vegetables; and when the war was over, he was in charge of converting his vast vegetable patch into a playing-field. He also had a highly talented collie dog which could do the High Hurdles race as a party trick on the morning of Games Day.

On May 22, 1931, a special meeting of the Directors was hastily summoned 'to consider and deal with' a letter from Mr Lyon, in which he tendered his resignation as Rector of the Academy; he had just been offered, and accepted, the Headmastership of his old school, Rugby. The Directors were greatly disappointed at losing Mr Lyon when things were running so smoothly, but they congratulated him on 'the great honour which had been paid to him' in being elected to the famous school which the Academy had already provided with a distinguished Headmaster – Archibald Campbell Tait. The Directors minuted their tribute: 'During his five years' tenure of the Rectorship he had proved himself an able and energetic Head, under whose rule the School had developed and prospered and its best traditions had been worthily maintained. Although his period as Rector had been all too short, Mr Lyon had thrown himself with great zeal and ability into his work, and his Rectorship had been distinguished by important developments in many spheres of the School life.'

At Rugby, Mr Lyon proved himself to be an administrator on the grand scale, and plunged into the sort of reconstruction schemes that the Academy could well have done with in the 1930s, when both Merchiston and George Watson's College were moved into brand-new schools. Almost at once there was expenditure of £20,000 on buying fields and land, and converting a House. The Governing body there-upon decided to call a halt on capital expenditure for the next five years; but as J. B. Hope Simpson wrote in *Rugby since Arnold* (1967), 'No Minute of the Governing Body, however, could prevent the Headmaster from planning . . .' By the time the moratorium on expenditure was nearing its end, in 1938, Mr Lyon presented an enormous scheme of reconstruction, involving a new Classroom Block, a new House, extensions to the Music School and Science School, and various other improvements, and estimated to cost £65,000. There was only time to complete the new House and new changing-rooms before war broke out; but as Hope Simpson says, 'But for the outbreak of war, Lyon's Headmastership would probably have been the greatest period of School building since the days of Temple [1858–69].'

Mr Lyon retired from Rugby in 1948, at the age of 55. From 1950–61 he was Director of the Public Schools Appointments Board.

History is full of 'ifs'. 'If' Hugh Lyon had stayed on at the Academy, would he have been able to give fuller rein to the zeal for rebuilding and reconstruction he showed at Rugby? The thirties were not a good time for heavy capital expenditure, and the Directors of the Academy were committed to a policy of caution and retrenchment rather than expansion. By putting off the kind of developments which were becoming essential, they unwittingly left the Academy in poor shape to face the rigours of the Second World War and the immediate post-war years. But hindsight is easy. How could anyone know that the German elections of September, 1930, when the Nazi Party increased their representation in the Reichstag from 12 seats to 107, or Adolph Hitler's assumption of the Chancellorship in 1933, would ensure that no development at all would be possible by the end of the decade? And how could the new Rector of the Academy, Mr Arthur Lionel Forster Smith, dream that the shouts of 'Sieg Heil' in far-off Germany would make his Rectorship the most critical in the Academy's history, with the Academy being rescued by Old Bailie Blackwood's successors – Edinburgh Corporation?

CHAPTER XVIII

'Alfie' Smith (1931-45): The War Crisis

And now ride e'en your ways; for these are the last words ye'll ever hear *me* speak, and this is the last reise that I'll ever cut in the bonny woods of Ellangowan.
(Sir Walter Scott, *Guy Mannering*)

HE was 'Alfie', of course, right from the beginning: Dr Arthur Lionel Forster Smith, C.B.E., M.V.O., M.A., LL.D. (Edin), LL.D. (St Andrews). He was the eldest of the nine children of A. L. Smith, Master of Balliol from 1916 to 1924. Young A. L. F. Smith went to the Dragon School, Oxford, and from there to Rugby, where he won an Open Classical Scholarship to Balliol College, Oxford, in 1898. There he gained a Second in Greats and a First in History, and was elected to a Fellowship at All Souls in 1904. From 1908 until 1914 he was Dean of Magdalen College, where he was one of the tutors of the Prince of Wales, later to be King Edward VIII.

All this put Mr Smith high up on the short leet when the Directors of the Academy were considering applications for the vacant Rectorship in 1931. They were just as impressed with the next part of his career. During the First World War he was on active service with the Hampshire Regiment in India and Mesopotamia, and in 1919 he resigned his Fellowship at Magdalen to return to Mesopotamia as Director of Education at Baghdad. He had a six months' spell as a temporary master at Harrow during a visit home in 1923, then returned to the East where he was Inspector-General and Adviser to the Ministry of Education in Iraq right up to the time of his application for the Academy Rectorship. (In 1932, when King Feisal of Iraq visited Edinburgh and the Edinburgh Academy, he said at a lunch at the City Chambers, 'No one has a greater place in the heart of Iraq than my dear old friend Mr Lionel Smith, Rector of the Edinburgh Academy.')

As if all this were not enough, the committee of Directors who interviewed him knew that Lionel Smith had outstanding athletic qualifications to match his intellectual attainments. He was the school skating champion at Rugby, played in the Cricket and Hockey XIs both at school and at Balliol, and twice won the lawn tennis singles. He was captain of the College Boat Club, and rowed in the winning crew for the Oxford Fours and in the crew for the Visitors' Cup at Henley in 1901. He won his Blue at hockey, and played hockey for England in 1903, 1904 and 1913. He excelled at Rugby Fives and also played a good game of soccer. As *The Times* said at the end of his long life, he was one of those rare people of whom, by reason of their talents, character and friendships, it was rightly said they could have done anything.

Yet here he was, at the age of 50, the friend of kings and adviser to governments, offering himself to the Directors of the Edinburgh Academy for a salary of £1,600 a year and no house. The wonder is that they did not snap him up on the spot; but the selection committee reported to the Directors that there was another candidate, Mr John Traill Christie, whose qualifications were also outstanding, and after interviewing both candidates the committee were unanimously of the opinion that 'each of them in respect of high character, academic record and intellectual ability, could justly be recommended for the post'. The crucial factor was that of age. Mr Christie was 31 against Mr Smith's 50, and the committee was equally divided on a fundamental question of policy: Was it in the best interests of the Academy as it found itself today to select a man of mature years with a wide practical experience, and with the reasonable expectation that the appointment would be more or less permanent – or a much younger man who appeared already to be marked for high distinction in his profession, and who might be called away to still further promotion after a comparatively short term of service at the Academy? Or to put it more bluntly – could the Academy afford the risk of another young Rector who might see the School simply as a stepping-stone to greater things?

The Directors went into what had been called since the days of Cockburn, Horner and Russell 'prolonged deliberation and discussion', during which a letter was read from Lord Clyde (the senior), who favoured Mr Christie, and one from Mr W. J. 'Pussy' Stuart, who opted for Mr Smith. To clarify the matter, they took a vote first of all on the general principle of youth versus age, and the result was 6 to 4 in favour of having a man of maturity and experience. The Directors then voted unanimously in favour of Mr Smith. (The defeated candidate, J. T. Christie, became Headmaster of Repton School the following year, and then Headmaster of Westminster School in 1937, before becoming Principal of Jesus College, Oxford.)

It is interesting to speculate whether they ever regretted, in later years, their decision to go for an older man. Certainly, no one ever regretted 'Alfie' Smith. Kindly, lovable and wise, with an infectious sense of humour and fun, he was liked by everybody, and he guided the Academy in peace and war with an unruffled calm and a good-natured refusal to let anything upset the quiet tenor of his ways. His lithe and active figure, in elegant bowler hat, rolled umbrella, pink Leander scarf, and slightly shabby raincoat, became a familiar sight in and around Henderson Row, Inverleith Place, and the New Club in Princes Street. When it became known that he had turned down the Headmastership of Eton in 1933, the bond between him and the Academy was complete. 'Alfie' could do no wrong: the Directors' foresight had been vindicated.

But (and there always seems to be a 'but' when contemplating Lionel Smith's Rectorship) his very niceness may have been a grave disadvantage to the Academy's future. The thirties were the lotus years, which had to be paid for after the war. The serene years, when the numbers stayed rock-steady at just under 700, should have been spent in reconstruction and renewal. The war crisis simply underlined the comparative weakness of the Academy in the forties, it did not entirely create it.

For Mr Smith did nothing spectacular at the Academy, and did not want to. He introduced no far-reaching innovations into the curriculum. There was no campaign to build or expand. True, he did repeatedly urge the Directors to build a swimming pool; he started swimming classes and entered the Academy in competitions against other schools, and lost no opportunity of pointing out how much at a disadvantage the Academy was in having to practise at the private baths at Drumsheugh. But the Directors were not in an expansive mood and could not see their way to meeting the expense of a pool, even though a parent offered to pay the costs of the excavation. And so the swimming pool that Rector Mackenzie had first wanted to build in 1893 at a cost of £2,750 was never built, and still is not built; because Mr Smith was not a Mackenzie who could dazzle a Board of Directors with his financial wizardry and blazing determination to get things done.

Besides, Mr Smith did not like change. He said it at the 1935 Exhibition, when he was announcing staff changes due to the prolonged absence through illness of 'Billy' Peel: 'I dislike change, and would rather not dwell upon it.' His annual *Reports* to the Directors invariably started with the comment that the past year had been 'comparatively quiet and uneventful', or 'has not been marked by anything of outstanding importance', or 'prosperous and uneventful', or 'nothing spectacular to report'. Yet during most of these years there were a lot of good things to report: in 1934 there were three Classical Scholarships, a Classical Exhibition and a Demyship in Classics to Oxford and an Exhibition in Mathematics to Cambridge; in 1935 the XV won all its ten matches for the first time since 1911, and the XI won four of its School matches and drew one. Both of these undefeated teams were captained by R. B. Bruce Lockhart, now Headmaster of Loretto. In 1939 there were four Open Awards at Oxford and Cambridge, three for Classics and one for Natural Sciences.

Yet in his *Report* for 1939, Mr Smith duly recorded 'no event of outstanding importance', despite the scholarships, and even more oddly, despite the fact that the opening of the School session in 1938 had been delayed for a week because of the Munich crisis, and despite the fact that every spare moment during the session had been spent digging trenches in New Field, building air-raid shelters and rehearsing the boys in getting under cover in the event of air-raids.

'Alfie' took it all in his stride. Perhaps it would have taken an earthquake to count as an 'event' to someone who had been pioneering education in the depths of Mesopotamia. Both during war-time and peace-time he applied himself to keeping the Academy ticking over; but in fact it was marking time.

It was not that he did not have enough interest in the Academy. Quite the contrary. There was no aspect of the School's activities in which he was not involved. He was a great performer in the squash courts at Raeburn Place (he won the Academical Club Squash Racquets Cup twice, in his fifties!) and at hockey, which he introduced as an alternative to athletics after the close of the football season. During the very severe winter of 1945-6, when the playing-fields and the School Yards were like sheets of ice, he arranged for busloads of boys to travel to Threipmuir reservoir in the Pentlands and taught them ice hockey, bewitching everybody with his weaving runs and his skill with the stick.

During the war, when part of the School was evacuated to Hartree, the Rector would visit them once or twice a term. He would take a train to Symington and walk the next five miles, wading the Clyde as a short-cut. He was also deeply interested in the Stockbridge Boys' Club that his predecessor had started, and often the affairs of the Club would take up more space in his annual *Report* than any item of School activity. He attended their pantomimes and concerts and football matches, joined them in rambles and hill-climbs, and visited them at their annual camp, always insisting on sleeping in the open. His interest in the Club brought him into contact with many families in the poorer districts of Edinburgh ('under-privileged' is the word nowadays), and often he helped them out of his own pocket without anyone else knowing about it at the time.

He encouraged the formation of an Angling Society, a Play-Reading Society, a Photographic Society, a Bird-Watching Society. He was passionately interested in nature and wild-life. He took a blind friend on a trip to the Highlands just so that he could hear again the splash of a salmon leaping, the harsh cry of an eagle, the roar of a stag.

Senior and not-so-senior boys warmed to his humanity and opened their minds to his broad and profound interest in the Humanities (one of his favourite writers was W. P. Ker, the author of *Epic and Romance* and other splendid books on literature). He also revolutionised morning Prayers and Bible disquisitions in the Hall. Where Reginald Carter had fired questions at some luckless class in Hall to see if they had been paying attention to previous talks, and Dr Ferard quoted constantly from Frazer's *Golden Bough* and 'Josephus, the Jewish historian', Lionel Smith with his intimate knowledge of the Middle East made the Old Testament spring to life as a historical document. Parents warmed to his sincere interest in their sons, and the bubbling sense of humour that accompanied it. When a parent wrote crossly during the war asking who was responsible for the shoddy geometry sets supplied by the School, the Rector replied that the responsibility belonged to the manufacturers, the Rector, and Adolf Hitler – 'and far be it from me to decide who should bear the brunt of the blame.' At an Exhibition he told the audience that there had been a number of complaints from parents saying that too much home work (prep.) was set at the Academy; he drew from his pocket a thick bundle of letters, saying, 'I have here, in fact, the letters of these parents – Oh, I do beg your pardon; these are the letters of parents who think that not enough prep. is set.'

He could charm the birds off the trees. And probably did. Everyone who came to him in wrath was disarmed and pacified, from the parent who objected to the School's staying open during the funeral of King

George V, to the mother of the boy who got a rusty staple in his lunchtime sausage. He did, however, put his foot down when there was a proposal to appoint a Headmistress to take charge of the Prep School (there was only a Senior Mistress in those days), and he continually championed the cause of the younger masters who supervised games – 'The Games Master, Mr West, has an occupation absorbing most of that time which other people in other professions call the schoolmaster's leisure.'

He paid much attention to the minutiæ of school life. In 1934, for instance, he arranged for a glass of milk, hot or cold, to be provided in the Dining Hall every morning at 11.15 for any boy who wanted it. The work of the VIIth was reorganised to allow boys destined for Science and Medicine to receive special tuition in Chemistry, Physics and Biology, so that it was now possible for a boy to cover all the necessary work to take the Cambridge first M.B. exam (in the September following his entrance into the VIIth) in Physics, Chemistry, Mechanics, and most of Biology. And on the principle that Old Boys tend to give most when they are satisfied with the School's progress or impressed by the Headmaster, he can surely claim some of the credit for the rash of donations for scholarships and endowments that happened in that 'no event of outstanding importance' year of 1938-9, when the announcement at the 1938 Exhibition of the foundation of a Scholarship by the three Salvesen brothers was followed up next day by an anonymous donation by an 'Old Academical' of £1,000 to endow a scholarship 'to assist boys already at school whose parents find themselves unable to continue the payment of full fees', and a further donation of £1,000 a few months later by a son of 'Skinny' Carmichael, the former Classical Master, to found a bursary in memory of his father to be tenable by a boy at the Academy.

But there were uneasy straws in the wind long before then. The numbers at the Academy remained obstinately below the 700-mark achieved by Mr Lyon. There was a decrease in the number of boys coming to the Academy from outside Edinburgh, and for the first time for many years there were vacancies in the Boarding Houses. A number of Boarding Schools were also finding their numbers dropping at this time; it was a symptom of middle-class apprehensiveness about the future, when unemployment was rife, money was tight, and war clouds were looming.

Meanwhile the man who had turned down the Headmastership of Eton was discovering just how multifarious were the duties expected of the Rector of the Academy. From the Directors' Minutes of March 13, 1934: after a Department of Agriculture expert advised fertiliser treatment to improve the condition of the turf at New Field – 'It was remitted to the Rector to arrange for a further application of sewage sludge, and also to arrange for sowing some seed if necessary.'

But the Rector was keeping the Directors busy too, in the most bizarre way. He had 'failed to report himself timeously' for medical examination by the Scottish Education Department, and as a result they were only recognising his service from 1933 instead of from 1931 for superannuation purposes. He appealed in vain, and the Board of Directors took up his case with the Department. It kept them busy almost to the end of his Rectorship. There was hardly a meeting at which 'Rector's Pension' did not figure on the agenda. Representations revealed that it was not just a matter of how much pension he should get, but whether he would be eligible to qualify for one at all under the Government pension scheme. Lawyers were consulted. The M.P. for West Edinburgh (Mr Erskine Hill) was called in, and he took the case up with the Secretary of State for Scotland. There was talk of raising the matter in Parliament. Eventually, in 1941, the Scottish Education Department agreed to lay a Special Regulation on the table of both Houses, amending the Superannuation Scheme for Teachers (Scotland) Act, 1926, to cover someone with a varied career like Mr Smith's. It became operative in May, 1942, and the Directors informed Lionel Smith that his pension was at last assured. It had been a noble effort on the part of the Directors, and it says a lot for them that they never let up even at a time when they were almost at their wits' end coping with the worst financial crisis in the history of the Academy. It was caused by the war.

THE ACADEMY ON ITS KNEES: 1939

The Directors have decided that the School should again return to its independent status, and that they will not seek further aid by way of Grant after 31st July, 1945.
(Directors' *Report*, 1945)

In February, 1939, when war seemed imminent and the air-raid shelters were going up in Henderson Row, when fears of wholesale bombing of cities and the need for evacuation were growing, the Directors sent a circular to all parents asking: In the event of war, do you wish your son to continue to attend school?

On September 19, sixteen days after war had been declared, when evacuation from cities was in full swing, the Directors met to consider the parents' replies. Out of a total of 439 boys in the Upper School the previous session, 102 would be leaving, 198 would be returning, 74 wished to be evacuated, and 65 did not reply. It was little short of a catastrophe: in one swoop, the numbers attending the Academy were practically halved. The staff too were decimated: within days or weeks, Messrs Quick, Scott, West and G. C. Wood (1935–9) were called up, and one new master due in October would not be coming to take up his appointment. Some of the Boarders were to be evacuated, along with any other boys whose parents felt the same way, to Hartree House, near Biggar, and that meant losing more staff – Mr Hempson, who became 'Rector' of this little Academy-in-exile, and Messrs Munro, A. O. Chesters (1927–40) and T. D. W. Whitfield (1935–45). To plug the gaps, Miss Millar and Miss McTavish moved into the Upper School, which now contained only 260 boys, compared with the normal average complement of 475; besides, the Prep School had to close because the shelter accommodation was not considered adequate. A rump of thirty Prep School boys (the normal pre-war complement was over 200) attended classes in Mackenzie House under Miss Tullo, Miss Smith and Miss Ogilvie; and a Lilliputian Academy-in-exile of fourteen small boys started up at Tullochgribban, a country house on Speyside, under the care of Miss Hagart, Miss W. C. Mitchell (later Mrs Doyle) and Miss K. Goldingham.

It was a crisis that made all earlier crises pale by comparison. For the session 1939–40 there were only 342 pupils in all: 260 in the Upper School, 30 in the Prep, and 52 at Hartree. How on earth could the Academy, which relied entirely on the income from school fees, remain solvent at that level?

The first move was to reduce staff salaries by 10 per cent; and the Minutes record the fact that the teachers received the news 'in a most agreeable manner'. Not only that – the staff felt they could do even more to effect economies in the running of the School, and requested a meeting with representatives from the Board of Directors to air their own suggestions. Today, this list makes historic reading:

1. That a staff member should be nominated to carry out an investigation, in conjunction with the Secretary & Treasurer, of all school services with a view to working out possible economies.

2 & 3. That Prep classes be moved back to Henderson Row immediately, and the Prep School as a whole should be reopened in

January, 1940 (in the event, the air-raid shelters were quickly brought up to the standard approved by the Dean of Guild at a cost of £100, and the Prep reopened at Henderson Row on January 10).

4. That the possibility of admitting *girls* to the Prep School for the duration of the war should be considered (this was not a unanimous recommendation; Dr Wightman thought it was the Academy's public duty, as well as a possible source of income, but the Prep staff did not favour it – for one thing, the lavatory accommodation was unsuitable – and the Directors agreed that it was not a practicable idea).

5. That the Academy expenditure on Raeburn Place should cease (this was remitted for further joint consideration, when it was pointed out that it might mean that the groundsman and cricket coach there, Joe Irwin, might lose his job; Joe stayed on, in fact, and retired in 1949, twenty-five years after he came to Raeburn Place from Durham).

6. That repairs and maintenance at the School should be carried out by the School Carpentry Instructor (this was agreed).

7. That the *Chronicle* should be limited to one issue per term, instead of two, and reduced in content (this was agreed, but 'Billy' Peel made a strong plea for the school match commentaries to be kept in, because he himself had enjoyed them so much in the trenches during the last war).

8. That the Masters should pay 6d a head per day for school dinners (this was turned down by the Directors, who felt that Masters should not have to pay for meals when they had to carve and keep discipline).

9. That the Masters should pay full fees for any sons they had at the Academy, or (10) should pay two-thirds fees (the Directors declined to accept this offer, 'unless members of staff particularly wanted to').

11. That Masters who left the School should not be replaced unless the remaining staff were fully employed (agreed, if possible).

12. That a Master be appointed to undertake 'unostentatious publicity for the School, by means of photographs and notices of school activities in the Press' (this was not approved, but it was agreed that any Master could send photographs and news items 'on his own responsibility').

13. That the possibility of raising a loan among members of the staff should be considered (but the Directors did not think it advisable for members of staff to become creditors of the School under present conditions – 'it would not be a good investment!').

14. That a 'Special Class' be formed, with a duty master to supervise work set by other Masters, to stop the 'flight to the crammer' (it was

agreed that this was purely a matter for the Rector and staff to decide).

It was a generous and self-sacrificing list of suggestions, and the Directors were duly grateful, even though they felt they could not let all the sacrifices be made. The first proposal – that an elected member of staff should investigate the running of the School with a view to working out economies – was the key one; it made practical sense, and in retrospect it was a step in the direction of the kind of 'Workers' Participation' that is being urged for schools nowadays. The Directors agreed willingly, and passed the job to the man who knew more about the Academy and its finances than anyone else – their Secretary and Treasurer, R. Arthur Morrison.

Mr Morrison was himself an Academical (1902–05). He qualified as a Chartered Accountant and later became associated in business with Mr C. E. W. Macpherson, who was Clerk to the Directors and later Clerk and Treasurer of the Academy for nearly fifty years (he was also Secretary of the Academical Club for twenty-five years, from its re-constitution in 1900 until 1925). Arthur Morrison was appointed Joint Clerk and Treasurer with him in 1925, and when his partner died in 1931, Morrison became the first holder of the combined post of Secretary and Treasurer. This was the first time in the history of the Academy that the office of Secretary was salaried; from the days of John Russell, the first Secretary, to Sheriff Charles Mackintosh (E.A. 1901–7, later Lord Mackintosh and a Chairman of the Directors), the office of Secretary had always been an honorary one. Morrison remained Secretary and Treasurer of the Academy for thirty-eight years, the last seven of them with a joint S & T, C. F. Sleigh (E.A. 1944–7), who succeeded him when he retired in 1969 and who is now the Secretary and Treasurer himself.

In December, 1939, then, Arthur Morrison met the staff, who had been assured that they could see the full accounts of the School (even though in law they were only available to the Proprietors of the School), and that there was no item of expenditure which the Board would be unwilling to expose to the staff. The staff were told that the previous year's accounts showed a deficit of £1,185, and that even with a small increase of fees for the 1939–40 session the accounts for the next year might show a deficit of up to £9,000. The staff then elected from amongst their number the Investigator who would work in conjunction with Morrison; he had to be 'a very tactful man', and the very tactful man they nominated was Mr Ferguson – 'Fergie'.

After a thorough investigation of all the Departments, they agreed that the only substantial economy that could be achieved was by reducing the number of staff; the other teachers were prepared to give up their free periods to enable the School to carry on with a staff of only fifteen.

(It is really rather touching for an Academical who was a small boy in the Upper School at the time to read in the Minutes of the solidarity and self-sacrifices of the teachers in their efforts to keep the School alive during the war; and to learn too that despite the financial crisis, the Directors continued, as in the previous war, to make up the difference between the Army pay and former school salaries of masters on active service. Mr J. S. Brown (1934–45) refused to accept any money from the School, and when Mr Quick was later promoted to Captain he wrote to the Rector that he would 'no longer be a burden on school funds' and thanked the Directors for their generosity; and in March, 1942, Jack S. Carter (E.A. 1906–10, Headmaster of St John's, Leatherhead, and later Head of Blundell's), the son of a previous Rector, wrote to the Directors offering to make an annual contribution to the School under a Covenant.)

Meanwhile the Finance Committee was wrestling with the problem of how to pay the mounting bills. The Directors decided to apply to the Carnegie United Kingdom Trust for a grant, but the Trustees replied they were sorry, but assistance to educational institutions was quite outside their field of action. However, the Finance Committee had three further recommendations to make:

1. That an enquiry be made as to the possibility of a grant from Edinburgh Corporation under Section 9 of the Education (Scotland) Act, 1918: what conditions would be attached to such a grant?

2. That an appeal be made personally by individual Directors to a limited number of Academicals with the object of raising a Guarantee Fund of £10,000.

3. That the donors of Bursaries be asked whether the capital funds could be used as security to the Bank. (The committee had decided that the Centenary Fund could not be applied for general school purposes because it was raised for specific purposes.)

The second and third suggestions were not taken up by the Board, although an anonymous Academical gave a loan of £500 without interest. It was the first suggestion that seemed to offer the best hope. The chairman of the Directors, Sheriff (later Sir) Robert H. Maconochie (E.A. 1892–97), had an informal meeting with the Edinburgh Director of Education, Mr Frizell, who explained the conditions that would be attached to a grant from the Education Authority. For one thing it would mean having representatives of the Corporation sitting on the Academy's Board of Directors.

Meanwhile, on March 21, 1940, the Secretary and Treasurer reported the sombre fact that he was doubtful whether he could continue to finance the School without additional facilities. He said that he was unwilling to approach the Bank for an increase in the School's overdraft in case it simply withdrew the facilities at present enjoyed. There was only one immediate hope: the Endowment Fund Trust held £686 1s 9d 3% Local Loans Stock, and if this were realised it might just enable him to pay the bills for the current term. By next term they should know whether they were getting a grant from Edinburgh Corporation. The Directors agreed, and gave Mr Morrison the go-ahead to realise the Local Loans Stock.

It was a desperately worrying time, worse than anything the School had known even in the great financial crisis of Dr Hannah's time, away back in 1848-9. Yet very few people knew anything about the grim battle for survival apart from the Rector and the Board of Directors – Sheriff Maconochie, Sheriff Mackintosh, Sir Patrick Ford, Sir George Rainy, and Messrs W. H. Fraser (E.A. 1886-94), 'Gibbie' Hole, 'Pussy' Stuart, A. Thomson Clay (E.A. 1874-80), William Greenhill (E.A. 1874-8), K. M. Oliphant (E.A. 1891-1903), 'Beaky' Druitt, A. T. Sloan, E. C. Somner (E.A. 1893-7), and Major Noel Salvesen.

Metaphorically squaring his shoulders, Arthur Morrison (who had cheerfully accepted a 10 per cent cut in his own salary, like all the teachers) called on the manager of the Union Bank of Scotland and explained the situation, including the possibility of a grant from the Corporation. To his relief, the Bank agreed to allow the Academy to overdraw its current account to a ceiling of £8,500. This gave the Academy a little breathing space until such time as the negotiations with Edinburgh Corporation were concluded. And on July 16, 1940, Academy history was made when Councillor Stewart Lamb of Edinburgh Corporation was present at a meeting of the Directors of the Edinburgh Academy. Sheriff Maconochie welcomed him, 'and expressed the opinion that the Board was sure that the representatives of the City would be most helpful and be of great benefit to them at their Meetings'.

A historic moment indeed. What would Lord Cockburn and

Leonard Horner have thought of it? Indeed, what would Old Bailie Blackwood have thought of it, for that matter? It seems now such a very small sum for which the Academy temporarily traded the independence it had guarded so jealously for 115 years – £3,000 was the size of the grant that was eventually approved by the Scottish Education Department on March 9, 1941.

The Academy was to remain a Grant-Aided School for the next four years; and in addition to Councillor Lamb, who served on the Finance Committee, three other representatives of the Edinburgh Education Authority served on the Board – Dr Guthrie on the Finance Committee, Councillor Gilzean on the Property Committee, and Sir William McKechnie on the House Committee. It was an amicable arrangement, but a confusing situation for the Directors, who found themselves wearing different hats when attending meetings both of the Governing Bodies of Fee-Paying Grant-Aided Schools and of the Association of Independent Schools at a time when the terms of the new Education (Scotland) Bill were being considered. The brunt of this work fell on Lord Mackintosh, as he was by 1944 when the Academy withdrew from the Grant-Aided Schools committee; he explained: 'All the matters discussed were really relative to direct Grant-Aided Schools . . . While, strictly speaking, the Academy is not a Grant-Aided School, in that it does not receive a direct grant, it is indirectly a Grant-Aided School at the moment . . .'

That was how it came about that an Edinburgh Town Councillor was chairman at the annual Exhibition of the Edinburgh Academy in 1941 – a sight that would surely have made Old Bailie Blackwood turn in his grave. Councillor Stewart Lamb told the audience that the Academy had maintained for over a century the ideals of its founders, who had never intended it to be a money-making concern but a home of Classical learning. As such it had added lustre to the fame of the city of Edinburgh, and now, when it was passing through the most difficult time of its long history, the Town Council had been glad to lend it a helping hand. How long the present arrangement would last he could not foretell.

In fact, the Grant Aid continued throughout the war, on an annual basis, each payment being based on the previous year's deficit, and each one never more than £3,000. The last grant that was received was for £1,500, to cover a deficit of £1,301 for the session of 1944-5. The Directors had decided, in December, 1944, that 'while expressing the very deep gratitude of the Directors to the City for the way in which they had come to the School's assistance financially when the serious result of evacuation arose . . . it would be desirable as soon as possible for the School to return to its independent status'.

And at the 1945 Exhibition the chairman was the man who had headed the Directors through the war crisis, their own chairman, Sheriff Maconochie. He began his speech by making reference to 'the generous help which the Edinburgh Education Authority had granted to the Academy from the early years of the war, without which its survival would have been well-nigh impossible. He was glad to say that, from now on, the Academy would return to its former independence with a deep feeling of gratitude to the Local Authority and particularly to those members of its committee who had rendered invaluable service on the Board of Directors.' (*Chronicle*, December, 1945.)

The worst of the crisis was over, and the Academy could get up off its knees again.

THE ACADEMY AT WAR – II

I would rather see hands stained with earth than stained with ink or begrimed with lubricating oil.

(The Rector, 1943 Exhibition)

While the Directors struggled to keep the Academy's head above the financial waters, the Academy itself was getting on with the business of carrying on as best it could in wartime conditions. It was a strange opening to the session of 1939–40: great gaps in the Hall, where the Geits' gallery was empty; no torrent of small boys with clackens and satchels streaming through the Yards each morning and yelling their heads off during break at eleven o'clock, only a trickle of larger boys festooned with gas-masks. The classrooms on the west side were lying empty, there were a dozen familiar faces absent from the ranks of the staff. The Classical, Modern and Science sides of the School were merged into one. Later there was a 22,000-gallon water-tank in the front Yards, and the Prep Yards filled up with an assortment of engines and machines as the Edinburgh Auxiliary Fire Service moved into the School; the west classrooms, the old Prep building, and two classrooms in the main block were used as quarters for the men. The sirens sounded a few times during school hours (welcome diversion!) and the boys were all marched down into the basement shelters. That was the only sound allowed, so the splendid old school bell from Armstrong's

Foundry fell silent after 115 years. Instead of the Janitor tolling the passage of the periods every day, he went around with a wee hand-bell which was inaudible in some of the classrooms (it gave a wonderful new lease of life to the time-honoured excuse of 'Please, sir, I didn't hear the bell'). Later, some rather feeble electric bells were fitted in each entrance lobby and in the Hall, until the sonorous notes of the school bell were heard again in the summer term of 1943 when the danger of air-raids had long since ceased. The school railings were removed for scrap iron, though the gates were reprieved after 'representations' had been made. But the old piece of German artillery that used to stand near the pavilion at New Field was sent off for scrap with positive glee, in the hope that 'it might serve a more useful purpose by being returned after transformation to its former owners'. Miss McTavish started a War Savings Group that soon embraced everyone in the School, raising £973 during Edinburgh Warships Week in 1942, £3,738 for the Edinburgh 'Wings for Victory' week in 1943, and the astonishing total of £17,589 for 'Salute the Soldier' week in 1944.

The numbers stayed sadly depleted to start with, and a second wave of evacuation in 1940 dropped the Upper School numbers to 223, and 'the Bud's' morning P.T. parade in the Yards was a shadow of its former self. The Academy accepted six Austrian refugees as pupils, and later eight Poles, even though three of the refugees were enemy aliens: the Directors decided to let them stay on at school until such time as they would be old enough to be interned. What really kept hope flying for the future of the Academy was the return of the Prep to Henderson Row in January, 1940. At first there were only 30 boys, then 69 boys, then 100 boys in the 1941-2 session, then 150, then 169, until by the session of 1944-5 there were 236 in the Prep. With the number of Academy evacuees at Hartree holding steady around the 50 mark, the growth of the Prep was entirely responsible for the recovery of school numbers as the war years passed, from 342 in 1939-40 to 439 in 1942-3 to 580 in 1944-5.

During the summer holidays parties of boys worked in forestry camps at Tomich in Strathglass and harvest camps at Balnagown near Tain. At school, compulsory horticulture frequently replaced compulsory games. Sheep were put to graze on part of the sacred turf at New Field, and the eight-acre extension at the western end, right up to East Fettes Avenue, which had been bought in 1936-7 but had not yet come into use as playing-fields, was put to the plough. The Midlothian Agricultural Committee wanted to plough up another six acres, but after a meeting with the Rector and Secretary they agreed to plough up Raeburn Place instead. The Army, which had taken over Scott House, dug up the tennis lawn without permission, and the Directors made a strong protest and demanded compensation.

The Academy was really rather good at growing vegetables. The man in charge of the operation to begin with was one of the Classics masters, Mr G. W. Rowe, who had joined the staff in 1925. A formidable disciplinarian, he had had much to do with the spate of Classics scholarships to Oxford that Academy boys had been winning in the thirties. It was he who organised the armies of boys, teachers and friends who planted the Extension at New Field, until he was appointed Headmaster of John Watson's School in 1941 and 'Fergie' took over.

The crops were reported in loving detail in the *Chronicle* as the yield grew better and better each year. In the autumn of 1940 the yield was seven tons of potatoes per acre; and twice a week an equipage drawn by a spirited little pony clattered into the School Yards laden with home-grown produce for the kitchens. The potato crop was up to ten tons per acre the following year, and 14.8 tons the year after that, with the surplus stored in an empty classroom at the Academy. Congratulations were sent in from the local agricultural committee, seven hundredweight of onions and an abundance of brussel sprouts, cabbages, turnips and leeks went into the store-rooms. The Directors' meetings began to sound more like gatherings of the National Farmers' Union as the latest crop yields were noted, and the Rector reported the bumper harvest of 1941–2 with as much pride as he did a Classical Exhibition to Balliol and 3,400 books collected for the Salvage Campaign. That particular potato crop was immortalised in the Agricultural Department's 'Notes for Farmers' as 'an exceptional crop'. Surplus vegetables were sold to local shops, and free gifts were given to the Royal Navy, and to the elephant at Edinburgh Zoo.

The annual Exhibitions became simply 'closing ceremonies' with little ceremony and a reduced prize list. But the work of the School kept producing gratifying results. In the first wartime session there were four open awards won – three in Classics at Oxford and one in Natural Science at Cambridge – and another four in 1943–4 (one in Mathematics at Cambridge, one in History at Oxford, and two in Modern Subjects at Oxford). The Rector reported in 1942 that the Academy passes in the Oxford and Cambridge School Certificate examination were 95 per cent – 18 per cent above the average.

Gradually things began to come back to normal. There had been no proper Exhibition in 1940, 1941 or 1942, but in 1943 it returned to its pre-war style, with the colourful hoods and academic gowns of the staff brightening the scene and the Hall packed with parents and invited guests. Professor Sir D'Arcy Wentworth Thompson was the Guest of Honour. He recalled his schooldays of seventy years ago under his old master, Dr Clyde, and the day that his whole class spent every penny they owned taking rides on the first horse-drawn trams in Edinburgh. 'Alfie' Smith, presenting a Rector's Address at an Exhibition for the first time since 1939, had to admit that 'though on the surface the School had appeared to be running its normal smooth course, this was far from being the truth. The schoolmaster's task in wartime consisted in making day-to-day improvisations and sudden decisions, and was not the tranquil life in the midst of a world at war that the uninitiated seemed to imagine'. But – 'in spite of the many conflicting claims on the time and energy of the staff and boys, the standard of work, as shown by examination results, had never been so high. Other activities had continued to flourish, on the playing-fields, in military training, and in agriculture where our six and a half acres of various crops might be considered the most remarkable of all our recent achievements.' (*Chronicle*, December, 1943.)

Close contact with the soil, he went on, warming to his favourite theme, was beneficial to the body and mind. He would rather see hands stained with earth than stained with ink or begrimed with lubricating oil. But as well as providing the School with an abundance of fresh vegetables, the boys stained their fingers with ink to good purpose the following year, the year of the four Open Scholarships. The Dux of the School that session was Geoffrey M. Shaw, who won the Ernest R. Balfour Music Prize for singing as well as the Academical Club Prize for the best in Classics. Geoff Shaw went on to become the Rev. Geoffrey Shaw, living in a room and kitchen in Glasgow's Gorbals as a Church of Scotland social worker. He is now Labour Party Chairman of the vast new Strathclyde Region.

Dear 'Alfie' Smith! There was so much kindliness about everything he said and did, such sweetness, even – if one can use such a word about one's old Rector. In 1943 he had that most blindingly difficult, impossible task that a Headmaster is ever faced with: finding the right words to say to parents of a pupil who dies. On February 22 of that year, a boy, Gordon F. A. Philip, died as the result of an accidental knock on the head during a game of football. He was 15 years old and had been at the Academy since 1933. He was in his first year in the Classical VIIth when he died; a marvellous boy, intelligent, hard working, full of zest and enthusiasm for life, always with a big, broad smile ready to break out all over his face, which perfectly matched his nickname of 'Guffy', made up inevitably from his initials. Memory, no doubt blurred by time and circumstance, recalls the Rector pressing a sprig of rosemary into the mother's hand and murmuring a line from *Hamlet* – 'There's rosemary, that's for remembrance; pray, love, remember.' Or was it from *The Winter's Tale*? – 'For you there's rosemary and rue; these keep/Seeming and savour all the winter long' . . . In remembrance of their son, Sir Randall and Lady Philip presented to the School an endowment fund to provide a bookcase and collection of books for the special use of the VIIths, known as the Gordon Philip Collection.

As the war drew to a close, so did Lionel Smith's Rectorship; he would be 65 in 1945, and in November 1944 they started looking for a new Rector to succeed him. 'Alfie' had no wish whatsoever to retire, but the Directors had to look to the future, which they knew would be a tough one for independent schools. It was time to start a new chapter, and on February 20, 1945, out of sixty-six applications, they offered the Rectorship of the Academy to C. M. E. Seaman, assistant master at Rugby.

At his last Exhibition in 1945, Lionel Smith did not pretend to be anything but miserable at having to leave the Academy. It was, he said, the last occasion on which he would speak from that platform as, though it was usually considered inadvisable to change horses in the middle of a stream, the powers that be had decided, in spite of all the inconveniences to horses and passengers alike, that the horses must be changed at the most awkward moment possible. During the fourteen years he had spent at the Academy, he said, there had been no unnecessary changes. Nothing had been abolished, no innovations had been made. He had done his best to maintain the well-established traditions of the School. And then this man who did not like change closed his speech by saluting all Academy boys, past and present, saying that he considered himself highly privileged to have been permitted to spend fourteen years working among the best people in the world; and he ended his Rectorship with the moving quotation from *Guy Mannering*:

'And now ride e'en your ways; for these are the last words ye'll ever hear *me* speak, and this is the last reise that I'll ever cut in the bonny woods of Ellangowan.'

The *Chronicle* of December, 1945, wrote of him: 'From the day he came to us, in October, 1931, till the day he left, his one ambition was to serve the Academy and to it he devoted all his energies . . . He was a leader who relied more on example than precept, more on good deeds done by stealth than on publicity. Many a lame dog he helped over a difficult stile, and the general public often did not know that the dog was lame. Too large-minded and too well informed to be dogmatic on most matters, he was uncompromising in his hatred of any forms of injustice or bureaucratic tyranny, and would never rest till wrongs had been redressed. Such a man inspired devotion in his colleagues and affection and respect in the boys who were fortunate enough to know him well . . . We shall miss him sadly.'

No one could ever disagree with these words. He was a great man, and a great headmaster; but the judgement of history must be that he was the wrong Rector for the Academy at that particular time in its history.

The gentle, brilliant Englishman who had been a globe-trotter all his working life before he came to the Academy was now content to spend the rest of his life, with his wife Mary, in their house at 84 Inverleith Place. And a long life it was. Dr Smith, as he now was, remained a familiar figure in the purlieus of New Field, crossing the turf to go and work in his allotment on the north side of the 1st XV football pitch, near the end of Kinnear Road. Here he continued his communion with the soil, digging and hoeing his vegetables for many years; he only gave up his gardening at the age of 89 when he was blown over by an Edinburgh gale and badly bruised. He donated his allotment to the school he had loved so much – 'Smith's Piece' it's called, and it has been levelled to provide an additional playing pitch. On his 90th birthday, the Directors of the Academy honoured him by creating a new Academy scholarship bearing his name. He died on June 3, 1972, aged 91.

CHAPTER XIX

C. M. E. Seaman: The Post-War Years (1945-51)

It is in truth a high privilege to be Rector of The Edinburgh Academy.
(Mr Seaman, 1951 Exhibition)

CLARENCE MILTON EDWARD SEAMAN, known to his family and friends as 'George', was 37 years old when he came to the Academy: a short, stocky man with a bright eye, a friendly deprecating smile, and a distinctly acquiline but small nose. He came to the Academy from teaching at Bedford School and at Rugby – the school which had given the Academy two Rectors (Lyon and Smith) and which the Academy had provided with two Headmasters (former pupil Archie Tait and former Rector Hugh Lyon). Mr Seaman had been educated at Christ's Hospital, where he had won an Open Scholarship in Classics to St John's College, Oxford; there he had gained Firsts in Classical Moderations and Greats, and a Distinction in the Diploma of Education, and had played for his college at cricket and rugby.

He became Rector of the Academy in 1945 at a time when it needed to be reborn, as in Mr Mackenzie's day; when it was seriously weakened by the effects of the war and the lotus years that had preceded it. It was a hectic period, with teachers coming back from active service and boys returning from evacuation. The paraphernalia of war had only recently been dismantled – the air-raid shelters, the trenches, the baffle-walls and the big water-tank – and the firemen were gone from the Yards. School uniform regulations had been relaxed during the war, and the new Rector had to stiffen the rules and tighten discipline to get the School back to normality and prepare it for the climb back to its former greatness.

Exactly 700 boys attended school for that first post-war session under Mr Seaman: 400 in the Upper School and 300 in the Prep. Of those 300 Prep boys, 100 little boys aged from 5 to 7 made their way not to Henderson Row but to Denham Green House, near Golden-acre, the gift of the Salvesen family, which was opened by the new

Rector as a Junior Prep School on October 3, 1945. In one gratifying leap, the numbers of boys at the School were back to the pre-war heyday; but that simply created more problems than it solved. Although the number of fees received meant that the School could be run without a deficit, the number of bodies soon had Henderson Row bursting at the seams again; not even the opening of Denham Green House did much to relieve the pressure.

After a year of working in these cramped surroundings, the Rector presented a *Memorandum* to the Directors in December, 1946. By now the numbers had jumped again, to 780 (a record), and the Rector urgently warned the Directors that the Academy was beginning to fall seriously behind what was required of a modern, up-to-date school. New Science buildings were required, particularly for the teaching of biology. Lavatory accommodation would have to be increased and modernised. More classrooms and increased dining accommodation were also required – and these were just the immediate priorities. Expansion was imperative – but as the Directors pointed out, where was the room in which to expand?

Lord Mackintosh, who had recently been elevated to the bench, had now taken over from Sheriff Maconochie as chairman of the Directors; and he suggested that before considering the Rector's *Memorandum* in any detail it was necessary to decide whether or not the Henderson Row site should be abandoned and the whole School moved to a new site. His own feeling was that, apart from the financial aspect, it was not feasible to consider moving the School. It was essential for the Academy, which was first and foremost a day school, to be as nearly as possible in a central position, and it was most unlikely that another suitable site in a sufficiently central position in the city could be found. He also pointed out that new playing-fields would have to be found if the School were moved to a quite different quarter of the city. After much discussion the Directors agreed that it was not practicable to contemplate moving the School to another site; instead, it was decided that a better alternative would be to try to move the whole of the Prep School, except the two Upper Classes, to the Denham Green House site or some other site in its vicinity. This would release sufficient accommodation at Henderson Row for the developments required. An architect was consulted as to the possibility of building upwards at Henderson Row without destroying the old building, or at least without interfering with the famous classical frontage; and meanwhile priority was to be given to modernising the lavatory accommodation 'down the hill' and extending the Science buildings.

The discussions and negotiations that followed were complex and protracted, but the upshot was that the Directors decided to acquire a fifteen-acre site at Arboretum Road at Inverleith, to the east of New Field, on which to build a new Prep School. It was agreed that the only way to finance such an ambitious project (as well as the cost of modernising and developing Henderson Row) was by making an Appeal to Academicals for a £100,000 Development Fund. But Academicals were already being appealed to for funds for the Academy War Memorial, and it was 1951 before the Development Fund Appeal was launched. By that time Mr Seaman was leaving the Academy; and it was not to be until 1960 that the new Prep School at Inverleith was opened.

But it was Mr Seaman who saw the needs, made the plan, and set the wheels in motion, showing foresight and a sense of urgency in the best traditions of the Mackenzie Rectorship; Mr Seaman, however, was up against a situation that Mr Mackenzie had never had to face – post-war building restrictions, raging price rises, labour problems, and shortages of building materials. He also had the disadvantage of the Academical dynamic, which Mr Mackenzie himself had created, being channelled towards the War Memorial – restoring the playing-fields at Raeburn Place, and founding War Memorial Scholarships. The first of these was awarded the year after Mr Seaman left; but in his last year he was present at the dedication of new panels on the 1914–18 War Memorial gymnasium, commemorating the 179 Academicals who were killed in the 1939–45 war.

Having made his Mackenzian move in 1946 and shown the Directors the directions in which he thought the School should develop, Mr Seaman left them to get on with it while he got on with the difficult job of running the School as it would have to be run until funds became available. One of his problems was the comparative lack of senior pupils: only twenty of the boys in school during his first session were over 17, and only a further fifty were over 16. As a result, the early post-war XVs and XIs were severely handicapped, and fared poorly. The burden of leading the School fell on all too few shoulders – George W. Burnet, for instance (E.A. 1934–46, now the School's Law Agent and brother of the present Headmaster of the Prep), who was Head Ephor, Captain of Football, Cricket and Athletics, and gained the distinction of being awarded the Old Members' Exhibition at Lincoln College, Oxford.

In that first session, Mr Seaman instituted a major change in the system of choosing the Dux of the School. The Dux Medal had always been awarded to the top boy in the Classical VIIth. Now Mr Seaman pointed out to the Directors that the top boy in the Classical VIIth (especially when there were so few seniors) was not invariably the most able boy in the School, and that adherence to the old rule was causing dissatisfaction among the staff. The Directors agreed that in any year when it appeared that 'a flagrant injustice would be done by adhering to this system', the Rector should report to them and recommend that the title and medal be given to a boy in another department. That year, 1946, for the first time in the 122-year history of the Academy, the Dux of the School was a Science pupil – S. R. Martin (E.A. 1937–47), who was awarded an Exhibition in Natural Sciences at Trinity College, Cambridge, and is now Senior Development Engineer with a firm of Chemical Plant Constructors in London. It was a decisive break with tradition, and succeeding Duxes during Mr Seaman's Rectorship covered a variety of subjects – I. S. Wheatley in 1947 (Classics), M. Magnusson in 1948 (English), J. K. Friend in 1949 (Mathematics), N. L. Lawrie in 1950 (Mathematics), and J. J. Clyde in 1951 (Classics).

New talent was soon bursting up from the lower school as the post-war years went on – boys like J. M. Allan (E.A. 1937–50), who came into the Cricket XI in 1947 at the age of 15, won his Blue at Oxford, and went on to play for two English counties (Kent and Warwickshire) and for both the Gentlemen of England and the Gentlemen of Scotland. In all, he was capped sixty times for Scotland. On the academic front too, improvement was rapid, measured in open awards at Oxford and Cambridge: none in 1946, two in 1947 (Mathematics and Natural Sciences at Cambridge), two in 1948 (Classics and English at Oxford), five in 1949 (three Mathematics at Cambridge, one Classics and one Modern History at Oxford), one in 1950 (Mathematics at Cambridge), and four in 1951 (two Classics at Oxford, one Natural Science and one Classics at Cambridge).

Oddly enough, the numbers at the Academy could have been slightly higher after the war if certain applications had not been refused. And this raises the question – distasteful to some Academicals, no doubt, but of interest to the social historian – of whether there has ever been a colour bar at the Edinburgh Academy.

Academy boys today would laugh at any suggestion of a colour bar at their school. There was a boy at the Academy from 1880–2 called

The Preparatory School

'The clacken . . .'

'Hailes' in the Yards: Ephors *v.* Seventh (1948)

Academical Clacken-and-Ball race (1949)

Ahmed Ruza, though the *Register* gives no information about him except that he became a medical student, and he might have been any colour; but in 1929 the Directors decided not to accept an application for a boy from Sierra Leone. The Minutes of the Directors' meeting of November 5, 1929, read as follows:

'The Rector [Hugh Lyon] raised the question of the policy of the Board regarding the admission to the School of boys of coloured races. The matter arose through the application by a native of Sierra Leone for the admission of his boy to the Academy. The father was a doctor and a graduate of Edinburgh University and the Rector, who had looked into the case, was prepared on his part to admit the boy. Various members of the Board expressed the view that if there were widespread objection among parents the Board ought to respect their view. After considerable discussion it was agreed to come to no final decision on the matter at this meeting and to consider the question again at the next meeting.' On December 3, 'the question of the admission of boys of coloured races was agreed to be dropped and no further action was taken in the matter, the application which came before the last meeting having been refused.'

Late in 1944 a letter arrived from His Imperial Majesty Haile Selassie of Ethiopia stating that he wished his son and grandson to be educated in Scotland; once again the Directors 'carefully considered the matter, having in view an earlier decision against acceptance of pupils of coloured races'. In the end the Secretary was instructed to pass the word to the intermediary who had been used to approach the Academy that the School was unable to accept the two boys. It seems that the main concern in the minds of the Directors was the problem of security as much as anything else: the war was not yet ended and the boys would have represented a serious responsibility in these troubled times.

During Mr Seaman's Rectorship the question cropped up again; he asked the Directors what he should do about an application for an Anglo-Indian boy. This time the Directors had no hesitation in letting the name go on to the Enrolments Applications list for such time as he would be old enough to become a Boarder. Since then the Academy has had boys of many nations and many shades of colour; and the list of places of parental residence of Boarders from one of the Houses in the summer term of 1974 reads like a committee meeting of the United Nations – Addis Ababa, Malawi, Canary Islands, Zambia, Madrid, Miami, Oman, Guinea, Washington, New York, Gilbert and

Ellice Islands, Hong Kong, and Indonesia, as well as a Norwegian from Sierra Leone and a Pakistani from Saudi Arabia (besides such 'locals' as Dingwall, Ayr, Aberdeen, Pittenweem, Berwick-upon-Tweed, Callander and Grantham).

There were many changes on the staff front in the post-war years. When Mr Seaman left in 1951, he estimated that more than half of the staff had been appointed during his six years, and an equal number of old faces had left the Academy – men like Wightman, Lockhart, Dawson, Quick, and Mr K. H. Hagopian (1928–50), who had taught Mathematics and Science and who designed the ingenious new scoreboard at New Field. The all-important sense of Academy continuity was bolstered by 'old-timers' like Messrs Hempson, Read, Atkinson, Scott, West, Munro, Cooke, and Mr P. R. L. Heath, who came to take up a 'temporary' appointment in 1934 and retired in July 1974 as Senior Master after forty years of service. For many years he played an enthusiastic part in school games (he was an Oxford Greyhound); and in the early post-war years, when the Rector was encouraging a renewed sense of partnership between staff and senior pupils, Mr and Mrs Heath opened the eyes of many boys to the pleasures of literature and drama at meetings of the Play-Reading Society in their hospitable home. Nor will any Academy boy forget Mr Heath's uncanny skill at solving *The Times* crossword – almost, it seemed, in his head during the brief walk from the Masters' Lodge to his classroom. *The Times* crossword is very much a schoolmasterly addiction, and Mr Heath won national fame as a finalist in the Cutty Sark crossword competition. On his retirement in 1974, he was senior by twelve years to any other member of the Upper School staff, the last of the notable pre-war intake that guided the School's post-war generations.

The new faces introduced by Mr Seaman soon began to make their influence felt as the School burgeoned again after the lean years. A remarkable number of them became long-timers in their turn, and the end of the session in 1974 brought a trio of retirements: W. H. Hook, who came in 1947 and refreshed the English Department as well as reviving the Shakespearian tradition at the Academy; P. D. L. Ford, Head of the Geography Department, who came in 1949 and took over the mantle of school productions of both Shakespeare and operettas; and S. W. J. Marshall, Head of the Mathematics Department, one of Mr Seaman's last appointments in 1951. Another six of the Seaman intake are still going strong: C. A. Head, who came in 1946 to teach

French and became Head of the Modern Languages Department; P. S. MacIlwaine, who has been teaching French since 1948; J. E. King (1949) who, besides teaching English and History, has helped to build up the impressive Careers advisory service at the Academy; J. H. Bevan (1949), Head of the English Department, who came with an Oxford rugby Blue and took over as coach of the 1st XV; J. McMichael, Head of the Science Department, who first came in 1948 for a six-year spell and returned in 1957; and B. Cook (1951), who teaches Mathematics and is now the timetables expert; he took over from T. C. Edwards (1943–60), who was for many years classmaster of IB in succession to 'Fushy' Lockhart and helped generations of Geits overcome the difficulties of transition from the Prep to the Upper School, as well as coaching future stars like J. M. Allan and Tom McClung (E.A. 1930–40 and 1942–4) in cricket and football.

Two other masters of the Seaman era have left an indelible mark on the Academy. One was W. S. Fieldhouse, who joined in 1951 from King William's College, Isle of Man, as Head of the Science Department in succession to Dr Wightman. During his time at the Academy (he left in 1965), Bill Fieldhouse presided over some tremendous developments in the Science Department, and no fewer than twenty-four Open Awards were gained at Oxford and Cambridge. His was an exceptionally successful and popular reign, and he developed boys' interests far beyond the confines of the classroom with his Science 'At Homes', his research projects, and with the Field Studies Group which he helped to found. Exploring and mountaineering and 'field studies' may be said to have a long and honourable tradition at the Academy, considering that there was an Academical (John Irving) with Franklin in the North West Passage in 1845; another (Lord Francis Douglas) joined forces with Whymper for the first ascent of the Matterhorn and died on the way down, and yet another (F. M. Bailey, E.A. 1892–4) after whom the Tibetan blue poppy is named.

The other major figure of the post-war Common Room was M. H. Longson, who came in 1946 and retired in 1971. In twenty-five years with the Classical VIIth he achieved about the same number of Classical Scholarships, a tribute to his fluent and inspired teaching of 'dead' languages that were living tongues in his classroom. But quite apart from his excellence as a teacher, Michael Longson was a splendid all-round 'character' on the staff. He was a devoted cricket enthusiast and became a familiar figure behind the stumps both as keeper and umpire; a fine pianist and organist, and a splendid singer who bolstered the basses while Mr Hempson led the tenors. Apart from all that he had a most versatile and witty pen, and contributed over a hundred comic ballades to *Punch*. His affectionate nickname of 'Hoppy' – short for 'Hopalong' – was a tribute to the zest with which he threw himself into school activities despite his pronounced limp.

Some changes had to be made to try to fit in all the increased range of work as the curriculum expanded to keep pace with the times. In 1948 the whole structure of the school day was altered, to allow for seven instead of six periods with a slight reduction in the length of each period; so now the week had thirty-five periods instead of thirty. (This change was commended in the report of the Schools' Inspectors for the session 1948-9.) Mr Seaman also introduced another innovation which was less successful, however; it was a Tutorial system, whereby each member of staff became 'tutor' to about twenty boys in whom he would take a continuing personal interest – an echo, here, of the original system of one-master classes moving up through the School from start to finish. This system, which was based on the collegiate model, was only marginally successful, and it was eventually abandoned a few years ago – perhaps the only one of Mr Seaman's ideas that didn't bear fruit.

Parents, too, tended to misunderstand it – some of them assumed that it meant 'tutor' in the old sense of 'coach'. That system, which was as old as the School itself, was also coming to an end at this time. One of the last breed of private tutors employed by parents to provide extra tuition for their boys at the Academy was T. H. Corfield, who died in 1949. He taught in the Tutor's Room at the Academy for nearly fifteen years; and it is pleasant to record that in his latter years, when the number of boys being coached was decreasing rapidly, the Directors went out of their way at the Rector's recommendation to guarantee him an annual income.

On the administrative side, Mr Seaman also started the process of gearing the Academy to the modern age. In those days the Rector had to do an extraordinary number of odd jobs on his own; he had to make up his own register of enrolments, with separate lists for boarders and day-boys; he had to keep a detailed Calendar for all the multifarious activities of the School; when Academy-bound staff needed lodgings, it was the Rector who wrote round the estate agents and even interviewed potential landladies on occasion. The only administrative staff at this time was the Rector's Secretary (the only typist at the School!), an office boy, and the Rector's Clerk, who at this time was that ageless Academy fixture, Mr Kennedy. Malcolm Kennedy had started at the Academy as a 14-year-old office boy in 1912, and later became a clerk in the office of the then Clerk and Treasurer to the Directors, C. E. W. Macpherson. He had succeeded James Jamieson as Rector's Clerk in 1930, which he remained until he retired in 1965 (he died in 1973). His successor is Ronald Smith; so far, these three Clerks have between them covered eighty-one years of Academy history and eight Rectors.

Quite clearly, the Rector's 'back-room' staff needed strengthening, and in 1949 the Secretary of the Academical Club, Bruce Stenhouse (E.A. 1920–30), was appointed Administrative Assistant to the Rector. Shortly afterwards his title was changed to Registrar. One of his many duties was to edit the *Chronicle* for twelve years: his main task now is in connection with admissions, but with his profound interest in all Academy affairs, past and present, he is now also the man in charge of the school records and archives, a veritable fount of Academy information. In his spare time he had much to do with the compilation of the first of the three *Edinburgh Academy Lists* that have been published since the war, with *One Hundred Years at Raeburn Place*, and with *The Edinburgh Academical Football Club Centenary History* in 1958. For the last twenty-five years he has contributed the *Annals of the Academy* feature annually to the *Chronicle*, looking back over the history of the Academy 25, 50, 75, 100, 125 and now 150 years ago.

It was not until 1966 that the Academy saw a further extension of Mr Seaman's administrative reforms, with the appointment of a Bursar to supervise the fabric of the School (it would probably be more accurate to call the post that of Factor). The first incumbent was an Academical, Captain J. E. P. Smeall, R.N. (retd), who had been at the Academy from 1923–6. When he retired in 1973, he was succeeded by the present Bursar, Squadron-Leader E. C. Waterer, R.A.F. (retd).

At the same time, the Board of Directors was itself being reorganised. Sheriff John (later Lord) Cameron, the Dux of the School in 1917, had joined the Board, as had I. A. (later Sir Ian) Johnson-Gilbert (E.A. 1903–8), a future Lord Provost of Edinburgh; in 1949 the Board was enlarged to twenty members, and a new executive or management committee of four Directors was appointed to deliberate and decide on matters which had formerly been handled by several different committees. The new executive committee would refer matters of general policy to the Board, and report to it at a full Board meeting at the end of each term. Sheriff Cameron, newly elected Dean of the Faculty of

Advocates, was the first chairman of this streamlined committee, which was appointed just in time to deal with a serious threat to the Academy's whole existence. It cropped up, unannounced, in the Civic Survey and Advisory Plan for Edinburgh which was published in 1949 – one of the flightier Town Planning fancies to emerge since the war. The Directors were astonished and not a little alarmed to see in it that the whole of New Field and the site of the School Boarding Houses had been arbitrarily proposed for compulsory acquisition to provide a site for three new Secondary Schools and their playing-fields. The executive committee, headed by Sheriff Cameron, went straight to see the Town Planning Officer; and Cameron was soon reporting to the Directors that the Planning Officer clearly had no idea whatsoever of the status of the Academy, of its constitution, or of its financial structure. He had, for example, airily suggested that the Academy might be moved to somewhere on the outskirts of the city; when he was asked if he had considered what the approximate cost of such a move would be, he had replied, equally airily, 'Probably a quarter of a million.' When questioned as to how this was to be financed, the Town Planning Officer had replied, 'By grant, or from the School's own resources.' It was also quite definite that the Town Planning Officer regarded it as essential that rate-provided schools should have priority in every way, including the provision of playing-fields. It was pointed out to him that in the case of a day school such as the Academy it was absolutely essential that the playing-fields should be easily accessible to the school.

The Directors decided to make the strongest possible protest to the Town Council, and girded themselves for the battle to save the Academy. Individual members of the Board took it upon themselves to lobby Town Councillors and drop discreet words in the right ears in St Andrew's House. Academicals were alerted and mobilised by the publication in the *Chronicle* (January, 1950) of a brisk exchange of letters between the Academy Secretary, Arthur Morrison, and the then Lord Provost, Sir Andrew Murray: 'If the proposals of the Advisory Plan were to be carried out, the Directors feel that the only result would be the extinction of the School permanently and, in these circumstances, unless any alternative suitable proposals can be suggested, they must continue their opposition by every means in their power.' The Lord Provost back-pedalled rapidly, agreeing that the Directors were quite right to resist the Plan, and hinting that the Town Council did not intend to accept it in its entirety, anyway. In the event, after further representations to the Town Planning Committee, the proposal to expropriate New Field was dropped (as was most of the Plan itself), and the danger to the Academy was averted.

However, this faintly ludicrous episode had highlighted the fact that something drastic would have to be done to cure the problem of accommodation at the Academy. The Rector was growing impatient to see some action over the development plan he had presented for discussion after his first session, and in 1950 he sent the Directors another *Memorandum*, emphasising that 'the School cannot contract – it must follow the ideals of Rector Mackenzie'. It was a reminder that very little had been done to implement the plan apart from re-equipping the Biology lab, which came into use that session. The executive committee asked the Board to give them a direction for formulating a scheme of development based on the lines of the Rector's new Memorandum. It was agreed that there should be a fund-raising campaign, and that it should start with a preliminary article in the *Chronicle* (May, 1950) as a shot across the bows, or purses, of the 'sole benefactors of the Academy' – the Academicals. School fees had recently been 'very substantially raised' (the start of the post-war spiral of rising prices and rising fees), and it was felt necessary to explain in detail precisely what was involved in running a school and why a major appeal for capital funds would shortly become necessary. There was still a widespread misapprehension that the Academy was 'well endowed' – a misunderstanding fostered by the occasional news of generous benefactions to endow scholarships, like the Close Scholarship to University College, Oxford, that had recently been endowed in memory of K. D. Thomson (E.A. 1892–1905, killed in action in 1916) by legacies of £3,000 each from two of his sisters. The *Chronicle* article, entitled 'The Finance of a School', was intended to clarify the position once and for all:

'The Academy has never been a rich school . . . It has very little in the way of endowment, and has to live from year to year almost entirely on the income which it draws from the fees of its pupils – a position which is at once precarious (as the experience which the School went through in the autumn of 1939 only too vividly demonstrated) and which makes it all the more necessary that the educational facilities offered at the Academy are kept well up to standard . . . The Academy must go forward with the times if it is to survive as a leading school, and it is only as such that it is worth while carrying it on on an independent basis. To go forward means development and extension, and that costs money. To find the necessary money, resort must be had to the Academy's one real source of wealth – the goodwill and loyal support of its sons. Now that the need is known – and it is both real and urgent – Academicals the world over will rally to the side of their old school. *Floruit florebit usque* must never be allowed to become an empty boast.'

Once more, Mr Seaman had got things moving. By July, 1950, the Directors were negotiating for ground at Inverleith and had decided to appoint an Appeal Committee. But there was still the War Memorial Appeal to clear out of the way; by 1950 it stood at £28,000, and would shortly have achieved its object in raising the funds required. But the situation at the School was becoming desperate; the numbers were at an all-time record of 831, and even with Denham Green House now equipped with an extra wing with recreation and dining-rooms, Mr Seaman was still having to cram 731 boys into Henderson Row. So in October, 1950, he sent a third Memorandum to the Directors, entitled *Time and the Academy*, arguing that there was simply not enough time in the school day to do everything that had to be done, with the accommodation and staff available. The executive committee, having considered the Memorandum, reported to the Board that they were convinced that drastic action would have to be taken to extend the time available for school; this would involve a reduction in the time available for games, and also the introduction of Saturday morning school for the first time since it was abolished a century earlier in 1851. (It never came to that, mercifully; for one thing, it would have severely limited the calendar of cricket and football matches against other schools which might not wish to play on Saturday afternoons.) But the real import of the Memorandum was to point up the difficulties of running a first-class school at all under existing conditions, and adding urgency to the preparation of a Development Plan. The Directors had obtained a five-year lease, with an option to purchase, of the ground at Arboretum Road on which they hoped to build a new Prep School and were beginning to plan the Appeal; and they had agreed to make it clear that if a sufficient sum was not raised to make building possible, the money would be used as a Capital Endowment Fund, and the site could be used for additional playing-fields. And at the 1951 Exhibition, the Chairman of the Directors, Lord Mackintosh, announced that an Appeal would be launched that autumn.

But Mr Seaman, the man who had striven so hard to get the School off its knees and get the Development Plan off the ground, would not be there to see it come to fruition. In October, 1950, he had informed the Directors that he had been asked to apply for another Headmastership, but had not yet decided whether to do so. Mr Seaman had been appointed in 1945 on the understanding that, as the Minutes put it, 'if he were offered the post, he would not consider that he was fulfilling his duty, either to the School or to himself, unless he continued as Rector for a period of at least ten years'. Nevertheless, Lord Mackintosh pointed out that there had been 'no legal undertaking sought or given' as to the duration of his Rectorship, and Mr Seaman must do exactly what he thought right. A few months later, in January, 1951, Mr Seaman informed the Directors that he was resigning to become Headmaster of Bedford School; and the Directors, as a long line of their predecessors had done since the day Rector Williams had announced that he was off to London, bravely accepted the resignation, expressed their cordial thanks for services rendered, and appointed a Selection Committee to find a new Rector.

As for Mr Seaman, the *Chronicle* accurately summed up the reaction to his resignation: 'No greater tribute could have been paid to him than the consternation felt, shown and freely expressed when his appointment to the Headmastership of Bedford was announced. We have lost an outstanding Rector, and one who has sown seeds that will bear good fruit after he has gone.'

He brought the Academy out of its wartime difficulties and increased the numbers by well over a hundred. He brought a civilising influence to replace the austere grind of wartime schooldays, by reviving suspended traditions like the Sunday services in the Hall, and 'Parents' Evenings' – a more intimate version of the pre-war 'At Homes', welcomed by both staff and parents as a pleasant and informal way of getting to know each other.

And he took a Mackenzian interest in the music of the School, which throve and blossomed during his Rectorship under Mr Robert Howells, who was appointed part-time Organist and Choirmaster in 1945 (he stayed until 1958), with his wife in charge of the embryo school orchestra. In no time at all, the number of pupils taking music was soaring. It was in those early post-war years that the foundations were laid for the spectacular achievements of Academy music today, under the present Director of Music, Mr Brian Head, with no fewer than four orchestras and a dance band, and a choir that can boast of having recorded Handel's *Messiah* and Benjamin Britten's *The Golden Vanity*. Perhaps the most interesting feature of the musical development at the Academy during Mr Seaman's Rectorship was the way in which the boys themselves took it over. In his last year, the Divisional Music Competitions were started and run by the Dux of 1951, James Clyde (the third of the Clyde dynasty to win the Medal), and the Head Ephor of 1951, Charles D. L. Clark (E.A. 1939–52), now an eminent publisher in London. At his last Exhibition, Mr Seaman described the concert which followed that year's Divisional Music Competition (prepared and presented entirely by the boys themselves) as 'the most interesting and exciting musical event' of his six years at the Academy: 'It does seem to me that when upwards of seventy boys give up their time – and in some cases very much time – for so good and so musical an enterprise, a very important process is at work. We have in the Academy a growing enthusiasm for music which I hope it will never be possible to make light of.'

As for the outdoor activities of the School, he confessed that he had always thought it his duty 'to resist an exaggerated emphasis on games, if it appeared; and in particular a tendency to "cry havoc" if a season was unsuccessful. But to make a last avowal, I admit that a great part of the enjoyment I have had has been on New Field, watching the exciting struggles of our teams with a partisan fervour I have done my best but failed to cloak.'

During his six years at the Academy, Mr Seaman had noted the success of Academicals in amazingly varied walks of life. Sir Thomas Innes of Learney (E.A. 1906–10) was the Lord Lyon King of Arms, and James Monteith Grant (E.A. 1910–21) was Carrick Pursuivant of Arms (he in turn became Lyon King of Arms himself). Two Academicals were Heads of Oxford Colleges – Keith Murray (E.A. 1908–21, later Lord Murray of Newhaven) at Lincoln and W. F. R. Hardie (E.A. 1911–20) at Corpus Christi. R. P. (later Sir Ronald) Morison was Dean of the Faculty of Advocates. Five Academicals were Members of Parliament after the 1945 election – Lt.-Cmdr. (later Sir) G. I. Clark Hutchison (E.A. 1909–16), as a Unionist for Edinburgh West; Major N. M. S. Macpherson (E.A. 1914–21, later Lord Drumalbyn) as a National Liberal for Dumfries; Major (later Sir) Basil Neven-Spence (E.A. 1897–1906) as a Unionist for Orkney and Shetland; J. S. C. Reid, K.C. (E.A. 1899–1908, later Lord Reid of Drem, a Lord of Appeal) as a Unionist for Glasgow Hillhead; and Sir J. Douglas W. Thomson (E.A. 1912–17) as a Unionist for Aberdeen South. They were joined in the Commons in 1950 by J. L. M. (later Lord) Clyde as Conservative Member for Edinburgh North, and A. J. (now Sir Arthur)

Irvine (E.A. 1919–26) as Labour Member for Liverpool Edgehill.

In the Army there were six Academicals of General rank on the active list – General Sir Alan Cunningham (E.A. 1897–99), General Sir Roy Bucher (E.A. 1905–13), who was the last C.-in-C. of the Indian Army, General Sir Gerald Templer (E.A. 1905–9), who became Chief of the Imperial General Staff, Major-General (later Sir) Kenneth G. McLean (E.A. 1906–15), Major-General J. E. C. McCandlish (E.A. 1910–12), and General Sir Philip Christison (E.A. 1902–12), G.O.C. Scottish Command and Governor of Edinburgh Castle.

In the Arts, W. M. Caverhill (1925–7) was receiving rave notices under his better-known name of Alan Melville for his songs and lyrics in London revues like 'Sweet and Low', 'Sweeter and Lower' and 'Sweetest and Lowest'. Gerald F. Shaw (E.A. 1924–5), who had made a great hit with his piano-playing at school concerts, was making a reputation as a cinema organist (he was latterly organist at the Odeon, Leicester Square, before his death in 1974). Kenneth Ireland (E.A. 1927–38) was pioneering in the Highlands as General Manager of the Pitlochry Festival Theatre. Harry Watt (E.A. 1920–5) directed the Australian film *The Overlanders*. Denis Peploe (E.A. 1920–31) was holding one-man art shows in Edinburgh to much critical acclaim. Bruce Marshall (E.A. 1906–9) published *The Red Danube* and *Every Man a Penny*, and D. R. Weir (E.A. 1922–8) published a Middle Eastern political thriller called *Red Flows the Barada*. I. S. Jehu (E.A. 1915–26) was Editor of *The Times of India*. Bruce Seton (E.A. 1920–7), the fencing champion, played Sergeant Odd in the film of *Whisky Galore*, and Donald Watson (E.A. 1932–7) held an exhibition of a hundred water-colours of Scottish Birds and Landscapes. David Cleghorn Thomson (E.A. 1907–17), formerly Scottish Regional Director of the BBC, was advising Rank on film-making and publishing slim volumes of poetry. George Waterston (E.A. 1918–29) bought Fair Isle and set up a bird observatory there.

Academicals were Convener of the National Mod of An Comunn Gaidhealach, President of the Bombay Chamber of Commerce, Director of Veterinary Services in the Gold Coast, Provost of Brechin, Stationmaster at Colne (London Midland Region), and President of the Glasgow Society of Sons of Ministers of the Church of Scotland.

And at the Commemoration of the War Memorial in May, 1951, which was organised by Mr Seaman, the opening hymn was 'Unto the Hills' in the version of the 121st Psalm by the Marquis of Lorne, the prayer was said by the Rev. Ian R. Gillan (E.A. 1898–1909), the address spoken by the Rev. Ronald Selby Wright (E.A. 1915–21, later to be a Moderator of the General Assembly of the Church of Scotland), and the lesson read by General Sir Alan Cunningham, deputising for his brother Viscount Cunningham.

'It is in truth a high privilege to be the Rector of the Edinburgh Academy,' said Mr Seaman in his farewell speech at the Exhibition later that summer. 'We have our problems – I shall not list them. I shall say rather that for those who will take what is offered, this school provides opportunity of education second to none. He is indeed fortunate who is Rector of it.' And he wished success to the 'fortunate man' who was to follow him into the Rectorship, Mr Robert Cameron Watt – 'a friend and former colleague [at Rugby], whom I have long admired and respected.'

Lord Mackintosh, the Chairman of the Directors, returned the compliment in full:

'In our School, unlike some other types of school, the Rector is not simply a head or leading master but is in the true etymological sense of the word the *Ruler* of the school – the Guider or Regulator of its educational policy . . . We soon realised that we had in Mr Seaman a Rector who had both vision to see the lines upon which our School should develop in the changing circumstances of our time and the courage and strength of mind to meet and try to overcome the many obstacles and difficulties which beset educationalists in all these rather bewildering post-war years . . . We were profoundly impressed with the masterly and almost uncanny way in which he managed to evaluate the strong and weaker features of our School and point the way to the improvement and strengthening of the latter . . .'

And so 'George' Seaman went off to be Headmaster of Bedford School, where he had once been on the teaching staff. He was the second Academy Rector to go there (Reginald Carter was the first, in 1910). He stayed there only four years, until he was appointed Headmaster of his own old school, Christ's Hospital, in 1955. He retired in 1970 and now lives near Oxford.

He had hardly left the Academy before the School launched the great Appeal that was to dominate the Rectorship of his successor, and published a book to record a hundred years of Academy history at Raeburn Place since the day it was all started by that unathletic Rector, Dr Hannah, in 1854 . . .

CHAPTER XX

R. C. Watt (1951-62): Years of Appeal

Except the gratitude of its pupils, it has nothing else to depend upon. Its founders are passing away, and in a very few years the place shall know none of them. It has no funds. Paying no interest, the heirs of even its solvent contributors cease to care for it. Its tone of manner and of education, superior to those of all other Scotch Schools, tho' it secures the admiration of the wise, impairs its vulgar popularity. Thus, it stands alone, supported by its own merits and by the recollections of worthy pupils; of these two, the last is the best.

(Lord Cockburn, Letter dated February 25, 1847)

LORD COCKBURN's letter to a young Academical, J. M. Morison, in 1847, which came to light a century later, is a marvellously concise and pungent statement of the Academy's position; and it was particularly appropriate at the time it was sent to the Directors in 1947 by the doctor in Liverpool who had come upon it. In December, 1951, another letter was read out at a Board meeting which must have gladdened the hearts of the Directors and the new Rector of the Academy, Mr Robert Cameron Watt. It came from Dr D. W. MacLean (E.A. 1932-9 and 1941-3), who had been assisted by a bursary for four years after his father's death while he was studying medicine at Edinburgh University. Now that he had qualified and was in practice, he and his mother were writing to say that they wished to repay the amount he had received: he would like it to be a thank-offering to the Development Fund.

It was a cheering and encouraging start to Mr Watt's Rectorship, this timely evidence of 'the gratitude of its pupils', because on the gratitude and recollections of thousands of worthy former pupils of the Academy was going to depend much of what would happen during Mr Watt's tenure of office, and indeed the whole future of the School; and the business of jogging that gratitude, harnessing it, and making it work effectively for the development of the Academy dominated the reign of the twelfth Rector.

The Development Fund Appeal to which young Dr MacLean had responded with such immediate warmth was being launched when the new Rector arrived in October, 1951. Like his predecessor he came from Rugby, where he was Head of the History Department and a Housemaster. He was an older man than George Seaman (he was 53 when he came to the Academy); he had taught History at Clifton College, and for two years before that he had been a lecturer in History at Queen's University, Kingston, Ontario (he had gone to Canada after serving as a lieutenant in the First World War).

Rob Watt was born in 1898, the son of the Rev. J. Gordon Watt of the Congregational Church, Secretary of the British and Foreign Bible Society. He won a scholarship from the Royal High School in Edinburgh to Fettes, where he became Head of the School. From there he won an Open Scholarship in Classics to Oriel College, Oxford, where he gained a First in Classical Moderations and a First in the Final Modern History School, and played rugby for the University XV. He was married to the daughter of the Bishop of Ontario, he had three sons, and he had always felt Edinburgh to be his home.

So here he was, back home, an Old Fettesian in charge of his former friendly rivals, at a time when the Academy was launching a life-or-death Appeal addressed 'to Academicals and others who love and are in the debt of the Edinburgh Academy':

> *This is an appeal for the resources by which a vital step may be taken to retain for the Academy its rightful place among the schools of Edinburgh and of Scotland . . . It is an appeal for a sum of money not less than £100,000.*

The Chairman of the Directors, Lord Mackintosh, had adumbrated the Appeal in his speech at the Exhibition on July 31, 1951 (a fact which miffed some Academicals who resented reading about it in the newspapers before they had been informed of it directly). When it arrived officially through Academical letter-boxes, it presented the aims and ideals that had been outlined by Mr Seaman early in his Rectorship. It explained that apart from sums earmarked for bursaries and scholarships, the whole of the Academy's endowments amounted to no more than £1,000. Because of this stark lack of financial resources, the Academy's fees (which had just been raised to £84 a year in the Upper Classes to cover a recent rise in salaries) were higher than at any Scottish day school. To reduce them by an average of £20 a year per pupil would require an endowment of £400,000!

Without any endowment at all, the Academy had to depend solely on its fees for its working expenses: the more boys, the more income; the older the boys, the higher the fees; and on the oldest boys, over 17 and 18, depended 'the management of the School and its reputation in different fields'. In October, 1950, the Academy had only 286 boys over 13, compared with 370 at Fettes, 660 at Rugby, and 390 at Sedbergh. There were only forty-four boys over the age of 17 at the Academy, and only nine over the age of 18, and educating them was a costly job. The thirty-five boys in the VIIth Class absorbed 'the equivalent of the complete teaching time of four masters'. Each of the groups taught could, if enough boys were available, be doubled without loss of teaching efficiency.

But where were those boys to be accommodated? It was ironical that the Prep School, which had been started in Dr Harvey's time to provide a nucleus of boys for the Upper School, was now crowding the Upper School out:

'The Academy needs these boys, but they are strangling it. They have invaded the classrooms of the Upper School; they have invaded the Upper School Yards. The Henderson Row site, which never between 1830 and 1908 contained as many as 500 boys at one time, now bursts from all its seams with the pressure of more than 700 . . . Those times when the Prep are in the Yards and the Upper School in their classrooms, or the Upper School in the Yards and the Prep in their classrooms, each party at play is disturbing, even deafening, the party at work.'

Because of the presence of the Prep boys there was no space to re-organise and re-equip the Upper School at a time when 'the material needs of an efficient school have multiplied'. Not much more had been needed in 1824 than some masters, some boys, and some classrooms; since then the conception of education had been transformed. The Academy had added a Gymnasium, Science Laboratories, a Wood Workshop and a Library. But the well-equipped school of 1950 needed much more than that – Geography and Mathematics specialist rooms, an Art Room 'that our status and needs demand', and better facilities for music – 'not only because Inspectors and Education Departments look for them, but much more because no education that lacks them can be satisfying to us.'

The conclusion was inevitable. The Prep School must be moved to another site. When an adequate Development Fund had been established, the Directors intended to build a Senior Preparatory School for 300 to 350 boys and move into it not only the Prep boys at Henderson Row but also the two lowest classes of the Upper School, leaving the Junior Preparatory Department in its present quarters at Denham

Green House. Then the Directors would get on with the job of modernising the Upper School.

But first must come the funds. Was £100,000 a large sum to expect? No, said the Directors, not if the object is 'the maintenance, the fortification for the future of a long-beloved institution'. Eton College, they pointed out, was in the process of launching an Appeal for £1,000,000.

There were at this time 2,000 members of the Academical Club, and perhaps as many as 3,500 Academicals altogether who might want to help: 'The Directors consider that it is not optimistic to hope that, out of this number, 300 will be able and willing to give, under a covenant scheme, a sum of £25 a year for seven years. This, together with a few larger donations, and many small ones, will enable the target to be reached.'

In fact it was eight years before the target was reached. Nearly £43,000 came in in the first year, and £50,000 was reached by the end of the second (November, 1953). By then the steam had gone out of it, and it crawled slowly to £66,000 by 1956. During this time, however, 'Fushy' Lockhart, the organising genius of the school time-tables, had come out of retirement to act as Organiser of the Appeal and inject new life into it. Mr Lockhart arranged an intricate network of Academicals who were each deputed to make a personal approach to ten fellow-Academicals, and organised a 'second subscription' drive on those who 'might not perhaps have given as substantial a contribution as might be expected'; and gradually the Appeal, which seemed on the point of grinding to a halt, took on fresh impetus; the original list of nearly 600 covenants and nearly 800 donations was buttressed by 160 second covenants or donations, and in December, 1959, the Development Fund broke through the magic £100,000 barrier. Considering that fund-raising in those days was not the highly sophisticated professional operation it is nowadays, and that all those involved in it did everything in their spare time, without any reward, it is really rather remarkable that the target was ever achieved at all, thereby confounding the pessimists who had not believed it possible.

Unfortunately, in the intervening eight years, costs had been rising at roughly the same pace as the Fund. The original plan for the Prep had to be trimmed and trimmed again, just as Mr Burn's original plan for the Academy itself had had to be trimmed. By the time the new Prep School was ready to be opened on its 13½-acre site at Inverleith, it was considerably smaller than had been envisaged, and there was no room to accommodate even the Geits from Henderson Row. By the

Royal Visit, July 5 1974

Her Majesty the Queen with the Rector, Dr. H. H. Mills

The Edinburgh Academy — 150 years old

time an additional wing had been completed at Inverleith in 1965, with extra classrooms to take boys for an additional year, a house for the Headmaster of the Prep and two houses for other masters, the total cost of the whole project had risen to around £176,000 – with the modernisation of Henderson Row still to come. So the Appeal for funds continued.

But by then Mr Watt, who had put up stoically with the overcrowding and lack of facilities, who had had to live with the Appeal night and day for eleven years, who had whipped up support for the Appeal and pinned the Academy's hopes on the Appeal, had retired.

SPORTING ANNALS: PLAY UP, PLAY UP!

> *'Then strip, lads, and to it, though sharp be the weather,*
> *And if, by mischance, you should happen to fall,*
> *There are worse things in life than a tumble in heather,*
> *And Life is itself but a game of football.'*
>
> (Sir Walter Scott)

Ageing Academicals tend to think that the School is going to the dogs all the time; but especially if the School is not doing particularly well at games. Victories on the field are what they want, to a degree probably unsurpassed in other Scottish day-schools (perhaps it is because the Academy has always had to measure itself against the strength of the great boarding-schools like Merchiston, Loretto and Fettes, which has conversely given it a great advantage over day-schools in the West of Scotland).

In the fifties, these unsuppressed yearnings for sporting glory were given free rein, when two historic landmarks were celebrated with much pomp and ceremony and back-slapping – the Centenary of Raeburn Place and the Academical Cricket Club in 1954, and the Centenary of the Academical Football Club and the annual Academy Games in 1957–8: the oldest Old Boys' Cricket Club in Scotland, and one of the oldest Football Clubs in the world.

The 1954 celebrations included an entire week of cricket matches in July, culminating in a magnificent two-day encounter between the Academical XI and the M.C.C. which ended in a thrilling draw: despite a hurricane 90 runs in 105 minutes from B. G. W. Atkinson, the Accies failed by 14 runs to overhaul the M.C.C. total before stumps were drawn.

There was a star-studded Centenary Dinner in the Music Hall in

Edinburgh, attended by 323 Academicals and guests, including what Ben Tod in his speech called 'a smattering of Headmasters'. That day too saw the publication of a short history of the Field, *One Hundred Years at Raeburn Place*; a free copy was given to every member of the Academical Club and to every boy at the Academy, to every player in the Centenary Week matches, and to every guest at the Dinner ('By so doing, not only was each guest provided with a pleasant memento of the occasion, but it also relieved the speakers of the necessity of overloading their speeches with a mass of historical detail,' according to the *Chronicle*, December, 1954). From then on, if the runs ever came slowly or the master wasn't looking, it was possible to browse through the remarkable record of prowess and performance at Raeburn Place since the founders of the Academy had promised in their first Prospectus 'ample space for playground'.

All that *they* had envisaged was an enclosed space, buttressed or unbuttressed, surrounding the main school building – the Yards. And for the first thirty years the Yards were all in the way of a playing-field that Academy boys knew, apart from those cricket matches on Brunts-field Links and the Meadows, and occasional sessions at the only cricket ground in town, the old Grange Club field in Grove Street where Academy boys would pay tuppence each to the Grange pro-fessional, 'Old Sparks', and were coached by William Moncreiff, one of the founders of the Grange Cricket Club and its captain from 1838–62, who had been a member of Mr Ferguson's Class the day the Academy opened. When the Field at Raeburn Place was opened in May, 1854, it was the first real school playing-field of its kind in Scotland, initiated by, of all people, Dr Hannah – 'this serious scholar . . . with no love for the ordinary games and active pursuits in which most boys delight', as the Raeburn Place History put it. And at the Centenary Dinner it was Dr Hannah's great-grandson, the Rev. John M. C. Hannah, Rector of St John's, Selkirk, who said Grace.

The Raeburn Place History recalled the delight of Lord Kingsburgh, who left the Academy in 1852, when he returned in 1858 from studying abroad to find 'my old school, the Edinburgh Academy, in possession of a splendid cricket field, and the boys turned out in white flannels. Matches were regularly played, and the Academy eleven went often long journeys by rail to contend with other schools at games. Such a thing was unheard of in my boy days. I think I can hear my father, if such a proposal had been made for his sanction, and the producing of the necessary railway fare, say in decisive tones: "The match of that for absurdity I never heard." '

He also described the changing accommodation available for the Academical Football Club, of which he was one of the original members when it started in 1857–8: 'We had not much luxury. A small loft over an outhouse in the garden of a villa in the corner of the field, approached by a wooden ladder . . . was our only pavilion. We played in old clothes of any sort, and coming off the ground we had no basins and no lockers. We used to sit and chat until it was dark enough to go home without observation.'

One Hundred Years at Raeburn Place and the Centenary Dinner brought it all vividly to life; and there were cheers for 'Gibbie' Hole, President of the Academical Cricket Club, who had been playing at Raeburn Place for sixty-five years, and for O. St J. Gebbie, a member of the Academy XV of 1896–7, who had travelled all the way from Buenos Aires to attend the Dinner.

It was the same story three years later at the Academical Football Club Centenary. There was a match on October 26, 1957, between the Accies and an International XV of veterans, which the Accies eventually won by 24–10; there were 5,000 spectators, and a special Football Club Centenary Flag. There was a Centenary Dinner in the Assembly Rooms and Music Hall that evening, attended by 468 members and guests; the flowers and menu cards were all in blue and white, and the place of honour behind the top table was given to the Kingsburgh Cup.

There were representatives of the seven clubs, including the Academicals, who had provided the entire Scottish XX (as it was in those days) in that first International against England at Raeburn Place in 1871, and glasses were raised to the memory of the Academy boys who had started it all, in particular Francis Crombie, who came to the Academy from Durham in 1854 at the age of 16 and became the first recorded Captain of Football. His brother Alexander (an Accie by association) was the first captain of the Academical Football Club in 1857–8. Dr Almond of Loretto is quoted as saying, 'So far as I know, Rugby football was introduced into Scotland in 1855 by a small knot of men connected with the Edinburgh Academy. Mr Alexander Crombie, of Thornton Castle, may fairly be said to be the father of the game in Scotland, for he was the chairman and organiser of the club. The hon. secretary was William Blackwood, the well-known publisher.' In fact, as *The Edinburgh Academical Football Club Centenary*

History pointed out, the actual Academical Football Club, the oldest football club playing under either Rugby or Association rules in Scotland, held its first Annual General Meeting in January, 1858.

Not long after the first A.G.M. of the Academical Football Club, on April 30, 1858, Raeburn Place staged 'The Academical Cricket Club Foot-Races': according to the *Edinburgh Evening Courant*, 'the first of its kind that have been held in connection with a public school in Scotland'. There were fourteen events, eight for the boys and six for Academicals. The Academy Games, as they are now called, have had the longest unbroken record of all the annual sporting events associated with the Academy; they have been held every year since 1858, though sometimes they have had to be postponed, as they were in the Centenary Year, from the traditional inclement date in March until the summer term. Another 'first' for Academy athletics was the annual Merchiston match, the first inter-school match in Scotland, which was held in 1922. It continued as a regular fixture for forty-nine years, but after 1970 it 'had unfortunately to be discontinued because of the changes in arrangements for athletics at Merchiston', as the *Chronicle* put it.

The boys' events at the first Games were the 100 yards, Mile, Hurdles, High Jump, Long Leap, and Throwing the Cricket Ball (for which the impressive record of W. M. Wallace, 105 yards 6½ inches, set in 1912, still stands); there were also the 100 yards and quarter-mile open to boys under five feet in height. In 1867 the Cricket Club Committee laid it down that the costume worn by competitors must meet with their approval, and it was customary to wear long trousers tucked into socks, or knickerbockers with stockings; but in 1872 at the Inter-Scholastic Games (held at Raeburn Place between 1866 and 1873), a daring boy from the High School appeared in shorts and socks. He ran in the open quarter-mile and won it, and though there was some talk of an appeal against him for wearing an illegal costume, from that time onwards 'the more rational dress was tacitly allowed' (H. B. Tristram, *Loretto School*).

But athletics have always been the poor relations on the Academy playing-fields. Since the days of Dr Hodson it was cricket and football that were the important items in Rector's *Reports*, as the tally of Academicals who won international caps mounted triumphantly (the latest score is eighty-five who played rugby for Scotland, five who played rugby for England, and thirty-eight who played 'representative' cricket matches for Scotland). The names of the great players are better known than the Duxes of the School – T. R. Marshall (E.A. 1860–7), who played in the first rugby International in 1871 against England, and later played cricket for the M.C.C. at Lord's; the extraordinarily versatile L. M. Balfour-Melville, who was captain of the Academy XX in 1871 and was only prevented by illness from becoming the first schoolboy to play in an International (he got his cap the following year, and numerous cricket caps thereafter); the magnificent Harry J. Stevenson, captain of both the school XV and the XI in 1885, who won fifteen rugby caps and even more cricket caps; Gerry Crole (E.A. 1899–1912), another double International, who played in the school XI for five years; Ben Tod, that prince of games-players in the Academy teams of the twenties; R. B. Bruce Lockhart, who captained both the school XV and the XI in an unbeaten season in the thirties and played rugby and cricket for Scotland; S. H. Cosh (E.A. 1930–8), captain of the school XI for two years and the Scottish XI thereafter; W. I. D. Elliot (E.A. 1936–9), the most capped rugby Academical of them all, with twenty-nine games for Scotland.

Athletics had none of this kind of glamour, despite the glittering presence of the magnificent silver Burma Cup, held aloft by three elephants on an ebony stand (it was presented in 1909 by Academicals in Burma for the best all-round athlete of the Games). It was only when athletics was reorganised under Mr Brian Cook as Athletics Master in the fifties, and later became an optional Summer term activity, with proper coaching and facilities at the Arboretum Field at Inverleith, that standards began to rise; by the sixties, the Academy athletics organisation was able to cope with the spectacular advent of David Jenkins, who ran the 440 yards in 1968 in 52.6 seconds as a 15-year-old to break the school record. In 1969 he ran the 400 metres in 51.4, and in 1970 he ran the 400 metres in the astonishing time for a schoolboy of 46.9, the 800 metres twice in under 2 minutes, the 200 metres in 21.1, and the 100 metres in 10.6. The Academy had found an athletics star who would not be playing second fiddle to football or cricket.

By 1971 the Rector, Dr Mills, was reporting 'a record year in games', in that Academy boys had been selected at International level in three major sports – rugby, cricket and athletics: C. R. M. Hook and A. C. Kinghorn, captain and vice-captain of the XV, for the Scottish Schools XV; A. V. S. Chedburn for the Scottish Schools Athletics team (800 metres); and R. G. Cosh (the son of S. H. Cosh) for the Rest v. Southern Schools at Lord's. (Academicals represented Scotland at the senior level in all three of these sports that year too.)

The early seventies, indeed, were vintage years for Academy sport. In 1972 the XI became the first undefeated team for twenty-two years, since J. M. Allan's XI of 1950. The XV won twelve and lost three, and next year only lost one game, while the XI was undefeated in School matches for the second year running. The Hockey XI was also undefeated, and the Academy Cross-Country team won the Scottish Schools Cross-Country Championships (a far cry from the days of those dreary runs 'round Fettes' or 'to Davidson's Mains and back' as a penalty for bad weather). Meanwhile the Athletics team was covering itself with glory as well: Chedburn's fine team of 1972 won all its seven School matches. David Jenkins had gone on to greater things, but by this time his younger brother, Roger Jenkins, was running the 100 metres in 10.1 seconds, as a 15-year-old; and the *Chronicle* noted, 'He is faster than David at this age, but is also much stronger.'

Athletics – the original Games of the Edinburgh Academy – had come out of the cold and the rain with a vengeance, to help to make the seventies the outstanding decade so far in the 150-year annals of sport at the Academy.

THE FIFTIES: YEARS OF ACHIEVEMENT

Whereas my predecessors were handicapped by the financial crisis of the Thirties, the catastrophe of the War, and the stringency of post-war years, I have enjoyed what cricketers call "a good wicket".

(Rector Watt, 1962 Exhibition)

In retrospect, the fifties at the Academy seem a welter of money-raising efforts and pneumatic drills as the Prep School rose and Henderson Row was partially reconstructed. Although the major efforts and resources were directed towards creating the new Prep at Inverleith, a great deal of modernisation was achieved in the Upper School as well during Mr Watt's Rectorship.

The major changes took place in the Science Department and other non-Classical areas. To start the modernisation plan, the Directors acquired in 1956 the ground-floor and basement flat at No. 38 Henderson Row, which provided two large classrooms and one small one for the Modern VIIth, and the following year they purchased a first-floor flat in No. 40. By moving classes into new quarters here, a start could be made to the complex programme of reconstruction while the School was still in operation. The front Yards were at long last asphalted in 1956, ending more than a century of gravel-scarred knees (the Prep and Gym Yards were converted to tarmac later). The whole School was rewired and converted from D.C. to A.C., the remains of the old bicycle sheds along the front wall were removed and new sheds built along the west wall of the Prep Yards, and the unsightly, dilapidated wooden boarding which stretched along the top of the front wall was removed and replaced by new coping-stones topped by a two-foot fence of strong interwoven wire. A completely new central heating system was installed, using solid fuel and equipped with automatic stoking and thermostatic control: in future, Janitors would have only one fully automated boiler-house underneath the back of the main building to cope with, instead of eight different boilers to tend as in the days of that prince of stokers, Janitor William Bell.

But the major project was the renovation of the Science Department, which started with the Lecture Theatre in 1954. Subsequently, Labs 1 to 5 were gutted and completely reconstructed, and a corridor was added to run the whole length of the Science Department: the main Chemistry and Physics Labs (1 and 5) were refitted in 1956 and the main Preparation Room renewed, the dual-purpose Physics and Chemistry Labs (2 and 4) and the Advanced Chemistry Lab (3) in 1957. In 1958 the two small classrooms running north and south at the back of the main building were transformed into an Advanced Physics Lab and a Preparation Room (these had formed one of the original classrooms in the School, which had been subdivided in the 1890s during Rector Mackenzie's time to cope with the 'population explosion' at the Academy). This conversion created a number of Prep School refugees, who camped in the inner Library and the ante-room of the Rifle Range until the new Prep at Inverleith was ready. (In the course of the reconstruction to provide the Advanced Physics Lab, the builders broke into one of the flues for the original warm-air central heating installed by the Sylvesters of Derby – the one that never worked. In it they found some thirty very old balls, mostly about the size of fives balls, which had fallen down the chimney at various times between 1824 and 1959 (the oldest one was dated 1833). Two of them were 'hollow india-rubber balls with holes in them', as had been specified in the *Rules of the Game of Hailes* that had been published in 1890, and were obviously original Hailes balls.

The departure of the Prep in 1960 to Inverleith set free nine classrooms at Henderson Row – three above the Dining Hall (which were taken over by the Geits), one at the north end of the west block (which reverted to its former use as an Upper School classroom), and five in the 'Prep Block' in the north-west corner at the back of the School. This was the original Mathematical and Writing Block of 1826, which had been taken over by the Prep when it began in 1888. The front (south) part was now converted, or reconverted, into a Mathematics Laboratory; this had been the last of the really big classrooms to be sub-divided (it was a single classroom between 1826 and 1953, and for a time in 1951–2 it had accommodated the whole of the Prep for prayers – 231 boys and a staff of ten!). The two classrooms at the back con-tinued as classrooms, but the lower classroom, which opens out on to the Lower Prep Yards, was converted into a music room. This was originally the 'basement room' in which the Rolands taught fencing from 1831 to 1889, and where the Academy Corps of Volunteer Rifles had met in 1859 (ch. 15).

To complete the first phase of the Science Department reconstruc-tion, in 1960 a Physics Lecture Theatre was created out of the double classroom that ran from east to west immediately at the back of the main block. (In 1973 it was converted again into a third Biology Lab.)

The successful completion of this burst of building-work in the fifties was marked by the dedication of the Advanced Physics Laboratory to the memory of James Clerk Maxwell in July, 1961, by Sir George Thomson. Two-thirds of the finances required to carry out these major developments was provided by the Industrial Fund for the Develop-ment of Science and Independent Schools, which was sponsored by leading industrialists in the United Kingdom.

The man who was instrumental in securing the substantial grant from the Industrial Fund was one of the School's most influential Academicals, Sir Keith Murray (E.A. 1908–21), now Lord Murray of Newhaven, K.C.B. He was a Director of the Academy from 1949–61. He had been Rector of Lincoln College, Oxford, until he was appointed Chairman of the University Grants Committee in 1953. In 1955 he alerted his fellow-Directors to the fact that a Fund was being raised by industrialists to make grants to schools for the purpose of developing the teaching of science, and advised them to apply at once on behalf of the Academy. Sir Keith was an invaluable contact with the world of Funds and Trusts, and his advice was continually being sought as to the best way of making an approach to possible sources of financial aid, and the Minutes are spattered with remarks like 'Sir Keith Murray has very kindly offered to give any help within his power'. He is a member of yet another remarkable Academical dynasty, the third of five brothers who all went to the Academy – D. C. G. Murray (1903–15), the eldest, who took up residence in Paris, C. G. Murray (E.A. 1905–6), who died while a schoolboy, Sheriff C. D. L. Murray (E.A. 1912–24), who was a Director just after the war, and F. H. Murray (E.A. 1914–27), who became a master at Rugby. Their father was C. D. Murray (E.A. 1875–82), later Lord Murray, who was for a long time Chairman of the Directors; and three of his own grandsons also went to the Academy – M.G. (E.A. 1930–41), the son of Paris-based D.C.G., and Iain C. (E.A. 1945–51) and S.M. (E.A. 1947–51), the sons of the late Sheriff Murray. (Iain Murray came back to the Academy as a member of staff between 1965–73, and is now Head of the Classics Department at George Watson's College.)

Amid the racket of Dinkum Diggers, Kango pneumatic drills, miniature bulldozers, stone-crushers, cement-mixers, mechanical saws and hammers, amid the chopping and changing of classrooms, the constant rearrangement of timetables, the improvisations and the annoyances, Mr Watt managed to make many distinctive contributions to the history of the Academy, not least in being the first Rector to bring the total number of pupils over the thousand mark – 1,024 at the start of his last session in 1961–2. And with rising numbers came a corresponding increase in the number of school activities. In Mr Watt's first session, the Scientific Society made an exciting expedition to Wester Ross – the first of what became regular Field Studies Group expeditions that were to take Academy boys to many inaccessible parts of the world, including the hinterland of Iceland. Scottish Country Dancing lessons were started. The Duke of Edinburgh's Award Scheme was introduced at the Academy in 1958, and two years later the Duke of Edinburgh himself visited the Academy to see Award demonstrations by candidates from the Academy, Fettes and Melville College. A few weeks earlier, J. T. Black (E.A. 1955–60), the first Academy boy to complete the course, had received the Gold Badge from the Duke of Edinburgh at Buckingham Palace.

There were academic successes too. In 1955, five Open Awards were won to Cambridge, in Maths (3), Natural Sciences, and Classics; indeed the Head Ephor, F. H. D. Walker (E.A. 1943–55), who was also captain of the XV, the XI, and the Athletics team, won his Exhibition in Mathematics to Clare College, Cambridge, on the day that he was chosen to play for the Scottish Schoolboys XV against the English Schoolboys at Richmond. (Walker's father, F. H. N. Walker (E.A. 1908–18), was also Head Ephor, and captain of the XV and the

XI in his time – a unique father-and-son record.) The Academy was the only Scottish school in a list of forty-three schools to gain five or more Oxbridge awards that year. The 1957–8 session produced another winner of the Old Members' Exhibition at Lincoln College, Oxford, which demands not only a good academic record but marked qualities of leadership – P. J. Burnet (E.A. 1944–58), who was captain of the XV, vice-captain of the XI, and the Scottish Junior Squash Rackets Champion. That year too, A. M. Kerr (E.A. 1946–58), who was Pipe-Major of the C.C.F. Band, the best shot at Bisley, and Hamlet in that year's Shakespeare production, won a new type of award; this was one of the University Apprenticeships awarded by industrial firms to help increase the country's supply of technologists. The firm footed the bill, but the scholar had to secure his own place at a University, and Kerr had already gained a place at Christ's College, Cambridge. (Oddly enough, Kerr is now a Writer to the Signet!) In the following session there were five Open Awards – two in Natural Sciences to Oxford and Cambridge, and the others in Classics, History, and Mathematics: 'a remarkable result, on which the Board congratulates the Rector and staff', said the Minutes.

In 1957 the Academy was granted its first Coat of Arms, and a flag bearing the new arms was flown on the occasion of the Exhibition on July 29, 1957. An Academical, Ian M. Campbell, W.S. (E.A. 1913–24), met the costs involved in preparing it and having it approved by the Lord Lyon. Represented on the Coat of Arms are the personal arms or crests of five of the original founder-Directors of the Academy – Robert Dundas of Arniston, the first Chairman (red lion on silver); Sir Walter Scott (blue stars and crescent on gold); Colin Mackenzie of Portmore (gold stag's head on blue); James Skene of Rubislaw (wolf's head on dagger, in silver and gold and red); and Lord Cockburn (red cock on silver). The crest is the familiar Homer's Head in a green chaplet, with the Greek motto from the organ case in the Hall – 'Always strive to excel'.

Unfortunately, neither Leonard Horner nor John Russell possessed family crests, so two of the three main founders are not represented on the Coat of Arms at all. Another Academical, Noel B. Erskine (E.A. 1926–37), offered to meet the cost of making the necessary blocks and of printing coloured reproductions of the Grant of Arms as a money-raising effort for the Development Fund, but there were so few advance orders for copies that the idea was dropped. Handsome as it is, the Coat of Arms has never really caught on with Academicals;

they seem to prefer old Homer's Head which still appears on the front cover of the *Chronicle* and other official school records.

Academicals were to the fore as usual in many various fields. At the Exhibition in 1958 the guest speaker, Graham A. Usher, C.A. (E.A. 1909–19), listed the Academicals to be found 'in almost all spheres of authority and leadership . . . amongst the Lords of Appeal in the House of Lords . . . in high office on the permanent staff of the House of Commons . . . as Heads of Colleges at the great Universities . . . in positions of great responsibility in the service of the Crown . . . bearing their full share and responsibility in the industries and professions of our country . . .

'In our own City . . . it is an Academical who holds the highest post in the Justiciary of this country, the Lord President of the Court of Session [Lord Clyde]; it is an Academical who is the Lord Provost of our great City [Ian Johnson-Gilbert]; and it is an Academical who presides over those 6,000 Scotsmen who are reputed to be found in every part of the world where the going is good, the members of the Institute of Chartered Accountants of Scotland, the oldest body of Accountants in the world [R. Ian Marshall, E.A. 1912–17].'

V. F. Noel-Paton (E.A. 1913–18) was one of the first people to receive a Life Peerage under the Act of 1958, and took the title of Lord Ferrier of Culter. A. G. (now Sir Andrew) Gilchrist (E.A. 1924–9), who is the present Chairman of the Highlands and Islands Development Board, was British Ambassador in Iceland at the time of the First Cod War (and later had his Embassy burned down over his head in Indonesia). James Gilbert (E.A. 1931–41), now the Head of Comedy at BBC Television, made an instant hit with the lyrics and music for *Grab me a Gondola*, and J. I. M. Stewart (E.A. 1913–24) was turning out best-seller thrillers under the pen-name of Michael Innes. Tam Dalyell (E.A. 1939) got into Parliament as the Labour M.P. for West Lothian at a by-election in 1962.

And a group of senior Academicals, twelve in all, had a ball to themselves in 1959 when they met for dinner to celebrate the 50th anniversary of their first day at school together on October 5, 1909, in the lowest class of the Prep, Class IB – Miss Moyes' Class of 1909–10. One had his first reading book with him in almost perfect condition – *Ned, Ted and Fred, the Sad Fate of Three Little Mice* (price 3d). Through that dinner they managed to get in touch with their old teacher, by then Mrs Margaret Murison, of Rogate, Sussex, a grandmother with eight grand-children, and they presented a teak seat to the Prep School at Inverleith commemorating their gratitude to her. She died in 1970, aged 88.

Meanwhile, much younger Academicals were setting up records for longevity of a different kind – at school. In 1956, J. B. Neill, the Head Ephor and captain of the XV, left school after fourteen years and one term. This record was equalled three years later by another two embryo Academicals – W. N. Mackinnon and C. McMartin (winner of a Major Scholarship in Natural Sciences at Caius College, Cambridge), who had both arrived in May, 1945, and left in July, 1959.

Not long after they left school, another Academical record was established with the arrival in Prep VC in September, 1961, of the first representative of a fifth Academical generation – P. A. Robertson Durham, the son of A. W. Robertson Durham, C.A. (E.A. 1921–32), grandson of A. W. Robertson-Durham, C.A. (E.A. 1887–95), who played rugby for Scotland, great-grandson of J. A. Robertson-Durham, C.A. (E.A. 1859–63), who was an Edinburgh Town Councillor, and great-great-grandson of A. W. Robertson, C.A. (E.A. 1828–32), an original member and first secretary of the C.A. Society of Edinburgh. In the following year this achievement was equalled by a descendant of Lord Kingsburgh, when A. N. G. Macdonald joined Prep IB in September, 1962. He is the son of N. A. M. Macdonald, W.S. (E.A. 1942–7), the Secretary of the Academical Club, grandson of Sheriff N. Macdonald (E.A. 1899–1906), great-grandson of N. D. Macdonald, Advocate (E.A. 1877–84), and great-great-grandson of J. H. A. Macdonald (E.A. 1845–52), Lord Kingsburgh himself.

A number of staff stalwarts reached the end of their careers during Mr Watt's Rectorship – Dodds, Ferguson, Hempson, Scott, Edwards, Read, and Atkinson. C. J. R. Mair (E.A. 1934–7), one of the rare Academicals to teach at the Academy, left in 1958 after ten years as a Classics master to become Rector of Kelvinside Academy in Glasgow; and another Academical member of staff left that same year – R. B. MacEwen (E.A. 1906–13), 'Bob Begg'. He became a master at the Academy in 1941, having spent fourteen years in the Indian Civil Service, and retired after seventeen years of teaching Latin and Greek. One of his classroom customs dated back to his own schooldays – awarding a 'penny bun' (later $1\frac{1}{2}$d) to the 'top man' in a round of questions round the class; it was a ploy he had picked up from 'Billy' Peel. Dr D. G. D. Isaac, known to all and sundry as 'Ike', left the Academy at the same time as Rob Watt, to become the first Head-master of the newly formed High School at Abergavenny, Monmouthshire, back in his native Wales. He won a wartime Soccer Blue at Oxford, but switched to rugby in Edinburgh, playing and coaching and acting as Hon. Sec. of the Academical Football Club; a man of boundless energy and enthusiasm both on the field and in the classroom, where he taught History with distinction. He also found time to do much careful research into the early history of the Academy, which the present chronicler was relieved and grateful to be allowed to use. 'Ike' is now Rector of Marr College, Troon.

In 1961 the governing body of the Academy was itself reconstructed with the granting of a third Supplementary Royal Charter. The former Proprietors (who had long since ceased to exist except on paper) and Board of Directors were replaced by a Court of Directors, consisting of a Chairman, Extraordinary Directors, Elected Directors, and Representative Directors. The Chairman (then Lord Cameron) is elected by the Directors for as long as they determine. The Extraordinary Directors are elected by the Court, and are more or less Honorary Directors. The Elected Directors, also elected by the Court, are limited in number to not fewer than fourteen and not more than eighteen; two retire each year and are not eligible for re-election until a year has elapsed. The Representative Directors, two in number, are appointed by the Council of the Edinburgh Academical Club and hold office for such period as the Council may determine.

Reconstruction remained the keynote of Rob Watt's Rectorship right to the end. Throughout his last session, 1961-2, work went on at the west side of the old Prep Yards, building four new classrooms as the nucleus of a new Modern Language Department, equipped with modern audio aids. Throughout the summer holidays, two Biology labs were constructed behind the Hall to complete the modernisation of the Science Department; and in the main building a new Geography Room was provided on the west side of the Hall by knocking down a partition and restoring 'Skinny' Carmichael's classroom to its original size, and a new History Room was created on the east side of the Hall. And 'down the hill' in the Lower Prep Yards, the toilet block was rebuilt and new cycle sheds put up; this was made possible by felling several handsome old trees behind the Dining Hall, and injured naturelovers had their distress mollified by the planting of a single tree 'in a more suitable position'.

But there was still a great deal more to be done, and Mr Watt's departure in 1962 on reaching the retiring age of 65 did not mean that the Years of Appeal were over. Far from it. The previous year, the Appeal Committee had announced a further target of £40,000 to complete the plans in hand. In his last speech at the Exhibition of 1962, Mr Watt said:

'It has been an exhilarating experience to be associated with a period of expansion of buildings and of numbers, and the educational developments of the past decade have made manifest the vision of those who decided that expansion and re-equipment must take place if the Academy was to maintain its position in the forefront, educationally, of Scottish schools. And I gladly repeat the tribute which I have paid before to the generosity of those who have responded and are continuing to respond. For an important part of the programme, as I have indicated, has yet to be tackled, and further financial help will be required.'

He left the Academy in very much better shape than it had been when he arrived in 1951. Numbers at school had topped 1,000 for the first time. In the previous five years the Academy had won eight Open Scholarships at Oxford and nine at Cambridge. But he saw the greater pressures that would be applied. He spoke of the increased competition for places at Scottish Universities, and the problem facing his successor of how to keep the ideals of a broad-based education and not reduce it to 'the technique of acquiring the requisite number of marks in the requisite number of subjects in the Certificate examinations held a year before leaving school, not even if one of these examinations is called "The Use of English". Boys must be helped to master that technique; God forbid that it should become the chief end of education.'

And with these eminently sound words, the Rector went on his way. He worked in the United States for a while as an assistant master in St George's School at Rhode Island, Newport, and did some work at Glenalmond and at his old school, Fettes. Like Dr Isaac, he did some further research into the early history of the Academy, to the continuing benefit of the present chronicler, and he edited the centenary edition of the *Fettes Register*. He is often to be seen at school matches at New Field; and all his old pupils and colleagues are delighted to see that when the Academy is playing Fettes, he invariably takes his place (at whatever cost to the tug of loyalties) on the Academy 'side'.

CHAPTER XXI

Dr Mills (1962 onwards): 150 Not Out

The Academy has been learning for nearly 150 years: no doubt there will still be a lot to learn, but it has never shown itself unwilling to do so nor to adapt itself to modern needs.

(The Rector, 1967 Exhibition)

THE Directors were well aware of the problems that would face the next Rector. Dr A. G. Donald (E.A. 1932–45), the Chairman of the Selection Committee, said they felt that this appointment might prove to be a critical one in the history of the School because of the difficulties which would almost certainly be encountered in the next ten years. These were:

1. Education – in respect of entry to the Universities.
2. Political – in respect of changes in the Constitution of the Independent Public School.
3. Economic – in relation to ever-rising costs.

The qualities which the Committee set themselves to look for were: a high academic standard; sympathy and understanding for the traditions and aims of the Academy; vision and foresight to anticipate the problems of the future; and, for good measure, he should preferably have a good games record and ability as an administrator.

The man the Directors unanimously chose was Dr H. H. Mills, who was then aged 42 and teaching at Sedbergh School – 'the candidate with the highest intellectual calibre contained within a modest disposition, and whose athletic record was unsurpassed by any other candidate'.

Dr Mills, a bachelor, was educated at Marling School, Gloucestershire, at Grenoble University, and at St Catharine's College, Cambridge – he was the first Cantabrigian to be appointed Rector of the Academy apart from Mr Sheepshanks. He was also the first non-Classicist to be appointed Rector of the Academy – he had graduated with First Class Honours in Modern Languages. He spent a year at the University of Philadelphia with a Commonwealth Fellowship doing research in medieval literature and history, and then was Assistant

Director of Education to the County of Hertfordshire before returning to Cambridge to carry out post-graduate research. For a time he was on the Editorial staff of *The Sunday Times*. In 1952 he got his Ph.D. at Cambridge for his thesis on 'Literacy of the Laity in the Middle Ages'.

He was a Rugby Blue at Cambridge, playing wing forward in the 'Varsity Match in 1947 and 1948, and was an England trialist and reserve in 1947–8. During the war he had commanded a company of the 7th Parachute Battalion, and dropped at Caen on D-Day. He was awarded the Military Cross during the Normandy campaign. As Brigade Major of the 5th Parachute Brigade he took part in the crossing of the Rhine and the advance into Germany, and he served against the Japanese in Malaya and Java. He was mentioned in dispatches three times. It is little wonder that the Directors were impressed by a record so versatile and so distinguished.

Dr Mills is still Rector of the Academy in this 150th Anniversary year, after twelve years at the helm. At this point, in J. B. Hope Simpson's words, 'we enter into the region of contemporary history. Lord Acton once said that "the living do not yield up their secrets with the candour of the dead", and if *de mortuis nil nisi bonum* is a sound maxim, perhaps, for the historian of a living institution such as a school, *de viventibus nil* would be an even sounder one'. But to end the 150-year story of the Edinburgh Academy at 1962 for that reason would be pusillanimous and a bit absurd. It will be the task of some future historian to assess properly Dr Mills's Rectorship in the sixties and seventies; but this book would not be complete without at least an outline of the events of the last decade.

The reconstruction and renovation went on. The fund-raising went on. By the end of the sixties well over £500,000 had been spent on renewing the Edinburgh Academy since the war. And the sixties were notable too for a major policy decision: it was the decade in which the Directors made a serious attempt to sell the old school at Henderson Row and rebuild it at Inverleith – and decided once and for all that it was financially impossible. (And not a few sweaty Academical night-caps were thrown in the air with joy when that principle was established.)

The early years of Dr Mills's Rectorship were taken up with pro-tracted discussions and negotiations about the physical future of the Academy. His predecessor had agreed with the Directors that a new

Appeal should be launched to raise money to expand the Prep School at Inverleith and remove the Geits from Henderson Row, and then improve the facilities for the Upper School. But after two terms of studying the Academy in operation and thinking hard about it, Dr Mills was having serious doubts about the wisdom of such a policy. There were three grounds for his concern:

1. That if substantial sums were spent on expansion at Inverleith, there would be very little left for Henderson Row.

2. That too great an emphasis on improving facilities at the new Prep School might well aggravate the problem of parents making use of the excellent facilities at Inverleith as a Prep School, with no intention of sending their children on to the Upper School of the Academy. The Prep must not be allowed to dominate the Upper School in the public eye.

3. That there would be difficulty in recruiting the extra male staff required for Inverleith. More than six new teachers would be needed, and existing staff at Henderson Row would be unlikely to want to move; and it would be much more difficult to get suitable teachers to work exclusively in the Prep than, as at Henderson Row, men who only had to devote a small proportion of their time to the lower levels of the School and could be offered some advance work with the Upper Classes.

The Directors heeded the Rector's arguments and agreed to delay action on the proposed move of the Geits to Inverleith, in order to give Dr Mills and the Executive Committee more time to assess the problem and obtain estimates of the costs involved; and they also agreed to postpone the launching of any new Appeal until the policy was settled. They had already decided that this time they would use a professional fund-raising organisation, Appeal Planning Limited, who were to do a preliminary survey of the potential to be tapped.

By October, 1963, when Dr A. G. Donald, the Chairman of the Executive Committee, reported the outcome of their discussions to the Court of Directors, the Directors agreed to change the priorities of the policy: the necessary development expenditure at Henderson Row should take place first, at once, and the removal of further classes to Inverleith should only be carried out 'as and when finances made this feasible'.

There followed months of hectic work – construction work at the

Academy as new porches were added to the east and west wings of the main building (the only external additions that have ever been made to the main building since 1824), the new Biology labs were equipped in the main building and the old labs under the Gymnasium converted into the Pottery part of the Art Department, and the Library was transformed with the help of a £5,000 bequest from 'Pussy' Stuart; and behind the scenes, a profusion of schemes and plans and designs, as Dr Donald produced and costed various alternatives. There was a strong move to build a new block of classrooms right across the front of the Yards, creating a Quadrangle, and discussions started up on the merits of a new Art block right at the back of the School, adjacent to Glenogle Road. Everything seemed to be happening at once – the Court approved a massive programme of redevelopment for the Boarding Houses, and agreed to build houses for a Prep Headmaster and two masters at Inverleith. But by July, 1964, no decision had been taken regarding the provision of the extra accommodation at Inverleith that would be necessary if the Geits moved there. By the autumn, however, conditions at Henderson Row threatened to become chaotic as the development project there bogged down in delays, so it was decided to authorise the building of four extra classrooms at Inverleith, to be ready for occupation by September, 1965, in order to relieve overcrowding at Henderson Row. Suddenly time was of the essence, and the Directors decided to initiate the Appeal without delay; meanwhile negotiations continued with the architects over costs and revision of plans for the Henderson Row project.

By March, 1965, the suspicion was growing that the plan to build across the front of the Yards might prove beyond the School's financial resources. When these doubts were reported to the Court a few days after a joint meeting of the Executive and Policy Committees, the alarming implication had to be faced: perhaps it would be physically impossible to develop the Henderson Row site at all with the money that would be foreseeably available? Perhaps complete removal of the whole School was the only feasible course after all? The Court estimated that such an undertaking would cost £500,000, but that they might raise £150,000 by selling off the old school to some other educational establishment.

The first thing to do was to try to find out how much money they could realistically expect to raise by an Appeal. The fund-raisers were instructed, in May, 1965, to conduct a feasibility survey based on alternative targets: (1) Complete removal from Henderson Row at an estimated cost of £350,000; (2) Keeping the Second Classes at Henderson Row and developing there for £200,000; (3) Moving the Seconds to Inverleith at a cost of £125,000 and doing no further major building at Henderson Row; (4) Keeping the Seconds at Henderson Row and only providing a part of the facilities planned for Henderson Row.

These were the permutations possible; everything depended on how much Academicals would be willing to subscribe to them. So the fund-raisers carried out detailed interviews with seventy-five Academicals and parents 'representing all age groups and degrees of wealth' to try to assess the appeal of each particular Appeal, as it were. Each selected interviewee was asked for his reaction to the idea of an Appeal with as its primary object the complete removal of the School from Henderson Row – any alternative would be 'in the nature of a second best'.

Their researches underlined a central problem where the Academy was concerned: 'The Academy has not produced many rich men. It has supplied men of good quality to the professions, business, and the Services, who will make their contributions from income rather than capital; and this class is particularly affected by the rise in the cost of living, inflation, educational expenses, and the withering away of private means.'

The basic conclusion was, however, that there would be loyal support for an Appeal, and that this would probably raise around £130,000 if the objective were announced to be the complete removal to Inverleith; but an objective of 'patching up' Henderson Row would severely restrict support, and might produce as little as £40,000. At the same time, doubts had been expressed by many interviewees as to the feasibility of carrying out such a mammoth project for as little as £500,000.

The Directors were now in a very tight spot indeed. The only objective that was likely to raise a reasonable sum of money was one which they might not be able to afford after all – and any other objective would not raise sufficient money to carry *anything* out. Obviously, the first move must be to get a realistic costing of the removal scheme. There was a possible buyer for Henderson Row in the market who might be interested in taking over the Academy buildings for £150,000; but what would the cost of rebuilding be? The Executive Committee led by the indefatigable Dr Donald got down to work with the architects, and feelers were put out towards the possible buyer; and meanwhile, all major works at Henderson Row other than the first phase of the Dining Hall were deferred 'pending clarification of plans for possible development at Inverleith'.

By October, 1965, the new classrooms at Inverleith were in use, and the top classes in the Prep, the Vths, stayed there for another year as the VIths, thus effectively 'moving' the lowest Upper School Class to Inverleith; and the Second Classes made history by being Geits for two years running. That part of the operation at least had all gone smoothly; but by November, the Court's own estimation of the probable cost of a total removal from Henderson Row had gone up to £800,000. The potential buyer was told that the price for Henderson Row would have to be £300,000 to £400,000 – and with that his interest evaporated.

On December 15, 1965, the Court heard the worst. The surveyor's realistic estimate of the total cost (excluding land) of removal from Henderson Row and rebuilding elsewhere was – £1,215,307. The maximum savings that could be effected by cuts, including the omission of a swimming pool (always the first to be sacrificed) would be only £100,000.

So the Court 'reluctantly concluded that . . . a complete removal from Henderson Row was not feasible. However, it was felt that the time and trouble taken in fully exploring this possibility had not been wasted, as it had established for posterity the fact that, however desirable such a move was, it would have placed an impossible financial burden on the School.'

So there it was. No removal. In July, 1966, it was agreed to launch the Appeal on a broad front, *The Development of the Edinburgh Academy*, with a target of £150,000. And on October 21, 1966, Lord Cameron, the Chairman of the Directors, officially launched the campaign at a small informal party in the old Hall in Henderson Row. The Directors led the way with a splendid corporate contribution of £20,000, and Lord Cameron explained why the Appeal was necessary, while Mr Craufurd-Benson, managing director of Appeal Planning Limited, explained the mechanics of the campaign.

The *Chronicle* commented: 'Many may doubt the wisdom of having an appeal for funds at this particular time – but is there an ideal time for launching an appeal? . . . In our case it had to be phased to fit in with the financial requirements of the School arising from the continued development which is so vital in order to maintain The Academy in the forefront of Scottish Public Schools.'

Nor did the Academicals let their old school down. Within a year, £80,000 had been subscribed, and by October, 1968, the total had reached £122,000, sufficient to keep the impetus of renovation and reconstruction going. The Boarding Houses were totally modernised, the VIths and VIIths got a Common Room at Henderson Row, and the Dining Hall was renewed, a Dining Hall block was built at Inverleith, and Denham Green House, the Junior Prep, was reconstructed and modernised after the fire that ravaged it in 1971.

And that should be where the story ends. Except that the story of the Edinburgh Academy has no ending. While all these momentous decisions were being taken, the School itself kept on generating its own alchemy. It kept on producing its only valid product – people. Every year a thousand boys of all shapes and sizes were being moulded, individually, into young adults, being taught and helped to make the most of themselves.

The brilliant boys made the headlines, like those able twins D. M. and J. B. St Clair, who in 1967 both won Open Awards in Classics to Oxford. D. M. St Clair won the Dux Medal that year, just as his elder brother, W. L. St Clair (E.A. 1948–56), had done before him (he wrote *Lord Elgin and the Marbles* and *That Greece Might Still Be Free*). And the Guest of Honour at the Exhibition of 1967 who handed St Clair his Dux Medal was himself a former Dux of the School, Sir James Dunnett (E.A. 1920–32), then Permanent Under-Secretary to the Ministry of Defence, whose two brothers had also been Duxes in their time – Sir George in 1925, and D. I. in 1935.

J. N. Sands (E.A. 1949–63) capped his distinguished school career as an all-rounder by becoming the fifth Academy boy to be selected to play at Lord's (the others were Gerry Crole in 1912, Ben Tod in 1926, Ian Syme in 1948, and Jimmy Allan in 1950). The XV led by John Crerar (1952–66) was being described as 'vintage' even before the season was over. A new generation of Accies was making its mark: Alick Buchanan-Smith (E.A. 1941–5) as an M.P. for North Angus and Mearns, Gordon Honeycombe (1946–55) as an immensely popular newscaster with ITV and a considerable writer, P. A. Pond (E.A. 1958–60) as 'Paul Jones', a member of the Mannfred Mann pop group, J. B. Neill (E.A. 1942–56), and R. J. Arneil (E.A. 1957–62) on the International rugby field.

The distinctions and honours keep rolling in – eleven Oxford and Cambridge awards in 1969–70, for instance. But now there are other awards in the list, for engineering and industrial training, at other, more technological universities. But Dr Mills is just as concerned with the 'rank and file'; up to 80 per cent of boys leaving the Academy go on to University, and they cannot all win awards, and Dr Mills is always looking to ways in which to create more opportunities in which they can develop other interests than the purely academic. There are at least fifteen school societies, including Industrial Archaeology, Oxfam, Motor, Railway, and Chess. There are at least a dozen different sports available, including sailing and ski-ing. In 1964, Dr Mills started a Pursuits session on Friday afternoons when boys can engage in various hobbies under the guidance of a member of staff. The pursuits followed include art, pottery, stone carving, boat maintenance, bookbinding, fishing-rod-making, fly-tying, hand-setting and printing, photography, public speaking . . .

Music flourishes as never before, with a magnificent choral society and four orchestras at present. Pupils can read Russian and A-level Economics. A parent put his son down for the Academy recently at the age of four hours. And Edwina Brown, the sister of an Academy boy, was given permission by the Court of Directors to attend certain Science classes at S level and won an Open Scholarship to Somerville College, Oxford, to study medicine . . . Who knows? It may be a straw in the wind.

Oh, yes, and there's a new Appeal afoot, a 150th Anniversary Appeal. The target is £325,000 – at least, that is the cost of the next phase of the Development Programme: a new Science Block at the Upper School, new Art Rooms and an Orchestra Room; a new Games Hall and Squash Courts at Inverleith, plus that extra classroom that will eventually complete the plan to move the two lowest classes of the Upper School; more classrooms at Denham Green House; and possibly even that elusive swimming pool!

No, it does not stand still, the Academy. It keeps changing, seeking the best of the new, keeping the best of the old. What would Lord Cockburn and Leonard Horner think of their brainchild today? They would be delighted – because they too were ahead of their time; the Academy was an instrument of change right from the start.

Their strictly Classical Academy has been transformed into a school that caters for all the modern demands of wide-ranging education; an exceptional school for Scotland, in that its examination system combines the best of both the Scottish and the English exams, and prepares boys for both Scottish and English universities. All boys take the English G.C.E. 'O'-levels in the IVth Classes (aged 14+), but not the puny Scottish 'O' grades in the S.C.E.; boys wanting to go on to Scottish universities then take the S.C.E. 'Highers', those heading for English universities take the G.C.E. 'A'-levels in the VIIths, where they are also groomed for University entrance and scholarships. The aim is to master the qualification for any University in Britain.

But more than that: I am convinced that it is possible to talk of 'an Academy education' as something distinct because it is the result of a coherent and deliberate policy of educating the whole person, an integrated education towards maturity in the fullest sense. The Academy's efforts are not directed towards creating an elitist education for a certain class of privileged people, but towards creating and maintaining a particular standard of excellence, a particular quality of education. One never hears of 'the kind of boy we want', only of 'the kind of boy we want to turn out'; never of 'the kind of money we want' – only of 'the kind of money we need to keep up our standards'. It is a school rooted in independence.

The cost of independence is high – even though the Academy is run on a shoestring compared with most State schools (when did you last see the annual balance sheet of your local secondary or comprehensive school?). Yet the kind of bills that are taken for granted by education authorities all have to be met from fees. Every penny has to be accounted for. There can be no wastage, no over-ordering, no frills – because if the fees go up more than they must, the field from which potential pupils are drawn gets smaller. The Academy still cannot afford the luxury of a swimming pool – yet what local authority would dream of building a school of the Academy's stature without one?

It's the price of independence, the price of keeping alive what Cockburn and Horner and Russell started 150 years ago. It has always been high, not just in terms of money but in terms of dedication and self-sacrifice. And it will remain high. But so too will the rewards of independence. The 15,600 Academicals who have passed through those familiar gates in Henderson Row in the first 150 years of the Academy can vouch for that.

Even Old Bailie Blackwood would probably admit it too.

Index

This Index is highly selective, and limited to entries with direct associations with The Edinburgh Academy and Academicals; there are no entries for other schools, for instance. Figures in brackets denote years spent at the Academy.